38.40

Advanced Series in Agricultural Sciences 1

Co-ordinating Editor: B. Yaron, Bet-Dagan

Editors: G. W. Thomas, Lexington   B. R. Sabey, Fort Collins
Y. Vaadia, Bet-Dagan   L. D. Van Vleck, Ithaca

A. P. A. Vink

Land Use
in Advancing Agriculture

With 94 Figures and 115 Tables

Springer-Verlag
New York Heidelberg Berlin 1975

Dr. A. P. A. Vink, Professor of Physical Geography and Soil Science,
University of Amsterdam, Amsterdam, The Netherlands

ISBN 0-387-07091-5 Springer-Verlag New York Heidelberg Berlin
ISBN 3-540-07091-5 Springer-Verlag Berlin Heidelberg New York

Foreword

The *Advanced Series in Agricultural Sciences* is designed to fill a long-felt need for advanced educational and technological books in the agricultural sciences. These texts, intended primarily for students of agriculture, should also provide up-to-date technical background reading for the many agricultural workers in extension services, educational systems, or international bodies.

The editors of *Advanced Series in Agricultural Sciences* will select key subjects relating to the agricultural environment, agricultural physics and chemistry, soil science, plant sciences, animal sciences, food technology, and agricultural engineering for a critical and synthetic appraisal. An initial theoretical presentation will be used by authors of individual volumes in the series to develop a technical approach—including examples and practical solutions— to each subject.

In addressing the advanced undergraduate and early graduate student of agriculture, selected authors will present the latest information, leavened with the lessons learned from their own experience, on precise and well-defined topics. Such books that widen the horizons of the student of agriculture can serve, too, as useful reference sources for the young specialist in the early years of his career.

Many specialists who are involved in teaching agricultural science are isolated from universities and research institutions. This series will bring them up-to-date scientific information, thus keeping them in touch with progress.

The basic objective of *Advanced Series in Agricultural Sciences* is to effect a structural integration of the theoretic and technical approaches to agriculture. The books will be particularly helpful to extension specialists who have an ever-present need for the latest information in the day-to-day solving of practical problems.

The increasing involvement of agricultural sciences in projects in developing countries has created a demand for clear, current texts on specific problems. The texts to be published in this new series, written by specialists from different countries, should provide this profession with the appropriate tools for insuring the effectiveness of schemes for agricultural development all over the world.

The normal activities of the editors of *Advanced Series in Agricultural Sciences* center around teaching and research, not publishing. It was our awareness of the scarcity of advanced texts that led us to accept Springer-Verlag's invitation to enter this field and to devote time to writing. We hope our endeavors will be met by the understanding of our colleagues—both scientists and teachers—and we hope that they will cooperate with us by using *Advanced Series in Agricultural Sciences* in the way we envisage, so making a useful contribution to agriculture.

The Editors

Preface

The Netherlands school of soil scientists has always had particular interest in the relationship between land use and land resources. Nearly thirty years ago the late Professor C. H. EDELMAN wrote a book in Dutch on *Socio-Economic Soil Science*. In 1963 the present author published *Aspects de Pédologie Appliquée* (A la Baconnière, Neuchatel, Switzerland). Our knowledge of the resources aspects of land use has since then grown continuously, thanks in particular to the work of the Food and Agriculture Organization (FAO) of the United Nations in Rome. This knowledge crystallized in the *FAO Expert Consultation on Land Evaluation*, held at Wageningen in 1972.

Latterly, the ecological aspects of land use and land resources have received increasing attention. This interest was much stimulated by the activities of the Division for Natural Resources Research of UNESCO, Paris, who sponsored the *International Symposium on Integrated Surveys and Environmental Management in Developing Countries*, held at the ITC/UNESCO Centre, Enschede, in 1972.

The request to the author to write the present book, made by Dr. BRUNO YARON on behalf of editors and publishers, therefore came at a propitious moment. There are still many problems to be solved in the relationship between land use and land resources, but at least we have reached a stage at which a coherent text can be written. I am very grateful for this opportunity, which has enabled me to make use of nearly thirty years' experience in this field of study, experience obtained in various parts of the world.

Agriculture is continuously advancing toward economic and social goals in accordance with the demands of human society. To this end, old and new technologies are being applied to the various kinds of land resources. A careful study of the kinds of land use and of the various resources involves a variety of methods of research and evaluation. Land management provides the means for maintaining a sound ecological balance together with optimal fulfillment of human demands. For a successful outcome, land use and land management have to be well adapted to the land resources and to the ecological conditions. Land improvement provides a further means of adapting land resources to human demand.

It is impossible to acknowledge in a personal manner the contributions made to this work by the many people with whom I had contact during this period. In a general manner I thank here most sincerely the farmers of the Netherlands, Indonesia, Luxembourg, Cameroun, Ruanda, Tunisia, Iraq, Switzerland and Italy, from whom I probably learned more than from anybody else. I also thank my colleagues from these countries as well as from FAO and UNESCO and from Belgium, Iran, Egypt, Portugal, Scotland, England, Ireland, France, the German

Democratic Republic, the German Federal Republic, Israel, and the United States.

A special word of thanks goes to my former colleagues at the Netherlands Soil Survey Institute and at the Agricultural University, Wageningen, as well as at the International Institute for Aerial Survey and Earth Sciences (ITC), Enschede. My present cooperation with staff and students of the Laboratory for Physical Geography and Soil Science of the University of Amsterdam, has considerably increased my insight into the subject and was therefore indispensable for the writing of this book.

Finally, I would like to mention by name a few persons who deserve my special thanks: the late Professor C. H. EDELMAN (Wageningen Agricultural University), Professor W. SCHERMERHORN (ITC), Dr. D. L. BRAMAO and Dr. R. DUDAL (FAO), Professor V. KOVDA (Moscow University), and Monsieur M. BATISSE (UNESCO).

Special thanks go also to all those who permitted me to use illustrative material from their publications.

Without the help and encouragement I received from the publisher and editors as well as from the administrative and secretarial staff of our laboratory, the attempt to write this book would probably not have succeeded. Without the work of our drawing office, the production of the figures would have constituted a major problem. I thank them all most sincerely.

Amsterdam, January 1975   A. P. A. VINK

Contents

Chapter 6: Land Evaluation

Chapter 7: Development of Land Use in Advancing Agriculture

Chapter 1   Introduction

1.1 Definitions

Land use is any kind of permanent or cyclic human intervention to satisfy human needs, either material or spiritual or both, from the complex of natural and artifactial resources which together are called "land". In this sense, true nomads with no fixed habitat do not practice land use; they do not systematically apply their energies to any specific tract of land, and they themselves are a natural part of an ecosystem, as are other living organisms. Land carries ecosystems; land use is the application of human controls, in a relatively systematic manner, to the key elements within any ecosystem, in order to derive benefit from it. Man, although an inherent part of the ecosystem in which he lives, places himself to some extent outside the system and tries to manipulate it. He may do this in a very intensive manner, as is seen in the paddy cultures of Asia or in the horticultural cultures of Western Europe, or in a very extensive manner, e.g. the semi-nomadic peoples of Africa. Hunting which is practiced as systematic game-cropping on specific areas of land falls into the category of land use. Although it is often the most extensive (low input) form of land use, it fulfills the essential qualification that man systematically applies his technological know-how to derive the required benefits. The same holds true for wildlife conservation, carried out systematically either for purposes of recreation or because man perceives that he cannot exist without obtaining a sufficiently steady state in his cultural ecosystems.

Land, being the carrier of those ecosystems which provide the most benefits to mankind, is the over-all natural resource. A resource is there to be used, and use takes place in specific areas and at specific localities. Although land may be viewed from a broad, holistic concept in natural science, its use always involves specific surface areas; land is therefore a truly geographical concept. The land as we see it today is in many areas the result of a combination of both its natural genesis and the human influences which have been brought to bear on it in the past and of those which are still active in the present. The human influences may be the result of positive human action, such as the construction of polders with dikes and pumping stations; it may also be the result of human negligence or lack of knowledge and foresight, as is seen in many severely eroded areas of the world and in areas covered by human, mainly industrial, refuse.

Land is a dynamic concept; it carries ecosystems, but is itself also a part of these ecosystems. One of its main components, the soil, is itself a complex ecosystem containing animals and plants of different sizes and activities. Natural processes occurring in the land derive energy from the sun as well as from mineral and biological sources. Relief, which is one source of energy, i.e., the energy provided by differences in height, is a specific attribute of the land surface. Land, although tending towards a steady state, is therefore never truly stable. The land, viewed as landscape, as observed today by both visual and other methods of perception, may achieve near stability from certain points of view, but this stability is the result of complex interactions of a multitude of phenomena and processes. We try to use this for our own ends and hope to induce those kinds of near-stability which will benefit us most on a long-term basis (CHORLEY and KENNEDY, 1971).

The best definition of land therefore is one which involves the geographical aspects of "a tract of land" and reads: "A tract of land is defined geographically as a specific area of the earth's surface; its characteristics embrace all reasonably stable, or predictably cyclic attributes of the biosphere vertically above and below this area including those of the atmosphere, the soil and underlying rocks, the topography, the water, the plant and animal populations and the results of past and present human activity, to the extent that these attributes exert a significant influence on present and future uses of the land by man." (Adapted from BRINK-MAN and SMYTH, 1973, and CHRISTIAN and STEWART in REY et al., 1968.)

This definition obviously includes all land resources, both natural and man-made, of a clearly permanent or cyclic nature. Vegetation and animal popula-tions, both natural and man-induced, are definitely included. Permanent artificial structures such as dikes, canals, metalled roads or stable terraces are also consi-dered a part of the land. Several institutional factors, however, are not included. Thus, a distinction must here be made. The concept of land as a natural resource does not include the institutional aspects; scientists adhering mainly to this con-ceptual approach prefer to include institutional aspects with the land utilization type. Land as a "tract", i.e. as a geographically defined specific area, does include the permanent or cyclic institutional attributes. Thus, the general field pattern and the system of ownership of a particular tract of land are attributes of the land itself, because they are relatively permanent. Whether a particular individual is at a certain moment the owner of a tract, which may be a subdivision of the above-mentioned one, is not an attribute of the land, because in many social systems ownership may be changed by a simple deed. National and administrative bound-aries, also relatively permanent, are attributes of the land as well. In some cases they may even have a marked influence on the resources of the land, as in water-districts of the Netherlands, boundaries have determined throughout the centu-ries all matters pertaining to drainage. In land development planning as well as in environmental management, these attributes often are highly significant: they offer both resources and limitations which may have to be adapted by rural reconstruction, in order to use the land to its best advantage.

The concept of "land use" is often considered a relatively stable subject, re-lated mainly to the use to which the land in a certain region at a certain time is put. One might infer this, for example, from the World Land Use surveys made under the aegis of the International Geographic Union and under the guidance of the late Sir Dudley Stamp, although the latter certainly did not mean this to be concluded from his work. Land use is the result of a continuous field of tension created between available resources and human needs and acted upon by human efforts. Some resources—climate and relief—are not readily responsive to human intervention and therefore induce a tendency towards stability. Other resources—

vegetation, water and soil—are obviously responsive to human intervention and make development, sometimes even over-development, leading towards degradation, possible. Human societies and human needs show tendencies towards stabilization as well as towards growth and development; their main effect, during the twentieth century, has been to promote growth and development.

Even when a new stability, leading to a better environment, is sought, human effort for changes in land use is often urgently needed. Any text on land use will therefore be concerned with the changes in land use as well as with the means for effecting them. A text on land use is therefore a text on actual as well as on potential land use. Because both types must be based on a careful evaluation of land resources, land evaluation is a principal subject for consideration.

Land use is carried out in many different ways. The broadest categories include:

A. Rural land use in its widest sense, including agriculture, forestry and game-cropping as well as wildlife conservation and the development and management of recreation grounds;

B. Urban and industrial land use, including towns, villages, industrial complexes, highways and mining activities.

In the present text, the emphasis is placed on rural, and more specifically, on agricultural uses of the land. In most parts of the world, however, all kinds of land use are becoming increasingly interrelated. Periodical references will therefore also be made to non-agricultural land uses.

Agricultural land use as such, including horticulture, grazing and forestry, is already a very diversified activity. To cope with this, a classification into land utilization types has been found to be effective. In principle, this concept is also applicable to non-agricultural uses. In this book more treatment of agricultural land utilization types is, however, indicated.

1.2 Anthropological, Historical, and Institutional Aspects of Land Use

Land use is the result of a scarcity of land. In a global context, and even when regarded per continent, this scarcity has generally been relative. Sufficient land of some kind was available, but originally fertile land producing sufficient fruits of nature for human sustenance without systematic land use became scarce many thousands of years ago on most continents.

This scarcity may provoke two kinds of reactions in human beings, both of which may be considered cultural responses. One response is to find new land, which still provides sufficient natural sustenance; the other is to put some effort into primeval land management to obtain the needed foodstuffs and materials at the same locality, thus leading to production of agricultural crops. The need for the latter is further enhanced by the nature of the land, which contains many natural barriers, and by the increase in world population, which has led to the establishment of many barriers in human society.

Less than ten thousand years ago, probably on the western fringe of Asia, a group of people began to use the land systematically, i.e., through agriculture. It is not our task to give an extensive treatise on the history and origins of land use, but to some extent the situation then created exists even today. Seen in a global context, there is still a relative abundance of land. Reasonable estimates indicate that the earth is capable of supporting about fifty billion people at a reasonable standard of living. The world today supports nearly four billion people. The present rate of population increase may lead to an absolute scarcity of land in the next millennium, which is a danger that must be seriously studied. A much more serious situation exists today, however, with regard to the serious regional scarcity of land, and in particular of productive land, in many parts of the world. We must look for appropriate cultural responses to this situation.

In the past, local scarcity of land led either to intensification of the existing type of land use, or to settlement of a part of the population in distant areas. As early as the Neolithic Age, which saw movements of people along the Danube into the fertile loess areas of Central and Western Europe, these peoples took with them their cultural and institutional achievements. A later age witnessed the spread of irrigated rice-growing in Eastern Asia, and a still later period, the nineteenth century, saw the mass-movement of farmers from Europe into the plains of North America.

Wherever land use is found in the world, it is the results of techniques and customs acquired by these peoples before their migrations as well as of their later adaptation to the regions of settlement. In Rwanda, Central Africa, the Bahutu are small arable land farmers with relatively well-developed techniques, including the use of refuse as manure; the Watusi, on the other hand, are semi-nomadic people with a feudal societal structure, who make their living by cattle-breeding in the same areas and on the same soils. The agricultural techniques of the Bahutu appear to be derived from the old agricultural civilizations of Egypt, as are many of the structures of the sedentary societies in this area (see OLIVER and FAGE, 1962). In central Cameroun, near the Sanaga river, tribal movements were still active until the end of the German colonial period (1914 seq.); even today, a tendency towards some internal migration can be observed by comparing the situation of the villages on fairly recent aerial photographs with their actual position as seen in the field. In this region, agricultural techniques are still similar to those used in the systems of shifting cultivation practiced over large areas by many peoples in Western Africa (see also DE SCHLIPPE, 1956). Potentially, many soils in central Cameroun are nearly as productive as the soils cultivated by the Bahutu in Rwanda; the difference in land use between these regions is largely the result of the difference in inherited agricultural techniques of the peoples, to some extent consolidated by the societal structures.

Some interesting examples from Indonesia have been described by G.J. VINK (1941). Indonesian farmers are restricted in their methods of land use by their genealogical or their territorial customs. These traditions determine the kinds of institutional rights on the land as well as the kinds of land use and the techniques used in agriculture (see also GEERTZ, 1971).

Land use may also reflect previous systems of settlement, whether descendants of the same people are still living in the area or not. In those parts of Europe and the Mediterranean area which belonged to the Roman Empire, many remnants of the field pattern of the Roman military colonies can be found. The centuriatios, almost perfect squares of 709×709 meters, indicated the area of a villa, a farm of one colonist, and were arranged in long lines, only slightly adapted to the local landscape, running in the same direction over many kilometers in two directions at 90 degrees to each other, thus covering many square kilometers with a perfectly quadratic system of land use. The subdivision of the centuriatios into passus, or rectangular fields, is often reflected in the field patterns used today (BRADFORD, 1957; EDELMAN and EEUWENS, 1959). In these cases, the present land use itself may have little connection with the Roman land use. In other cases, land use of many thousands of years ago may still be reflected clearly in the land use of today, although the farmers of today may be only distantly related descendants of their agricultural ancestors. Such is the case in Mesopotamia, where today's Iraqi farmers practice methods of basin irrigation which are very good copies of the land use practiced in the different Babylonian empires (BURINGH, 1960; VINK, 1963 a). This even holds for the manner in which silted-up irrigation canals are being circumvented by new canals. The institutional arrangements of the Babylonian empires and of the well-organized Arab empire have, however, fallen down; it is only now that a comparable system is being reconstructed with modern methods.

Previous land use systems, practiced either by the same people in a different country or in the same country by different people, often exhibit divergencies in appropriate land management. One such divergence, i.e., insufficient adaptation to the prevailing restraints of the land resources, may lead to land degradation; such was true for the opening-up of the American midwestern prairies by European farmers with steam ploughs.

Land degradation may also be aggravated by an increasing population density, which leads to land use of too great intensity without proper changes in land management, as occurred in many parts of Mesopotamia. Occasionally, however, local populations have themselves found the right technical and institutional arrangements for adapting land management to the prevailing circumstances, even with a growing population. The best examples of this are perhaps the paddy-growing on the Isle of Bali, which has a highly institutionalized system of land and water management, and the waterdistrict system in Holland (the western part of the Netherlands), which is run today broadly along lines established during the twelfth century, and which is still adaptable to new needs of pollution control.

The system of land use established during the early Middle Ages (600 to 1200 AD) is still reflected in the patterns of land use and settlement as well as in the nature of the soils and landscapes, in the slightly undulating "coversand landscapes" of the Netherlands and of the adjoining parts of Germany and Belgium. A careful analysis of the field pattern and of the local field names (EDELMAN et al., 1958) indicated that the old settlement system of the village of Bennekom ("Bero-ingha-hem" cf. villages called "Beringen" in southern Germany and in Switzerland) is still closely reflected in the field pattern and in the toponymy. Furthermore, this system led to increased soil fertility on the arable lands of these regions by the formation of "Plaggen soils" (EDELMAN, 1950; PAPE, 1970; FINK, 1963; DUCHAUFOUR, 1970). Land use in other landscapes shows comparable traces of the past systems of settlement (HOFSTEE and VLAM, 1952). In some cases, e.g. in the peat-polders near Amsterdam and in some horticultural areas of North Holland, land use has also led to a build-up in soil fertility.

Even in prehistoric times, the costs of reclamation were taken into account. The best soils were not always reclaimed first, but rather those soils which were not too densely vegetated and, therefore, easier to clear. The same phenomenon is still seen today in parts of Western Africa. Only at a more advanced stage of technology does this phenomenon become less important. Modern mechaniza-tion may, in fact, lead to the clearance of areas without sufficient consideration of their potential fertility and conservability. The same is also true for areas cleared in primitive systems by repeated burning, which may even be for the pupose of hunting rather than of stable land use.

Stable land use over long periods, such as has been practiced in much of Western Europe since the early Middle Ages, tends to adapt itself to local land resources and tends to produce a steady state which closely approaches ecologic equilibrium, thereby producing a true cultural ecosystem. Adaptation to changing economic circumstances may also occur within these systems. For example, in the fine, loamy-sandy soils ("coversands") of the Netherlands, a considerable amount of flax was grown in every village until the early part of the twentieth century (around 1914). Apparently, flax was grown in these areas throughout the Middle Ages mainly for the use of the farmer's family and perhaps for local exchange. Later, local industries used the flax as one of their basic materials. Today, the cultivation of flax has completely disappeared from these regions. Economic conditions, for example the importation of inexpensive cotton from overseas countries, caused this disappearance. The system of land use adapted itself to a mixed system, in which the arable land is used to provide fodder crops for cattle breeding. Today, an additional change is evident as a result of the economic situation within the European Community and of the increased cost of produc-tion, i.e., cultivation of arable land has become less feasible in these areas. The land is now used almost exclusively for grassland farming for cattle breeding and milk production. The more highly developed technology for producing high qual-ity winter fodder from grasslands has also enhanced the change.

Land use is always strongly linked with advances in human technology. In Western Europe, before 1900, it would have been considered impossible to grow crops on dry, poor humus podzols. Around 1900 the use of chemical fertilizers made it possible to reclaim large areas of these soils. Some of these are now highly productive, albeit with enormous applications of chemical fertilizers, which is reflected in the cost of production. Today's economic situation, together with the increasing need for recreation grounds and the not quite negligible hazard of pollution of adjoining waters and of nature reserves, has induced a change of land use in these areas. This change is particularly enhanced by the growing interpene-tration of rural and urban land uses in the industrial areas of Western Europe.

In many of the preceding cases, institutional structures play an important role. Systems of landownership and of land tenure often determine the feasibility of certain systems of land use and of the appropriate kinds of land management belonging to these systems. The ownership of large tracts of lands, e.g. by Arab sheiks, combined with primitive systems of tenure, was adaptable, with few problems, to a comparatively low-input kind of land use with equally low-input methods of land and water management. Agrarian reform, badly needed to obtain decent standards of living and of general human welfare, requires different institutional arrangements, particularly for the appropriate management of land and water in irrigated agriculture. Patriarchal family systems in Western Africa, adapted to seminomadic shifting cultivation, do not provide the best means of land management for sedentary agriculture on small or medium-sized farms with cocoa and other marketable products. The governmental and administrative institutions must be adapted to modern kinds of land use. In some countries historic developments in relatively democratic societies led to some solutions: national and provincial institutions for land and water management provided coordination and technical assistance for regional and local water management institutions. Depending on the available resources, institutional and other human aspects of land use, inherited from the past, must be adapted and perhaps even revolutionally changed, to provide adequate solutions for present and future problems.

1.3 Resources-Aspects of Land Use

Land resources comprise many elements, which fall into two main categories: (1) natural land resources and (2) artifactial land resources. The former constitutes the largest group and includes subgroups such as: climate, topography, geology, geohydrology, hydrology, soils and vegetation. The second category includes the products of past human activity such as dikes, polders, roads, canals and terraces. General aspects of the subgroups of land resources will be discussed here. A more detailed discussion will be given in Chapter 4. Our attention in this section will be directed towards their relative importance and towards some of their interrelationships.

Climate

Climate covers a range of factors: sun, precipitation and atmospheric circulation. The sun provides almost all the energy which is applied to land use. Solar radiation, falling on land areas, is of the order of 28000×10^{12} watts per year, whereas the total depletable supply of mineral fuels is of the order of 1400×10^{12} watt-years. Hydropower produces a maximum of 3×10^{12} watts per year (STARR et al., 1971). More than 99% of the total energy input of the world comes from solar radiation. Nearly half of this is directly converted into heat, 23% energizes the processes of evaporation and precipitation and about 0.02% is utilized in photosynthesis (40×10^{12} watts per year).

Even more important for land use is the distribution of this radiation over the land area of the world, also taking into consideration the prevailing temperatures. The latter are of particular importance for determining the growing season of the plants and the intensity of photosynthesis (DE WIT, 1966). Theoretical calculations have been made of the total potential production by photosynthesis, expressed in kilograms of carbohydrates per year for the different latitudes. The highest potential production, found between 10° and 20° North latitude, is 124×10^3 kg carbohydrates per hectare per year. Agricultural production in general does not reach this high figure because of limitations imposed by other land conditions as well as by the available genetic composition of the plants. The lowest figure given by DE WIT (1966) is 12×10^3 kg carbohydrates per hectare per year for 70° NL and 50° SL, respectively. At 50° NL and 40° NL these figures are 59×10^3 and 91×10^3 kilograms of carbohydrates per hectare. At these latitudes, at which the highest producing land use types of most industrialized countries are found, relatively low percentages of potential production are realized in present-day agriculture.

Available solar radiation, even when considered together with factors such as local exposure, cloudiness etc. is not an absolute limitation for quantitative production of calories. It is, however, often a serious limitation with regard to quality of products and kinds of crops, in particular when taken together with the temperatures originating from solar heat production. Precipitation differs considerably in different parts of the world, and is a dominant factor in determination of land uses. Distribution of precipitation and even lack of precipitation can to some extent be corrected by irrigation; human effort, organized in land utilization, has more impact here than in the cases of solar radiation and temperature, where only extremely specialized kinds of land use, with hothouses, can supply extra energy. Atmospheric circulation, apart from its influence on cloudiness and precipitation, also has a direct impact on plant growth and on agricultural production; this impact is, however, much more local and specific in nature than are the main climatic influences.

All other land resources have their impact on land use within the general context of a given climate. Even so, many of these land resources have been, and are, influenced by climate during their formation. Climate is one of the main genetic factors in the formation of relief ("topography") and soils. It has been an important factor, e.g. paleoclimates, at the origin of the lithology of geological formations. It is the main agent determining the water balance in geohydrology and hydrology. Finally, climate largely determines the nature of the natural vegetation in any given area. Interactions between climate, relief and soils are particularly important for land use. Both the main climatic conditions, the "macroclimate", and the local climatic conditions, the "mesoclimate" or "topoclimate", are of the greatest importance. The "microclimate" prevailing within certain crops is dependent also on human management.

Geology and Hydrology

Geological formations, in mountainous and hilly, as well as in flat alluvial areas, determine the main materials and structures of the land. They determine the main features of the relief, including altitude, which is an important ecological factor, as well as the general directions of both surface and subsurface waterflow. Geological formations also have a decided influence on the formation and degradation of soils and landscapes; a detailed knowledge of geological conditions is often necessary for understanding these processes. Geohydrology, the study of the subsurface water, also includes hydrogeology, which is the study of the deeper underground water. The latter may consist partly of "fossil" quantities of water which have been formed under different ecologic conditions in previous geological epochs and are therefore depletable resources. The study of geohydrology is essential for understanding land use in all areas where lack of water for irrigation, for human or animal consumption or for industrial uses exists. It is also highly necessary in all cases where water pollution may be expected to occur. In large drainage projects, including the essential drainage works in all irrigation projects, the study of geohydrology is an essential requisite for sound land use planning. The study of geohydrology also provides the only means for explaining the natural processes of salinization (KOVDA, 1964; KOVDA and EGOROV, 1964; KOVDA et al., 1973; YAHIA, 1971).

Hydrology, the study of surface waters and water balance, and soils will be treated in Chapter 4. These are the two main resources with which land use is continuously concerned. Water and soils are, on the one hand, the stable resources on which all land use must be based; on the other hand, they can, to some extent, depending also on their position with regard to the other resources of a given region, be manipulated and adapted to man's requirements. Knowledge of soil and water conditions is indispensable for the understanding of past und present land use as well as for the prediction of future uses.

Vegetation

Vegetation within our context includes all natural and semi-natural vegetation which is not purposely and continuously manipulated by man for any of his systematic land uses. Vegetation may be used by man for satisfying material needs, e.g. gathering of products (timber, fruits, rubber, medicinal herbs, food) as well as for satisfying spiritual needs, e.g. "beauty" and "quietude" for recreation. It may also satisfy scientific or artistic needs. Finally, natural vegetation as a habitat for wild animals is the natural hunting ground for many people as well as the habitat of animal pests and their predators. In terms of land use, natural vegetation is often regarded as a hindrance: e.g. densely forested tropical areas make reclamation of land difficult, and hedges and lanes prevent the laying-out of large fields for mechanical cultivation. Man has sometimes utilized the natural regrowth of vegetation for the regeneration of his land, e.g. in well-balanced shifting cultivation (REYNDERS, 1962), or even in systematic adaptations of the original systems (DE SCHLIPPE, (1956). Land use has also benefitted from natural vegetation by the use of natural species to breed more resistant varieties of cultivated plants. Only lately has attention been drawn to the possible importance of natural vegetation for healthy, ecologically balanced land use. The ecosystem concept of land management (VAN DYNE et al., 1969) has thus far not been clearly developed for the more sophisticated land use systems. Within the more "natural", less intensive systems of land use such as range grazing and forestry, some ecological concepts have always been maintained to produce an optimum efficiency with a minimum of hazards.

Natural or semi-natural vegetation is characterized by a great variability of species which are well adapted to the ecological conditions under which they have developed; they are therefore internally stable, i.e. occasional disturbances within the ecosystem are easily compensated by the system itself without running into the danger of a disequilibrium. The same holds true for natural disturbances caused, e.g. by severe winters, dry summers or exceptional storms. Their external stability, i.e. their stability versus unnatural and man-made disturbances, is not always great; much depends on the kind of ecosystem and on the kind of disturbance with which it is confronted. An oligotrophic ecosystem will be very unstable towards strong eutrophic influences, whereas a eutrophic system may be fairly stable towards influences of an oligotrophic nature. Some pests may be easily counterbalanced by an ecosystem in which a large variety of appropriate predators occur, but in others this may not be the case. This is also true for the influence of areas of natural vegetation within a large area of intensively used land. These areas will be agreeable to the human eye and thus have a beneficial influence on the ecosystem for mankind. Whether they will also have a stabilizing influence on the cultural ecosystem within which they exist, will depend largely on the nature of the ecosystem itself. Basically, variability always tends to produce greater stability (see e.g. VAN LEEUWEN, 1966) and therefore some stabilizing influence can always be expected. Any cultural ecosystem which allows for a certain amount of natural variability is therefore from an ecological, and ultimately also from a production standpoint, preferable to a completely monotonous system under comparable conditions. More research is urgently needed, however, to determine the true value, importance and quantitative effects of ecosystems in the long run.

Artifactial Land Resources

Artifactial land resources are an essential part of the land in terms of land use. Man, as a result of past efforts, has for example created land from sea and from inland waters: e.g. the polders of the Netherlands and of many other countries. Construction of these polders produces the land, and drainage works within the polders make land use possible. Often, however, continuous annual activities of pumping water from the polders, is necessary i.e. in all cases where excess water is caused by periodic, often seasonal, precipitation excesses and by seepage. In all cases, a careful system of land and water management is required, particularly for the maintenance of canals and ditches. Artifactial land resources usually are not self-sustaining, whereas natural land resources under suitable natural or cultural ecosystems often need little or no specific management.

In addition, artifactial land resources may lead not to the creation of new lands, but to the development of usable from non-usable land. Such usable land has been produced by centuries-old systems of irrigation, in arid countries such as Egypt, Iraq and Iran and in humid tropical countries, e.g. Ceylon and parts of India and Indonesia. Similar systems exist in more subtropical parts of the world, e.g. China and Japan (KING, 1910). This artifactial system of land modification consists essentially of the construction of bundterraces; in "rainfed" irrigation systems, this may be the only essential feature. In more sophisticated systems in

a

b

Photo 1. Irrigation in Iraq. (a) Irrigated young barley on saline soils. (b) Irrigated wheat on desalinized land

Photo 2. Irrigated rice fields in Indonesia. (Photo W. P. v. D. KNAAP †)

which surface water is used for irrigation, the construction of irrigation canals and ditches is also an essential feature. In most old irrigation systems the construction of specific systems for drainage is absent or negligible.

In both preceding cases, the artifactial construction or modification of land resources has also led to relatively permanent modification of one or more of the natural land features. The soils are nearly always influenced by the construction of dikes and drainage works: in many cases the loose, anaerobic, "unripened" sediment is made into soil by the systematic drainage. When deep polders have been constructed near highly permeable lands, the latter may have undergone a definite modification of their hydrology through loss of water by seepage into the polder (VOLKER et al., 1969). In humid tropical countries, centuries-old irrigation has led to a marked change in soil development. Continuously wet conditions, in areas such as Western Java, have caused the formation of ironpans at a depth of approximately 60 cm below the soil surface. In seasonally dry tropical areas, such as Eastern Java, soil formation has undergone a still clearer change through the development of montmorillonitic clays which exhibit chemical and physical properties very different from the original kaolinitic clays formed under normal conditions (see SCHEFFER and SCHACHTSCHABEL, 1970; MOHR, VAN BAREN and VAN SCHUYLENBORGH, 1972). These tropical irrigation systems also exhibit clear relationships with the hydrology of more high-lying areas; they are particularly sensitive to modifications of the natural forest vegetation in the source areas of the water.

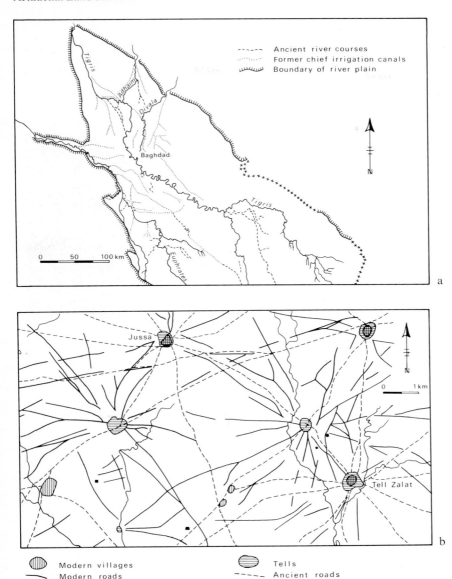

Fig. 1.1a and b. Irrigation and land use in early historic times in Iraq. (a) Ancient river courses and chief irrigation canals. (b) Tells and former roads about 12 miles west of Mosul, Iraq. (After BEEK, 1972)

Irrigation systems in arid lands have often had a complex influence on land development. Irrigation in Iraq, which was begun in the fourth millennium BC, led to local modifications of the soils by salinization; this effect has, however, been exaggerated. YAHIA (1971) has shown that the influence of natural salinization probably has been a more important process. In the Mesopotamian Plain, irriga-

Photo 3. Background: Remnant of an old irrigation canal from Abassid times near Baghdad, Iraq; foreground chloride-saline soils

tion has clearly resulted in the deposition of silty deposits, often more than 1 m thick. These silty deposits have been caused by the high silt content of the water of the two rivers, the Euphrates and Tigris, which is brought into the irrigation canals, a process which still continues today. Thus, silt loams of generally poor structures and low porosity have been deposited on top of the original, often more fertile, Mesopotamian alluvial soils. In some localities, notably in strips along the old irrigation canals, more sandy sediments, similar to natural river levees, have been deposited; where these have been sedimented on top of older heavy clays a definite improvement of the natural conditions has resulted. The landscape of Mesopotamia has also been affected by the ruins of the old banks of irrigation canals from Old Babylonian times (approx. 2000 BC) until the period of the Abassid Empire (approx. 1200 AD) (ATUJAH, 1968; BURINGH, 1960; SOUSA, 1969; VINK, 1970b; YAHIA, 1971) (Photo 3).

Other artifactial land features have a considerable impact on land use. Extension of urban areas and construction of highways and canals may have both favorable and unfavorable influences. The opening up of lands by roads and railways always has a clear influence on land use. Typical examples are found along the railways constructed at the beginning of this century by the Netherlands Indies Government on the island of Sumatra; until recently, some Hevea-rubber plantations could be reached only by railroad. The same influence, although perhaps less realized today, is found in many countries of the Old and of the New World with the construction of roads and railroads, such as the new road-construction projects in Central Brazil. Occasionally, the construction of roads may also have deleterious effects on drainage in arid lands; it may seriously aggravate the already existing problems of soil salinity. The influence of road construction and of other comparable disturbances of the landscape on erosion and on land-slides and other mass movements is well known but not always sufficiently real-ized. Particularly in areas with a strong natural instability, this often causes serious problems (FLAWN, 1970) (see also Photo 10, page 88).

1.4 Present and Potential Land Use

Present land use is the result of different causes, many of which are directly related to the nature and quantity of land resources, others of which have their origin in cultural, social and economic conditions of the past and their developments within the context of history. As a result present land use is only rarely in accord-ance with the interplay of today's resources and human society. Often, it is even less adapted to the requirements of tomorrow in so far as these can be estimated by a projection of today's ideas, which may lead to more intensive production or to a more balanced ecological use of land, or, which is more important, to a suitably balanced compromise between the two. Thus, potential land use is often different from what is presently being done. Present land use, therefore, must always be, if not continually, at least periodically, tested against other possible methods of land use. Such methods may prove more suitable to human needs as well as to the need for conserving or establishing a healthy biosphere. Different kinds of potential land use should therefore be treated in any book on land use. To systematize this approach, the categorizing of the different types of land utilization has proved very effective.

The crucial point, however, is how to determine land suitability or land use capability, i.e. the potential capacity of a given tract of land to support different types of land utilization under given cultural and socio-economic conditions. Land utilization types must be selected with regard to the kind and quantity of available land resources, paying particular attention to their stability and to the hazards of growth and production of plants and crops. Land use, therefore, should be studied in relation to land resources. The land resources, their nature and the methods of investigating them, must be carefully considered.

In using the land, land resources should be managed in a manner appropriate to their nature and to the desired results to be obtained from the particular type of land utilization. If this is not done, the result is often degradation, which is of serious importance in many parts of the world. Some features of the processes leading to degradation of available land resources will therefore be mentioned; this may also serve the useful purpose of avoiding exaggerations of their impact. The serious dangers which have led and still may lead to continuation of these processes will also be discussed.

Although man undoubtedly must adapt land management to the land re-sources, he need not always take these as they are found in nature. Land improve-ment has been practiced by human societies for thousands of years. Today, land improvement provides a wide range of tools to adapt land resources in a manner suitable to the needs of mankind. The kinds of improvement and their results depend on the nature of the land and on the techniques to be applied. Their feasibility also depends both on the land utilization type and the socio-economic context where they are applied. Knowledge of the general range and impact of the various methods of land improvement is therefore an essential part of any study on land use.

Given land resources, land utilization types, land management and land improvement, all seen within a cultural and socio-economic context, how can the best potential use of a tract of land be determined? There is no simple solution. In most cases several kinds of potential land uses must be considered and compared. None of these is without hazards and constraints, just as most land resources and most human societies have their hazards and constraints. Only in rare cases are simple solutions applicable, because only very few lands in the world are so productive that any kind of land use will yield good results. It is also true that a relatively small percentage of the lands of the world have such poor resources that no kind of land use may be considered. For most lands, a delicate evaluation of the land resources and their interactions as well as of the human resources and their interactions with the land has to be made. For this purpose, the discipline of "Land Evaluation" is now being systematically developed. Reliable methods of land evaluation are an essential tool for solving, by interdisciplinary methods, the present-day problems of land development and environmental management.

Today's literature often divides the world into three parts: the Eastern World, the Western World and the Third, or Developing, World. For Land Evaluation this is an unsatisfactory division. We prefer a simple subdivision into two parts: those areas of the world where the interplay of human society and land resources may make further development of production necessary and feasible within the next decades, and those parts where industrialization and the resulting standard of living have led to a partial shifting of priorities in land use from production to environmental management. It would, however, be a serious distortion of the truth to think that the former occur only in the so-called "Third World" and that the latter are found only in the industrialized countries. Only a careful study and evaluation of land resources and of the needs of human societies can provide suitable solutions for the various lands of the world as well as for the world as a whole. The lack of well-balanced knowledge of land resources and of the uses to be made of them is one of the most serious drawbacks in the world of today.

Chapter 2   Land Use Surveys

2.1 Principles of Land Use Surveys

Within the context of this book, the term "land use survey" includes all those surveys used to register the different aspects of land use as they exist at the moment of survey. Land use surveys are therefore "surveys of present land use". As in all surveys, the contents of such a survey depends on the scale of the map, the special purpose of the survey and the nature of the region. All of these factors are additionally elaborated by persons who have their own special knowledge and preferences, their "reference level" (VINK, 1970a). Most land use surveys are made primarily to register the occurrence of crops in their more or less regular geographical distribution. The "World Land Use Survey", initiated by the late Sir Dudley Stamp under the auspices of the International Geographical Union, is a typical example of a general land use survey (STAMP, 1950, 1953, 1954, 1958, 1961a). Other comparable crop surveys have been carried out in different countries. They all reflect to some extent the ecological conditions under which the crops are grown, but the past and present economic conditions of the area have equally had their impact on present land use, as was discussed in Chapter 1. A special kind of survey is the "soil use survey" in which the quantity of crops grown is compared statistically with the types of soils in a given area. "Crop disease surveys", in which particular crops are investigated for the nature and geographical distribution of diseases and other kinds of crop damage, are of major interest today. In other cases, one particular crop is surveyed to obtain an inventory of its present or future production under the existing management conditions.

In systems of "Economic Land Use Classification", the emphasis is on the system of farming, including the nature of the farm buildings, rather than on the geographic distribution of individual crops. Field pattern surveys and land allotment surveys are concerned with different aspects of land use, in particular with the size and shape of the fields on which the crops are grown. Like the crop surveys, they register what is being done today and are not concerned with potential land use. The same is true for cadastral surveys, which register the ownership aspects of land use; together with other cartographic indications, e.g. of administrative boundaries of various kinds, they provide data on the institutional aspects of land use.

All of the preceding types of land use surveys are of considerable scientific interest. As a means of characterizing human activities in a region, they provide one means of characterizing the geographic regions of the world (cf. WEAVER, 1954a,b). They are an indispensable tool for international and interregional exchange of data and experiences. Within a country or region, but lately also for the whole world, the data from land use surveys provide the best possible basis for agricultural statistics. Much depends on the accuracy of these statistics, since many important governmental decisions are based on them. Also international prognoses, e.g. for the World Food Program, could not be made without reliable data on the surface area of crops grown in the different countries of the world. In particular cases, e.g. for irrigated rice growing ("paddy") in the humid tropics, even monthly predictions on the surface area to be harvested have been made.

Land use surveys are of fundamental importance for land development planning. Only when all aspects of the present situation are known, can further developmental plans be made. Although knowledge of how the land is presently being used is in itself insufficient, it is, next to the knowledge of the land resources to be developed, an essential prerequisite. Decisions on changes in land use should be made only after the present land use is investigated from all viewpoints, including cultural, socio-economic and ecological conditions. These conditions often have also a direct bearing on the planning of land improvement, e.g. in soil conservation and land reallotment projects. The ecological importance of existing land use obtains special attention in modern industrialized countries; the disturbance of existing cultural ecosystems, with a variety of habitats established through ages of well adapted land use, has many serious ecological effects which have often been neglected in the past.

Usually it is impossible to derive sufficiently accurate conclusions on the ecology of a region from present land use maps only. Though it may be possible, as mentioned by PAPADAKIS (1938, 1964), to make some such conclusions in a broad global sense, more detailed conclusions require a study of the natural resources of the land itself. Still, the observation that a particular crop is grown on a certain tract of land at least proves one important thing, which may sound obvious, but is often not treated as such: i.e. that *at least* under the prevailing type of land utilization, the land is *at least* suitable, though perhaps not most suitable, for the production of that crop. The reverse may then prove true for adjoining tracts of land utilized in the same manner under the same circumstances, but great care must be taken with this conclusion.

Land use surveys, perhaps even more than other surveys, benefit from modern survey methods. Of these, the use of aerial photography and of other kinds of remote sensing, generally air-borne, are of the greatest interest (see Para. 2.3).

2.2 Various Kinds of Land Use Surveys

Characteristic Crops

In a global context, PAPADAKIS (1964) indicates that the following groups of crops characterize the main ecological regions of the world:
— *cryophilous* (cold-needing) *crops*, such as wheat, barley, oats, rye, Pisum, field beans, flax, potato, beet, turnip, cabbage, cauliflower, lettuce, celery, onion, Phleum, Poa, Festuca and other grasses, clovers, lucerne (alfalfa), apple, pear, plum, peach, grapes, olives;

— *non-cryophilous crops*, such as maize, sorghum, millet, rice, Phaseolus, soybean, cowpea, tobacco, tomato, sweetpotato, hemp, coffee, cacao, citrus, oilpalm, coconut, datepalm, Hevea, sugar cane.

"Cryophilous crops need cold before flowering; when grown continuously under sufficiently high temperatures their flowering is delayed or inhibited. In non-cryophilous crops, such continuously high temperatures do not delay or inhibit flowering." Cryophilous plants are also long-day plants whereas non-cryophilous crops are short-day plants. The former are also relatively winter-resistant, whereas non-cryophilous crops have little or no resistance to winter. This division of all crops of the world into two categories is admittedly very broad. It does no more than divide the world roughly into the tropical and the temperate zones with the subtropical areas as transitional regions. Neither does it take into account the cultivation of crops in tropical mountain areas, such as tea, which is grown in Northern India with a relatively short-day period and a winter with some frost, as well as in the mountainous areas of Java. Such a division does, however, stress the point that there is a basic physiology of all crops which responds in a more or less typical manner to the main climatic regions of the world and therefore acts as a guiding principle in world land use.

The Land Use Survey of Britain

The land use survey of Great Britain stood as an example of the World Land Use Survey of the International Geographical Union, which was carried out in different parts of the world, e.g. Cyprus and Hong Kong. The original work done in Britain was by far the best described and documented and will therefore be taken as the most typical example of the work of Dudley Stamp and his school of workers. The survey was begun in 1930 and continued in the following years. The single intention was to gather and map land use data in order to obtain a better geographical knowledge of Great Britain. By the end of 1934 nearly ninety per cent of the field work, which was organized per parish, had been completed. At the beginning of the Second World War, with ensuing changes in land use, all field work had been completed and a large part of the cartographic work, based on a scale of 1 inch to 1 mile (1:63360) had been carried out.

The need for utilizing arable land for food production during the war suddenly rendered this relatively academic exercise into a practically applicable tool which could be used by County War Agricultural Committees and by the Service Ministries. During the war, a total of 8000 map sheets were loaned for practical application, not counting the use of the already published sheets. Gradually, the work itself was more and more directed towards the needs of the Ministry of Agriculture for an assessment of the productivity, fertility and classification of the land.

In addition, as the need for basic material for town and country planning became more urgent, more basic data on soils and landscapes were collected. These data were finally integrated into a Land Classification of Great Britain, some aspects of which are discussed below. In this highly pragmatic manner, based on the considerable knowledge of land resources collected largely as a by-product by the geographers who led the land use survey, a land classification

Table 1. Land use survey of Britain 1931–1938 (STAMP, 1950)

Notes on the classification

1. *Forests* and woodland are usually marked on the six-inch maps, but all the areas must be checked. Care must be taken to include the newly planted areas. When this has been done the woodland must be classified as follows:

    (a) High Forest, big trees, sufficiently close for their crowns to touch; also state whether the trees are Coniferous, Deciduous, Mixed.

    (b) Coppice, or coppice with standards, woodland that is cut over every few years, for fencing, posts, etc.

    (c) Scrub, any small bushes or trees unfit for cutting.

    (d) A Forest, cut down and not replanted. This requires a note stating its present character. A note should also be made against any forest or woodland which is not intended to supply timber, but is ornamental, for screening houses and gardens, etc.

    In practice it has been found that the simplest way of dealing with forest or woodland on the field map is as follows:—Mark each piece of forest with the letter F; then distinguish its character according to the above classification as Fa, Fb, Fc, Fd. Then distinguish coniferous (c), deciduous (d), or mixed (m), thus Fa^c, Fb^d, Fb^m, etc. Any woodland not intended to supply timber may be shown by underlining the symbol thus: $\underline{Fa^d}$. There is sometimes room to mention in brackets the chief trees, e.g. (oak) (beech), etc.

    Plantations of trees intended for timber should be marked Fa, with a note "plantation".

2. *Meadowland and Permanent Grass.* Care must be taken not to include rotation grass (grass grown in rotation with crops) under this classification.

3. *Arable* or tilled land includes rotation grass and fallow land. Rotation grass is often indicated by a large proportion of clover. At the present time, when much land which was recently arable is being converted to permanent grassland, its appearance, showing evidences of recent cultivation, gives rise to doubt as to whether it is Arable or Meadow. In such cases, information should be obtained from the farmer. A point, easily recorded, which may well be added to the map is the crop actually being grown at the date of the Survey. *Market Gardens* are arable, being merely a special form of agriculture and should accordingly be marked A. Where it is quite clear that they are market gardens, they should be marked A (M.G.).

4. *Heathland, Moorland, Commons and Rough Hill Pasture.* This type of land is usually already distinguished on the six-inch maps. Swamps and marshes are often used as rough pasture, and should be included here. It is advisable to make a special note against any land where there is any doubt, saying what use is made of it.

5. *Gardens, Allotments, Orchards, Nurseries, etc.* Houses with gardens sufficiently large to grow a few vegetables or even flowers should be marked G (garden) since the area is productive. Backyards and other areas agriculturally unproductive should, however, be marked W. Allotments are merely gardens at a distance from the house. *Orchards* are usually already distinguished on the maps (but should, of course, be checked). They must be marked G. In some orchards, in addition to the fruit trees, the ground is used for grazing or for agriculture. In such cases they should be marked G(M) when used for fruit and pasture, or G(A) when used for fruit and ground crops. The addition of the world "orchard" is useful.

6. *Unproductive Land.* This includes buildings, yards, mines, cemeteries and waste land, i.e. all ground of which the soil is not productively used. It is advisable to make a special note stating the character of all considerable areas marked (W).

    Parks should be classified according to the use of the land, e.g., pasture, woodland, gardens, etc. Public parks are large gardens used by the public, and should be marked G.

Table 1. (continued)

Notes on the classification

Golf Courses can sometimes be used for grazing, and then are permanent grassland (M). Others are heathland and moorland (H). Mark them also with the words "Golf Course".

Sports Grounds are usually grassland, but where devoted entirely to sports, they should be specially distinguished, e.g., M (Sports).

Poultry Farms usually occur on meadowland. A special note should be made against them.

New Buildings, Roads, etc., made since the map was printed should be sketched in as far as possible. In the case of a new building estate it is not necessary to mark in every house, but the general plan of the roads and lines of houses should be indicated, and in the case of undeveloped estates the approximate boundaries should be ascertained and a note made of the estates. When a whole area is marked off as "Building Estate" a note should be added as to whether it is undeveloped (lying waste), partly developed (scattered dwellings), or more fully developed.

system was developed. Due to the sound practical knowledge and the large amount of common sense which were integrated with the actual survey data, this system led to a useful basis for the first stage of land use planning in postwar Britain.

Such a system was very necessary at the time, because the proper survey organizations for the study of the land resources themselves either had not yet reached a sufficient stage of development or were only concerned with the academic exercise of studying the soils as natural phenomena. From the point of view of land use planning, this situation was highly regrettable, since a distortion in the approach to land evaluation could thus not be avoided. It was also regrettable that, because of the initial successes of Stamp's system of land classification, the use of sound land evaluation practices by international bodies was delayed by at least ten years.

This fact does not, however, detract from the value of Stamp's land use survey as such. The combination of historic data, derived partly from the 11th century Domesday Book, with factual data of land use at the time of survey and with interesting, although pragmatically collected and often superficial, data on the land itself, led to a very interesting result. The fact that the land resources data available to Stamp were insufficient is not to be held against his original effort; the same could be seen in other countries where the needs of rural planning could not yet be met by the soil survey organizations. The German Bodenschätzung and the original land classification systems of the U.S. Soil Conservation Service (1933 to 1950) and of the U.S. Bureau of Reclamation (1953) provide comparable examples.

The succes of Stamp's land use survey depended primarily, apart from the energy and talent of Stamp and a small group of scientific co-workers, on the large number of volunteer workers, many of whom were schoolchildren, who were recruited from all over the country. About 22000 quarter-sheets on a scale of six inches to one mile (approx. 1:10000) were covered by a nearly equal number of volunteers. They were given a leaflet of instructions with a simple legend and

Table 2. Types of farming in Great Britain (STAMP, 1950)

A. In England and Wales

Pasture Types

A. Predominantly dairying
B. Dairying supplemented by other enterprises
C. Grazing and dairying
D. Rearing supplemented by several livestock enterprises
E. Mainly rearing and sheep grazing

Intermediate Types

F. Mixed farming with substantial dairying side
G. Mixed farming with substantial rearing or feeding side
H. General mixed farming
I.   Corn, sheep and dairying
J.   Farming based largely on wheat and cattle
K. Other intermediate types, with fruit, vegetables or hops

Arable Types

L. Mixed farming based on arable production
M. Mainly corn and sheep farming
N. Corn and sheep farming, supplemented by cash crops
O. Mainly cash crop farming
P. Market gardening
Q. Other arable farming types

Various (not types)

R. Land of small agricultural value
S. Marshes
T. Varied farming on mixed soils, or unclassified

B. In Scotland

Arable with livestock feeding
Livestock rearing with arable
Dairying
Hill sheep pasture
Crofting
Early potatoes
Seed potatoes
Soft fruit
Timothy hay for sale

with sufficiently clear and simple explanations on how to use this legend and to produce the field sheets. A specimen of a finished map was included with the instructions. The essential notes on the classification from these instructions are reproduced in Table 1.

During the course of this survey, many other remarkable data on land use in Britain were gathered or synthesized. In particular the descriptions of the grasslands of Britain and geographical and statistical data on cattle breeding are still worth reading. Also of interest are segments of the chapters on the separate land uses distinguished in his survey and many of the cartograms included in these chapters.

Of particular importance are Stamp's discussions on the types of farming, partly because of their content, and partly because they are being followed up in the studies on types of land utilization which are presently being carried out by Stamp's successors in the International Geographical Union. These studies will be discussed in Chapter 3. Table 2 contains a list of the types of farming recognized by STAMP (1950).

Other Land Use Inventories

The World Atlas of Agriculture, produced by MEDICI et al. under the aegis of the International Association of Agricultural Economists (World Atlas of Agriculture, 1973) comes nearest to STAMP's original concept of a Land Use Survey. Strictly speaking, however, it is not an original survey but a compilation of available data. Because it is a world atlas, the maps are produced on a very small scale, e.g. 1:2 500 000, whereas the scales of STAMP's documents range from 1:50 000 to 1:250 000. Some of STAMP's original intentions are, however, at least for global use, being met by this interesting new venture.

Some interesting data published by WEAVER (1954) came not from direct field surveys but from census data. In this case, the land use survey did not support the census, but the census data (statistical data per county) were used to compile a kind of land use map on a very small scale: crop-combination regions. Some interesting conclusions can be made from this study, for example, by comparing data from different years. The development and change of the crop-combination regions in the Middle West of the U.S.A. is clearly a part of a general evolution of agriculture. The four crop combination of corn-oats-hay-wheat (COHW) was the most prominent in 1919 and 1929. In 1939 and 1949 this crop combination had been reduced to a remnant of what previously was *the* dominant combination, at least in the areas east of the eastern margin of the Great Plains. In the Northwest a general and substantial increase of the barley acreage and a concurrent reduction of the wheat acreage led to the development of the crop combinations corn-oats-hay-wheat-barley (COHWB) and even to corn-oats-hay-barley (COHB). In more southern parts of the area, combinations which included soybean came into being. The reasons for these developments were both ecological and economic: i.e., the relatively poor suitability of the northern part of the area for both winter and spring wheat and the increasing specialization of farmers towards dairying.

In recent years, different land utilization studies have been carried out in Eastern European countries (SARFALVY et al., 1967). The methods used for these surveys were derived from STAMP's system, described previously. Initially, the project was begun in Poland and from there developed into a coordinated effort in which other countries took part, i.e. Hungary, Czechoslovakia, Yugoslavia and the German Democratic Republic. The project was also coordinated with similar work, including land evaluation, being carried out in the Soviet Union. This work, directed primarily towards a detailed study of the characteristic features of land utilization itself, tends towards a more thorough study of the natural and socio-economic conditions of land use. It also points towards systematic research into questions of ownership (structures agraires = agricultural structures) and of organizational and technical matters leading to the elaboration of land utilization systems. The ultimate goal of this work is clearly not only to register how the land is being used at present, but to study this critically with a view to land evaluation. The latter includes a critical study of the relative suitability of the existing types of land utilization to the lands on which they are being practiced. This objective is clearly expressed in a publication from Rumania (GRUMAZESCU in: SARFALVI et al., 1967), in which the suitability of different types of landscapes and "biotopes" is discussed.

The Eastern European system is not directed exclusively towards agricultural land use. The main headings of the legend include:

    I. Ownership boundaries and administrative boundaries,
   II. Agricultural land (agrarian structures, rotations on arable land, perennial crops, permanent grasslands, animal breeding),
 III. Forests (density, dominating species, brushwoods),
 IV. Waters (kinds of water, water control, water utilization),
  V. Settlements and non-agricultural land (residential areas, industrial areas, mining areas, agricultural-industrial areas, commercial areas, communication areas, public utilities, recreation areas, other constructions of tourist interest),
 VI. Unproductive land (because of natural conditions, derelict lands),
VII. Special areas.

Thus, from the relatively simple system of STAMP, a complicated structure for describing land use has been developed. The particular importance of land utilization systems or types will be discussed separately in Chapter 3. The development of this system towards a method of land evaluation, although seemingly based on more elaborate data on natural and socio-economic conditions than were available to STAMP, may nevertheless possess the difficulties inherent to its being primarily based on present land use instead of on land resources. Some of the knowledge and experience gained from this work will, however, no doubt prove to be essential contributions to a more balanced system of land evaluation.

The Canada Land Use Inventory, although based partly on investigations of present land use, is primarily executed as an ad hoc evaluation of land use capabilities; it is therefore primarily to be treated as a system of land evaluation (MCCORMACK, 1971).

Surveys of present land use constitute a well-known part of many land resources surveys for development projects; they are particularly useful in areas where both irrigated agriculture and dry farming exist, such as in Syria (VAN LIERE, 1965) AND IRAQ (BURINGH, 1960; YAHIA, 1971). In areas with much acreage in perennial crops, particularly in the humid tropics, the survey of these crops is also particularly significant (SCHWAAR, 1971). In all of these cases, land use is characterized by one or more long-term features which, although not really permanent, come near to being parts of the land resources themselves. The same often holds true for forest inventory surveys and surveys of permanent grasslands in semi-arid lands and in other cases in which natural or seminatural vegetation types must be considered, for ecological or for economic reasons or both, to be essential parts of a particular tract of land.

Soil use surveys represent a particular kind of survey of the present land use. They differ from the preceding land use surveys not so much in the manner in which they are executed, as in the manner in which the results are compared with soil survey data, in particular with detailed or semi-detailed soil maps. The results from soil use surveys have, in most cases, not been published separately, but have been incorporated in the general system of land evaluation for which they were made.

The soil use survey of the area around Wageningen, made in the summer of 1955, was published (DE VISSER, 1956) as a methodological exercice. In this survey, for each separate plot of arable land the standing crop was noted. The actual condition of the crop was described roughly as being "good", "medium" or "poor". The coherent grassland area as well as separate plots of grassland were also noted. Afterwards, for every soil type indicated on the soil map (scale 1:10000), the percentages of the different crops were calculated according to the number of the plots for each crop. It was found that according to the differences in land use, the soil types could be divided into four major groups (A—D), each of which could be further subdivided into a number of land use classes. Group A consisted almost exclusively of arable land, and within this group some interesting differences in crops were found. Group B contained arable land and grasslands in nearly equal quantities, and orchards occurred within this category. The soils found in Groups C and D were used predominantly for pastures containing different species of grasses and herbs. This survey contributed significant insight into the actual adaptation of the land use of the time to the ecological conditions of the landscapes and the soils. It also provided important information which was later used to evaluate land in pasture areas (VINK and VAN ZUILEN, 1967, 1974).

The Cornell system of economic land classification (CONKLIN, 1957) was also based primarily on a particular kind of survey of the present land use, i.e., on the kinds of structures of the farm buildings and of other buildings in the surrounding areas. In this survey, the farms of New York State are classified as business units. Too often, an inventory of the relatively permanent artifactial structures of the land is neglected. These structures constitute an important part of the land itself, and knowledge concerning them contributes to a better understanding of present land use and provides essential data for the reorganization of rural structures.

One aspect of rural land use structures is the way in which the fields are organized, both within the village or parish area and by individual owner and tenant. The Land Division Survey of the Netherlands (BIJKERK et al., 1970) is a computerized system for the inventory of all those aspects which may be of importance for rural reallotment projects and for similar projects of rural reconstruction. The data are presented in tables and on maps. The tables include:
— all basic data per holding,
— basic data per land users' districts,
— socio-economic data,
— horticultural data,
— data on sites of farm buildings relative to lots, on use by farmers who are not living in the area and on kind of culture,
— data on the distribution of holdings,
— data on distance,
— data on accessibility,
— data on slope of lots and roads (when applicable).

The following maps are produced:
— map of land users' districts,
— map of land users' holdings inclusive of use by absentee farmers,
— map with sites of farm buildings,
— map of compound lots,
— distance map (to farm buildings),
— accessibility map,
— slope map (where applicable).

For planning purposes, these data are also compiled into concise categorical print-outs. The results of this survey, which is now being conducted over areas totalling more than 600000 hectares, are being used for benefit-cost analyses of rural reconstruction measures. They are also being tested as a means of predicting the future development of the actual sizes of holdings and for different kinds of physical planning. They provide, in conjunction with data on the natural land resources, an essential means for modern planning of rural projects.

Studies on the history of land use are an indispensable tool for understanding present land use. They can often only be carried out with a thorough study of historical as well as of sociological data. The study by DE SCHLIPPE (1956) of the Zande system of agriculture in Central Africa is a well-known example. The history of land use in arid regions (STAMP et al., 1961), a monumental example of this type of study, was compiled by a large group of extremely well-qualified experts, and is an essential background document for understanding present land use in the Old as well as in the New World.

2.3 Modern Survey Techniques

Aerial Photography

For almost all purposes for which natural resources surveys are made today, modern survey techniques are essential for covering large areas within a reasonable time and with sufficient accuracy. These surveys nearly always utilize material collected from an aerial vantage point, in particular aerial photographs, and occasionally thermal infrared photographs and radar scannings. Aerial photographs can be made with panchromatic film, with film sensitive to the "near infrared" (wavelengths of up to 1000 nanometers), with color film sensitive to the normal spectrum or with color "ektachrome" film, which is in addition sensitive to the near-infrared wavelengths; the latter was originally called "camouflage-detection film" and now is often called "false-color" film. The proper term for this kind of film, of which there are several types, is "spectrozonal film", a term often used in the Soviet Union; this term indicates properly that the film is sensitive to particular selected zones of the spectrum (REY et al., 1968; Symposium 1962, 1966, 1970; COLWELL et al., 1960).

The different types of aerial photographs can be taken with various kinds of cameras and from various types of vehicles. The latter are of particular importance, since the type of vehicle determines the altitude from which the photo can be taken, and thus the magnitude of the scale of the photo. The scales of photos taken from air planes are relatively large, while the scales of those taken from satellites are relatively small. The scale of the photo may be increased by enlarging the print, but enlargement does not affect the mathematics of the images, which have often been taken at very great altitudes (see also SHAY et al., 1970).

These photographs are analyzed using photogrammetry and photointerpretation techniques and then incorporated into the survey results. It is not within the scope of this book to discuss these techniques in detail (VINK, 1968, 1970a; ALBERTZ, 1970). Special instruments and special knowledge are needed for the photogrammetric and systematic photointerpretation techniques which are truly useful in modern surveys. In all such surveys, some systematic field investigation is also indispensable.

In land use surveys, these modern techniques are applied to the study of land use in historic and prehistoric times as well as to the study of present land use and of the land resources. The latter two features are used as the basis for determining how the land could be used in the future.

Remnants of Former Land Use

The study of the remnants of former land use is of particular interest for understanding the settlement and the field patterns of today. It can also lead to a better understanding of erosion processes and other kinds of land degradation. A classic example is found in the pre-Roman and Roman patterns described by BRADFORD (1957). Patterns from Medieval times have been described by CHEVALLIER (1963, 1964; and BURGER, 1966) and by NEWCOMB (1966). Many interesting examples are also found elsewhere (Symposium 1962, 1966, 1970). (See also the discussion of the remnants of historic land use presented in Chapter 1 (pp. 5–7). Surveys of historic land uses also often include the use of topographic maps, both old and new, and of cadastral maps. In addition, a regional study of toponymics, which entails careful analysis of the linguistics of field names originating from different settlement periods, often produces remarkable results (EDELMAN et al., 1958; EDELMAN and EEUWENS, 1959).

NEWCOMB (1966) developed a key for the historical interpretation of aerial photographs. This key consists of two parts: (1) a selective key for the historical interpretation of aerial photographs in general, and (2) a dichotomous elimination key for the interpretation of enclosed features of ancient types of British fields. The former recognizes five different kinds of features:

1. Areal features: mostly agricultural features such as Celtic fields;
2. Linear features: travelling earthworks, boundaries, alignments and transportation lines, e.g. Roman Road, Wansdyke, the Old Bath Road, the Kennet and Avon Canal;
3. Focal features: Ritual centers, settlements, habitation complexes and communication junctions, e.g., the Avebury Complex, Windmill Hill;
4. Point features: Monuments, small enclosures and isolated buildings, e.g., Silbury Hill, Knap Hill Fort;

5. Complex features: Overlaps in position and usage, usually reflecting ori-
                            gins at different times: overlapping land uses and mili-
                            tary or political frontiers, e.g. the Avebury Circle, occu-
                            pied since the Bronze Age.

The dichotomous elimination key for the interpretation of enclosed features of
ancient British field types is specifically directed towards the determination of old
land uses. This key is reproduced in Table 3; the sketches of the phenomena are
reproduced in Fig. 2.1. The same keys, or similar ones developed especially for
local uses, can be utilized in many countries. Linear features, most often indicating old irrigation canals, and focal features indicating old settlements ("tells"),
have been mapped from aerial photographs in Iraq (BURINGH, 1960; BEEK, 1962).

In a recent study, NEWCOMB (1971) applied his method to Celtic fiels in Denmark, which probably date from the Iron Age. With the use of panchromatic
aerial photographs, at a scale of approx. 1:25000, he mapped the Himmerland
area of Jutland, an area of 2500 km^2. He proved the extensive occurrence of these
fields over the entire area studied and was able to delineate many of the fields in
great detail. The ancient fields in general show up as dark crop or soil marks
within the present crop pattern. The pattern is very regular and intricate, with a
rough North-South, East-West orientation. These investigations contributed
markedly to a better understanding of Iron Age land use in Denmark. They
indicate a clear resemblance to similar finds of a less extensive nature in other
European countries, e.g., the Netherlands. Similar studies have been carried out
on urban land uses (e.g., CHEVALLIER, 1966).

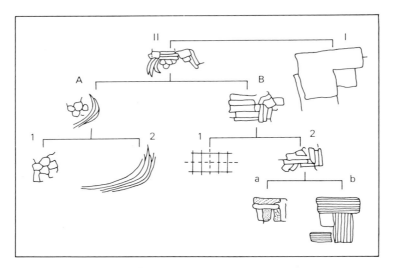

Fig. 2.1. Illustration of a dichotomous elimination key for interpretation of ancient field types
(NEWCOMB, 1966)

Table 3. A dichotomous elimination key for the interpretation of enclosed features of ancient British field types (after NEWCOMB, 1966).

I. *Size* of Enclosed Area large	agricultural enclosures such as ranch boundaries, cattle corrals, pastoral enclosures and estate boundaries
II. *Size* of Enclosed Area small	
A. *Shape* of Area irregular	
1. Irregular but rectilinear	corn plots of Neolithic and Bronze Ages
2. Irregular but long and narrow	strip-lynchets, lynchets, terraces
B. *Shape* of Area regular	
1. *Pattern* or Relationship with other Enclosures highly regular	Roman fields, e.g. centuratios
2. *Pattern* or Relationship with other Enclosures irregular	
a) *Cultivation marks* absent, although may have slight scratching marks of cultivation, usually 2 sets crisscross	Celtic fields
b) *Cultivation marks* present, banks and hollows or ridge and furrow in elongated strips bundled into rectangular groupings	Ridge and Furrow

Purposes and Methods of Land Use Surveys

Surveys of present land use are carried out in different manners and for different purposes by various kinds of persons and organizations. General land use surveys, indicating the broad divisions of rural and urban land use, constitute a normal part of any topographic mapping; these surveys are executed by photogrammetrists and topographic surveyors with the use of photointerpretation and some essential field checking. Crop surveys are carried out to delineate more accurately the crops grown in a specific area. Crop disease surveys are increasingly executed to obtain accurate information for combating agricultural pests and diseases and to locate especially noxious environmental influences, e.g. the influence of city gas mains on trees. The efficiency of field pattern surveys for reallotment projects is enhanced by the systematic use of up-to-date aerial photographs. Surveys of grassland vegetation and of the influence of grazing practices on natural or seminatural grasslands, in particular in developing countries, are unthinkable without the proper use of appropriate aerial photographs; aerial photographs are also helpful in conducting inventories of the cattle actually grazing in an area (HAEFNER, 1964, 1967; KREIG, 1970).

Forest inventories, including forest mensuration and typology, generally include the use of photogrammetry and photointerpretation. Normal black-and-

white photography is most often used, including black-and-white infrared photography (see e.g. STELLINGWERF, 1967). For typological studies, full-color and
false-color photography are increasingly used; they are, however, useful only for
large-scale images, because the atmospheric haze, even with suitable film-filter
combinations, tends to distort the color. Nevertheless, recent experiments have
shown that, even with satellite photography at great altitudes, false-color film
often aids in a better interpretation of the photographic images.

The following methodological points are pertinent to the use of photographic
images in land use surveys. STEINER (1962, 1966, 1970a and b, 1971; and MAU-
RER, 1969) studied in detail the influence of the season during which the photos
were taken on the interpretability of aerial photographs for detailed crop surveys.
In general, for a detailed crop survey, a careful study of the periodicities of growth
of the different crops is necessary before decisions on the season of photography
are taken. COLWELL (COLWELL et al., 1960) investigated extensively the use of film-
filter combinations for the detection of crop damage; his studies, as well as many
later investigations, showed false-color photography to be an exceptionally good
tool for this purpose. In many industrialized countries, such as the Netherlands,
false-color photography is used as a routine, not only for agricultural purposes
but also by municipal administrations concerned with the health of trees and
other crops in public parks and roads. The use of special film-filter combinations
often has proved worthwhile for crop surveys (MEIER, 1967; MEIENBERG, 1966;
PHILPOTTS and WALLEN, 1969; NEUBERT, 1969; FRINKING, 1972; GAUSMANN et
al., 1970). In particular cases the use of "multiband photography", which produces
simultaneous images in different parts of the spectrum, has provided very satisfactory information (PESTRONG, 1969).

Satellite Photography

Satellite photography, i.e. the use of images transmitted regularly from especially
constructed earth satellites over periods of some months or more, does not replace the kinds of photography described above. Rather, it introduces a new
dimension into the techniques of modern survey. In particular, it permits: (1) the
production of a regular sequence of images from approximately the same areas at
fixed periods in different seasons, and (2) the simultaneous production of different
kinds of high-altitude photography. The systematic use of "sequential photography" for land use and land resources surveys has often been advocated. It is,
however, difficult to achieve using the normal photographic systems, for technical, organizational and often also financial reasons. Satellite photography, which
is multipurpose, multidisciplinary and multinational, lacks these disadvantages
because the sequentiality is an essential element of the tool itself. Satellite photography does not always produce the same kind of image-definition produced by
conventional photography, and it is more difficult to use stereoscopically. In
addition, existing interpretation techniques must be specially adapted for use with
this system. Once this is done, satellite photography facilitates the acquisition of
information, in particular on the development of land use around the world, as
well as predictions on acreages of crops to be harvested in different areas of the
world during different seasons (see COLWELL, 1965; SHAY et al., 1970; SYMPO-

SIUM, 1966, 1970). Under certain conditions, special purpose photography with a rocket as a vehicle has advantages, with regard to timing and quality, over the use of satellite photography. This was shown in recent British experiments with the "Skylark"over a large area in Argentina (R.A.G. SAVIGEAR, 1974, oral communication).

In satellite photography, the entire range of the electromagnetic spectrum, which includes wavelengths of from 0.3 microns to 20 microns, is systematically used in so far as this is permitted by the atmospheric penetration of the various wavelengths. In principle, the same results can be achieved using an apparatus mounted in a conventional aircraft; in fact, the latter is sometimes even more successful because of the relatively low altitudes of the recording vehicle. As mentioned previously, the basic difference is one of organization. The electromagnetic spectrum is divided because different apparatus is necessary to record the different wavelengths (see e.g. VERSTAPPEN et al., 1970; SHAY et al., 1970). To facilitate general understanding, the recording apparatus are divided into two groups: (1) photographic recorders, which record wavelengths within the visible spectrum, from 0.3 to 0.7 microns, and the "near-infrared" wavelengths, 0.7 to 1.0 microns. The recording systems include the film-filter combinations mentioned previously, i.e., "normal" or "panchromatic" photography, "full-color" and "false-color" photography and "black-and-white infrared" photography. All apparatus used within these photographic groups of apparatus use the "camera-concept" of recording system. (2) non-photographic recorders: For those parts of the electromagnetic spectrum which have wavelengths of between 1 micron and 20 microns, different scanners are used. Many of these work according to the principle similar to that used in television systems. Mechanical scanners of a mirror type, which transfer their information to magnetic tapes, are used to record thermal infrared waves (4—20 microns). The information is later transformed into photographic images by special instruments. All of these systems passively record either solar reflected radiation or thermal radiation emitted by the earth's surface and by the objects (plants, animals, machinery) present on the surface. The usefulness of a particular system for a specific purpose depends on the quality of the radiations emitted by the objects to be distinguished, e.g. for a crop survey, a crop disease survey or an animal inventory. The usefulness of a system may be partly determined by previous reflectance measurements, from the air, the ground, or both, of the objects in question.

Radar systems, which utilize short waves of a kind comparable to radiowaves (between 0.5 cm = 5000 microns and 1 m) which are recorded by scanning microwave radiometers, have also proved applicable. The kind of reflectance, and therefore the use, depends on the wavelength and on the angle under which the waves are emitted and recorded. Radar systems have thus far in particular been used as "Side-looking Airborne Radar" (SLAR) in airplanes and have yielded interesting results on land use and on land forms. Interesting data on the use of SLAR in mapping mangrove vegetation in Panama has been published by LEWIS and MACDONALD (1972).

Several kinds of these "sensors" are mounted in the earth resources satellites, e.g., ERTS and SKYLAB (Earth Resources Technology Satellite and Apollo Applications Program, respectively), to record different earth resources, including features pertaining to land use. Useful data with respect to present land use as well as to the essential earth resources, applicable to future land use, are being systematically obtained using these systems.

A test to ascertain the feasibility of these programs was carried out in the Phoenix, Arizona area (DRAEGER and PETTINGER, 1972). The analyses prepared by a number of interpreters, including estimates of the acreages of different crops (wheat, barley, other land uses), were compared with ground survey data. The results indicated that a fully operational agricultural inventory which utilizes Apollo-9 space photography is not beyond the scope of present technology. Another experiment group (NUNNALLY and WITMER, 1970) found that careful, systematic development of systems of terminology and classification markedly enhanced interpretation of the photos. Other features clearly connected to land use, such as the quality of the environment, e.g., air, water and social quality, were also interpreted from satellite photography (WOBBER, 1970). Interesting data on ground temperature were obtained with thermal infrared photos (BASTUSCHEK, 1970).

SLAR proved extremely useful for site-selection for engineering structures for urban land use (BARR and MILES, 1970).

Tsetse Habitats

Separate mention must be made of the use of air-photointerpretation techniques in locating the habitats of the tsetse fly in Central Africa. The cases described by VERBOOM (1965) and by BUYCKX et al. (1966) are both good examples of what,

Photo 4. Riverine forest belt in Zambia savannah, tsetse habitat (Syzygium association, from VERBOOM, 1965)

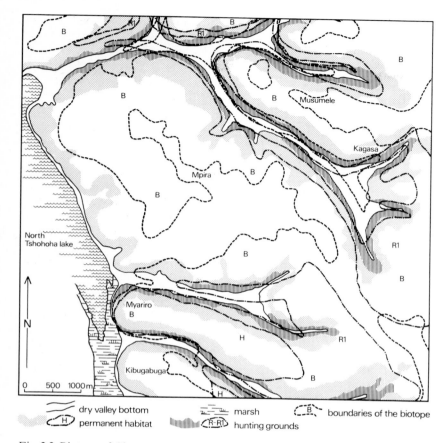

Fig. 2.2. Biotope of *Glossina morsitans* Westw. (Rwanda). (BUYCKX et al., 1966)

given a good understanding of the problems at hand, can be achieved by systematic interpretation of the available conventional aerial photography. Ground
observations indicated that the species of tsetse flies in question (mostly *Glossina
morsitans* Westw. and some *G. pallipedes*) require damp, shaded habitats. In the
area in Zambia, the following areas met these requirements (VERBOOM, 1965):

1) the riverine tree belt, a dense forest-like belt with different species of trees
and liana-like plants,

2) the dambo-grasslands with tree cluster,

3) the dambo-fringe vegetation, low shrubs and low-branched trees at the
edge of the dambo-depressions. Dry woodland, on soils suitable for arable land,
was not normally a fly habitat.

In Rwanda, it was possible to delineate the habitats as: H, permanent habitats
("Hotel" areas) and R, hunting grounds of the fly ("Restaurant" areas). Furthermore, the limits of the biotope of the fly could be exactly delineated. Part of the
map, scale 1:50000, is reproduced in Fig. 2.2.

In both cases, the surveys led to well-directed, carefully adapted methods for combating these very noxious flies. These methods occasionally involve destruction of the vegetation, but often other means are preferred for reasons of environmental conservation.

A Comprehensive View

Aerial photographs and other means of remote sensing are extensively used in all resources surveys pertaining to predicting and planning of potential and future uses of the land. Reference to these will be made in Chapter 4 (GOOSEN, 1967; REY et al., 1968). Particular mention must also be made of the publication by MARINET (1964), which includes a comprehensive view of the use of aerial photography for land use planning. He mentions that in the course of this work, photointerpretation was used for the following purposes:

1. Inventory of lands already in use.
2. Inventory of the crops being cultivated and of their importance, particularly perennial crops such as Hevea, coffee, tea, including indication of whether they are grown under shadow (VINK, 1953), and of crops such as pepper, which are grown with supporting crops or poles.

    Particular attention was also paid to young plantations of crops such as oil palm and in general to the age and growth of the crops (SCHWAAR, 1971).
3. Inventory of the possibilities of cattle breeding in a region: occurrence and kind of savannas, relief, watering points, possible occurrence of tsetse habitats, periodically flooded areas and the periods of flooding (also indicating possible periods for grazing, see also VERBOOM, 1961).
4. Inventory of forest resources (ZSILINSKY, 1964; VERSTEEGH, 1966).
5. Inventory of mineral resources.
6. Inventory of the geology of a region with special attention to hydrogeology and engineering geology.
7. Inventory of water resources, including indications of old management structures and predictions for future management.
8. Inventory of the population, including the settlement pattern, the settlement size and density and a broad estimate on population density within a development area; also indications on more or less regular movements of the population, the latter if possible with the use of sequential photography.
9. Inventory of roads of access to the area and to the various parts of the area, or of lines along which access roads might be constructed.
10. Study of the topography of the area as a general basic document for all other operations.

Special attention should be made in all these studies, as well as in the related studies of land resources, to the limitations imposed upon land use by the nature of the area. For an extensive treatment of these and related subjects, reference is made to the following chapters.

Chapter 3   Land Utilization Types

3.1 General

A typology of land use in its most elementary form is based on the kinds of crops grown. This approach is, however, not sufficient in itself. The same crop may be grown within completely different enterprises: e.g. intensive (high input) wheat growing in rotational systems on small farms in the Netherlands, extensive (low input) wheat growing in dry farming systems with ploughed fallow in the dry regions of the U.S.A., or irrigated wheat in Iraq. On the other hand, markedly similar systems may yield quite different crops, e.g. mixed farms on family holdings of restricted acreage in many parts of the world, or large plantations, whether they produce tropical crops in Asia or Latin America or cultivate vineyards on a large scale in southern Europe. Thus, for the characterization of land use, a typology of the systems of land utilization is just as essential as that of the kinds of crops grown, e.g. the better known crop surveys.

One can also distinguish different land utilization types for both rural and urban non-agricultural purposes. The treatment of urban land utilization is outside the scope of this book. Rural non-agrarian land utilization types are, however, increasingly developing along lines resembling those of agricultural systems and having points of interference with agriculture, i.e., recreation grounds and conservation areas in developing as well as in industrialized countries. General points abouth both the agricultural and the non-agricultural types of land use will be discussed first.

Kinds of agricultural land use have interested students of agriculture from early ages onwards. More or less systematic descriptions are found in descriptions of foreign countries from all periods. In modern literature, ALBRECHT THAER (1811) was one of the first authors to apply systematic methods in his work on land evaluation, which even today provides interesting reading. Many other systems for indicating "types of farming" have been developed, of which the classification of types in Britain was mentioned previously (STAMP, 1950). As a direct consequence of the original World Land Use Survey, geographers have begun to pay more attention to the need for systematization, and soil surveyors and agronomists have developed similar ideas for use in land evaluation (SARFALVY et al., 1967; KOSTROWICKY, 1972; BEEK and BENNEMA, 1972, 1973; BRINKMAN and SMYTH, 1973).

A typology of agricultural land utilization is based on well-defined economic units of production even if sometimes, in traditionally nomadic or seminomadic agricultural systems, the boundaries may be somewhat vague. In all of these systems, however, there is a clear relationship between inputs and outputs and between these two and the two other main aspects of land use: human resources and land resources. In non-agricultural rural land utilization, the units to be characterized are much less clear. Many of the main management units, which often correlate with certain land resources, are not economic units. Also many of these units are not primarily established to yield results which can be easily expressed in terms of production. There is as yet no general direction in which non-agricultural rural systems of land use can be characterized. Some suggestions may, however, be given.

Basically, all types of land use can be characterized by noting the following points:

(1) Purpose of the land use,
(2) Kinds of plants, animals and/or structures maintained and/or produced,
(3) Capital invested for long-term purposes,
(4) Capital invested for short- and medium-term purposes,
(5) Yearly inputs for maintenance and production,
(6) Social, economic, cultural and institutional contexts within which the land use takes place.

In considering the priorities of the points within this sequence, one might well argue that the social, economic and cultural contexts as well as the institutional conditions are of such importance that they dominate all other points. Especially today, however, rapid developments in all parts of the world often render these conditions, for any particular case, more fluid than those contained in the other points. On the whole, all six points are of equal importance and all must be utilized in characterizing any particular type of land use.

Purposes of Land Use

Point 1, purpose of the land use, has to some extent, however, precedence over all ot the other points, in that a broad distinction can be made between agricultural land use and non-agricultural rural land use. The main objective of the former is to obtain material gain by the production of agricultural crops or of animals. The material gain obtained may be expressed in terms of amounts of food, clothing and housing, as is the case in some of the less developed regions of the world; it may also be expressed in terms of net financial gain. Non-agricultural rural land use may have either material or other objectives. Different kinds of mining provide typical examples of non-agricultural rural land use with material objectives. These include the exploitation of lands for the production of materials for road construction, for brick production, for the construction of houses, dams and various structures for conservation, irrigation and drainage and for the removal of solid, liquid or gaseous mineral ores. Many of these activities include both the extraction of the materials and the related industrial processing. e.g. for the production of bricks or for the rough processing of ores. These industrial activities are strongly tied to the land and should therefore be regarded as rural land uses, in contrast to other industrial activities which are more urban in nature.

Many non-agricultural rural land uses have purposes which are less directly linked to material or financial gain, though someone, somewhere is usually able to satisfy his material needs from the construction and/or maintenance of such projects. One can say that the primary purpose of a recreation area is to provide spiritual gain for those, usually urban, people who visit it. One cannot gainsay, on the other hand, that a recreation area provides material means of living for the many people associated with its recreation facilities such as hotels, playgrounds, swimming pools and campgrounds. The primary purpose of conservation areas and of nature and wildlife reserves is to conserve the land and its natural or seminatural plants and animals, i.e. to protect the ecological balance and the ecological riches of a region; on the other hand, the same area can often be used for recreational purposes.

Thus, conservation and reserve areas may indirectly support purely economic enterprises. Apart from this, if one concedes that the ecological balance of a region is of considerable economic interest on a long-term basis, such areas are, in their own right, economically significant in the long run.

Combined Purposes

In fact, many kinds of land use, which are geared toward one major objective serve other purposes as well. Roads are often originally laid out to open up an area for economic development, but they serve as a general means of communication for other cultural and recreational objectives. The primary function of dikes in the Netherlands is that of protecting the land, however, they nearly always

Photo 5. "Naardermeer", a nature reserve of particular biological interest developed in a "mined" peat bog (Photo H. P. GORTER, Natuurmonumenten, Amsterdam)

Photo 6. "Loosdrecht-lake", recreation on "mined" peat bogs (Photo KLM Aerocarto B.V., The Hague)

contain roads and often villages, and in many places, they are of scenic interest as well. Many large pits, dug for mining substrata, e.g. sand and gravel for road construction, have been developed as swimming pools and recreation grounds. Peat areas, originally mined to obtain turfs as household fuel, have become famous bird reserves such as the "Naardermeer" near Amsterdam (Photo 5). Other lakes of similar origin have become well-known sailing areas, i.e., the "Loos-

Photo 7. Tea plantation with shade trees in the volcanic area of Java (Indonesia)

drecht" lakes near Amsterdam (Photo 6). Wildlife reserves around the world are used for game cropping and thus result in material gain, in the shape of essential protein foods, for people in the area (BROWN, 1967).

The essential purpose of agricultural land uses, i.e., the production of plants and animals, is also not always the only one. Forestry has always served conservation purposes, particularly in mountainous areas of Europe and other parts of the world. In Indonesia, then the "Netherlands East Indies", as early as the middle of the nineteenth century, all mountain forest areas of Java were established as "Forest Reserve", i.e. cutting of timber was sharply limited and in most cases completely prohibited, to conserve the erodible forest areas and to allow the forests to act as the main regulators of the island's hydrology. Also on Java, extensive areas of well-maintained perennial crops, particularly tea and Hevea plantations, served the same purposes.

Well-maintained tea plantations, particularly those with the leguminous shadow trees grown extensively before the incidence of the "blisterblight" (*Exobasidium vexans*) disease, cover the soil surface very well and, because of their extensive root systems, hold the soil even on rather steep volcanic mountain

Fig. 3.1. An area "The Omval" near Amsterdam (etch by Rembrandt, 1643) (courtesy Museum "Rembrandt Huis", Amsterdam)

slopes (Photo 7). Even after the incidence of the afore-mentioned fungus disease, when the shadow trees had to be cut to avoid complete destruction of the tea crop, careful maintenance and increased nitrogen fertilizing made it possible to keep the tea as the main soil-conserving crop in many areas.

Hevea plays the same soil-conserving role on the lower slopes and other hills which tea plays on the middle volcanic slopes. When grown together with carefully maintained, preferably leguminous, ground cover, and when necessary with the proper terraces and drainage systems, it can be simultaneously a highly productive crop and a better soil-conserving agent than most other land uses of the same soils. Occasionally interplanting with leguminous trees *(Albizzia sp.)* or bushes *(Leucaena sp.)* contributes both to production and to conservation. In areas where landslides occur, in particular on hills consisting of tertiary shales, the planting of bamboo bushes along the valley sides stabilizes lands which otherwise would be unsuitable for any kind of agriculture. Throughout the centuries, agricultural land use has, to some extent, played a recreational role for urban populations. The art of different periods clearly reflects this role. Some of Rembrandt's (17th century) most beautiful etchings depict the rural areas around Amsterdam (Fig. 3.1), and the paintings of Van Gogh would be unimaginable without the extensive wheat fields and olive groves of southern France.

Today, as agriculture advances together with industrial and urban development in many countries, agricultural land uses may become even more involved in recreational functions. During the 17th century and continuing through the 18th and 19th centuries, planted forests had a clearly recreational function in many regions of Western Europe. Landscape gardening on large estates in England and often, although less markedly, in other Western European countries, clearly reflects this function. In most cases, planted forests were, and occasionally still are, combined with timber production. During the first part of the 20th century, planted forests in Europe were used increasingly for recreational purposes, even though their main purpose was the production of timber. Most of this timber, especially from pine trees, was used by the coal mining industry. With the development of modern mining techniques and with the subsequent closing down of many mines, timber production dwindled, in particular after the early 1960's. At the same time, growth of the urban populations and the increasing standard of living greatly enhanced the need for recreational areas. In the Netherlands today, these forests serve mainly as recreation grounds and the way in which they are managed has shifted accordingly. The financial burden for state forests and for forests owned by non-commercial private organizations, although certainly not negligible, can be borne by, or with the aid of, the national government. For forests owned by private persons and institutions, subsidies provided by the state, under certain conditions, offer at least a partial solution.

Conflicting Purposes

Advancing agriculture, essentially an economic venture for material or financial gain, has a natural tendency towards increasing efficiency to fulfill its primary purpose. This tendency occasionally leads to a conflict with the tendency of the urban culture to place primary emphasis on the recreational features which, in traditional agricultural systems, are almost always a by-product. Agriculture in industrialized countries, in its quest for advancement, has to contend with the continuously increasing standard of living of the industrial and related labor forces. It must, therefore, look for means of increasing the productivity of labor on the farms. The result is often extensive mechanization, which in turn leads to larger fields and larger enterprises. The logical consequence is the establishment of large rural reconstruction projects in which areas of many thousands of hectares tend to take on a monotonous aspect. Such projects lend themselves well to the efficiency necessary in modern agriculture, but not so well to the development of attractive recreational areas. Another important result is the destruction of the natural habitats of the plants and animals, and thus the shifting of the ecological balance of the region. The ecological shift should not, however, be confused with the recreational aspect, as is too often done. This confusion is understandable, because the natural habitats of plants and animals may enhance the value of an area for recreation, but this does not imply that the two are the same.

Advancing agriculture may also find its way in a modern industrial state by very strong intensification, leading to the development of sophisticated horticultural systems. In exceptional cases, these may even strikingly enhance the recrea-

Photo 8. Glasshouses in the horticultural district between The Hague and Rotterdam (Photo KLM Aerocarto B. V., The Hague)

tional value of an area. The flowerbulb fields of the Western Netherlands and areas in Europe where flowers, e.g. roses, are grown extensively, contribute well-known examples. Fruit trees such as apples, pears and cherries, have a marked recreational value during their flowering period, which is sometimes clearly exploited for its recreational value. On the other hand, the development of intensive sophisticated horticultural land uses can lead to the complete destruction of the recreational by-product of more traditonal kinds of agriculture, e.g., the construction of glass-houses over large areas. The completely industrial nature of a large district of continuous blocks covered with glasshouses destroys all of the area's recreational possibilities (Photo 8).

Air pollution caused by oil-heated glasshouses can spread over adjoining areas of many square kilometers. Plastic houses in still relatively small areas in southern Europe have produced similar effects.

These tendencies, which in themselves are fully legitimate trends in advancing agriculture, explain some of the conflict and confusion which exist today concerning rural land use in industrialized countries. Perhaps what is needed is a new definition of the purpose of agriculture, a new understanding of how specific regions within a country can be set aside for a particular purpose. Such regions have been called "landscape parks", i.e. large park areas of at least some square kilometers, where agriculture is maintained primarily for its recreational features. Acceptance of these areas would, however, require a thorough revision of present social, economic, cultural and institutional values. In contrast to present land uses, these "landscape parks" would yield by-products of plant and animal materials. They may also serve ecological functions. Products obtained from these areas may even be of special value for biologically oriented consumers.

Social and Cultural Problems

The purpose of the average agricultural enterprise has, in the preceding discussion, been formulated as one of material or financial gain. There is no doubt that even the most primitive kind of agricultural land use serves a primarily economic purpose, i.e. the procurement of scarce materials to fulfill certain needs. In addition, however, some regional and even national social functions are fulfilled. Even without reverting to any kind of mystical *Blut und Boden* theory, it is clear that the existence of a healthy rural population with a good standard of living contributes to the wellbalanced functioning of a region and of a nation. Many developing countries are experiencing considerable problems in this respect. Large towns, e.g. capitals, coastal towns with extending harbors and industries, are growing faster than the agricultural regions. This unbalanced growth of the urban populations, often resulting in the creation of shanty towns or *Bidonvilles*, constitutes a serious problem for these countries. Advancing agriculture, although perhaps satisfactory, cannot compete with the rapid growth of industry and its related services. Furthermore, it is always to some extent bound by traditional social, cultural and institutional constraints. Rapid population growth increases this effect considerably. For agriculture to fulfill its social functions under these conditions, careful reevaluation of its primary objectives under different land conditions is essential.

Under a given set of social, economic, cultural and institutional conditions, any system of land use must yield certain goods, i.e., material goods, cultural goods obtained through communication or spiritual goods obtained by recreation. Once specific structures, e.g. man-made structures such as roads and dams or ecological structures such as biological habitats, have been created, they have to be maintained, and in some systems of land use, this becomes the primary activity. There is, here, a sufficiently clear boundary between the normal agricultural systems and all other systems of rural land use. The former can always be defined in terms of clear units of production, with a specific size and with clearly definable inputs and outputs. The latter, as was shown above, must often be defined in different terms. Some types, particularly mining, can never be described in terms of sustained productivity. Within this book, our attention will primarily be focussed upon agricultural land utilization types. Other types, which are interrelated with agriculture, will be discussed later at some length.

The remaining characteristic points mentioned previously are: capital invested for long-term purposes, capital invested for short- and medium-term purposes, and yearly inputs for maintenance and production. Both agricultural and non-agricultural land utilization types can be defined using this terminology. Together, they represent the inputs which are an essential feature of any kind of land use. Long-term capital investments include roads and buildings as well as structures for conservation, irrigation, drainage and flood protection. Many of these are of a regional nature and may even be said to become artifactial parts of the land itself. Similar and even the same structures are used for agricultural as well as for non-agricultural purposes. Short- and medium-term capital investments include heavy machinery and small structures which are from the beginning more directly related to a particular land utilization type. The latter is especially true for the yearly inputs of labor and materials for maintenance and production, which can, for the most part, be used to distinguish individual land utilization types.

3.2 Agricultural Land Utilization Types

A Key Concept

The concept of "land utilization type" is a key concept for understanding land use in agriculture. It includes many broad categories and their sub-divisions as well as the levels of management which may exist within certain defined types of land use. Because the term "agriculture" is used here in its widest sense, the broad categories include kinds of natural product extraction as well as forestry and range grazing. Even some kinds of systematic game cropping are included in our concept of agricultural land utilization.

Recently two attempts were made to arrive at a modern typology of world agriculture in terms of land utilization types (BEEK and BENNEMA, 1972; KOSTROWICKY, 1972). These two systems, which were developed independently by two different groups, show many similarities. They will be used together in the following text. In addition, data from other sources, cited in previous paragraphs, as well as the present writer's personal knowledge and experience, have been incorporated (see also BRINKMAN and SMYTH, 1973). Land productivity, although mentioned briefly by KOSTROWICKY (1972) as one of his variables for characterizing World Agriculture and certainly interrelated with land utilization types, is not treated in this paragraph. Land productivity is a result of the interrelations between the inputs utilized within a land utilization type on the one hand and of the nature of the land resources on the other. It is therefore not a proper variable for characterizing a land utilization type as such and will be treated separately in following chapters.

The following categories of variables are useful for characterizing agricultural land utilization types:

(a) social characteristics in their widest sense,

 b) infrastructural characteristics insofar as directly related to the land use,

(c) produce ("outputs") of the land use,

(d) initial inputs (long-term capital, development cost) for the land use,

(e) annual production inputs (short-term capital),

 (f) labor intensity,

(g) source, kind and intensity of farm power.

Social Characteristics

The social characteristics embrace several subvariables which have a great impact on the land utilization type and on the level of management within a certain type. These include:

— system of land tenure,
— other social and/or administrative systems directly related to land use,
— size of farms,
— level of cultural development.

The following systems of land tenure are indicated by KOSTROWICKY (1972):

A. Common—operated under tribal or traditional communal forms of tenure: tribe, clan or part thereof;

B. Tenancy—holdings operated by tenants in exchange for services or by the share-cropping system;

C. Owner-operator and fixed-rent tenancy—holdings operated by a landowner or by a tenant under a fixed rent system;

D. Corporation and Cooperative—holdings operated by profit organizations, corporations or cooperatives;

E. Collective and State—holdings operated by a group of persons working together/collectively, on land owned by the collective or by the state, according to instructions from central planning.

The "other social and/or administrative systems" which may be directly related to the land use include written systems, e.g. legal rights of inheritance, or unwritten, e.g. patriarchal systems in areas where the land tenure itself is to be considered as an individual right. These systems may also encompass written or unwritten obligations for land and/or water management, e.g. the "subak" system of irrigation on the isle of Bali or the written ordinances of the polders and water districts in the Netherlands. All of these may have a direct bearing on the kind of land use, e.g. they may facilitate and regulate irrigated agriculture or facilitate, by the common system of drainage and pumping, either pastures or arable land farming in certain areas. The presence of such systems may either facilitate or retard advancing agriculture. Their absence in many countries is certainly deleterious to development (VINK, 1970b).

To some extent, farm size is a characteristic of some land utilization types. The production of irrigated rice, e.g. on tiny farms of 1 hectare or less in parts of Southeast Asia, constitutes a type of land use which differs considerably from that observed in some areas of western Asia and southern Europe, e.g. middle class rice production, and from that in other parts of the world, e.g. highly mechanized production of rice on farms of several hundred or more hectares. The same holds true if one compares the very small farms, usually with vineyards or olive orchards, common to many Mediteranean countries, with the large, almost industrialized, enterprises for the production of the same crops often found in the same areas. Still another example is provided by comparing the production of Hevearubber and tea on family-sized farms of the local population, with that of adjoining large plantations operated by state corporations or foreign companies in Indonesia. In this case, a kind of symbiosis often exists between the two types. Often the large plantation has led to the establishment of the family-sized enterprises. It provides planting material, instruction and sometimes also fertilizers for example, and buys the products of the family farms to be processed in its factory. The small-farm owners often work as seasonal or part-time laborers on the plantation, thus finding some degree of material security as well. This symbiotic type of land utilization has been found to be very satisfactory for development; it should be noted as a separate land utilization type in those areas where it has attained a measure of importance.

The level of cultural development of farmers around the world can be ascertained in broad categories. In some countries or regions it is often worthwhile to distinguish more precise subdivisions. The broad categories include the distinction between those farmers who are illiterate and those who can read and write well enough to absorb modern information on proper methods of land use. A further distinction can be made between those who have attended some kind of secondary agricultural school and are therefore usually more open to procedures necessary for regular agricultural extension, and those who have not yet attained this goal. In many areas also the special technical know-how required to operate farm machinery, which always includes daily maintenance and small repairs, is a distinguishing criterium. These cultural levels, which may or may not correlate with financial considerations for creditability, do influence the land utilization type in general, but perhaps even more so, the level of management to be obtained within the common land utilization type.

Levels of Management

Level of management has been defined (Soil Survey Staff, 1951) as the management practices followed by various groups of farmers within a certain region; these practices are often indicated as "poor", "average" or "superior". For the purpose of soil survey interpretation, they have been indicated more precisely as follows:

Level 1.—The most common combinations of management practices followed by the majority of successful farmers using the soil being dealt with.

Level 2.—The superior combinations of management practices followed by the leading farmers using the soil, perhaps 1% or perhaps over 10%.

Level 3.—The optimum combinations of management practices developed on pilot-research farms, if any, or on other farms that represent the best (or "ceiling") that can be done in the present state of the agricultural arts.

Wherever possible, these broad definitions should be replaced by definite figures of inputs. Not all differences in management levels can, however, be indicated by different levels of inputs. A better farmer, within the same land utilization type and on the same soil, is often distinguished not by the higher quantities of inputs but by their correct dosage and timeliness. Differences among land utilization types on the same soil may often be expressed in quantitative figures, but differences in levels of management within one land utilization type can only be expressed in this manner after careful study, and then only occasionally. The boundary between what constitutes a different level of management within one land utilization type and what is a different land utilization type is not always clear. Many land utilization types of relatively similar natures are distinguishable in terms of their different levels of management. Only a careful study of agriculture in a given region can lead to the best solution.

In some cases, near-industrial enterprises such as tea plantations may show sets of practices which are very similar to those used in indigenous tea farms. In other large plantations, more intensive sets of management practices are used. The reverse is also true in various kinds of agriculture. The land utilization type is, however, generally determined by a large number of criteria, which may or may not result in characteristic sets of management practices. The level of management is only determined by the study of the management practices, which may or may not coincide with other criteria. In situations in which differences in management practices coincide with a fairly large number of other criteria, a different land utilization type may be found to exist.

Infrastructural Systems

Infrastructural systems may have a tremendous impact on land use without really being useful criteria for determining the type of land use, e.g., roads and other systems of communication, which do not have any direct connection with the type of land use. The opening up of a region may result in better facilities for transporting bulk and thus lead to extensive wheat or sugar beet farming in large enterprise. It may also lead to better transportation of perishable goods and therefore to intensive market gardening in small units.

Other infrastructural systems have a direct impact on the land utilization type and may be used as an inherent characteristic for determining a particular type. The systems of dikes, polders and resulting precise water management in the Netherlands have a direct relationship to some land utilization types. Dikes against flooding permit the presence of intensive land utilization systems in areas which otherwise could only support summer grazing by cattle and sheep. The effectiveness of the dikes is clearly demonstrated when one considers those coastal areas which at present are not surrounded by a system of dikes, the situation in the Netherlands in the early Middle Ages and similar situations in other regions of the world which are subject to periodic flooding. The polder system has also led to relatively careful water management, formerly with windmills and later with steam-, diesel- and electric pumping stations, which has provided a means for good arable and horticultural production in areas which otherwise could be used only for grazing because of high ground-water levels. The most typical case is the water management of the Hoogheemraadschap (Top-level Water District) of "Rhijnland", between Leyden and Haarlem, where precise water management has permitted the growth of flower bulbs since the eighteenth century.

Infrastructural systems are equally important in irrigated agriculture. The existence of fully regulated technical irrigation systems, combined with suitable drainage systems, is a main determinant for land utilization types in North Africa and western Asia as well as in the tropical regions of Asia and elsewhere. A fully reliable technical irrigation system which is continuously well managed is the only way to assure reliable water supplies and, in arid countries, desalinization, which permits the production of good arable and specialized horticultural crops.

Particularly in humid tropical areas, some interesting land utilization types can still be maintained without such a system, but they are always sufficiently different from those with fully organized irrigation systems to be distinguished as different land utilization types.

Produce

Produce is usually the primary factor used in characterizing land utilization types. Although it is an essential factor for this purpose, it is often not sufficient in itself to distinguish land utilization types without the use of other factors. The division between types which yield primary biological products—crops used directly by man—and those which yield secondary biological products—animals—is not always clear. In "mixed farming", the arable crops are at least partly fed to the animals, which are an inherent part of the land utilization type. Another portion of the crops may be sold directly. Different kinds of mixed farming occur in Europe as well as elsewhere in the world. It can be carried out under a traditional system or with modern industrial methods. The actual nature of the system at a certain time is strongly influenced by the socio-economic circumstances prevailing in a region.

Land utilization types which produce the same crop often differ in all other aspects. We mentioned previously the difference between the production of perennial tropical crops on small holdings and on large plantations. The same is valid for the production of annual crops, e.g. tobacco, cassava (*Manihot utilissima*) and rice. Cassava in particular is grown as an important crop in systems of shifting cultivation but also as a dry-season crop on farms with paddy cultivation and as a fully commercial crop on highly mechanized, large-scale industrial enterprises. Grassland types of land utilization also have different farm sizes and different degrees of intensity of land use: e.g., seminomadic "transhumance" systems, extensive ranches and many different types of land use with inputs depending on the land resources, including climate, as well as on the human resources of the area.

On the other hand, close resemblances are often found among land utilization types with ostensibly different crops, particularly if one compares types from different climatic regions. Medium-sized family farms with orchards (cherry, apple, pear or citrus and sometimes even cocoa or coffee) as well as arable land (rye, oats, wheat, maize, sorghum, paddy) and grassland show many interesting points of similarity. Many large enterprises which produce perennial crops (vineyards, citrus, olives, Hevea, tea, coffee, oilpalm, sisal, sugar cane) show a resemblance to those which produce annual crops (rice, tobacco, sugar cane, cassava).

Nevertheless, produce is an indispensable natural means for characterizing some important aspects of a land utilization type. Within a particular region with specific land and human resources, it may even serve as the main indicator, because, under given circumstances and often due to historical causes, it correlates well with other aspects of land use. But these correlations may be broken, and often are, by the introduction of new land utilization types with beneficial results for the advancement of agriculture.

Initial Inputs

Initial inputs for agricultural land utilization types play an important role in land development. Capital outlay as a long-term investment may completely determine the feasibility of a developmental project. In old, established agricultural systems, this may be less so. Infrastructural investments in dikes, roads, canals and dams may have been largely or wholly amortized even if, calculated at present-day value, they represent a large capital investment. They have truly become artifactial parts of the land resources and are usually treated as such. The needs for their regular maintenance are considered as legal obligations fulfilled by means of annual inputs of labor, materials and machinery. Even the financial obligations inherent in these needs, which for many polders in the Netherlands may consist of annual contributions of the order of Hfl. 50,—to Hfl. 150,—per hectare per year ($ 20 to $ 60 per year) to the general administration of the polders, belong under the category of annual inputs rather than of capital investments. The following are some data for a polder near Amsterdam:

The polder was diked, drained and reclaimed in the middle of the nineteenth century. The original investments for construction have been completely amortized. During the last decades, due to the need for renewal of pumping machines and for modernization of the entire drainage system, new capital investments of approximately Hfl. 160,—($ 65) per hectare have been made. Other capital investments in roads and bridges, made in recent years, have been utilized partly for agricultural land use in the polder, partly for traffic to and from the urban areas in and near the polder. The latter investments are of the order of Hfl. 400,— ($ 160) per hectare. Amortization of all these investments is carried over periods of from 15 to 50 years, depending on the nature of the structures invested in.

If new projects, e.g. land reallotment, are carried out within the old, established land utilization types, new capital investments are made. These investments, e.g., for a modern land reallotment project in the Netherlands consisting of complete rural reconstruction, are of the order of Hfl. 2000,— to 3000,— per hectare. About 65% of this is carried as an annual expenditure on the government budget and is therefore directly amortized. The remaining 35% is paid by the land owners either as a lump sum or as an annuity over 30 years. These rather heavy investments have, however, the nature of capital investments, as can be seen from the types of resulting permanent structures for land improvement.

For the most part, such projects result in very few changes in the land utilization type. At the utmost, 10% of the surface area in any project is converted from agricultural into non-agricultural land uses: e.g., urban, industrial, recreational. Of the remaining area, the farm size shows some increase because of emigration of farmers to the newly reclaimed polders and because of the buying-out, with government funds, of older farmers who prefer to retire. All aspects of farm management are, however, greatly facilitated, and rural life obtains many of the modern conveniences which were, until recently, only obtainable in urban areas. The land utilization type, which always allows for a certain margin in all characterizing variables, is only very rarely changed.

Similar situations can be found in many old agricultural systems with irrigation. Some remarks about the infrastructural apsects of these systems were made previously. In arid regions, whether or not a specific type of irrigated agriculture is carried out with or without systematic drainage and ensuing desalinization, can be so important that this fact in itself can be construed as a definite difference in land utilization type.

In addition to infrastructural constructions, capital investments, in many land utilization types, include farm buildings and some kinds of fences. They also include the more elaborate on-farm construction of conservation structures such as terraces and weirs, and investments in farm drainage, e.g. in tile systems. All of these can be considered characterizing variables for land utilization types. In general, the systematic occurrence of the different capital investments indicated serves as a means for characterizing land utilization types, whether they are considered to be capital in the economic sense or not, under a given set of conditions.

Annual Production Inputs

Annual production inputs (short-term capital) nearly always provide an important means for characterizing land utilization types. They can be used to make broad distinctions among "traditional" agricultural systems, "industrial" agricultural systems and a third category, "low intensity industrial" systems (VINK, 1963a). The inputs of fertilizers and pesticides are often the two most important variables, particularly in relation to the nature of the available land resources. The combination of pesticides and fertilizers often not only indicates a rise in level of management, but also includes so many changes in the whole land use pattern, that a completely different land utilization type results. Tea growing in Indonesia in the early 1950's provides a good example.

Plantation tea growing was introduced in Indonesia on a fairly large scale during the nineteenth century. It expanded in particular on the slopes of the many volcanoes of the island of Java, altitudes between 250 and 2000 m above sea level. The tea was grown under a shadow crop of leguminous trees (Photo 7, page 39). These trees provided a natural source of nitrogen and at the same time, particularly within the lower range of altitudes (between 250 and 1200 m), they induced a favorable microclimate for the growth of young tea leaves which were harvested in regular rounds by hand plucking. Even more important was the influence of the microclimate on the balance between tea growth and the growth of the main pest, a fly, *Helopeltis antonii*, which damages the tea leaves and stalks, thus giving rise to serious necroses. Annual inputs were low because no satisfactory pesticides against this fly existed. Thus, the efficiency of chemical fertilizers on most soils within the resulting cultural ecosystem was relatively low. Just before World War II, the use of Derris powder as a pesticide resulted in an increase of annual inputs. A larger increase of annual inputs occurred after the war, when DDT, HCH and other pesticides proved very effective against *Helopeltis*, and the use of these pesticides together with nitrogen fertilizers resulted in clearly increased yields, particularly from the young, rich volcanic soils. The subsequent introduction, through direct communication by air transport, of the "blisterblight" disease, caused by the fungus *Exobasidium vexans*, gave a new stimulus to the reorganization of the land utilization type by means of much larger inputs. This disease, which is endemic to the tea plantations of northern India (Assam) and is not especially important there, caused excessive damage to the tea plantations of Indonesia.

Combating this disease necessitated the rigorous cutting of all shadow trees, because the microclimate under these trees was very favorable to the growth of the fungus. As a result a new land utilization type, with large annual inputs which included fungicides against the blisterblight, pesticides against *Helopeltis*, and much larger dressings of chemical fertilizers, was found to be the best, at least on the young, very fertile volcanic soils. The high yields thus obtained easily paid for the higher annual inputs and at the same time for the concurrently increased labor costs. Pruning cycles and plucking rounds also had to be adjusted, and these changes resulted in a product of better quality and a more regular distribution of labor throughout the year (VINK, 1953, 1962a). This land utilization type was found to be much less effective on the older, poorer soils, which led to a shift of the land use towards the better soils (see also Para. 5.4.4).

Annual inputs, also within one land utilization type, may vary considerably, depending on the nature of the land. Differences in annual costs of fertilizers may be of the order of hundreds of guilders per hectare per year, as shown by DE SMET (1962). Different soils may also require different combinations of chemical fertilizers and imported food for animals. When two farms of a mixed type—arable land and grassland—in a sandy area of the Netherlands were compared, it was found that the farm on the drier soil had a much lower density of cattle per hectare than did the farm on humid sandy soil. Annual inputs on the drier farm were much lower because of the soil difference. Fertilizer was much less effective on the drier soil, and therefore lesse fertilizer was applied. As a result, grass production was lower, particularly in midsummer when the dry soil also showed drought effects, and fewer cattle could be supported the year round. Fewer cattle required a lesser amount of imported food per hectare; in addition, the quantity of imported food per cow was lowered, because on the drier soil the cattle left the barn at an earlier date in the spring and were stabled somewhat later in autumn, grass production as well as general grazing conditions on the drier soil being particularly favorable during these periods.

Annual inputs may also vary on different soils within the same land utilization type because of differences in feasibility of these inputs with regard to erosion hazards. Good examples have been given by BALL et al. (1957). Modern developments in no-tillage agriculture on erodible soils show the same tendencies.

Annual inputs of irrigation water depend heavily on the water requirements of the different crops under given conditions. DOUGRAMEJI (1970) computed the monthly water requirements of crops in the Baghdad area (Iraq). His figures, converted into millimeters per annum, are given in Table 4.

Labor intensity in average man-hours per hectare per year is another means of characterizing different land utilization types. This average figure is a rough measure, because it depends very much on socio-economic circumstances, kinds of crops, farm size, farm power and other inputs. All kinds of labor intensity are found in many different land utilization types. High intensity-labor occurs in sophisticated systems of horticulture as well as in primitve systems of agriculture. Low intensity-labor occurs in highly mechanized farming systems as well as in

Table 4. Water requirements of some crops in the Baghdad area (Iraq). [After DOUGRAMEJI (1970)].

Crop	Water requirements mm/annum	Growing season (months)[a]
Flax	700	8 (w)
Cotton	1300	8 (s)
Soybean	760	5 (s)
Corn	960	5 (s)
Wheat	520	6 (w)
Barley	560	6 (w)
Alfalfa	2070	9 (s)
Cauliflower	440	5 (w)
Lettuce	210	4 (w)
Carrot	660	9 (w)
Potato	730	5 (l)

[a] Between brackets: w = winter, s = summer, l = spring.

several types of traditional agriculture. To characterize a land utilization type without giving some data on the labor intensity is very unsatisfactory. To give precise data on labor intensity in any type is, however, not possible without careful studies of farm management.

An even more complicated variable is labor productivity, indicated by KOS-TROWICKY (1972), and defined as "gross agricultural production in grain units per 1 person active in agriculture". It could, tentatively, be calculated per man hour, man day or man year. This factor seems, however, hardly possible for use in international comparisons. The relatively simple data for labor intensity, as calculated or estimated from the number of people working primarily on a farm, in persons per hectare, might be more feasible for this purpose. Many land utilization types, because of the seasonal character of the crops grown, are also characterized by a seasonally high demand of labor, e.g. for harvesting (vineyards, grain crops with low mechanization), which can never be satisfied by the amount of labor normally available on a farm. This need may be overcome either by communal systems (neighborly help, in Indonesia: *tulung menujung*) or by a seasonally available labor force of sufficiently great numbers, which is distinguished by many different social implications: structural idleness, different social groups (gypsies, school children, roving teams of laborers). The inherent necessity for this kind of labor within a land utilization type should also be used as a characterizing variable.

Farm power is characterized primarily by its source (BEEK and BENNEMA, 1972) and as such "symbolises to a great extent the accompanying set of agricultural implements". Four main categories are distinguished: a) four-wheel and crawler tractors, b) two-wheel and one-wheel power-operated machinery, c) animal power, d) manpower. Manpower has already been treated as "labor", but here it is meant as an indicator that no other source of power is used in a certain land utilization type. It may be possible to give a rough quantification of the various power sources used within a specific land utilization type. Such a list is useful, since, in many cases, more than one source is used. KOSTROWICKY (1972) proposes the following classes:

Inputs of labor: *Number of people active in agriculture per 100 ha of agricultural land:*

Class 1   — below 10
Class 2   — 10–20
Class 3   — 20–40
Class 4   — 40–80
Class 5   — over 80

Inputs of animal power: *Number of animal conventional units per 100 ha of agricultural land:*

Class 1   — below 4
Class 2   — 4– 8
Class 3   — 8–15
Class 4   — 15–25
Class 5   — over 25

Inputs of mechanical power: *Number of tractors in conventional—15 HP—units per 100 ha of cultivated land:*

Class 1   — below 0.5
Class 2   — 0.5–1
Class 3   — 1 –2
Class 4   — 2 –5
Class 5   — over 5

These or similar classes may be useful in developing a systematic approach to characterizing land utilization types in terms of farm power. Whether farm power should only be related to the surface area of cultivated land depends largely on the definition of the latter. "Cultivated land" should also include orchards and other tree crops as well as certain kinds of improved pastures.

Other sources of farm power not mentioned above may be of local importance. Attention is drawn to the use of windmills on farms for local field drainage, and on ranches as well as in nomadic tribal areas for the pumping of drinking water for cattle. Windmills as a source of electricity are also not always negligible as a source of farm power on medium-sized farms.

3.3 Typology of Agricultural Land Utilization

Both KOSTROWICKY (1971) and BEEK and BENNEMA (1972) have attempted to develop a general typology of agricultural land utilization. Kostrowicky's aim is to provide a general world typology as a follow-up to the previously mentioned World Land Use Survey, while that of the latter researchers is to develop a system

Table 5. Selected diagnostic features and variables for the typology of world agriculture. (KOSTROWICKY, 1972)

No.	Variables	Expressed by
Social and ownership characteristics		
1.1	System of land tenure	A–E symbols
2.2	Average size of farms	1–5 classes
Organizational and technical characteristics		
3.3.1	Inputs of labor	1–5 classes
4.3.2	Inputs of animal power	1–5 classes
5.3.3	Inputs of mechanical power	1–5 classes
6.4.1	Organic manuring	1–5 classes
7.4.2	Chemical fertilizing	1–5 classes
8.5.1	Extent of irrigation	1–5 classes
9.5.2	System of irrigation	A–E symbols
10.6.1	System of land use	A–E symbols
11.6.2	System of crop or land rotation	A–E symbols
12.6.3	Intensity of land use	1–5 classes
13.6.4	Cropping system	A–E symbols
14.6.5	System of livestock breeding	A–E symbols
Production characteristics		
15.7.1	Land productivity	1–5 classes
16.7.2	Labor productivity	1–5 classes
17.8.1	Level of commercialization	1–5 classes
18.8.2	Degree of commercialization	1–5 classes
19.9.1	Percentage ratio of animal to crop production in gross production	1–5 classes
20.9.2	Percentage ratio of animal to crop production in commercial production	1–5 classes

which is applicable to land evaluation (see also BRINKMAN and SMYTH, 1973). Neither is as yet finalized, but some outlines and examples have been provided.

The selected characterizing variables used by KOSTROWICKY (1972) are reproduced in Table 5. The use of these variables, some of which were discussed previously, leads to a system of "Model Types of World Agriculture", which is characterized by a formula in which the various classes of variables give rise to different types. In this manner 33 model types have been developed. These are grouped into a number of main types:

I. Primitive agriculture
    1. Shifting (long fallow) agriculture,
    2. Nomadic herding.

II. Traditional agriculture
    3. Current fallow agriculture,
    4. Continuing, extensive, mixed agriculture,
    5. Labor intensive, non-irrigated, crop agriculture,
    6. Labor intensive, irrigated, crop agriculture,

7. Labor intensive, irrigated, semi-commercial crop agriculture,
8. Labor intensive, non-irrigated, semi-commercial crop agriculture,
9. Low intensive, semi-commercial crop agriculture
10. Large-scale, low intensive, semi-commercial agriculture, latifundia.

III. Market-oriented agriculture
11. Mixed agriculture,
12. Intensive agriculture with fruit growing and/or market gardening dominant,
13. Large-scale, specialized agriculture with livestock breeding dominant,
14. Plantation agriculture,
15. Specialized irrigated agriculture,
16. Specialized, large-scale grain crop agriculture,
17. Specialized large-scale grazing (ranching).

IV. Socialized agriculture
18. Mixed agriculture,
19. Specialized fruit and/or vegetable agriculture,
20. Specialized industrial crop agriculture,
21. Specialized grain crop agriculture,
22. Specialized grazing,
23. Labor intensive, non-irrigated crop agriculture,
24. Labor intensive, irrigated crop agriculture.

Within each type, several subtypes are in principle suggested. Some indications are already given on the regional occurrence of the various types. The characterization is also carried out by the construction of "typograms" for each land utilization type.

As stated previously, the system being developed by BEEK and BENNEMA (1972) is designed primarily for use in land evaluation. Less emphasis is placed on the socioeconomic aspects of the land utilization types and more on the kind of produce and on the nature and quantity of the different inputs. This emphasis is understandable, because these features are more directly related to land resources and to the means of obtaining the various kinds of production related to them. The system has not yet been developed to include all possible kinds of land use in the world. Some examples have been elaborated and are reproduced in Table 6.

Both systems make essential contributions to the development of a more systematized approach to the study of land utilization. The development of a typology of land utilization is of considerable importance for a better understanding of the systems used today as well as for more careful land evaluation and for better directed land development. There is reason to doubt the feasibility of producing one all-purpose typology of world agriculture, even ignoring land utilization types such as forestry, with different purposes and intensities, which thus far has not been treated by KOSTROWICKY and only briefly by BEEK and BENNEMA. It is perhaps reasonable to expect that two or more typological systems may be developed within the near future, depending on their main purposes and on the persons involved in their development. It is highly commendable, however, that the preceding authors have drawn our attention to the importance of this work for scientific as well as practical purposes and that a good starting point for further development has been reached.

Table 6. Land utilization types (BEEK and BENNEMA, 1972)

Examples of land utilization types	Produce											
	Crops							Grazing		Forestry	Mixed	
	Annual			Semi-Annual		Perennial		Natural	Cultivated		Annual crops + cultivated grazing	
	fruits and vegetables	industrial	field	fruits	industrial	fruits	industrial				industrial crops + c.g.	field crops + c.g.
No irrigation												
Dry farming												
small holding, hand labor			×									
animal labor			×									
modern			×									
Horticulture												
annual fruits and vegetables, hand labor	×											
annual fruits and vegetables, modern	×											
perennial fruits, hand labor						×						
perennial fruits, modern						×						
Mixed farming												
field crops, cultivated pasture, animal traction												×
field crops, cultivated pasture, modern												×
Agriculture												
annual industrial crops, hand labor		×										
annual industrial crops, animal power		×										
annual industrial crops, modern, small plots		×										
annual industrial crops, modern, large plots		×										
annual field crops, hand labor			×									
annual field crops, animal power			×									
annual field crops, improved, animal power			×									
annual field crops, modern, large plots			×									
annual field crops, improved terraced cultivation		×										
semi-annual industrial crops, hand labor					×							
semi-annual industrial crops, improved, labor intensive					×							
semi-annual industrial crops, modern, labor extensive					×							
perennial industrial crops, labor intensive							×					
perennial industrial crops, labor extensive							×					
Grazing												
natural grassland								×				
natural grassland, improved								×				
cultivated grassland (meat)									×			
cultivated grassland (milk)									×			
Forestry												
commercial timber traditional										×		
commercial timber, intensive										×		
Irrigated												
annual fruits and vegetables	×											
annual industrial crops, labor extensive		×										
annual industrial crops, labor intensive		×										
annual field crops, labor extensive			×									
irrigated rice, fully mechanized			×									
irrigated rice, labor intensive			×									

Capital						Farm power				Employment			Farm size			Technical know-how level		
Development Inputs				Recurring Inputs														
low	medium	high	very high	normal	high	hand	animal	tractor 2 wheel	tractor 4 wheel + crawler	low	medium	high	small	medium	large	low	medium	high
×				×		×					×		×			×		
×				×			×				×		×			×		
×				×						×					×		×	×
	×			×	×				×		×		×	×		×	×	×
×				×		×							×			×	×	×
×	×	×	×	×	×	×		×			×		×	×		×	×	×
	×			×	×	×					×		×	×	×	×	×	×
	×			×			×				×			×	×	×	×	×
×				×			×			×	×		×			×	×	×
×				×					×	×				×	×	×	×	×
×	×			×		×						×	×	×	×	×	×	×
	×			×	×			×				×	×		×			
	×			×	×				×	×					×			
×	×			×		×	×				×		×	×		×		
×				×			×			×	×		×	×	×	×		
×	×			×	×				×	×	×			×			×	×
	×			×			×				×	×			×		×	×
	×			×								×		×		×		
	×			×		×						×		×	×		×	×
	×			×					×	×				×			×	×
	×			×	×				×	×					×			
	×			×		×						×		×	×	×	×	×
	×			×			×				×			×	×			
×	×	×		×		×				×	×				×	×	×	
×	×	×		×					×	×				×	×		×	
				×					×		×				×		×	×
×	×			×	×		×			×	×				×	×	×	×
	×	×	×	×	×				×	×		×	×		×		×	×
		×	×	×	×		×		×	×		×	×	×	×		×	×
	×	×	×	×	×				×	×		×	×	×	×	×	×	×

Table 6. (continued)

Examples of land utilization types	Produce											
	Crops							Grazing		Fores-try	Mixed	
	Annual			Semi-Annual		Perenn-ial		Na-tural	Culti-vated		Annual crops + cultivated grazing	
	fruits and vegetables	industrial	field	fruits	industrial	fruits	industrial				industrial crops + c.g.	field crops + c.g.
Supplementary irrigation semi-annual crops perennial crops annual fruits and vegetables	×			×			×					
Permanent drainage „polder" modern, field crops			×									
Vineyards, Mediterranean type, traditional, no irrigation												

3.4 Non-Agricultural Land Utilization Types

Types of non-agricultural land utilization include use of the land for industrial and urban economic purposes, including mining, as well as for recreation and for the conservation of wild life and nature. The latter, although they are often economically significant, cannot be strictly seen as economic enterprises. Non-agricultural land uses include activities with a very high intensity of different inputs as well as those with a low intensity of labor and of other annual inputs and/or capital inputs. Apart from broad categories, no over-all system of classification comparable to those discussed above for agriculture can be mentioned. In addition, discussion of such a system is beyond the scope of this book which is directed primarily towards the problems of advancing agriculture.

Because agriculture advances in a world which also supports many other enterprises, its land use is influenced by these other kinds of land utilization. Non-agricultural kinds of land utilization will therefore be viewed in terms of their relationship to and effect on, agricultural land uses. The following main categories are useful for this purpose:

— Concentrated urban land uses
— Concentrated industrial land uses
— Concentrated mining areas
— Dispersed urban land uses
— Dispersed industrial land uses
— Dispersed mining areas
— Predominantly urban and national or regional systems of roads and/or canals
— Predominantly rural road systems
— Recreation areas
— Conservation areas.

Capital						Farm power				Employment			Farm size			Technical know-how level		
Development Inputs				Recurring Inputs														
low	medium	high	very high	normal	high	hand	animal	tractor 2 wheel	tractor 4 wheel + crawler	low	medium	high	small	medium	large	low	medium	high
	×	×	×	×					×	×				×				×
	×	×	×	×					×	×				×				×
	×	×	×	×				×					×	×				×
	×	×	×	×					×	×				×				×
×				×		×		×			×		×	×		×	×	

All of these influence agricultural land uses in one way or another and may either hinder or stimulate the advancement of agriculture. The influence of concentrated urban and industrial land uses is primarily economic, as was recognized in principle by VON THÜNEN (1783—1850), who described the different kinds of agricultural land uses which were grouped in circles around the town of his *Isolierter Staat*. This basic concept, with suitable modifications, can still be observed today in many parts of the world. Another important influence of concentrated urban and industrial areas today is the fact that they often form islands with a much higher standard of living than has thus far been reached in the surrounding agricultural areas. These areas may have a healthy effect on agriculture, because they draw excess labor from the farms and thus help improve the standard of living in agricultural areas. In case of labor-intensive agriculture, the drawing-off of excess labor may, however, create problems: in particular in regard to the need for mechanization, towards which neither the land utilization as such nor the technical know-how of the farmers may be very well attuned. Urban and industrial waste disposal may create problems in the surrounding farming country, but part of this waste may, if processed to compost, also help to improve agricultural production. The influence of concentrated mining areas is similar.

The influence of predominantly urban and national or regional road systems is in some ways similar to that of the preceding concentrated land uses. They also have, however, some particular influences of their own: they tend to cut rural systems of roads and canals, a fact which does not always receive sufficient attention when the roads are planned and executed. The construction of a new national highway through any area of the Netherlands almost always has to be accompanied by a rural reallotment project to prevent the farmers from being cut off from part of their fields and from public facilities. In addition, proper measures for maintaining efficient drainage systems must also be considered. Soil salinity increases along the main highways in Iraq because the highways obstruct part of the natural drainage system of the Mesopotamian Plain. The construction of roads in unstable areas may cause landslides of previously unknown dimensions and thus cause the deterioration of adjoining agricultural lands. Regional and national canals are subject to the same problems, and in addition, they may cause serious disturbances in the water conditions of the soil in the surrounding areas. Serious drought effects of a similar nature may be caused by the regular pumping of large quantities of water from the subsoils for urban and industrial uses.

Heavy competition exists between the preceding land uses and agricultural land use for the little surface area available for all land uses in some countries. The total amount of land taken by urban and related land uses from agriculture in the Netherlands during the present century has been of the same order of magnitude as the total area reclaimed from the Zuyderzee (approx. 200 000 hectares).

The influence of dispersed urban, industrial and mining activities on agriculture is in many respects comparable to that of concentrated activities of the same kind. The effect may be advantageous in that these activities tend to enhance the penetration of technical know-how, and of small amounts of capital in the agricultural areas. The presence of these activities may also induce the development of "part-time farming" by providing farmers who are partially underemployed in their own family enterprises with the opportunity of earning more money. This effect may or may not be beneficial to agriculture itself, depending on circumstances. Occasionally, the agricultural work becomes neglected, because the farmer is able to earn more money in industry, with less work. On the other hand, money earned in industry is invested in new machinery or other inputs for agriculture. In such cases, agricultural development is effectively enhanced.

Dispersed mining activities of several kinds also may noticeably affect the agriculture of an area. For example, the digging of clay for brick factories is an age-old activity in the Netherlands and in some adjoining regions which has sometimes benefited agriculture, i.e. in places where heavy clay topsoils were removed, the underlying calcareous loams and clay loams were made available for agricultural use. On the other hand, the removal of good calcareous loams has caused the deterioration of good land into poor land or sometimes even to unproductive water. Similarly, many hectares have been destroyed by the removal of gravel from the subsoils. These activities must be carefully controlled by local and provincial legislation and supervision. Local mining of natural gas from shallow deposits with primitive means sometimes causes the salinization of surface waters because of the nature of the older marine deposits in which the gas is found. Larger mining activities in the deeper substrata also occasionally have deleterious effects on agriculture, e.g. by subsequent subsidence of the terrain which causes disturbances in the drainage and irregularities in the land in general.

Predominantly rural road systems perform a natural function in agricultural land use. Still, their construction or modernization poses several problems. In unstable hilly areas, e.g. consisting of shale, the relatively light construction of rural roads with light embankments may induce periodic landslides after heavy rains. Their construction and maintenance must be relatively inexpensive, since the cost must be borne by the rural community, which fact may pose serious local problems. Well-constructed rural roads located near overcrowded main roads tend to be used as by-pass roads by non-rural traffic. Once again, the construction

and financing of these roads are inadequate for this purpose, and similar problems are liable to occur. Another common problem develops when rural roads
attract the attention of the urban population because of their recreational possibilities.

Rural roads of age-old origin, sometimes even from Roman times, e.g. in
various parts of England, have become part of the cultural ecosystem of a landscape and have often acquired a particular kind of beauty. Over the years they
have acquired a particular kind of vegetation, of trees and bushes and related
plants and even some interesting animals, e.g. birds. They are often no longer
adapted to the needs of modern agricultural techniques, which include the use of
tractors and other agricultural machinery as well as heavy trucks for transport to
and from the farms. The tendency in agricultural areas is, therefore, to construct
wider roads, as straight as possible and with not too many trees and bushes. In
areas where the agricultural landscape has, in addition, attracted attention for
recreation purposes, grave problems result which are not always solved in a
manner satisfactory for all parties concerned. Local solutions may either be based
on the economic needs of agriculture, which results in unavoidable damage to the
recreational as well as to the ecological aspects, or the latter are stressed without
finding a satisfactory solution for the needs of agriculture. Only a careful assessment of the land utilization types and their needs as well as of the available land
resources may in the future provide better solutions.

Land use for recreation or for conservation, or for a combination of both, is in
some ways closely related to agricultural land use. Usually, both of the former
involve land use in rural areas, although recreation which is more urban in
nature, and conservation which is cultural are also of interest. We shall, however,
pay closer attention to the rural kinds of recreation and conservation. Depending
on the type of recreation practiced and on the measure of conservation wanted,
these two land uses may or may not conflict. Occasionally, they may even be said
to be interdependent. Both are in some ways closely related to agricultural land
uses (see e.g. KIEMSTEDT, 1967). Furthermore, interesting concepts, equivalent to
land utilization types, have been developed for recreation. These concepts are
playing an increasingly important role in determining rural land use for industrialized regions. As tourism, which itself is a multifaceted form of recreation,
becomes increasingly important in developing areas, the consideration of recreational land utilization types in conjunction with agricultural land use will serve a
useful function.

To recreate is "to refresh, entertain, agreeably occupy or amuse oneself" (Concise Oxford Dictionary). This may be done in many different ways by many
different persons at many different times. MAAS (1971) provides some figures for
different recreational areas in the Netherlands; these figures are reproduced in
abbreviated form in Table 7. A long list of recreational land uses included in the
Canada Land Inventory (DEPARTMENT OF REGIONAL ECONOMIC EXPANSION,
1969) is reproduced in Table 8.

It is clear that the very pragmatic Canadian list, which was made for a first
quick national inventory, does not in itself constitute a classification of land
utilization types. Several of the mentioned features are, however, indicative of

Table 7. Recreational land uses in the Netherlands (after MAAS, 1971)

Environ-ment	Facility	Density (pers./ha)	Surface area (ha)
A	crowded beach	3000	2—5
	sport stadium	over 3000	5
B	beach	1000	5—10
	open-air pool	1000	5—10
	zoo	500	20
	sports field with tribune	1000	5
	racecourse	500	30
C	camping	120	10—25
	quiet beach	100	10
	playgrounds in park	100—200	various
	beaches, lakes forest-fringes	100	various
	sports fields	100	20—30
D	small sailing lake	20	50—100
	golf course	20	50
	forest-park	10—20	50—100
E	productive forest (easily penetrable)	3—10	over 250
	heather (easily penetrable)	3—10	over 100
	agric. area in recr. zone	5	over 200
	large lakes	10	over 200

Table 8. Recreational features from the Canada Land Inventory (DEP. REG. ECON. EXP., 1969)

Angling	Upland wildlife
Beach	Cultural landscape
Canoe tripping	Topographic patterns
Deep inshore water	Rock formations
Vegetation	Skiing area
Waterfalls and rapids	Thermal springs
Glacier	Deep water boat tripping
Historic site	Viewing
Gathering and collecting	Wetland wildlife
Organized camps	Miscellaneous
Landforms	Family boating
Small surface waters	Man-made features
Lodging	

specific types. Others could be combined to form types which could be organized along lines similar to those used by MAAS.

KIEMSTEDT (1967) presented a method for evaluating the landscape for various kinds of recreation. The following table from his publication gives rough estimates of the recreational values attributed to different rural land uses (Table 9). The figures given by KIEMSTEDT are combined with other factors, e.g. of climate and relief, to produce a combined index of recreational values for different kinds of landscape. These figures are of course a rough approximation, but they are of value because they represent an attempt at a relative evaluation of agricultural lands for recreational purposes.

Table 9. Evaluation in points of the major land uses according to their suitability for recreation (after KIEMSTEDT, 1967)

Major land use	Suitability for the kinds of recreation			Originality factor	Total weight
	Walking	Play etc.	Bathing etc.		
Arable land	2	2	—	2	6
Grassland	5	5	—	5	15
Forest	7	5	—	7	19
Heather c.a.	7	7	—	7	21
Water	—	—	50		50

The problems inherent in areas with a mixture of agriculture and recreation in the Netherlands were the subject of a recent series of lectures at the Agricultural University of Wageningen (WERKGROEP, 1970—1971). Ways and means of why and how agricultural and recreational land uses should and could be combined, were discussed. Primarily, a certain percentage of the land is needed for very intensive use (urban c.a., intensive horticulture) and a certain percentage must be reserved for very extensive use (water, forest, nature conservation). The remaining land, therefore, must be divided among various purposes in an acceptable manner. The percentages are:

	very intensive	very extensive	rest
Netherlands	11%	$28^1/_2$%	$60^1/_2$%
Europe (excl. USSR)	8%	56%	36%

Clearly, this is one of the reasons why the Netherlands is felt to be a very crowded country (HELLINGA in WERKGROEP, 1970—1971) and why combined intensive multipurpose land use is particularly urgent in this country. The same tendencies, however, exist in other regions and may be analyzed in a similar manner. The actual solution in a given area depends largely on the available land resources and on the kinds of demands which are made on the area. To achieve such a balance, it will be necessary to develop new land utilization types which combine the different purposes of land use in a manner which makes them feasible for planning, execution and management. In order to do this, the rather vague ideas proposed for the development of generally large landscape parks, i.e., those comprising whole districts, in which agriculture should primarily serve recreation and conservation, should be presented as a more feasible blueprint, whereby a reasonably efficient agricultural system, although bound by definite restrictions, can be maintained.

Conservation may serve recreational needs to the extent that the recreation density does not have any deleterious effects on the lands and landscapes to be conserved. Nature and soil conservation can, therefore, often be combined with the less dense activities mentioned by MAAS (1971) and with "dispersed activities" mentioned in the Canada Land Inventory. Conservation of various kinds often serves agriculture more directly. Soil conservation can be, and often is, a regular practice in agriculture, and with appropriate land classification, also allows for conservation of wildlife and vegetation on the less productive, more erodible

lands. Conservation of natural forest vegetations is often indispensable for the
hydrology of an agricultural area. In other cases, the natural balance of the
ecosystems may help to a certain extent to maintain the balance in the cultural
ecosystems of agriculture. Reasons exist for distinguishing land utilization types
in nature conservation, even if only that systemization might lead to a clearer
perception of their different roles and thus to a more efficient application in rural
land use planning.

The first step in developing such a system should be to make a clear distinction between conservation practices applied within agricultural land utilization
types and those which lie outside the domain of agriculture in its widest sense.
The former include various methods of soil conservation and range management
(see e.g. LEWIS in VAN DYNE et al., 1969) as well as proper forest management
practices (see also: NELSON and CHAMBERS, 1969). The latter are in general poorly
defined and are therefore difficult to handle in practical land use planning.

Conservation in its broadest sense includes the conservation of natural or
semi-natural ecosystems for purposes which range from those of purely scientific
interest to those which are purely practical, i.e., directly applicable to the fields of
hydrology, of recreation or of the ideologically based but practically important
conservation of a minimum amount of natural biological variability within a
given region. These purposes, when combined with reasonable wishes for dispersed recreation and for education, lead to management practices which might
well be said to constitute different land utilization types. Conservation for purely

Photo 9. Heather moor in the Netherlands (Photo WIM K. STEFFEN, Natuurmonumenten,
Amsterdam)

scientific purposes, e.g. to study the development of a natural succession, may involve a total "non-management" approach. Conservation for any other purpose may lead to management practices which are geared to the preservation of a certain step within a succession which results in a particular kind of landscape of definite historical and recreational interest.

The heather-moors on the sandy soils in some parts of Netherlands (Photo 9) are a typical example. These moors (dominated by *Calluna sp.*) were created in early Medieval times from the natural oak-birch forests by sheep-grazing, as an essential part of the then prevalent agricultural land utilization type. The latter deteriorated after the use of chemical fertilizers became a common practice in the first decades of the present century. Now three different kinds of management are practiced: (1) sheep grazing is continued on a non-economic basis to maintain the moors and to provide a special recreational asset, (2) the small-tree growth which would eventually replace the moors is demolished by mechanical means, (3) all small-tree growth is demolished but the *Juniperus* bushes are conserved. Similar combinations of different management systems are found in other seminatural ecosystems, many of which have their origins in old human activities, e.g. the digging of peat from lowland marshes.

Agriculture is concerned not only with the conservation of terrestrial ecosystems, but also with that of aquatic systems, and it may in turn be influenced by these (see e.g. MACAN and WORTHINGTON, 1968). The definition of land utilization types may, in the future, also include combined types of agricultural land and water management which would involve typical conservation features as well as those of agricultural land use.

Chapter 4   Land Resources

4.1 General Introduction

Definition

Land resources include all those features and processes of the land, which can, in some way, be used to fulfill certain human needs. As can be seen from the definition of "land" given in Chapter 1, these resources are numerous and complex. To study land resources as a general academic excercise is not impossible, but it can only be done with major simplifications. It is easier therefore to study land resources from a more defined standpoint. For this text, the self-evident standpoint to take is that of the use of land resources within agricultural land utilization types. Only occasionally will some reference be made to other rural land utilization types.

For agriculture, the most important land resources may be indicated in broad groups:
  a) climate,
  b) relief and geological formations,
  c) soils (including soil hydrology),
  d) water (including geohydrology),
  e) artifactial elements of a stable nature,
  f) vegetation and related biological features.

In Para. 1.3, the resources aspects of land use were indicated briefly. This chapter is devoted to the description of those aspects of land resources which are of particular importance for agriculture. For more fundamental aspects of these land features, reference is made to the many good textbooks existing on climatology, geomorphology, geology, soil science or pedology, hydrology and biology.

From our viewpoint, the land resources may be divided into three groups: (1) very stable resources (climate, relief, geological formations, (2) moderately stable resources (soils and water, some artifactial elements of the land), and (3) relatively unstable resources (vegetation and related biological features). The stability of a particular resource is seen in relation to its period of formation as well as to the ease with which human activities can influence it, causing either degradation or improvement.

Very Stable Resources

Climate is a very stable resource in the sense that, apart from very local activities, e.g., glasshouses, it is almost completely free of man's influence. When viewed in relation to the duration of climatic conditions occuring over a period of millions of years, it is, however, less stable. The climatic changes occurring during the Pleistocene period (approx. 2 million to 10000 years ago) included at least three major cold periods (Glacial Ages) in those parts of the world which are now characterized by a temperate climate. Within each of these major periods, fluctuations of considerable ecological impact occurred (stadial and interstadial periods). Similar fluctuations of a somewhat different nature, often indicated as the Pluvial and Interpluvial Ages, greatly influenced many parts of the now subtropical zones of the world. Also during the present Holocene period, several climatic fluctuations occurred (STAMP et al., 1961; KOCH, 1947) which influenced land use in areas such as the polar regions and the arid zones. It is, however, almost impossible to predict either the present or future course of these fluctuations, and the impact of intentional human activities on climate does not go much further than certain aspects of microclimate; there is, however, some evidence that unintentional human influences on the climate, e.g. air pollution, may be very important locally.

Major relief features as well as geological formations have their origins mostly in ages long past. The Precambrian formations which are found on the surface in continental areas of America, Africa and Asia are more than 800 million years old. Most of the mountainous formations of the world are between 70 and 600 million years old. The remaining areas of the world consist primarily of formations of between 1 and 70 million years of age. Formations of the Quaternary, or the youngest, period are often found as covers over the older formations and rarely exceed a thickness of more than 100 m. Human influence on these formations as such is limited to local mining exploitation. Modifications of these formations for agricultural land use is out of the question apart from the contruction of tunnels for easier communication by road and railroad or for the transport of irrigation water.

The major relief features of the world belong to age classes which are similar to those of the younger geological formations. They are influenced by the nature of these formations as such, but their actual forms have been caused mainly by processes which influenced their formation at various times during the last 100 million years. Their development continues today, but it can only be superficially influenced by human activities. Relief features of smaller dimensions, usually 10 m or less, can, however, at a relatively heavy cost, be modified to suit agricultural land use, e.g. irrigation. Modification of these features, by levelling or otherwise, is concurrent with modifications of the soils and of the water regime.

Moderately Stable Resources

Most soils date from the Quaternary period, although several kinds of soils have inherited features of soils formed during older periods. The formation of a particular soil can take anywhere from hundreds of years to many thousands of years, to an order of magnitude of about 1 million years. The actual duration depends on the intensity of the action of the soil-forming factors, of which climate, parent material and vegetation are of particular importance. The other soil-forming factors—relief, water conditions, animals and human activity—induce modifications such as the kind and depth of soil formation. Human activity may lead either to building up of a particular soil (Plaggenboden), the modification of certain soils ("paddy soils") or to the partial or complete destruction of soils by erosion and degradation. Soils are therefore less stable than climate, relief and geological formations and more easily modified by man. Soils are more vulnerable to degradation but can also be positively influenced by soil management and soil improvement. Stability of water conditions as a resource is similar to that of soil conditions. Water conditions are primarily a result of the climate of a region, by means of which the basic quantities of the water balance—precipitation and evapotranspiration—are regulated. This fact endows this resource with a certain basic stability. In more detail, water conditions are strongly influenced by the relief and by the nature of rocks and soils as well as by vegetation and human land use. The quantity of water at a given time may, in addition, be strongly influenced by man. The quality of water is also partly a result of the over-all, rather stable, conditions of the landscape, but it is very dependent on the natural or man-influenced aquatic ecosystems as well as on human acitivities, deleterious or otherwise. Water quality is determined by the biological and chemical characteristics of organisms and of substances in solution and suspension as well as by the mechanical aspects of silt or mud content.

Soil, microrelief and water, as well as some artifactial features of the land, have in common that they are stable enough to have a permanent and continuous influence on agricultural land use and that, on the other hand, they are flexible enough, within certain limits, to be improved or modified for land development. This also implies that they are vulnerable to human pollution, degradation and destruction.

Relatively Unstable Resources

Instability and vulnerability are typical characteristics of the biological features of the land. Natural biological communities, particularly those which are not too far from the hypothetical, "climax", have a considerable internal stability, i.e. they can compensate internally caused changes as well as some externally caused natural fluctuations, e.g. climate, if they do not last too long. Long-term climatic changes, e.g. hundreds of years or more, as manifested during the Pleistocene period, cause great changes in the natural ecosystems. The transitional periods of these broader fluctuations are important periods of over-all instability of the land.

The vegetation and its changes have a very great influence on the stability of the soils and thus on the impact of processes of erosion and degradation on land forms and parent materials.

The external stability of the biological features of the land is very low, as can be seen by the way in which, ever since the Neolithic Age, they have been manipulated by agricultural land use and, perhaps even in earlier periods, by the destruction of vegetation through burning for hunting over large areas. The everpresent problem of pests and diseases of agricultural crops is of a somewhat different nature, as it may be considered to be caused by the unnaturalness of the agricultural crops as ecosystems. The weed problem in agriculture may be seen as essentially an aspect of the stability of natural plant communities which continuously try to encroach upon the man-induced monocultures.

The instability and vulnerability of the plant and animal communities of the land have different degrees of importance in different areas. A heavy tropical forest may, by its relative stability, provide serious problems for land clearing and therefore for land development. At the other extreme, the fragile constitution of the few remaining natural or semi-natural ecosystems in some industrialized regions may constitute a grave problem of environmental deterioration. Systems of forest management (DUFFY and SHEPHERD, 1969) and of grassland management, particularly in the natural grazing areas of the arid and semi-arid countries (Integrated Surveys, 1967), provide examples of vegetation management for the dual purposes of optimum sustained yields and of maintaining an element of ecological stability.

Levels of Classification

All land resources may be considered at various levels of generalization, which may be roughly indicated by the size of the regions considered:

a) the world as a whole,

b) continents or large regions, including the very large countries (U.S.A., U.S.S.R., Brazil, China, India),

c) national areas,

d) large regions within countries and some small countries,

e) project areas and sample areas.

Each level of generalization corresponds to a phase of land use planning and to the details of resources data as they are for example indicated on resources maps of different scales. The first level, (a), corresponds to very general planning of world resources such as are found for instance, in the Indicative World Plan (FAO, 1969); the related map scales lie between 1:1 million and 1:10 million. Level (b) corresponds to regional and large national planning and to map scales between 1:500000 and 1:5 million. Level (c) is typical for national planing and corresponds in general to map scales between 1:250000 and 1:1 million. Level (d) is typical for the planning of project priorities and in general corresponds to map scales of between 1:100000 and 1:250000. Level (e) includes all work for the planning and execution of projects for land use planning and land development; it is carried out on the largest scales of land resources maps which may vary, depending on the stage of planning or execution and on the size and nature of the region involved, from 1:2000 to 1:100000. Each of these map scales has to correspond to the appropriate detail as determined from field observations, air photo-interpretation and laboratory analyses and has to be cartographically represented in a corresponding manner (VINK, 1963a, b, 1968). The following paragraphs contain a discussion of the nature of these resources and of their impact on agricultural land use at the different levels of generalization. Repeated reference will be made to the "checklist" recently made under the aegis of FAO by J.L. UNGER (BRINKMAN and SMYTH, 1973).

4.2 Climate, Geology, Relief

4.2.1 Climate

The following climatic features all have a considerable impact on agricultural
land use (see also RUBINSTEIN et al., 1956; RUMNEY, 1968):

- a) temperature,
- b) precipitation,
- c) insolation,
- d) wind velocity,
- e) evaporation,
- f) various extremes and hazards.

Of these, the first four are basically independent factors, whereas evaporation
is largely a function of the first four factors combined. Other "secondary" climatic
factors also affect agriculture, such as relative air humidity. Evaporation and
evapotranspiration, which includes the influence of plants ("transpiration"), have,
however, such a great impact on land use, that they must be considered as factors
of primary importance. The main climatic factors may also be viewed in terms of
averages and of the periodic fluctuations determined from the calculation of the
former, such as: duration of summer and winter periods, of periods of drought
and rainy seasons, of periods with different lengths of daily insolation. These
fluctuations are very important for agricultural land use and their use in different
classification systems is common, as will be shown below. Extreme fluctuations of
these factors often, however, have particular effects which far surpass their rather
short periods of incidence as well as their relatively low frequency of occurrence.

Because many of these climatic extremes and hazards are known to be extremely deleterious to plant growth and agricultural production: night frost, cold
winds, hot and dry winds, extreme wind velocities or hail storms, less attention is
paid to the beneficial effects of some extremes. Some nights with frost are needed
for the vernalization of winter crops. An occasional frost may also act as a
constraint to the development of certain pests and diseases, e.g. of the fungus
Exobasidium vexans ("blisterblight") in tea cultivation in the northern provinces
of India. The occasional occurrence of extremely high temperatures may also
create favorable conditions for certain kinds of agricultural production. This
situation exists, e.g., as a result of the "Föhn" winds, in the vineyards of Switzerland north of the Alps, e.g. those growing in the area around the Lakes Geneva
and Neuchâtel (SCHREIBER, 1968). These winds occur particularly in spring and in
autumn. The wind occurring in the spring enhances the early development of the
young shoots, and that occurring in autumn, known as the "grape cooker" (*Trau-
benkocher*), ensures a harvest of good quality.

Classifications of Climates

The best known world system for the classification of climates is that made by
KÖPPEN during the first decades of this century. Although it is one of many
different kinds of classification systems, it has gained wide acceptance because of

Table 10. Climatic types of the world according to KÖPPEN (after KÖPPEN and GEIGER, 1928)

Zone A: Tropical rainy climates (average monthly temperature never below 18° C)
1. Humid and warm:
Af: always humid, at least 60 mm precipitation in the driest month (rain-forest climate)
Am: monsoon climate with moderately dry season
2. Periodically dry:
Aw: savanna climates with dry winter
As: savanna climates with dry summer (rare)

Zone B: Dry climates (determined by the relation between annual precipitation and annual temperature)
BS: steppe climates
— BSh: hot B climate
— BSk: cool B climate
— BSk': cold B climate
— BSn: B climate with frequent fog
BW: desert climate

Zone C: Warm-temperate rainy climates (between the 18° C and 3° C isotherms of the coldest month)
Cw: warm climates with a dry winter (precipitation in the wettest month is 10 times that in the driest month)
Cs: warm climates with a dry summer (precipitation in the wettest month is 3 times that in the driest month)
Cf: humid temperate climates
further subdivisions: a = hot summers, b = warm summers, c = cool summers.

Zone D: Subarctic climates with a cold winter (between − 3° C in the coldest month and 10° C in the warmest month and with more precipitation than is required for Zone C (boreal- or snow-forest climates)
Df: continuously humid
Dw: climates with a cold, dry winter
subdivisions as in Zone C

Zone E: Polar climates (tundra climates rich in snow) (warmest month between 10° and 0° C or even lower)
ET: tundra climates
EH: climates of high altitudes (more than 3000 m above sea level)
EF: climates of permanent frost

its very generally acceptable characteristics and of its clarity for educational purposes (HAURWITZ and AUSTIN, 1944: RUBINSTEIN et al., 1956). It is based on relatively simple values which can be measured or estimated with sufficient accuracy in most areas of the world. It is therefore also useful for a general comparison of climatic resources and constraints of the various land utilization types of the world. The main variables used in this system are:

— temperature of the coldest month (occurrence or not of summer and winter seasons),
— temperature of the warmest month,
— occurrence of a dry period (either in summer or in winter).

Subdivisions are made according to quantitative data on precipitation in relation to temperature. Further subdivisions are made according to specific quantitative temperature boundaries. A generalized version of the climatic types of KÖPPEN, which can be reproduced even on very small-scale maps (1:10 million and smaller), is given in Table 10.

Some interesting classifications, with special references to agricultural problems, were made by PAPADAKIS (1938, 1966). The considerations upon which these were based were also used in drawing up the Indicative World Plan (FAO, 1969). The generalized version has been produced by PAPADAKIS (1966) on a scale of 1:50 million for the whole world. The total detail can be produced on maps of scale 1:50 million and can thus be compared with the World Soil Map, which is being produced as a joint effort by FAO and UNESCO (DUDAL, 1969], 1970 AND FAO-UNESCO, 1971). PAPADAKIS (1938) originally divided the world into zones according to the growth of characteristic agricultural crops and characterized by specific temperature regimes:

A: summer insufficiently long and warm for the ripening of the small grains
.... 1. Polar zone,
B: summer sufficiently long and warm for the ripening of the small grains
I. winter too severe for the winter grains
.... 2. Zone of summer wheat,

II. winter sufficiently mild for winter wheat,
a) winter too severe for oats
.... 3. Zone of winter wheat,

b) winter sufficiently mild for oats
1. winter too severe for citrus
.... 4. Zone of winter oats,

2. winter sufficiently mild for citrus
i) two seasons (one colder: winter
and one warmer: summer)
.... 5. Citrus zone,
ii) no seasons with regard to temperature
.... 6. Equatorial zone.

This broad system is subdivided into a whole set of climatic types for each zone. It has some similarities to all other world systems, but it has certain advantages for comparing different agricultural land use types.

In his newer system, PAPADAKIS (1966) introduced a specific kind of climo-diagram which does not indicate mean temperatures and average figures for precipitation; these figures have been replaced by others which give a better indication of crop-ecological extremes and other values. They include, e.g. the duration of the frost-free season and the potential evapotranspiration. An example is reproduced in Fig. 4.1.

PAPADAKIS' system as it stands today recognizes 10 "fundamental groups" of climates. Each of these is characterized by specific temperature- and humidity-regimes and is subdivided into a number, usually 8 or 9, of more precisely defined climatic types. As far as possible, these types are characterized by the kind of crops which can be grown as well as by the localities and kinds of landscapes in which they are found. Further subdivisions are made according to more precise indications of humidity and/or temperature. In some cases the month of incidence of the dry season is used as a differentiating variable. This extensive, elaborate system is not easy to handle and therefore is too difficult for educational purposes. The data required are, however, relatively simple, and therefore the system could be used with the kind of information which exists in nearly all countries. Its

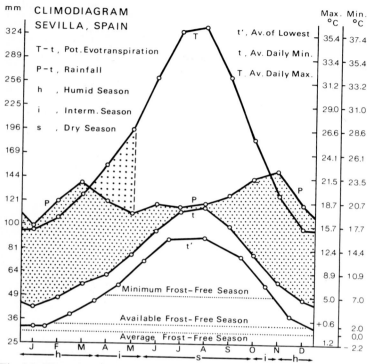

Fig. 4.1. Climodiagram (PAPADAKIS, 1966), in the scale of millimeters (for pot. evapotranspiration, and rainfall) 5 cm correspond to 25 mm, 10–100, 15–225, and so on; this diagram begins with 25 mm, because the lower 5 cm are not needed. The scale of maximum teperature (T) is according to a table 0.6 ° C corresponds to 36 mm, 8.9–64, and so on. In the scale of minimum (t and t') 7° C corresponds to 5 maximum, 10.9–8.9, and so on. In this way the difference T-t is equal to pot. evapotranspiration. Rainfall is shown by the shaded area above t; the half-shaded area shows evapotranspiration from water stored in the soil. To plot T we find in a table the mm corresponding to each temperature and extract the square root; this gives the ordinate of T in centimeters; t and t' are plotted in the same way, but we substract first 2° C. To plot rainfall we add to it the millimeters corresponding to t-2° C and we extract the square root; this gives the ordinate of P in centimeters. T, t, and P are plotted at the middle of the month; t' at the beginning, when the temperatures are rising (spring), and at the end when they are falling (autumn). This climodiagram can also be used to show the conditions of a particular year, or of a long series of years, in the latter case the diagram is very long, it includes 240 months for a series of 20 years; and 720 if it is done by decade; t' is the lowest temperature registered in each of these months, or decades, and it is plotted at the date it has been registered. The distance, to be more exact the ratio in mm T/t, is a good index of air humidity, cloudiness and radiation. The distance t-t' is an index of interdiurnal variability. We added a column (y), which gives directly the ordinate (distance from 0 mm) for the preparation of this climodiagram

careful consideration of the ecological requirements of the principal agricultural crops makes it particularly interesting for further study and use when investigating different climates for agricultural land use.

A very abbreviated outline of the main categories is given in Table 11 for the tropical part of the system. Of the several small-scale systems for the regional

Table 11. Abbreviated review example of the climates of the world according to PAPADAKIS (1966)—Tropical Part

1. Tropical	— permits growth of perennial crops very sensitive to frost; summer crops can be grown regardless of season; cryophilous crops cannot be grown.
1.1 Humid semihot equatorial	— climate of equatorial tree crops (coconut, oil palm, rubber, cocoa), good for sugar cane, robusta coffee, sisal, citrus and banana, rain fed rice and maize with some restrictions, yams and cassava extensively grown, irrigated rice especially in 1.13 and 1.14. The more humid climates (1.11, 1.123) too humid for cocoa, the drier ones (1.135, 1.14) too dry for cocoa and rubber.
1.2 Humid semihot tropical	— too cool for equatorial crops (rubber, coconut, oil palm, cocoa); good for all other crops that require a frostless climate (sugar cane, banana, pineapple, sisal etc.), irrigated and rain-fed rice, cassava and sweet potato yield good; nights are too warm for arabic a coffee.
1.3 Dry semihot tropical	— too dry for rubber, oil palm, cocoa; coconut is grown in subirrigated sands; good for maize, groundnuts; cotton can be grown but with serious phytosanitary problems, good for irrigated rice and sugar cane; cassava, yams and sweet potato extensively grown; sisal too.
1.4 Hot tropical	— too dry (with a few exceptions) for equatorial crops; annual crops are grown: sorghum, millet, groundnuts, cotton, sesame; irrigated rice extensively grown; important crops: sugar cane, banana and sisal but with irrigation in drier subdivisions; banana responds to irrigation everywhere.
1.5 Semiarid tropical	— drought-resistent crops: sorghum, millet, groundnuts etc.; in some subdivisions even these crops are submarginal; rice, cotton and sugar cane yield good, with irrigation.
1.6 Cool tropical	— good for all crops that require a frostless climate (banana, sugar cane etc., except the equatorial ones; in addition cryophilous crops (wheat, potato, etc.) during the cool season; rice, maize, cassava are important.
1.7 Humid tierra templada	— moist monsoon climate; arabica coffee is typical; cool nights favor maize and rice; in some climates winter is too warm for wheat and other cryophilous crops. In some climates sugar cane and/or cotton can be grown.
1.8 Dry tierra templada	— dry or semi-arid monsoon climate; too dry for coffee; maize and beans can be grown where 3 or more months are humid; where climate is drier, maize is replaced by sorghum, millet or eleusine; in some subdivisions sisal, cotton and groundnuts can be grown and in 1.84 and 1.85 wheat, potatoes and other cryophilous crops can be grown with irrigation in winter. Sugar cane and cotton require irrigation; cotton can be grown without irrigation in 1.81, 1.84 and the less dry parts of 1.82 and 1,85.
1.9 Cool winter hot tropical	— winter is cool and permits growth of wheat, flax, rape, chickpea, colza and potato; equatorial crops are not grown; rain-fed rice can be grown on adequate soils where the humid season is longer than 5 months, but is usually irrigated or flooded. Maize can also be grown where the humid season is 4 months or more; in the drier subdivisions sorghum, millet, cotton, groundnuts and sesame are grown; they are harvested at the beginning of the dry season. In the moister subdivisions banana grows without irrigation, but in the drier ones irrigation is needed. Jute is an important crop, but it requires fertile soils and long days, which delay development and produce tall plants (latitude 20° or more). Sugar cane, banana and citrus are important, but they require irrigation in the drier subdivisions.

2. Tierra Fria/Non/Frostless Tropical Highlands: not elaborated in this example.

Fig. 4.2. Climatic map of South America (FAO-UNESCO, 1971)

classification of climates which exist only those made for South America (EIDT, cited by FAO-UNESCO, 1971) and for the Mediterranean area (UNESCO-FAO, 1963) will be discussed briefly. Of a more limited scope is the work by MOHR-MANN and KESSLER (1959).

The system used by EIDT is based largely on the same characteristics introduced by PAPADAKIS (1966). Nine different types of summer and 10 different types of winter are distinguished. Furthermore, 14 different humidity regimes are recog-

Table 12. Key to climatic map of South America (EITH in FAO-UNESCO, 1971)

	Climate	Temperature regimes	Humidity regimes	Main locations
1.1a	Humid semi-hot equatorial	Eq	HU Hu MO Ln 1000 mm	Amazonia
1.1b	Humid semi-hot equatorial	Eq	HU Hu MO Ln 1000 mm	NE and NW coastal regions
1.2	Humid semi-hot tropical	Tr	HU Hu MO	Rio de Janeiro coast
1.3	Dry semi-hot tropical	Eq Tr	HI 0.44-1	Dry NE and NW coastal regions
1.4a	Hot tropical	EQ TR	MO Mo	Campos cerrados of Brazil
1.4b	Hot tropical	EQ TR	MO Mo (inundated in humid season)	Llanos of Venezuela and Colombia, Beni of Bolivia, Mato Grosso of Brazil
1.5	Semi-arid tropical	EQ Eq TR	mo	Brazilian caatinga, Venezuela, Ecuador
1.7a	Humid tierra templada	Tt tt	MO	Brazilian planalto
1.7b	Humid tierra templada	Tt tt	Hu	Andean countries
1.8	Dry tierra templada	Tt tt	MO Mo	Dry planalto of Brazil, NW countries
1.92	Cool winter semi-hot tropical	tR	Mo	West lowlands of Sao Paulo, Brazil
2a	Low-high tierra fria	TF Tf tf	HU Hu MO Mo mo	Highlands from Argentina north, S Brazil
2b	Low and high Andean	An an	HU Hu MO Mo mo	Altiplano of S Peru, Bolivia, NW Argentina
3.1	Hot tropical desert	TR	do	N Peru, Venezuela
3.2	Hot subtropical desert	SU	da do	Argentina
3.34	Cool tropical desert, summer g	tr	da	Coastal Peru
3.36	Cool tropical desert, summer 0	tr	da	N Chile coast
3.5	Andean desert	tf An	do	Peru, Bolivia, Chile
3.8	Pampean desert	PA TE	da de di do	Argentina
3.9	Patagonian desert	Pa pa	de	Argentina
4.1	Humid subtropical	Su	HU Hu	S Brazil, Uruguay
4.2	Monsoon subtropical	SU	Mo mo (dry spring)	N Argentina
4.3a	Semi-arid hot semitropical	Ts	mo	Bolivia, Paraguay, N Argentina
4.3b	Dry and moist monsoon, hot semi-tropical	Ts	Mo MO	Paraguay, N Argentina
4.4	Semi-hot semitropical	Ts	Hu	S Brazil, Paraguay

Table 12. (continued)

	Climate	Temperature regimes	Humidity regimes	Main locations
5.1	Typical pampean	PA	St	E Argentina
5.3	Subtropical pampean	SU Su	St	NE Argentina
5.6	Monsoon pampean	PA	Mo mo	Argentina
5.7	Semi-arid pampean	PA	si	Argentina
5.8	Patagonian grassland	pa ma	St	S Argentina, S Chile
5.9	Semi-arid Patagonian	Pa pa Ma TE	me si	S Argentina
6.2	Marine Mediterranean[a]	MA	ME	Central Chile
6.6	Cold temperate Mediterranean[a]	pa	ME Me	S Chile, S Argentina
6.8	Subtropical semi-arid Mediterranean[a]	MA	me	Central Chile
6.9	Cold semi-arid Mediterranean[a]	te	me	Central Chile, Argentina
7.1	Warm marine	MA Mm	HU Hu	Chile coast
7.2	Cool marine	Ma	HU	S Chile
7.3	Cold marine	ma	HU	S Chile
7.8	Humid Patagonian	pa	HU Hu	S Chile

[a] "Mediterranean" refers to Mediterranean Sea, not to parts of South America locally known by this term.

nized. The result is the differentiation of South America, on a map of Scale 1: approx. 35 million, into climatic regions, each of which subdivided into a number of climates. EIDT's system is reproduced in Fig.4.2 and in the accompanying Table 12.

The system used for the "Mediterranean Zone" of the world is based on a different approach, e.g. the "bioclimatic approach", which was described by EM-BERGER (1955). This approach is based largely on the construction of "ombroth-ermic diagrams" and on the use of a "xerothermic index". The former give a rather conventional, but in Mediterranean climates very useful, relation between monthly precipitations and temperatures; the latter gives an indication of "hot drought" and is based on the number of days in a month "which can be deemed

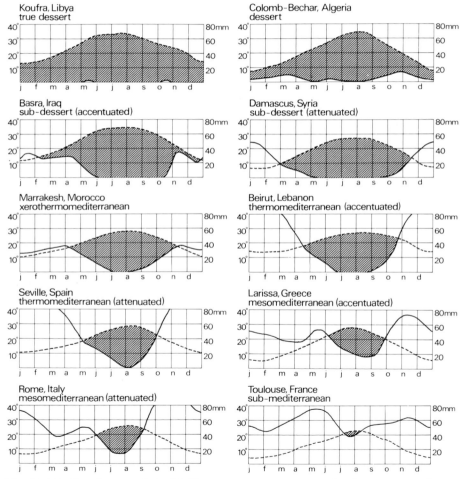

Fig. 4.3. Bioclimatic map of the Mediterranean zone – some ombrothermograms of warm and warm-temperate climates (reprinted from Bioclimatic Map of the Mediterranean Zone, Explanatory Notes, Arid Zone Research-XXI, by permission of UNESCO (© UNESCO, 1963)

dry from the biological point of view" (UNESCO-FAO, 1963). As a result, in the warm zone of the world, two desert climates, two subdesert climates, six mediterranean climates, three axeric ("near mediterranean") climates, four warm tropical climates, four "temperate" tropical climates, two "bixeric" climates (with two dry periods) and two tropical axeric climates are recognized. The system is interesting for those areas of the world which are more or less mediterranean in character, since it uses variables which bring out with great clearness important ecological differences within this climatic zone. Several diagrams from the Mediterranean area are reproduced in Fig.4.3 (see also DI CASTRI, MOONEY et al., 1973).

The world systems and the large regional systems for the characterization of climates are extremely important for facilitating, by systematic comparisons, the transfer of knowledge and experience on the present and potential uses of the agricultural lands in various regions of the world. As such, they can be used together with other world-wide systems, e.g. soil resources, which will be dealt with in a following paragraph. For more detailed regional use, minor differences of climate may be of extreme importance in agricultural land use. This is particularly so if a crop is grown near the limits of its true ecological range, either because of the general characteristics of the climate or of the nature of the soils or both.

Detailed Studies of Climate

One of the problems inherent in a more detailed study of climatic differences is the difficulty in obtaining sufficient quantitative data. As a result, these differences must usually be delineated using relatively indirect methods. The most accurate measurements and calculations can perhaps be made to determine insolation, because the maximum insolation at various degrees of slope can be derived from the latitude by calculations based on the various directions of exposition. The actual insolation can then be derived by measurements or estimates of cloudiness and of shadow-effects.

The characterization of local differences in climate, of which insolation often has particular importance, must be supported by investigations on the relief. The relation between relief and climate has been extensively discussed by RUBEN-STEIN et al. (1956). They state that the influence of relief on climate is great and takes many forms; in particular, the climate in mountainous areas is strongly influenced by the development of particular circulation systems in the valleys. Mountainous areas also have a considerable influence on the circulation systems in the neighboring plains. The radiation balance changes with altitude, and the difference between air temperature and soil temperature differs sharply when various parts of the relief are compared. Many observations from various parts of the Soviet Union point to interesting differences in relative air humidity at different altitudes and on different parts of the relief. The same is shown for the influence of relief on cloudiness, precipitation and snow-covers. Climatological differentiations related to relief differences are therefore an important aspect of the ecological mapping of landscapes.

For regional use, several interesting solutions have been found for the representation on maps of regional climatological variables, which are of importance for agricultural land use. BIRSE and his colleagues (BIRSE and DRY, 1970; BIRSE and ROBERTSON, 1970) using all available data from meteorological stations, assessed the climatic conditions of Scotland by computing the following variables:

— accumulated temperature,
— potential water deficit,
— exposure,
— accumulated frost.

Accumulated temperature was defined as "the integrated excess or deficiency of temperature with reference to a fixed datum, usually called the base temperature, over an extended period of time". For their purpose the base temperature was taken at 5.6° C, "approximately the level at which plant growth commences". Potential water deficit was used to indicate the effective wetness of the climate by using existing tables based on the methods of PENMAN. Exposure was defined as "the influence of air movement over an extended period of time on the development and survival of living organisms" and was applied by the measurement of the average wind speed in meters per second over a period of one year, based on the monthly weather reports over the period 1956—1968 for 34 stations in Scotland. Accumulated frost is "the integrated deficiency of temperature with reference to a fixed datum, usually called the base temperature, over an extended period of time"; the base temperature used was 0° C. Finally, these four variables were classified in separate classes for each and reproduced on two maps, one for the former two, and one for the latter two variables, respectively. The map legends indicate the combinations of variables, two for each map, as well as the kinds of relief in which they occur. These classifications are represented in Table 13. The maps are at scale 1:625000.

For a much smaller area in Switzerland, MARR (1970) produced a *Geländeklimatische Karte* ("terrain-climatic map") on scale 1:25000, which shows similar interesting features. His main variables are:

— insolation,
— temperature,
— annual precipitation,
— fog,
— wind direction.

Some of these variables were calculated (radiation intensity), some were obtained from existing stations (precipitation) and the remaining were measured in the field (horizon observations for the correction of sunshine duration, temperatures, some rain gauges). The data obtained and the resulting map contain many promising features for application to agricultural and other land uses.

Phenological studies are still another approach to more detailed investigations of local climates. Some interesting results have been published by several authors (WEISCHET, 1955; WEISCHET and BARSCH, 1963; SCHREIBER et al., 1959, 1967; SCHREIBER, 1968; HAEBERLI, 1968, 1971a,b,c). All these investigations have provided links between variations of the topoclimate, or mesoclimate, i.e. the climate as it is influenced by the different aspects of the landscape, e.g. relief and altitude, on the one hand and specific requirements or sensitivities of crops on the other hand. With this approach, one looks at the climatic variables which have

Table 13. Climatic Types of Scotland (after BIRSE et al., 1970)

1. Accumulated Temperature above 5.6° C and Potential Water Deficit

a) Classes of Variables

Accumulated temperature divisions (daydegrees C)
more than 1375:   warm, symbol E
1100–1375:   fairly warm, symbol L
825–1100:   cool, symbol M
550– 825:   cold, symbol S
275– 550:   very cold, symbol V
0– 275:   extremely cold, symbol Z

Potential water deficit divisions
more than 75 mm: dry, symbol E
50–75 mm: rather dry, symbol H
25–50 mm: moist, symbol M
0–25 mm: rather wet, symbol R
0 mm: wet, symbol V

The wet category is subdivided to show the area where the summer rainfall (April to September) exceeds summer evapotranspiration by at least 500 mm of water (indicated by V+).

Physiographic divisions (altitudes)
0–200 mm: Lowland
200–400 mm: Foothill
400–800 m: Upland
more than 800 m: Mountain

These divisions are used in description of climatic regions.

b) Legend of the Map

Lowland, warm dry . . . . EE
Lowland, warm rather dry . . . . EH
Lowland, warm moist . . . . EM
Lowland, warm rather wet . . . . ER
Lowland, warm wet . . . . EV and EV+
Lowland, fairly warm and dry . . . . LE
Lowland, fairly warm rather dry . . . . LH
Lowland, and foothill, fairly warm moist . . . . LM
Lowland and foothill, fairly warm rather wet . . . . LR
Lowland and foothill, fairly warm wet . . . . LV and LV+

Lowland, cool rather dry . . . . MH
Lowland and foothill, cool moist . . . . MM
Lowland, foothill and upland, cool rather wet . . . . MR
Foothill and upland, cool wet . . . . MV and MV+

Foothill and upland, cold rather wet . . . . SR
Upland, cold wet . . . . SV and SV+
Upland and mountain, very cold wet . . . . VV and VV+
Mountain, extremely cold wet . . . . ZV+

2. Exposure and Accumulated Frost

a) Classes of Variables

Exposure divisions (wind speed in meters per second)
less than 2.6 m/s: sheltered, symbol e
2.6–4.4 m/s: moderately exposed, symbol m
4.4–6.2 m/s: exposed, symbol p

Table 13. Climatic Types of Scotland (continued)

6.2–8.0 m/s:	very exposed, symbol v
more than 8.0 m/s:	extremely exposed, symbol z

Accumulated frost divisions (daydegrees C)

less than 20:	extremely mild winters, symbol e
20– 50:	fairly mild winters, symbol f
50–110:	moderate winters, symbol m
110–230:	rather severe winters, symbol r
230–470:	very severe winters, symbol v
more than 470:	extremely severe winters, symbol z

b) Legend of the Map

Sheltered with fairly mild winters	ef
Sheltered with moderate winters	em
Sheltered with rather severe winters	er
Moderately exposed with extremely mild winters	me
Moderately exposed with fairly mild winters	mf
Moderately exposed with moderate winters	mm
Moderately exposed with rather severe winters	mr
Exposed with extremely mild winters	pe
Exposed with fairly mild winters	pf
Exposed with moderate winters	pm
Exposed with rather severe winters	pr
Exposed with very severe winters	pv
Very exposed with extremely mild winters	ve
Very exposed with fairly mild winters	vf
Very exposed with moderate winters	vm
Very exposed with rather severe winters	vr
Very exposed with very severe winters	vv
Extremely exposed with extremely mild winters	ze
Extremely exposed with fairly mild winters	zf
Extremely exposed with moderate winters	zm
Extremely exposed with rather severe winters	zr
Extremely exposed with very severe winters	zv
Extremely exposed with extremely severe winters	zz

particular influences on specific crops, thus making it of more direct importance than is often the case with climatic data in general. At the same time, the phenological characteristics of various wild and cultivated plants are used as indicators of relative climatic differences within fairly short distances. These relative differences often are the result of variations of temperature and insolation; they can be consecutively checked and quantified by absolute measurements at well-selected locations, which could never be done with any efficiency without the use of the previously obtained information on plant phenology. The published maps are usually at scales of 1:50000 or 1:100000, but maps at smaller scales (1:300000 to 1:1 million) have also been published. The contents of the maps range from phenological data (time of flowering of tree crops or of small grains, wind deformation of tree crowns) to specific maps on climatic zones and on the incidence of night frosts or of warm winds. The maps provide important informa-

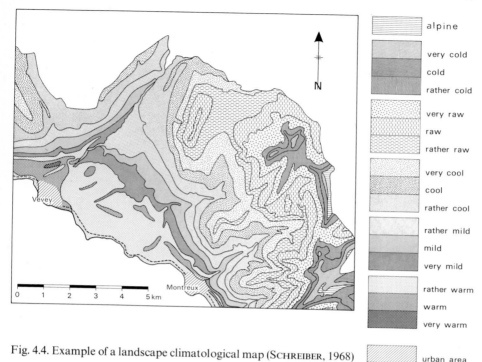

alpine

very cold

cold

rather cold

very raw

raw

rather raw

very cool

cool

rather cool

rather mild

mild

very mild

rather warm

warm

very warm

urban area

Fig. 4.4. Example of a landscape climatological map (SCHREIBER, 1968)

tion for agricultural land use, particularly for those crops which, in a certain area, are near the limit of their growth or have specific requirements as to quality, e.g. vineyards. This approach of "landscape climatology", together with other data on land resources, leads to a more comprehensive landscape ecology. (see Fig.4.4).

The importance of insolation measurements in some situations was made clear by observations on teagrowing and the incidence of blisterblight *(Exobasidium vexans)* in the mountains of Java (Indonesia). A good positive correlation was found between insolation and teaquality on the volcanic ash soils at altitudes greater than 1000 m; insolation figures showed a good negative correlation with the incidence of the fungus disease. General observations on the importance of insolation for the growth and quality of specific crops are known in various parts of the world; few of these observations have, however, been systematically published, and more quantitative investigations would no doubt be worthwhile in many cases where more careful agriculture land use is foreseen.

Data on the climatic variables of precipitation and evapotranspiration are of extreme importance for all areas where land use with irrigation is practiced or planned (ISRAELSEN and HANSEN, 1962), as well as for areas where drainage of excess water is an essential feature of land use (see e.g. KINORI, 1970). Such data are essential for determining the water balance of an area, from which can be determined the necessary specifications for the design of irrigation and drainage structures. In these calculations, data on water retention capacity of the soils are

Table 14. Leaching of soluble salts from drained plots in Turkey as affected by precipitation (BEYCE and CELENLIGIL. In: Salinity Seminar, 1971)

Location:	Tarsus-Alifaki		Izmir-Menemen		Central Anatolia	
Precipitation:	523 mm		453 mm		300 mm [a]	
Date:	8 11. 60	30. 5. 61	2. 12. 58	12. 4. 59	Autumn 1963	Spring 1969
Depth cm	$EC_e \times 10^3$		$EC_e \times 10^3$		$EC_e \times 10^3$	
0–30	16.9	6.4	4.8	2.1	10.0	3.2
30–60	20.3	19.1	23.3	13.0	13.0	8.0
60–90	23.4	24.3	59.3	37.9	13.7	9.0

[a] This refers to annual precipitation; the plots were drained at a spacing of 300 m. No corrections have been made for capillary resalinization, rewetting of soil, etc.

often used in a generalized manner (MOHRMANN and KESSLER, 1959), which is usually sufficient. In saline areas, precipitation may considerably improve the soils by leaching, once a proper drainage system has been installed (see Table 14). In areas where only slight water deficits are liable to occur, these climatic data, given in monthly figures over several years, have the additional advantage of providing the limits for judging the probability of water deficits occurring during the growing season.

SONNEVELD (1957) calculated the incidence of water deficits in various parts of the Netherlands. His figures clearly indicate that, in the southeastern part of the Netherlands, soils with the same water retention capacity as those in the remaining part of the country show water deficits sooner in normal years. One can also see from his data that, in the former area, soils with a water retention capacity of over 150 mm available water will only rarely show water deficits and that soils with a water retention capacity of over 200 mm have very little risk of water deficits occurring except in extremely dry years, which occur only about three to four times in a century. These observations are in perfect agreement with practical agricultural experience; the latter soils are loess soils, which are, with few exceptions, the best agricultural soils of Europe. Similar observations have also been published in "Climate and Man" (Yearbook, 1941).

4.2.2 Geology and Relief

The nature and structures of geological formations have many indirect influences on agricultural land use. Geology and relief are so closely tied that they will be treated together. Geological formations provide the basic materials and structures for the parent materials of the soils. Through the relief, furthermore, geological formations have a strong impact on climate and hydrology. Some aspects of geology have, however, an even more direct influence on land use, i.e.:

a) engineering geology,
b) hydrogeology,
c) environmental geology (FLAWN, 1970).

Geology

The science of geology consists of a number of specific subdisciplines: structural geology, historical geology and stratigraphy, paleontology, geophysics and petrology. Even a brief description of the contents and methods of these would exceed the limits of this book. The importance of geophysics for engineering geology has been described briefly by MEYER DE STADELHOFEN (1967). Information concerning its impact on environmental geology has been presented by FLAWN (1970). A thorough study by competent geologists is essential for investigating the problems of geology connected with land use, and is more often necessary than is sometimes understood by agronomists.

Engineering geology is concerned with the study of geological formations with respect to their suitability and requirements for the construction of man-made structures such as roads, bridges, dams and canals. It is also often essential when planning the construction of new urban sites. It may include engineering surveys, based on data collected by photogrammetric and other methods (Integrated Surveys, 1969), to determine the best sites. The type of information needed depends a great deal on the nature of the engineering works under consideration. The engineering geologist must provide sufficient detail to allow the engineer to make an engineering and economic appraisal of each alternative construction site. Often the assistance of a soil mechanical engineer or of a specialist in rock mechanics is required.

The types of investigations depend also on the nature of the area under consideration. In mountain regions, slope stability may be of major importance, cut and fill problems must be studied and tunnel alignments may have to be surveyed. In a desert environment, it may be vitally important to distinguish between areas of moving sand and zones in which sand dunes have become stabilized; the occurrence and effects of sheet flood and the zones of active erosion and sedimentation must be investigated. In tropical regions, the probable magnitude and frequency of floods and the occurrence of waterlogged zones or eroding zones are important features (VOÛTE in Integrated Surveys, 1968). Engineering geology has strong ties with engineering soil science or "soil mechanics". The former deals with the nature and structures of consolidated materials, "hard rock", whereas the latter is concerned with the engineering properties of unconsolidated materials.

Hydrogeology

Hydrogeology is the study of the availability and movement of water in the deeper subsoil. It is closely connected with geology because its observations have to be based on a sufficiently detailed knowledge of rocks and their structures. It is also closely connected with geochemistry, because water movement in the deeper subsoil often involves geochemical processes; these may, for example, cause the natural salinization of large areas (YAHIA, 1971). Geochemical methods are also helpful in prospecting geological formations for water movements. It is clear, finally, that hydrogeology is also a branch of hydrology and that it is interrelated with the other branches of hydrology such as geohydrology, the study of the water

Table 15. Volume of fresh water stored on the Earth (after R. Nace, cited by Ambroggi in Integrated Surveys, 1969)

Location	Volume (km^3)	% of total
Vapor in atmosphere	13000	0.17
Lakes	126000	1.47
Rivers and streams (average)	1300	0.02
Soil moisture and seepages in the unsaturated zone	67000	0.78
Ground water within a depth of half a mile	4200000	48.78
Groundwater, deep-lying	4200000	48.78
Total fresh water	8597300[a]	100.00

[a] 0.65% of the water on the earth

in the substrata directly below the agricultural land, soil hydrology and surface hydrology. Ambroggi (in Integrated Surveys, 1969) gives some data on the volume of fresh water stored on the earth (see Table 15).

Clearly, by far the largest amount of fresh water is found in the deeper formations which are studied by geological methods. For various reasons, relatively little of this water has thus far been used. The development of scientific knowledge and of pumping techniques has only during the last decades facilitated its utilization for agricultural land use. When used in conjunction with surface water, it may prove to have a great impact on land development in the near future.

Hydrogeology, therefore, may contribute to the mobilization of water from the deeper substrata for agricultural use. Such a project, however, necessitates a thorough study of the water balance of a region, because much of this water may have been collected during earlier geological periods. This water is called "fossil water", since it is not replenished after exhaustion. Its use depends on the amount of available water and on the intensity of its use. Fossil water is a mining resource similar to coal and oil; its use may be stimulating but there is a definite end to it. Side-effects similar to those occurring with other kinds of mining extraction, e.g. subsidence of soils in the area of exploitation, must be studied, and the influence of its extraction on a much larger area than the one for which its use is foreseen, must be determined.

Hydrogeology is also concerned with the movement of water through various kinds of rocks and unconsolidated materials in the deeper and shallower rock formations. Data on the permeability and on forms and directions of the geological structures are essential for obtaining a better understanding of the processes involved. Knowledge of the connections existing between underground aquifers is often essential for understanding the irrigation and drainage requirements in development areas, particularly in the arid zones of the world, as well as for determining whether a certain aquifer is recharged and what quantities are involved. This information is necessary in order to arrive at a reliable plan for adapting local water use on a long-term basis (Al-Jawad et al., 1970a,b). These and similar investigations (Haddad et al., 1970) may well be crucial in deciding on a project of limited supplementary irrigation.

The permeability of the subsoil of an area can have a considerable effect on drainage and desalinization projects. On too loose grounds, a particular area is assumed to have a very permeable substratum. Because water movement between ground surface and the surrounding area proceeds along curved lines which usually go at least 50 meters deep, the occurrence of less permeable layers in the deeper substrata may cause serious drainage problems. Over larger areas, even deeper aquifers must be carefully studied; if sufficiently capacious aquifers are found at a suitable depth, desalinization by pumping wells, such as have been used in projects in Pakistan, may well be practicable. In other, more complicated situations, only thorough investigations by bore holes and other geophysical methods can provide sufficient data for satisfactory water management. The neglect of these aspects may retard land-use planning because insufficient allowance is made for unsatisfactory drainage through the substrata.

Environmental Geology

Environmental geology to some extent comprises the aspects of engineering geology and hydrogeology described above. It is certainly closely tied to these. FLAWN (1970) described additional aspects of environmental geology:

a) earth processes, including earthquakes, results of volcanism, mass movements such as landslides, changes in sea levels and the processes of subsidence, erosion and sedimentation;

b) earth resources, including "high value resources" such as oil and iron ore, which are transported over long distance because of their value as a general commodity, as well as "low value resources" (sand, gravel etc.) which are only transported over short distance from the location of their mining; water is included among the latter, although recent developments include the planning of long distance pipelines for this essential commodity for agricultural and other land uses;

c) interactions between man and the geological elements in his environment, including the disposal of solid and liquid wastes, and the resulting environmental management activities.

The importance of these aspects in environmental management in the industrialized areas of the world is obvious. Waste disposal in the deeper substrata by chemical industries for example cannot be accepted unless detailed geological and hydrological studies show that no unacceptable effects need be feared within the entire drainage basin in which they are located; side-effects in adjoining areas must also be minimalized below an acceptable level. Land subsidence, which may cause serious deterioration of drainage in large agricultural areas, must be avoided or at least predicted in such a manner that appropriate corrective measures can be taken. Changes in river courses and in their flow characteristics have to be studied before serious damage is done and in such a manner that appropriate construction can be developed. Landslides and seepage, as well as deterioration of drainage, caused by engineering structures such as roads, dams and canals, have to be seen in a sufficiently detailed geological prospect and over a sufficiently large area (Photo 10). Environmental geology is rapidly developing into an essential tool for many aspects of land use.

Photo 10. Locality of subsequent landslides along a river course in Northern Italy

Relief

The influence of relief on agricultural land use is multifaceted. Relief is the expression of the interaction of several different phenomena and processes within the earth's crust and on its surface. Its forms and dimensions are primarily related to geological formations and to the climate, both past and present, which have either directly or indirectly acted upon these formations. The indirect action of climates and the effect produced by the natures of the geological formations on the relief occurs through the processes of weathering and soil formation and through the influence of living organisms, including plants, animals and man. Relief is therefore typically connected with many of the other land resources. For this reason also, it is extremely important in all methods of air-photo interpretation for the mapping of land resources (REY et al., 1968). Relief itself also has a strong influence on processes and phenomena connected with the land. Its influence on climate was mentioned previously. Its influence on hydrology derives directly from the fact that gravity is the dominating force in nearly all hydrological processes. Relief is also one of the most important factors in soil formation, including its negative aspect of soil degradation: both natural and accelerated processes of soil erosion are largely dependent upon the nature of the relief.

The phenomena and processes which underlie relief formation and differentiation are treated by the discipline of geomorphology. The latter is one of the subdisciplines of physical geography, although it is closely related to structural geology, particularly in regard to the major relief forms. For information on the development of relief forms and on their further evolution, reference is made to the literature on geomorphology (MABBUTT and STEWART, 1963; TRICART, 1965; CARSON and KIRKBY, 1972; CHORLEY and KENNEDY, 1971; SMALL, 1970).

Agricultural land use is strongly influenced by the size and shape of the relief forms. With regard to size, a division into three categories is often useful:

a) macrorelief, including all relief forms with height differences of more than 50 m;

b) mesorelief, including all relief forms with height differences of between approximately 10 and 50 m;

c) microrelief, including all relief forms with height differences of less than approx. 10 m.

The following categories are often superimposed on the previously indicated ones: macrorelief forms often carry on their surfaces forms of meso- and microrelief, mesorelief forms often carry microrelief forms on their surfaces. This fact is known to anyone who is acquainted with mountainous and hilly landscapes. Its direct and indirect influences on agricultural land use are, however, not always realized.

Relief shows many differences in shape, which in general has both a horizontal and a vertical component. Relief patterns include both hill patterns and drainage patterns, the dimensions of which may belong to any of the preceding size categories. Hill forms and slope forms may have many different shapes, all of which have a vertical and a horizontal component and include such generalized models as:

a) straight, flat, convex, concave;

b) long, short (slopes);

c) regular, irregular (slope forms, surfaces);

d) narrow, wide (depressions, valleys).

All of these factors have a direct impact on land management and may have a considerable significance for land improvement. They may to a great extent determine whether certain land utilization types are feasible in certain areas or not.

Relief may be divided into positive and negative forms, the former being elevations above a more or less arbitrarily chosen reference plane, whereas the latter are depressions below this plane: e.g., hills, hummocks etc., and valleys, watercourses etc., respectively. Cross sections of both positive and negative relief forms, either schematic or precisely quantitative, are very useful for many purposes (Fig. 4.5).

Relief, being three-dimensional, has a content which, in particular for microrelief forms of loose unconsolidated materials, is expressed in cubic meters (m^3). This notation is particularly useful for land improvement projects, such as levelling and/or the construction of terraces and embankments, and the construction of roads, canals and dams, where materials must be removed (cutting roads or canals through hills) or brought in (road fills, dam fills, road surfaces, canal linings, dike construction). Quantitative measurements of relief, as well as of other elements of topography, are performed by geodesy, with or without the use of photogrammetry. The use of photogrammetry is usually the cheaper and more efficient method, provided that good photogrammetric specialists are consulted (JERIE in Integrated Surveys, 1968 and 1969). The production of quantitative data on the relief in conjunction with photogrammetry is then accompanied by the production of topographic maps of excellent quality; at the same time, the aerial

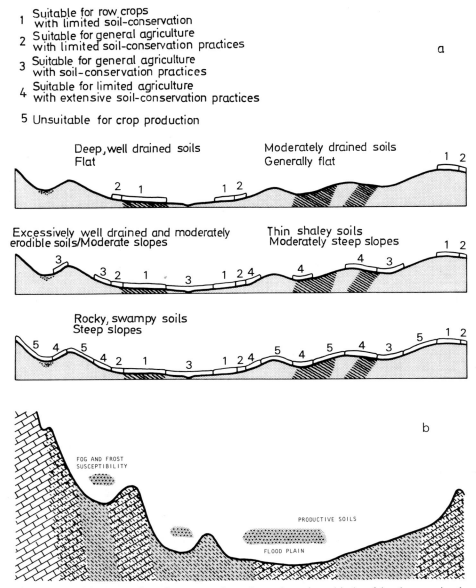

1 Suitable for row crops
   with limited soil-conservation
2 Suitable for general agriculture
   with limited soil-conservation practices
3 Suitable for general agriculture
   with soil-conservation practices
4 Suitable for limited agriculture
   with extensive soil-conservation practices

5 Unsuitable for crop production

a

Deep, well drained soils   Moderately drained soils
Flat   Generally flat

Excessively well drained and moderately   Thin shaley soils
erodible soils/Moderate slopes   Moderately steep slopes

Rocky, swampy soils
Steep slopes

b

FOG AND FROST
SUSCEPTIBILITY

PRODUCTIVE SOILS

FLOOD PLAIN

Fig. 4.5.a and b. Examples of cross sections through various kinds of landscapes in the
Potomac River Basin (McHARG, 1969)

photographs taken can often be used for airphoto interpretation, which is an
essential tool for land resources surveys. In some cases sufficiently accurate measurements of relief may be made from existing topographic maps with appropriate contour lines (CLARKE in DURY et al., 1966). Quantitative measurements of
relief are of particular importance for calculating the balance of materials in

projects in which the movement of earth (levelling, filling of gullies, digging of canals) is considered. The trend of trying to reduce both the quantity and distance of earth movement, because of extremely high costs, should be based on accurate calculations as to the nature and quantity of the material to be moved.

4.3 Soil and Water Resources

4.3.1 Soils

The term "soil" is handled differently in two different disciplines: (1) "soil mechanics" or "engineering soil science", and (2) "agricultural soil science", which in general is considered to include the more genetical aspects; the latter are also separately indicated as "pedology" (VINK in REY et al., 1968). Engineering soil science treats as soils all unconsolidated materials which in some manner are related to engineering structures (roads, canals, bridges, dams, air fields) either for foundations or as construction materials. This aspect has been briefly discussed in a previous paragraph. This approach is very useful in some land development projects, but its relation to agricultural land use is either very localized or relatively indirect.

Agricultural soil science is the soil science which is treated in the International Soil Science Society as well as in various national soil science societies. This discipline views soil as one of the land resources which has the most direct and continuous impact on agricultural land use. In this context, soil is defined as follows (BRINKMAN and SMYTH, 1973): "A soil is a three-dimensional body occupying the uppermost part of the earth's crust and having properties differing from the underlying rock material as a result of interactions between climate, living organisms (including human activity), parent material and relief over periods of time and which is distinguished from other 'soils' in terms of differences in internal characteristics and/or in terms of gradient, slope-complexity, microtopography, stoniness and rockiness of its surface."

Soil as a three-dimensional body of the earth's surface is "a piece of landscape" with its own surface and land form as well as soil profile and internal characteristics such as: phase distribution (solid, liquid, gaseous), chemical and mineralogical composition and physical properties. In this sense, soil is a central, dominant part of the wider concept of "land" (see Chapter 1). Soil is a narrower concept because it does not embrace the climate above the ground and the regolith below the solum. The concept of "soil" also differs from that of "land" in that soils are natural bodies and as such belong to the natural sciences. The natural science, "pedology" is the study of soils as natural phenomena, in particular of their genesis and classification and their relationships with other natural science concepts such as climate, relief, parent materials and living organisms. Soils are studied as objects of natural science also in soil physics and soil chemistry.

Table 16. Chart showing the more important groups of organisms that commonly are present in soils. The grouping is very broad and general as the emphasis is to be placed, not on classification, but upon biochemical activity (BUCKMAN and BRADY, 1969)

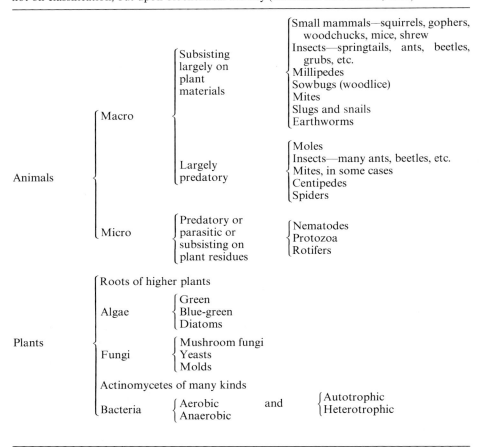

Soils are also natural bodies in the sense that they are the ecotopes of complex ecosystems. Soils, although often incorrectly indicated as "abiotic" factors of the environment, contain in fact complex systems of living organisms, from simple bacteria to vertebrates (moles, mice, etc.). BUCKMAN and BRADY (1969) included a chart showing the more important groups or organisms that commonly are present in soils. This chart is reproduced in Table 16. See also DUCHAUFOUR (1970), RODE (1962) and SCHEFFER and SCHACHTSCHABEL (1970).

Soils may be mapped as natural bodies for the sole purpose of studying regularities in their distribution. These investigations in general lead either to very small-scale maps (1:500000 to 1:20 million), or to maps on very large scales (1:1000 to 1:10000). In the former case, particular attention is paid to the correlations between soils and climates and related main types of vegetation. Often, too, correlations between these factors and the dominating geological formations and

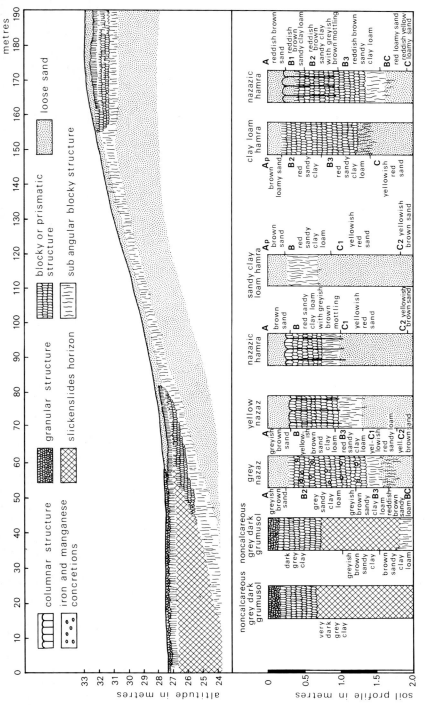

Fig. 4.6. Section through the Netanya Catena, Israel (DAN et al., 1968)

relief features are indicated; broad indications of agricultural land use are often included as well (Dokuchaev Soil Institute, 1963; TAVERNIER et al., 1966; FAO-UNESCO, 1971; DAN et al., 1972). In the latter case, very large-scale soil maps are made for studying in detail the relationships between soils and landscapes; the latter often also lead to the detailed study of soil catenas. The result is better insight into the natural phenomena and processes of soil formation, and often also into those of landscape formation. Large-scale maps of relatively small surface areas are often relevant to agricultural land use, but their use for this purpose is considered a by-product by most authors, which is reflected in the legends of the maps. An example of a soil catena is given in Fig. 4.6 (DAN et al., 1972).

These fundamental studies on the formation of landscapes are essential for all other soil surveys. Soil survey efficiency depends largely on a good understanding of the relationships between landscapes and soils. Only in this manner can efficient soil survey methods, including the systematic interpretation of aerial photographs, be used (VINK, 1963; VINK In: REY et al., 1968). The relationship between soil and land is a very fundamental one: Neither one can be sufficiently understood without a knowledge of both.

Soil Resources

Soil resources as an essential part of land resources are the main object of soil surveys. In many cases, the results of a soil survey are taken as the most essential part representing all other land resources. This viewpoint is occasionally acceptable as a pragmatic approach since all good soil surveys comprise the most essential data on those land resources which have a direct bearing on agricultural land use. Still, in principle, this approach is one-sided, and in several instances soil surveys have proved disappointing, not because of any lack of quality in the surveys themselves, but because other data on land resources and often also on human resources, were lacking. Much depends on whether the advancement of agriculture is determined largely by those variables which are normally mapped in a good soil survey and on how far a specific soil surveyor is prepared to adapt his survey legend. This legend may have to include land characteristics which are less interesting from a pedological viewpoint but which are essential, key variables, for land-use planning. For the latter purpose, land resources may be indicated by using a physiographic soil map legend and, additionally, by use of appropriate soil phases indicating land characteristics such as relief, erosion and soil hydrology. Often, particularly in irrigation projects, several other land characteristics have to be investigated and mapped in a more quantitative manner than can normally be done by a soil surveyor (see e.g. MALETIC and HUTCHINGS, 1967).

Soil maps for land-use planning are made on many different scales, varying from very small (1:5 million), to very large (1:5000). The scale of a soil map is of essential importance as it has a direct correlation with the detail with which the field investigations are carried out. The maps on different scales are thus applicable to different kinds of land use planning. Very small-scale maps can only be used for the general planning of large areas. The World Soil Map, on scale 1:5 million can e.g. only be used for very general projects such as the Indicative World Plan (FAO, 1969) and for similar planning of continents and large regions. For the execution of intensive projects such as irrigation schemes or horticultural development projects, maps on large scales e.g. 1:25000 or larger, are often needed. The detail and usefulness for planning are most properly expressed by the use of the "basic mapping unit" and of the "basic planning unit" (VINK, 1963). These terms indicate, respectively, the smallest area which can still be indicated on a map and the smallest area on this map which is sufficiently reliable to be used as a planning unity. Information concerning the essential characteristics and applications of different soil map scales which have been found to be useful in many cases are given in Table 17. Also included is information about the kinds of soil map units which can be expected to be represented in the legend of the various maps. It should be stressed that in all of these maps, with the detail depending on the scale, the different phases (relief, drainage, salinity, stoniness) may be indicated to represent some essential variables for land-use planning. In Fig. 4.7 a reconnaissance soil map at scale 1:250000 from Iraq is shown. Other soil maps are reproduced in Figs. 5.2, 5.13, 5.17 and 6.5.

The contents of the legend of any soil map for land-use planning should always embrace aspects of the following:

a) Soil taxonomy preferably in a internationally recognized system;

b) Soil materials, including not only their texture but also their chemistry and mineralogy;

c) Soil depth (either to the bottom of the pedological solum or of rooting depth, whichever is deepest) and soil hydrology;

d) Soil topography (slopes, complex relief forms, microrelief) and surface characteristics [gilgai, erosion features, indications of mass movements: e.g. escarceos (GOOSEN, 1971)].

The manner and detail in which these characteristics are indicated at different scales and for different areas depend on the nature of the area and, to some extent,

Table 17. Soil surveys at various scales

Scale	Units	Basic mapping unit (ha)	Basic planning unit (ha)	Phase of planning to be used in
1:5 million	association	64000	800000	international
1:1 million	association	2500	20000	international and large national
1:250000	association	160	960	small national and large national
1:100000	association	24	96	pre-investment and project planning
1:50000	association + family	6	24	project planning and execution
1:25000	series + family + association	1.50	3	project execution
1:10000 and smaller	series + type	0.25	0.50	project execution

NB. In all scales "soil complexes" may also have to be mapped, i.e. associations, the components of which cannot be separated at detailed survey scales.

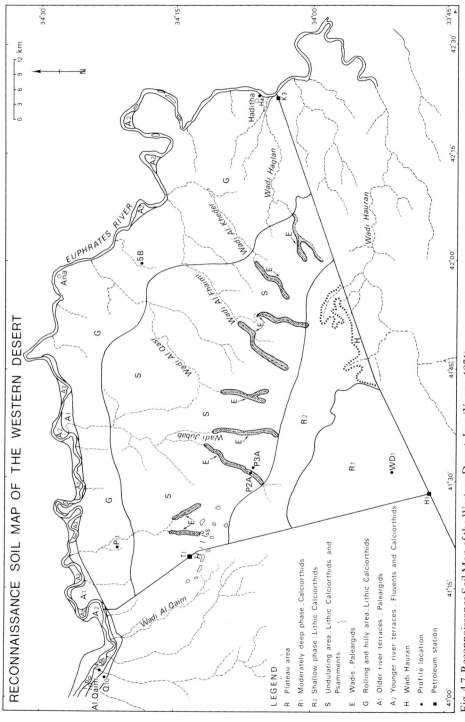

RECONNAISSANCE SOIL MAP OF THE WESTERN DESERT

LEGEND

R   Plateau area
R₁ Moderately deep phase - Calciorthids
R₂ Shallow phase - Lithic Calciorthids
S   Undulating area - Lithic Calciorthids and
    Psamments
E   Wadis - Paleargids
G   Rolling and hilly area - Lithic Calciorthids
A₁ Older river terraces - Paleargids
A₂ Younger river terraces - Fluvents and Calciorthids
H   Wadi Hauran
●   Profile location
■   Petroleum station

Fig. 4.7. Reconnaissance Soil Map of the Western Desert, Iraq (YAHIA, 1971)

on the purpose of the survey. It is the responsibility of the soil surveyor to see that all essential key variables for land use planning which are related to the soils are mapped in as much detail as is compatible with the scale of the map.

Soil Taxonomy

Within the context of land use planning, the importance of soil taxonomy for soil surveys is sometimes underrated. Soil taxonomy as a general outline of soil conditions is, however, at least as important as the ever necessary data on climate. Most planning for land development in advancing agriculture occurs by transfer of knowledge and experience from one region to another. In most cases quantitative data, at least at the essential early stages of planning, are lacking, and the time required for a comprehensive investigation of all possibilities never exists. Careful and systematic comparison with other regions is therefore always practiced often, however, without sufficient attention to the essential similarities or dissimilarities of conditions. Only the combination of climatology and soil taxonomy can provide a satisfactory basis, often together with similar information on other land resources, for reliable comparisons.

The use of classification systems which cover sufficiently large regions is essential for making reliable comparisons. National soil classification systems are often satisfactory for soil studies within a certain country, but, unless they can be easily translated into more internationally recognized systems, a large part of their usefulness for land use planning is lost. The only system for classifying soils which is now universally recognized in the world is the Legend of the Soil Map of the World (DUDAL, 1970, 1974). It is not a complete taxonomy, but it is very useful for classifying soils for practical purposes, both in the construction of soil map legends on larger scales and for the transfer of practical knowledge and experience from different parts of the world.

The American Soil Taxonomy (Soil Survey, 1970), better known today as "Seventh Approximation", because of the preliminary forms in which it has thus far been published (BUCKMAN and BRADY, 1969; BRADY, 1974), is a more precise tool for describing, classifying and comparing soils from around the world. It is essential for the careful description and classification of representative profiles in any region of the world. It requires, however, a specialized knowledge and experience for handling; in some cases data are required which cannot be obtained within reasonable time limits. Its scope, although based on numerous contributions from experts in many countries, is less satisfactory than is the scope of the World Soil Map Legend. Other systems of soil classification which are widely recognized and used in large regions are the French soil classification (DUCHAUFOUR, 1970) and the soil classification of the U.S.S.R. (RODE, 1962); elements from both have, together with data from the U.S. Soil Taxonomy, largely contributed to the comprehensiveness of the Legend of the Soil Map of the World (Table 18).

The use of soil taxonomy in soil surveys for land use planning is also a means of stimulating careful research on the internal characteristics of the soils. The need for critical description of many features in a systematic sequence contributes to research as such and thus provides a means of recognizing characteristics of the

Table 18. General review of the orders of the U.S. Soil Taxonomy and of the Soil Groups of the Legend of the Soil Map of the World, with their main diagnostic characteristics

Main diagnostic horizon and/or characteristics		Soil Orders U.S. Taxonomy	Some other diagnostic horizons or characteristics, important for subdivisions (suborders, soil groups)	Comparable soil groups of the soil map of the world
Terminology	simplified explanation			
none	none	Entisols	characteristics associated with wetness, soil climate, texture	Fluvisols, Regosols, Lithosols, Arenosols, Rankers
Vertic characteristics	indications of repeated swelling and shrinkage e.g. slickensides, cracks, gilgai	Vertisols	char. assoc. w. wetness, soil climate	Vertisols
Umbric epipedon or Cambic horizon	dark humose A-horizon with "acid" humus or structural B-horizon	Inceptisols	char. assoc. w. wetness, soil climate, mineralogy, alkalinity, fragipan	Gleysols, Andosols, Cambisols
Desert climate, Calcic, Gypsic, Salic horizons	Characteristics indicative of desert soils	Aridisols	Cambic horizon, natric horizon, argillic horizon	Solonchaks, Solonetz, Yermosols, Xerosols
Mollic epipedon	Dark, humose A-horizon with mild humus	Mollisols	Char. assoc. w. wetness, argillic horizon, natric horizon, soil climate, calcic horizon	Rendzinas, Kastanozems, Chernozems, Phaeozems, Greyzems
Spodic horizon	"podzol"-B-horizon	Spodosols	Char. assoc. w. wetness, histic epipedon, soil climate, fragipan, non-accumulation	Podsols
Argillic horizon with high to medium base saturation	Clay illuviation B-horizon with high to medium base saturation	Alfisols	Char. assoc. w. wetness, natric horizon, soil climate plinthite, duripan, fragipan, agric horizon	Solonetz, Luvisols, Podzoluvisols, Planosols, Acrisols, Nitosols
Argillic horizon with low base saturation	Clay-illuviation B-horizon with low base saturation	Ultisols	Char. assoc. w. wetness, color, soil climate fragipan, plinthite	Acrisols with low base saturation
Oxic horizon	"Kaolinitic" horizon	Oxisols	Char. assoc. w. wetness, plinthite, gibbsite, organic matter	Ferralsols
Histic epipedon	Peat-horizon	Histosols	Parent material, soil climate, water saturation decomposition, sulfuric horizon	Histosols

soils which otherwise might have been neglected and which later are found to be of essential importance for land use. In particular in soils which are considered for irrigation projects, information about processes existing in the soils often can only be found by careful study of soil genesis and classification, thus separating the results of fossil processes from those which are presently active. These data facilitate, particularly through comparison with similar soils which already have been under irrigation for different periods of time, the ability to predict changes in the soil processes and phenomena under irrigation. These changes may include the formation of secondary precipitates of calcium carbonate under arid conditions, the formation of vertisols under semi-arid conditions and the precipitation of oxides of iron and manganese under equatorial circumstances as well as several other processes which can only be detected after careful studies of soil formation. A soil survey, together with all investigations of land resources, is a research system; this system may yield data which indicate constraints as well as the existence of beneficial effects. Unsatisfactory research, always viewed within the planning phase for which it is carried out, contributes unsatisfactory results and may lead to unsatisfactory uses of the land.

The relations between the many aspects of a soil survey and their applications in land use are manifold. Soil characteristics, other soil survey data and examples of land use planning are given in Tables 19 and 20. The actual evaluation of such

Table 19. List of determinations generally carried out in a soil survey (Soil Survey Staff, 1961; 1970)

1. *Diagnostic Horizons:*	*Epipedon:* Mollic, Anthropic, Umbric, Histic, Ochric, Plaggen. *Subsurface horizons:* Argillic, Agric, Natric, Spodic, Cambic, Oxic. *Pans:* Duripans, Fragipans.
2. *Other horizons:*	Calcic, Gypsic, Salic, Albic.
3. *Other Soil Characteristics:*	Abrupt textural change, Crusty, Dry, Gilgai, Moist, Mineral soils, Organic soils, Mottles, N-value, Permafrost, Plinthite, Self-mulching, Slickensides, Soil temperature, Tongues of albic horizons.
4. *Criteria for Families:*	Texture, Mineralogy, Reaction classes according to pH in water, Bulk density, Permeability, Characteristics associated with wetness, Moisture equivalent, Consistency both moist and dry.
5. *Criteria for Soil Series:*	All differentiae used in the above plus any other properties as long as they have relevance to soil genesis, to plant growth, or to engineering uses or if they are very obvious.
6. *Description of Soils:*	Soil color, Soil texture, Coarse fragments, Stoniness, Rockiness, Soil structure, Soil consistency.
7. *Routine Laboratory Analyses in Soil Surveys:*	pH (in water, KCl and/or $CaCl_2$), texture, organic matter, organic C-content, N-content, Cation-exchange capacity, $CaCO_3$-content, Exchangeable Ca, Mg, K, Na, NH_4, H-ions.
8. *Other Analyses often Carried Out in Soil Surveys:*	Organic P, Inorganic P, K (25% HCl), Moisture at different pH, salinity and/or alkalinity, structure, mineralogy.
9. *Soil Phases:*	Slope, erosion (wind, water), stoniness and rockiness, depth, thickness, drainage, physiographic, buried, silted.

Table 20. Some examples of special aspects of soil surveys in the determination of soil qualities and/or limitations (see also Chapter 5)

Special aspects	Use purpose
homogeneous soil profile	— special horticultural crops
homogeneous soil pattern	— reallocation
flat surface	— mechanized land use
depth below surface of highest ground water level in winter	— drainage projects, town planning, sport fields
depth below surface of loam	— ditto
thickness of the surface humus layer	— crops, sport fields
depth below surface of peat	— drainage, road construction, town planning
depth below surface and lime-content of subsoil	— soil improvement
special requirements of texture	— growth of special crops and/or application of mechanized treatment, soil conservation
special requirements of summer ground water level	— growth of special crops, use for pastures, use of mechanized equipment
water retention capacity	— growth of crops in relation to climate and/or irrigation
permeability	— soil conservation, irrigation, drainage
occurrence of hardpans	— crops, drainage, irrigation, road construction
occurrence of fragipans	— ditto
acidity of topsoil and/or subsoil	— crops, soil improvement
availability of plant nutrients	— crops, fertilizer requirement
mineral reserve	— future development
clay minerals	— crops, chemical and mechanical soil management
plasticity	— mechanical management
salinity, alkalinity	— crops, soil improvement, irrigation

data in a given case has to be done by soil survey interpretation, which is a part of land evaluation and will be discussed in the following chapters (see also SCHEL-LING et al., 1970).

Laboratory Investigations

Micropedological investigations for determining important soil characteristics for land use are partially carried out within a good soil survey. Special micropedological investigations are, however, often called for in particular circumstances (see e.g. JONGERIUS et al., 1967). Micropedological investigations together with studies of the larger soil pores and with measurements of physical characteristics of soils have proved to be particularly useful for land use.

Physical measurements of soils comprise many different investigations both in the field and in the laboratory on undisturbed and disturbed soils. In the field, measurements of drainage- and infiltration rates, although always approximate in nature, are often essential for characterizing soil as a land resource. They are particularly useful in areas where erosion could become or already is a dangerous process and in all projects where artificial drainage, with or without irrigation, is considered. In certain conditions, e.g. in peaty areas, conus measurements of the carrying capacity of the soil surface, for human and animal use, are of increasing importance. Conus resistance measurements in soil profiles have also proved to be of considerable interest in some horticultural investigations (VAN DAM, 1973). Determinations of soil porosity and soil structure belong to the essential observations used in characterizing all soil profiles.

In the laboratory, determinations of soil moisture characteristics (pF, available water, permeability) are essential for most land use projects. Other values, such as Atterberg limits, cohesion, angle of internal friction, compressibility, bulk density, are important in land use planning where different kinds of structures have to be designed. More theoretical considerations are used, with or without sophisticated measurements, in studying the basic phenomena, processes and principles of soil physics. Some of these, such as electrical and numerical models for the moisture regime of soils, have found their way into studies which are directly connected with land use. Many other soil-hydrological aspects, particularly those related to the overly important unsaturated upper part of the soil profile, have not yet become operational for practical purposes. Soil technology will benefit from these at a later stage.

Since the discovery by JUSTUS VON LIEBIG in the 1840's of the basic principles of plant nutrition, soil chemistry has played an important role in determining the properties of soils as land resources for plant growth and agricultural production. The application of chemical methods to the study of the processes of soil formation has also led to a chemical branch of pedology, the science which is concerned with the theoretical study of soil formation and soil taxonomy. The mainstream of soil chemistry has, however, always maintained its interest in the fundamental and applied aspects of plant nutrition, leading to the study of soil fertility. In this sense, soil chemistry is an investigation of soil characteristics which are relatively stable or cyclic in nature, such as soil reaction (pH) and soil salinity as well as the basic characteristics of ion-adsorption, -transport and -fixation, which together are essential factors determining nutrient availability. The determination of "total available nutrients", including both macro-, meso- and micronutrients, data which are closely related to soil mineralogy, also indicates essentially stable characteristics of the soil as a land resource. Determinations of humus and of the nitrogen cycles, together with microbiological determinations, which have very strong ties with soil fertility, also are "reasonably stable or predictably cyclic attributes of the biosphere". The determinations of "available nutrients", although essential for land use, are more ephemeral and therefore are often more closely related to the land utilization type and to the human resources, in terms of inputs, than to the land itself. There is, however, no doubt that no clear boundary can be drawn, since the available nutrients, certainly in less intensive land utilization types, are often closely connected to the basic land resources.

The approach of soil chemistry and sometimes also of soil physics to the soil as a land resource occasionally differs from that described for soil survey. Land is geographically defined, and soil and land are natural bodies with regional and local differences. Many predictions from soil chemistry are of a more general nature, and soil chemical investigations tend towards the establishment of broad general laws rather than to a determination of regional situations, which is a typical aspect of the "land". The generalizations are perfectly valid in some major instances, e.g. with respect to the general processes of availability, transport and ion-exchange mechanisms, provided that for each individual tract of land the correct parameters are determined and used. However, many papers on soil chemistry are published without sufficient reference to the parameters of the particular tracts of land on which the investigations were carried out; the inclusion with each investigation of information concerning the soil series, although a regular procedure in some countries, is as regularly lacking in many others. If these parameters are omitted, two essential aspects are neglected: (1) the contribution to a better knowledge of a particular tract of land, as well as of other similar tracts on the basis of a justified transfer of knowledge and experience, has a low validity; (2) the generalizations made, although perhaps justified in some cases, cannot be properly checked and compared with results obtained on other tracts of land with other parameters.

Investigations of available nutrients are usually executed for individual farms and on specific tracts of land in the sense of land use parcels or fields. In such cases, there is, without doubt, a well-defined geographical delineation. Within a certain field, however, essential differences of land characteristics may occur in such a manner that different soils exist within the same field. The field is then influenced by two different systems which interact upon each other and upon the availability of nutrients: (1) the natural characteristics of the different land resources as represented by the different soils and (2) the influence on the land of previous land uses, which may have been homogeneous over the field for a long time. In this case, the proper geographical definition and delineation of what consists a true "tract of land" has to be carefully studied befor any predictions on behavior of the land with regard to future land use are made. For a proper definition of soils as land resources, therefore, soil chemistry and soil survey must work together to obtain the desired results.

Soil Salinity

Soil salinity is a particularly important aspect of soil as a land resource in many parts of the world, including all arid and semi-arid regions as well as areas which contain salts accumulated from other causes. As was pointed out by KOVDA (1964) and by KOVDA and EGOROV (1964), there are laws for the migration of salts on continents and also in more detail, salt accumulations are related to aspects of the landscape (see also YAHIA, 1971; KOVDA et al., 1973).

In the broadest sense, the movement of different kinds of salts is largely determined by their solubility. A second influence, which determines the context within which this solubility is acting, is the climate, in particular precipitation and temperature and the resulting processes of evapotranspiration. Of the salts which are produced by weathering, sesquioxides (mainly iron and aluminum oxides) and silicates (including secondary clay minerals) are found over the largest surface areas and in all climates. Next comes the accumulation of carbonates (particularly calcium and magnesium carbonates but also sodium carbonate) and of gypsum ($CaSO_4 \cdot 2H_2O$), which is found extensively in semi-arid climates (savannahs, monsoon tropics, forest steppes and steppes) as well as in particular circumstances (lakes, bogs, some alluvial areas) in other climates. The accumulation of

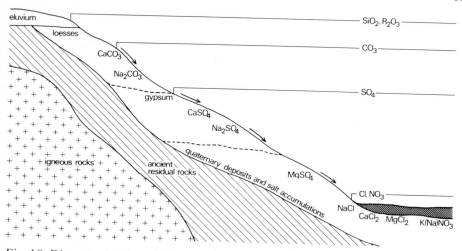

Fig. 4.8. Diagram of differentiation of compounds during salt accumulation on continents (after KOVDA, 1964)

Table 21. The main types of landscapes in irrigated territories (mainly after KOVDA and EGOROV, 1964)

Zone	Territory	Effects of irrigation	Need for drainage
A. Dry steppe, savannah, pampas	1. with natural drainage	— local waterlogging and salinization	— local
	2. with inadequate natural drainage	— rising ground water in lower parts, with salinization, increased by seepage	— deep, particularly in lower parts
	3. without natural drainage	— depressions with natural salinity, often to be left without irrigation	— extensive
B. Semi-desert and desert	1. with natural drainage		
	a. well-drained high loess plains	— no risk of salinity but risk of erosion	—
	b. ancient piedmont plains and upper river terraces	— slight	— local
	c. lower terraces	— local influence of seepage	— local
	2. with inadequate natural drainage	— strong salinization	— deep and extensive
	3. virtually without natural drainage	— strong salinization and waterlogging	— deep, narrow spaced and extensive, not advisable in lower parts

Table 22. Limits of salinity classes according to the American system (Soil Survey Staff, 1951, cited by YAHIA, 1971)

Class	Percent of salt	Conductivity of extract mmhos/cm at 25° C
Class 0: Free	0—0.15	0—4
Class 1: Slightly affected	0.15—0.35	4—8
Class 2: Moderately affected	0.35—0.65	8—15
Class 3: Strongly affected	>0.65	>15

Table 23. Types of salinity according to the Russian classification system, after BAZILEVICH and PANKOVA (1969), cited by YAHIA (1971)

Chemistry (type) of salinization	Ratios of meq anions		
	Cl/SO_4	HCO_3/Cl	HCO_3/SO_4
Chloride	>2.5		
Sulphate-chloride	2.5—1		
Chloride-sulphate:			
a) with small amount of gypsum	1—0.2		
b) with increased amount of gypsum	1—0.2		
Sulfate:			
a) with small amount of gypsum	<0.2		
b) with increased amount of gypsum	<0.2		
Sodium carbonate–chloride	>1	<1	>1
Sodium carbonate–sulphate	<1	>1	<1
Sodium chloride–carbonate	>1	>1	>1
Sodium sulphate–carbonate	<1	>1	>1
Sulphate- or chloride-bicarbonate	Any	>1	>1
a) $CaSO_4$ <1%			
b) $CaSO_4$ >1%			

Chemistry of salinization	Ratios of meq cations		
	Na/Mg	Na/Ca	Mg/Ca
Sodium	>1	>1	—
Magnesium-sodium	>1	>1	>1
Calcium-sodium	>1	>1	<1
Calcium-magnesium	<1	<1	>1
Sodium-magnesium	<1	>1	>1
Sodium-calcium	>1	<1	<1
Magnesium-calcium	>1	<1	<1
Magnesium	>1	—	>1

sodium- and magnesium sulfates and of sodium chloride occurs in much smaller areas, i.e. in regions of submerged alluvium, in deltas and in depressions of dry steppes and deserts. In the central, driest parts of deserts, over relatively small surface areas, the most soluble salts accumulated are sodium- and potassium nitrates, magnesium chloride, sometimes sodium carbonate. This sequence is particularly clear in large continental basins in the central parts of the Soviet Union, but similar tendencies can be found e.g. in the large basins of western Asia, such as Mesopotamia and surrounding areas. A diagram of the accumulation of salts in a

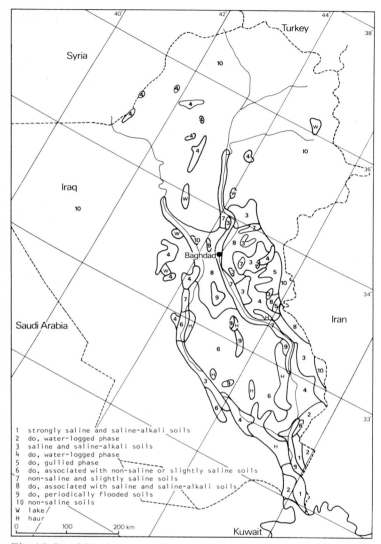

Fig. 4.9. Provisional map of saline and water-logged soils in Iraq (EL DUJAILI and ISHMAIL.
In: Salinity Seminar, 1971)

continental basin, with increasing aridity towards the center (right-hand part of
the figure), is given in Fig. 4.8 (after KOVDA, 1964).

On a lower level of generalization, that of the landscapes within each continent, salinization is closely connected to climate, lithology, relief and hydrological
conditions. The lithology of surrounding geological formations may have important consequences for salinization in a basin, as was indicated by YAHIA (1971) for
the case of Mesopotamia. Hydrological conditions refer primarily to natural
drainage, but artificial drainage and irrigation also have strong influences on

salinization (BURINGH, 1960). An excerpt from a list of the main types of landscapes in irrigated territories, as indicated by KOVDA and EGOROV (1964) (see also KOVDA in: Integrated Surveys, 1966), is given in Table 21.

The exact conditions of salinity vary widely according to the factors mentioned previously. Within many of the main types of landscapes mentioned, particularly in the semi-desert and desert areas, regional and local variations are found. These have to be accurately studied to evaluate the soil resources of any given area. When amelioration projects are being planned, careful consideration of the kinds of salinity in relation to the nature of the landscape and of the soils is essential. Special reference must be made to the general hydrology and the soil hydrology, as well as to particular soil characteristics, such as soil porosity and the compostion of the substratum. Determinations, both in the field and in the laboratory, are indicated in well-known U.S.D.A. Handbook 60: "Saline and Alkaline Soils" (Salinity Laboratory Staff, 1954). They are very useful for quantifying some aspects of the salinity of the soil as well as of the ground water and of the irrigation water. The scope of this handbook is, however, not wide enough to cover all problems of salinity in all parts of the world, because the book has a tendency to concentrate on the problems of sodium salinity (alkalinity). YAHIA (1971) has pointed out that, for Iraq and in particular for the Mesopotamian plain, other criteria, derived from Russian authors, must also be applied. In Tables 22 and 23 (after YAHIA, 1971), both kinds of criteria are indicated in a general manner (see also JANITZKY, 1957). In Fig. 4.9 the salinity of the different physiographic regions of Iraq is outlined.

Soil Hydrology

In the preceding discussions of soil hydrology, special attention was given to ground water in relation to salinity, because in many arid countries, it is the dominant factor for land use in agriculture (see also Table 24 and Fig. 4.10).

Ground water is, however, an important part of the soil as a land resource. It is primarily connected with the hydrology of a region and of a landscape in general, but it cannot be viewed apart from the soils. The usefulness of a particular soil for land use depends largely on the prevailing ground water conditions. In all soil surveys, some attention is given to ground water conditions as a factor in soil formation: these are reflected, for example, in the "Gleyic horizon" of the World Soil Map Legend and in the "Aquic" suborders and subgroups of the American Soil Taxonomy. The information obtained in this manner may, however, be partly superseded by the results of artificial drainage. The kind of information given in this manner is, however, insufficient for land use.

The actual drainage of a soil has, therefore, for many years and in many surveys been separately mapped from the more general taxonomic indications as a soil drainage phase. The U.S. Soil Survey Manual (Soil Survey Staff, 1951) indicates that soil drainage is a broad concept which contains three narrower concepts: (1) run-off, (2) soil permeability, and (3) internal soil drainage. Run-off may be defined in 6 classes: 0. ponded, 1. very slow, 2. slow, 3. medium, 4. rapid, 5. very rapid.

Table 24. Water and salt balance in the Bol Guini Polder (Chad) (DIELMANN and DE RIDDER, 1964)

	Oct.	Nov.	Dec.	Jan.	Feb.	March	April	May	June	July	Aug.	Sept.	Total average
1. Water level of Lake Chad (m + sea level)[a]	282.10	282.30	282.50	282.50	282.45	282.30	282.15	282.00	281.85	281.70	281.70	281.90	
2. Average ground water table (m + sea level)[a]	278.05	277.95	277.85	277.75	277.65	277.55	277.45	277.45	277.45	277.65	278.10	278.10	
2A. Average ground water table, in m below surface	0.05	0.15	0.25	0.35	0.45	0.55	0.65	0.65	0.65	0.45	0	0	
3. Difference between the levels 1 and 2, in m	4.05	4.35	4.65	4.75	4.80	4.75	4.70	4.55	4.40	4.05	3.60	3.80	4.4
4. Precipitation, in mm [b]	0	0	0	0	0	0	0	0	5	70	190	50	315
5. Seepage supply, in mm per month	155	165	175	180	180	180	180	175	165	155	135	145	1990
5A. Seepage supply, in mm per day	5.1	5.4	5.7	5.9	5.9	5.9	5.9	5.7	5.4	5.1	4.5	4.7	5.4
6. Evapotranspiration, in mm [c]	170	195	215	205	205	205	205	175	170	175	195	195	2315
7. Salt concentration of seepage water, in ma hos/cm							0.8						
8. Salt supply to the root zone, in g per 100 g of dry soil[d]	0.016	0.016	0.018	0.018	0.018	0.018	0.018	0.018	0.017	0.016	0.014	0.014	0.2

[a] Derived from PIAS and BARBERY. Years with exceptional levels have been left out of consideration.
[b] Average of 1946—1960.
[c] Assessed from lines 2, 4 and 5 (natural drainage being absent). The porosity of the upper 25 cm of soil is taken at 33% that of the 25—65 cm layer at 25%, the difference being partly due to variation in organic matter content.
[d] Accumulation in the upper 50 cm of soil, for which the apparent specific gravity amounts to 1.

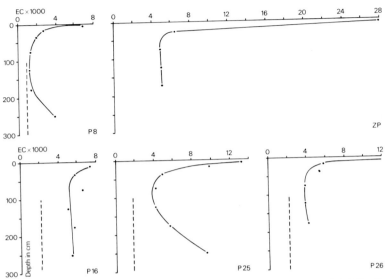

Fig. 4.10. Salt distribution (ECe) of some soil profiles in Bol Guini (Chad) (DIELEMAN and DE RIDDER, 1964)

"Soil permeability is that quality of a soil that enables it to transmit water or air"; it is defined in seven classes from 1. very slow (less than 0.05 inches per hour) to 7. very rapid (more than 10.00 inches per hour). In this system, permeability is measured through saturated undisturbed cores under a $\frac{1}{2}$-inch head of water. Field determinations in auger holes are widely used also for determining the saturated permeability of soils; the latter is often expressed in meters per 24 hrs and runs from less than 0.10 meters to over 10 meters per 24 hrs. Permeability or "hydraulic conductivity" may also be indicated in 10^{-5} cm/sec. This is demonstrated in Table 25 (after KINORI, 1970) where classes of hydraulic conductivity and "K-values" of soils are indicated. Measurements of the unsaturated permeability are often carried out by more or less perfected methods for determining the infiltration rates; the actual figures depend largely on local conditions and on the methods used.

"Internal drainage is that quality of a soil that permits the downward flow of excess water through it." The American manual recognized six classes from 0. none to 5. very rapid. Finally, general relative soil drainage classes have been defined in a descriptive manner. These are: 1. poorly drained, 2. imperfectly or somewhat poorly drained, 3. moderately well drained, 4. well drained, 5. somewhat excessively drained, 6. excessively drained. The same relative terms can be used for natural drainage and for altered, artificial drainage. The incidence of flooding is noted in a separate group of classes, usually by estimating wherever relevant the frequency and often also the duration of flooding.

In the Netherlands, more particular attention is paid to soil drainage. The seasonal fluctuations of ground water in different soils and under different condi-

Table 25. Hydraulic conductivity of soils (KINORI, 1970)

a) Hydraulic conductivity values

Class	Seepage	Hydraulic conductivity $(10^{-5}$ cm/sec)
1	Very slow	$<$ 3
2	Slow	3—15
3	Medium slow	15—60
4	Medium	60—170
5	Medium quick	170—350
6	Quick	350—700
7	Very quick	>700

b) The hydraulic conductivity of various soils

Soil	Sign	Hydraulic conductivity $(10^{-5}$ cm/sec)
Fat clay, non-organic, high plasticity	CH	$K < 3$
Organic clay, plastic	OH	
Lean clay, non-organic, low or medium plasticity sandy clay, silty clay	CL	
Elastic silt, silty sand	MH	
Organic silt, organic clay with silt, low plasticity	OL	$60 > K > 3$
Clayey sand, medium plasticity	SC	
Gravelly, clay gravel-sand-clay	GC	
Silty sand, poorly graded, non-plastic	SM	
Non-organic silt, very fine sand	ML	$60 > K > 3$
Silty gravel, sand-silt-gravel, poorly graded, non-plastic	GM	
Sand, well-graded (up to 5% fines)	SW	
Sand, poorly graded (up to 5% fines)	SP	$700 > K > 60$
Gravel, well-graded (up to 5% fines)	GW	
Gravel, poorly graded	GP	$K > 700$

K is used in the Darcy-formula: $Q = $ A.K.J. in which Q is the discharge, A. is the cross-sectional area of the flow, K is the coefficient of hydraulic conductivity and J is the hydraulic gradient.

Table 26. Ground water table in the Soil Survey of the Netherlands, scale 1:50000 (after HEESEN. In: SCHELLING et al., 1970), in centimeters below ground surface level

Water table class	I	II	III	IV	V	VI	VII
Mean highest water table ("winter")	—	—	<40	>40	<40	40–80	>80
Mean lowest water table ("summer")	<50	50–80	8–120	80–120	>120	>120	>120

tions of natural and artificial drainage are specially relevant (HEESEN in SCHEL-
LING et al., 1970). These fluctuations are shown on the Soil Map of the Netherlands, scale 1:50000, as separate ground water phases according to the classes
indicated in Table 26.

Apart from measurements at many locations, regional correlations have been
worked out for mapping these classes in the field; they can be used to estimate the
classes by correlation with other soil characteristics. Due to differences in the
general hydrological situation, these correlations can only be used per drainage
basin and with variations for different kinds of soils. For specific purposes of
detailed mapping, subdivisions of the preceding classes are used, e.g. VIIa
(MHW = 80—120, MLW = more than 200) and VIIb (MHW = more than 120,
MLW = more than 200).

4.3.2 Water Conditions

Next to the soil, water is by far the most important land resource which is
simultaneously relatively stable—and can therefore provide relatively permanent
supplies as well as permanent restraints—and rather easy for man to manipulate.
In the whole world fresh water is a scarce resource. The main difference between
water and soil is of course that water is mainly liquid, although it also carries solid
and gaseous components, and soils are mainly solid. Both water and soil are the
carriers of relatively complicated ecosystems in which many kinds of plants and
animals, from bacteria to vertebrates, live in a balance with their natural environment. Under natural conditions flowing water carries different quantities of solid
materials, depending on the kind of climate, relief, lithology, soils and vegetation
in the source areas and on the kind of action present in the different parts of the
stream; the latter are often differentiated into the upper, middle and lower
courses. In the upper course, there is an increasing sediment load away from the
stream's sources, in the middle course the sediment load remains approximately
equal and in the lower course the sediment load is gradually deposited along the
sides of the river and in the territories flooded. Particularly heavy sediment loads
are often carried by streams in glaciated areas and in many regions with seasonal
or permanent aridity.

Water is perhaps the most typically cyclic resource of all land resources. The
main quantitative aspects of the world hydrological cycle are shown in Table 15
(see p. 86). KELLER (1962) gives more detailed quantitative data for many parts of
the world. Some of his data are given in Table 27 and Fig. 4.11. Figure 4.12 (after
OLSON, 1970) contains a qualitative model of the hydrological cycle.

Table 27. Precipitation, surface flow and evaporation from land and
sea surfaces of the world (after KELLER, 1962)

	Land = 29% of surface	Sea = 71% of surface
Precipitation	67–75 cm/year	83–96 cm/year
Surface flow	25 cm/year	—
Evaporation	42–50 cm/year	93–196 cm/year

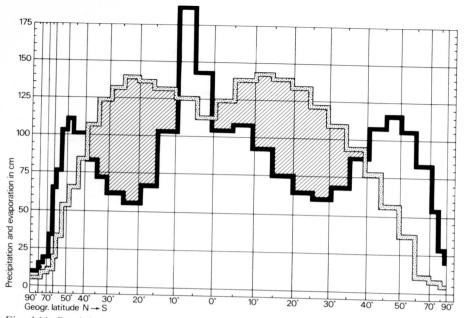

Fig. 4.11. Precipitation and evaporation from the sea at different geographical latitudes (KELLER, 1962)

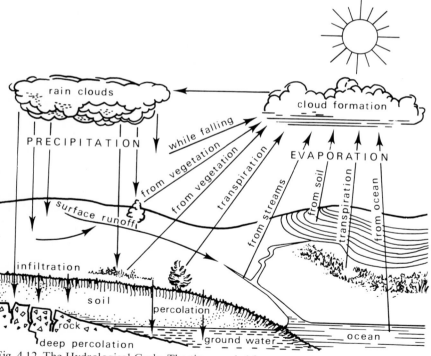

Fig. 4.12. The Hydrological Cycle. The time needed for water to complete the cycle from the ocean surface back to the ocean may be as little as a few hours or days or as much as thousands of years. (From WATER. In: The Yearbook of Agriculture, 1955, p. 42, courtesy U.S. Department of Agriculture, cited by OLSON, 1970)

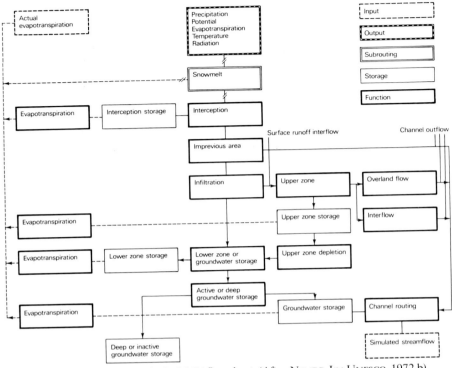

Fig. 4.13. Stanford Watershed Model IV flowchart. (After NEMEC. In: UNESCO, 1972 b)

Water Resources

A large amount of interesting information on the water resources of the earth has been collected during the International Hydrological Decade. Some of this is now being published and includes relatively simple and fairly comprehensive curricula and teaching aids for courses in hydrology (UNESCO, 1972a,b). The use of electric analog models for hydrological studies is an important means for research and demonstration in this discipline. Many other models are also used for the study of this cyclic resource. A watershed model flow chart is reproduced (after UNESCO, 1972b) in Fig. 4.13.

The use of water resources and their planning is always closely connected to the use of land resources (Water Resources Council, 1970). The latter are connected with the quantity as well as with the quality of the available water. As was shown previously, the available quantity of fresh water in the world is relatively low. Water as a resource in land use may be said to be more scarce than land. This is even true for such countries as the Netherlands, where for many centuries water was thought to be extremely overabundant. But even in the Netherlands, due to greatly increased consumption for industrial and civilian uses, water use has to be well managed and carefully planned. In more arid countries, where serious precipitation deficits exist either during the growing season of the main agricultural crops or throughout the year, the calculation of water availability and of water consumption in general is the major determinant of agricultural land use.

Water as an agricultural resource is used by plants, animals and men. Part of this water is temporarily stored in their tissues. A large part is, however, returned to the hydrological cycle through transpiration, which, together with direct evaporation from free water and land surfaces, is returned to the atmosphere as "evapotranspiration". For calculating evapotranspiration as an essential part of the water balance of a region, several useful formulas have been developed. The most generally accepted formula is that of PENMAN, but the more approximative formulas of THORNTHWAITE, LOWRY-JOHNSON and BLANEY-CRIDDLE have also proved useful, particularly in those regions where insufficient data are available for using the PENMAN formula. For these formulas and their application, the reader is referred to the many textbooks on hydrology and on irrigation, some of which are both easy to read and sufficiently comprehensive for many users (see e.g. ISRAELSEN and HANSEN, 1962).

Water consumption by agricultural crops differs considerably according to the kind of crop. It is also to some extent dependent upon the heat regime of the area under consideration. Table 4 (see p. 52) contains data on consumptive use of water by crops in the Baghdad region of Iraq.

Next to total water consumption, the consumption per month is very important, particularly, in reference to the monthly distribution of precipitation. Even in humid, temperate countries such as the Netherlands, a considerable water deficit may occur during the growing season. For grain crops in the Netherlands, this deficit is of the order of 150 mm in an average growing season. As a result, in soil with a water retention capacity lower than 150 mm, drought incidence is likely to occur even for relatively drought-resistant grain crops. Several other crops can only be grown when ground water is near enough to provide an extra water resource, e.g. oats and mangolds ("fodder beet"). Grassland vegetation in this climate is also very dependent upon ground water. In soils with an insufficient water retention capacity, only drought-resistant grasses can be grown and often even these, if intensively used, require a system with leys, i.e., sown grasslands, of limited duration, up to 10 years, after which several years of arable land cultivation are needed before grassland can be sown again.

Ground water as a water resource is therefore intimately connected with the soils. Excess of ground water leads to insufficient air in the soils and is therefore deleterious to many plants. VAN LYNDEN (1967) indicated the water requirements as well as the tolerance for high ground water (air requirements) of several wood species in the Netherlands. These are given in Table 28.

Excess water may be caused by excess precipitation on soils of poor permeability. Intensive artificial drainage may therefore be necessary in rather unexpected localities. Examples are found in Western Europe, e.g. the pseudogley soils of Germany, and in the humid tropical areas, where intensive artificial drainage of Hevea plantations as well as of tea gardens on moderately steep to steep hills often produced remarkable results. Drainage is also essential on many hilly tea plantations in northeast India (GRICE, 1971).

Excess surface water is a landscape characteristic which is intimately connected with the periodicity on the flow of rivers as well as with local relief. The effects on

Table 28. Water requirements and tolerance for high ground water of
some wood species in the Netherlands (VAN LYNDEN, 1967)

Species	Water requirements	Tolerance for high ground water
Pinus sp.	low	high
Larix sp.	high	low
Picea sp.	high	high
Pseudotsuga Dougl.	low	low
Poplars	high	high
Willow	high	high
Beech	high	low
Oak (*Quercus robur*)	high	low

land use of not-too-rapid flooding over short periods differ from those of inundations of long duration. These effects which can be both favorable and deleterious,
depend heavily on the quality of the water, which is viewed in terms of contents of
materials in suspension (silt and clay) and of contents of material in solution,
either natural or artificial. Deleterious effects may be due to natural salinity or to
man-made wastes, i.e., excessive amounts of salt and of heavy metals, which may
be harmful for plant growth but even more so for animal and, indirectly, for
human consumption.

Irrigation Water

The quality of irrigation water depends on the materials in suspension and in
solution, respectively. The accumulation of natural silt on cultivated soils has
often been considered very beneficial for soil fertility. In some cases, where easily
weatherable minerals, e.g. of volcanic origin, are deposited in not too large quantities, this may certainly be the case. In other cases, however, the silt content of
irrigation water has relatively deleterious effects on land use. Silt may reduce the
capacity of dams and reservoirs as well as that of secondary and tertiary irrigation
channels. The cleaning of these works is often difficult and costly in terms of
human effort and material expenditure. The amount of silt may grow to such
proportions that either new channels must be dug or considerable tracts of land
must be used as depot areas. The former is the classical approach utilized by Iraqi
farmers. They cleaned the channels until the walls along them became so high that
no more silt could be piled on them; the next step was to dig a channel around the
affected part to make a new connection (SCHILSTRA, 1962). The result is, of course,
not very beneficial to efficient land use. The theoretical approach of constructing
channels with gradients which are sufficient to keep the silt in suspension until it
is dispersed over the fields, evidently does not work; in any irrigation system some
spots occur where stream velocity diminishes. In these areas, large accumulations
of silt regularly occur and provide new sources of materials for reducing the
efficiency of other channels. The only solution in areas where large quantities of
silt regularly occur in the water sources for irrigation is to construct special
sedimentation basins as a first step in irrigation; the excess silt is allowed to settle
in these basins before the water is brought into the actual irrigation system. This

system, which e.g. was installed at the Amara Sugarcane Plantation in Iraq, seems to provide the only reliable solution. The system is provided with a dual pump, which at regular intervals is used for pumping silt from the sedimentation basin back into the Euphrates River.

A continuous sedimentation of silt on irrigated lands may also be deleterious to land productivity. The measure of this effect depends strongly on the kinds of original soils, on the kind and quantity of the silt and on the conditions under which the silt is deposited. The latter in particular may provide difficulties. If silt is deposited under saline or alkaline conditions and with little or no vegetation, the structure of the sediment after drying may become very dense and not very porous. As a result the drainability of the land may become greatly reduced, thus increasing the danger of salinization. The translocation of carbonates may further increase this danger, because the few existing pores may be filled with poorly soluble carbonates.

The materials in solution in irrigation water may to some extent provide extra nutrients to plants and may thus be beneficial to land use. Materials in solution may also tend to change the processes of soil formation even more than would be the case if irrigation with nearly pure water were applied. The trend of many soils of the humid tropics, which originally were of the kaolinitic ("oxisol" or "ferral-sol") type, to change under irrigation into montmorillonitic ("vertisol") soils is partly due to the additional amounts of silicates and cations, e.g. magnesium, which are continuously supplied by the irrigation waters. This process differs from another chemical influence on soil formation, i.e. that caused by the reduction under anaerobic circumstances of iron and manganese in many irrigated subtropical and tropical soils and which often leads to the formation of iron-manganese hardpans at specific depths.

The danger of salinization or alkalinization of lands as a result of irrigation, although present in many arid areas, has perhaps been somewhat over-empha-sized in the past. The increasing salinization of old irrigated areas such as Meso-potamia has probably at least partly been caused by natural circumstances, i.e. the flow of strongly saline ground water from the sides of the basin into the central depression. There is, however, no doubt that the problem has been aggra-vated throughout the millenia by irrigation without drainage. Furthermore, irri-gation of one area, necessarily high if soils are saline, caused the lateral flow of into adjoining areas, which then become even more saline than they originally were. There is sufficient evidence, however, that irrigation with good, intensive drainage, which provides the path for leaching of soluble salts and which also prevents the rising of saline ground water and the lateral accumulation of salts, offers a reliable solution to these problems. There is, however, one essential prerequisite, i.e. that the proper maintenance of all drainage works is assured. This requires not only a good set of technical management practices, but also suitable institutional arrangements. The age-old institutional arrangements of the rice-growing countries of Southeast Asia as well as those of the polders and polder-districts of the Netherlands provide interesting examples, albeit under somewhat different circumstances.

Scarcity of irrigation water in arid countries often results in the necessity of using water with a rather high content of soluble salts. For a long time, French

Table 29. Quality of irrigation water, expressed in total salt contents, according to different systems (VAN HOORN. In: Salinity Seminar, 1971)

Total salt content

Total salt content, expressed in g/l, me/l, ppm or by the electrical conductivity in mmhos/cm gives an indication of the water's quality with regard to the salinity hazard. Several classifications exist in this respect:

Classification of the US Salinity Laboratory:

Salt content

g/l	$EC \times 10^3$/cm	Evaluation
<0.2	<0.25	C_1 Low salinity water can be used for irrigation with most crops on most soils with little likelihood that a salinity problem will develop. Some leaching is required, but this occurs under normal irrigation practices, except on soils of extremely low permeability.
0.2–0.5	0.25–0.75	C_2 Medium salinity water, can be used if a moderate amount of leaching occurs. Plants with moderate salt tolerance can be grown in most instances without special practices for salinity control.
0.5–1.5	0.75–2.25	C_3 High salinity water, cannot be used on soils with restricted drainage, special management for salinity control may be required and plants with good salt tolerance should be selected.
1.5–3	2.25–5.0	C_4 Very high salinity water, is not suitable for irrigation under ordinary conditions but may be used occasionally under very special circumstances. The soils must be permeable, drainage must be adequate, irrigation water must be applied in excess to provide considerable leaching and very salt tolerant crops should be selected.

USSR classification:

Salt content in g/l	Evaluation
0.2–0.5	Water of the best quality
1–2	Water causing salinity hazard
3–7	Water can be used for irrigation only with leaching and perfect drainage.

Classification of Durand for North Africa:

Upper permissible conductivity limits of irrigation water in mmhos/cm for three groups of plants and five groups of soils, assuming good irrigation and drainage conditions.

Soil texture	Plant tolerance group $EC_e \times 10^3$					
	<4.0	4.0–10.0	>10.0			
			Dates	Vegetables	Fodder	Field crops
Sandy	2.5	6.5	15–20	8.0	12.0	10.0
Loamy sand	1.6	4.0	6–10	4.5	7.0	6.0
Loamy	1.0	3.0	8.0	3.5	5.0	4.5
Loamy clay	0.8	2.0	6.0	2.4	3.5	3.0
Clay	0.4	1.0	3.0	1.2	1.8	1.6

Table 30. Quality standards and leaching requirements in Pakistan (S. M. ISMAIL. In: Salinity Seminar, 1971)

Water quality grade	Chemical composition parameters[a]	Leaching requirements (water to be drained)	Water available for consumptive use[c]	Remarks
River waters				
1. Excellent quality	EC less than 450 RSC nil SAR less than 2	10%	90%	
Ground waters				
2. Good quality	EC less than 750 RSC less than 1.25 meq/1 SAR less than 7	20%	80%	Can be used without mixing with canal water but with 10% additional leaching requirements over and above those prescribed for Class 1 quality.
3. Satisfactory quality	EC 750–1500 RSC less than 1.25 SAR less than 5	37%	63%	Can be used without mixing with canal water but will require additional 27% leaching requirements over and above Class 1 quality.
4. Poor quality	EC 1500–3000 RSC 1.25–2.50[b] SAR 5–10	75%	25%	Not fit. Requires mixing 1:1 canal.
5. Bad quality	EC 1500–3000 RSC 2.5–5.0[b] SAR 5–10	75%	25%	Not fit. Requires mixing 1:2 canal.
6. Bad quality	EC 1500–3000 RSC 1.25–2.50[b] SAR 10–15	75%	25%	Not fit. Requires mixing 1:2 canal.
7. Worst quality	EC more than 3000 RSC more than 5 SAR more than 15	100%[b]	nil	Unfit. Not to be used.

[a] EC = electrical conductivity expressed in micromhos/cm. SAR = sodium adsorption ratio. RSC = residual sodium carbonate.
[b] The values of RSC and SAR in this group pertain to all water with EC ranging from 0–3000.
[c] The calculation is based on a fixed volume of available water.

scientists investigated the possibilities of using such water under the conditions in the North African countries. They demonstrated that, on sufficiently permeable and well-drained soils, water which contains large quantities of soluble salts may still be used with good results, provided that the manner of application and the crop to be grown are carefully determined. Lately, special research teams provided by United Nations agencies (UNDP, UNESCO, FAO) have carried out intensive, systematic investigations on these problems, in particular in Tunisia (DE FORGES, 1970; UNESCO/UNDP 1970; Salinity Seminar, 1971). Results obtained at two research stations under very different conditions, the lower Medjerda Valley and the oasis of Tozeur, respectively, showed that saline water could be used for irrigation in Tunisia, provided that special precautions are taken and that somewhat lower yields than normal are accepted. The basic requirement is "that water should flow everywhere and stagnate nowhere". The salinity of waters used was of the order from 2.0 to 2.5 g/l soluble salts (see also Chapter 5). Some data are given in Tables 29 and 30.

Drinking Water

Drinking water for cattle is of the utmost importance in semi-arid grazing areas, which occur particularly under monsoon climates (Integrated Surveys, 1967). The interrelationships between locality and availability of water on the one hand and of land resources and human resources on the other hand have to be very nicely balanced to provide a sufficiently reliable system of land use. The seminomadic systems, often called "transhumance", include the seasonal migrations of tribes or families with their cattle from the drier lands, which are used in the rainy season, to floodplain areas which can only be used after the river floods have retreated. In the dry areas particularly, special attention must be paid to the problems of drinking water, i.e., the available drinking water must be in good proportion to the carrying capacity of the grazing lands. If not enough water is available, either the other land resources tend to be underutilized or periodic drought may damage the herds, sometimes even catastrophically. If too much drinking water is available locally, the danger of over-grazing is everpresent and may lead to permanent damage to the carrying capacity of the lands. No definite solution to this problem has been found. The forced closing of wells provides great social and psychological difficulties. Prospecting for water to provide better land use with high carrying capacity does not always produce the desired results.

Seepage

Water is the ever-flowing resource. Even superficially stagnant waters may have underground connections with other water areas. The study of this resource therefore implies the study of coherent water areas, catchment areas, drainage basins or "watershed areas". A proper hydrology, regardless of purpose, is therefore always "watershed hydrology". Even then, the exact delineation of the coherent area is made difficult by the phenomenon of seepage, i.e. the underground flow of water from one catchment area to another. In its simplest application, seepage, e.g. in limestone areas with "carst" phenomena, may be used to explain gaps or excesses in the quantitative water balance of an area. From a more serious vantage point, seepage may induce pollution or salinization by underground flow to areas at considerable distances from the original source. Seepage may also cause the drying-out of areas, because large-scale drainage projects have been carried out in regions at some distance.

The "Veluwe Lake" is an example of the latter. The situation is indicated in Fig. 4.14 (a—c) (after VOLKER et al., 1969).

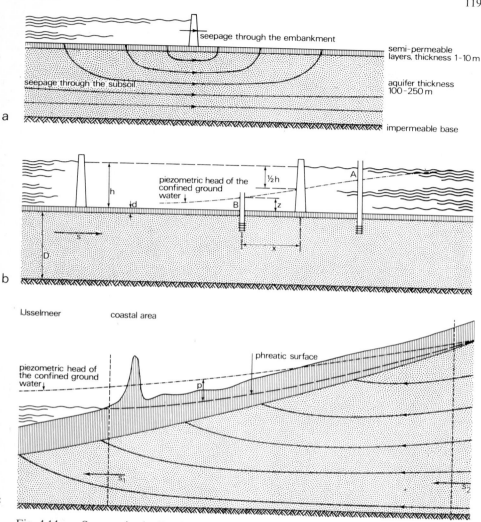

Fig. 4.14a–c. Seepage in the Zuyderzee Polder Area, the Netherlands. (After VOLKER et al., 1969)

In a, the principle of dike seepage and deep seepage is indicated in a general manner. In b the system of calculation of the deep seepage is sketched. In c the generalized cross section of the landscape with its hydrology is indicated.

The general outline of this situation is as follows. After the Northeastern Polder ("N.O. Polder") of the Zuyderzee Works had been drained, serious drought effects were observed on the lands directly adjoining this polder; it was proved that these effects were due to deep underground seepage from the "old" land, situated near Ordnance Datum (O.D.) Level, or slightly higher, towards the polder, situated at approx. 4 to 5 m below O.D. and drained by pumping stations. Before the subsequent polders were constructed, the soils, the geo-

Table 31. Water loss by seepage from earth channels (KINORI, 1970)

Type of soil	Seepage loss $(m^3/m^2/day)$
Impervious clay loam	0.07–0.10
Medium clay loam, impervious layer below the channel bottom not exceeding 60–90 cm in depth	0.10–0.15
Clay loam, silty soil	0.15–0.23
Clay loam with gravel, sandy clay loam, gravel cemented with clay particles	0.23–0.30
Sandy loam	0.30–0.45
Sandy soil	0.45–0.55
Sandy soil with gravel	0.55–0.75
Pervious gravelly soil	0.75—0.90
Gravel with some earth	0.90–1.80

Remarks: (1) The area, m^2, in this table is the wetted perimeter along one meter of the channel. (2) All the values in this table are quite general; the soil type definitions give large soil groups and the experiments on which they are based ignored such important factors as the shape of the channel, the depth of an impervious layer and the depth of the ground water surface. The values are to be considered as general information only.

logic substrata and the hydrological conditions, e.g. piezometric heads and deep flow, were studied. In addition, the effects of lowering of ground water tables on crop yields in the area adjoining the future polders, an area of sandy soil situated at some meters above O.D., were investigated. From these studies it was determined that the future hydrology would benefit considerably from the construction of a border lake between the new polders and the old land, in order to maintain sufficient hydraulic pressure on the deeper waters of the old land, thus avoiding excessive underground flow resulting in deep seepage. The width of the lake at different locations was determined by the underground hydrology. This project, in the main, proved successful; drought incidence on the old land has been kept to within reasonable limits and extra water flow into the new polders, with resulting water logging and/or extra pumping costs, has largely been avoided (see however Para. 5.4.5).

Seepage also has deleterious effects in quite different conditions, e.g. saline conditions in which saline water is brought in either from hydrologically connected lands by natural seepage or by excessive irrigation of the higher situated areas. This situation has been clearly proved even for relatively flat areas in Mesopotamia. Some quantitative data on seepage from earth channels in irrigation and drainage works are given in Table 31.

Hydrologic Inventories

Many special observations on the water resources of an area can, and often must, be made. UNGER (1972, cited by BRINKMAN and SMYTH, 1973) indicates for different land developments projects several items, listed under "geohydrology" and "hydrology", respectively. These are reproduced in Table 32. It is clear that for the selection of the best criteria in a given case and for the systems of qualitative and quantitative measurements and evaluation, more information is necessary than can be provided within the context of this book.

Table 32. Hydrologic Data Required for Land Development Projects (after UNGER, 1972)

1.	*Geo-hydrology*
1.1	Qualitative appraisals of safe yield, safe seepage
1.1.1	Geological information, see 3.1–3.1.1.8
1.1.2	Qualitative appraisals of seepage:
1.1.2.1	Water-saturation phenomena as reflected by the soil profile
1.1.2.2	Water-saturation phenomena as reflected by the soil vegetation
1.2	Quantitative appraisals of safe yields, safe input, seepage
1.2.1	Isohypses and seasonal fluctuations
1.2.2	Equipotentials and seasonal fluctuations
1.2.3	Depth to and thickness of aquifers
1.2.4	Aquifer characteristics such as:
1.2.4.1	Transmissibility
1.2.4.2	Piezometric gradient
1.2.4.3	Non-capillary porosity
1.2.4.4	Hydraulic resistance of aquicludes or overlying strata
1.2.4.5	Storage coefficient
1.2.4.6	Water quality
2.	*Hydrology*
2.1	Runoff characteristics
2.1.1	Approximate discharge determinations
2.1.1.1	with the aid of the dimensions and shape of water courses and their stage marks
2.1.1.2	by means of rainfall-runoff relationships
2.1.1.2.1	following the curve-number method (Handbook of Hydrology, S.C.S., U.S.D.A.)
2.1.1.2.2	following the method of Krayenhoff van de Leur
2.1.1.2.3	following the unit hydrograph method
2.1.1.2.4	following the rational method
2.1.2	Discharge measurement data
2.1.2.1	Location of gauging stations
2.1.2.2	River stage data
2.1.2.3	River cross-section data and stage-discharge relation
2.1.2.4	Other discharge-measurement data
2.1.3	Sediment load
2.1.4	Water quality
2.2	Tidal characteristics
2.2.1	Approximate determinations
2.2.2	Location of gauging stations and tidal-fluctuation data
2.3	Location and capacity of existing natural or man-made drainage outfalls

Recently, special attention has been paid to geologic and hydrologic maps for land use planning in the U.S.A. (PESSL et al., 1972). The hydrologic data given for Connecticut include the delineation of drainage areas with special attention to selected sites, i.e., stream-gauging sites, outlets of surfacewater impoundments, surface-water sampling sites and mouths of tributary streams. Supplemental sites are recorded; these show highway and railroad bridges, outfalls from sewage-treatment plants and the main stems from mouths of tributary streams. These data are used for regional streamflow analyses in order to facilitate the design of water-supply and waste-disposal facilities and to determine the flow direction of discharged wastes. Other data recorded in these surveys are: availability of ground water, depth to water table, flood-prone areas, low flow of streams (lowest average daily flow), maximum concentration of dissolved solids, location of wells and test-holes (where subsurface information is available), sites of solid-waste storage and liquid-waste discharge and sanitary and water-related facilities and their use. Modern land use, which is multi-purpose land use, needs these different data for well-balanced planning of the use of its water resources in conjunction with human resources and land resources.

4.4 Other Land Resources

4.4.1 Artifactial Resources

Other land resources of particular importance for agricultural land use include many permanent, or nearly permanent, artificial, man-made structures as well as natural and semi-natural vegetation. In many areas of widely varying land utilization types, at least one or more of these plays an important role in land use. Their rather abbreviated treatment in this section is not meant to detract from their importance. These resources, and their absence or presence, are, however, so varied in regional and local situations that a generalized discussion, within the context of this book, necessarily has to be even less comprehensive than that of the resources indicated in the previous paragraphs.

Artifactial land resources are found in nearly all parts of the world. They are often of very old and very specialized construction, completely adapted to the natural land conditions of an area by the age-old artisanship of the local peoples. The paddy terraces of several Southeast Asian countries, e.g. Ceylon and Indonesia, are good examples. Many of these terraces were built as early as the 11th century A.D. and are, through careful maintenance throughout the centuries, still fully operational today. A view of such terraces is shown in Photo 2. Another extremely old example is the "khanats" or "khareez" of arid countries of Southwest Asia. These are ingeniously constructed subterranean irrigation canals which fulfill even today a very useful function for the irrigation of arable land and horticulture in such countries as Iran and Iraq. They are particularly effective for conducting water from the top parts of large, mainly gravelly, alluvial fans of the footslopes of mountains towards the more productive soils at the bottom of the fans. A schematic cross section (after ISRAELSEN and HANSEN, 1962) is given in Fig.4.15; a surface view of some khanats in Iran, near Teheran, is given in Photo 11.

River embankments are also often among the very old artifactial land resources. Embankment of the Rhine and Meuse rivers in the Netherlands commenced in the Middle Ages. These embankments have been gradually built up and strengthened through subsequent centuries; they constitute essential land resources for all kinds of land use in the deltaic areas of the Netherlands (Photo 12). Similar constructions, of older or younger date, fulfill similar functions in many other countries. Man-made canals are often very old artifactial land resources which have become essential for both transport and drainage functions. Two large waterways in the Netherlands were dug by Roman legions under the command of two well-known Roman generals: Drusus and Corbulo, the historical

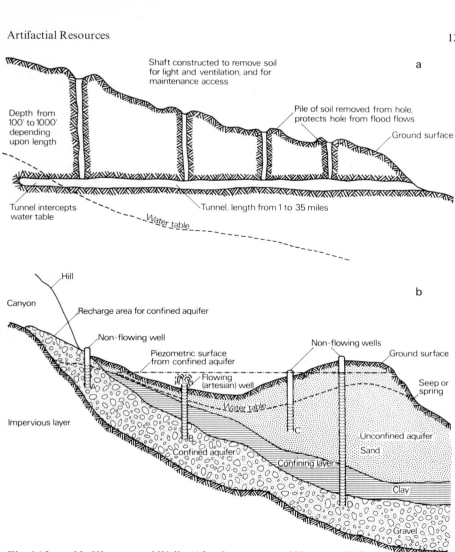

Fig. 4.15a and b. Khanats and Wells. (After ISRAELSEN and HANSEN, 1962)

authencity of these waterways being proved by reliable documents. For a long time, however, their exact location was unknown, because they had become fully integrated into the natural systems of water-ways. They still act today as important waterways and drainage ways in the eastern and western parts of the Netherlands, respectively.

Perhaps the most important artifactial land resources are the polders which were constructed from the 15th century onwards in the Netherlands, Belgium and elsewhere, e.g. Lincolnshire in England. The construction of these polders, which must be regularly maintained and often also regularly drained by pumping stations, was made possible by the perfection of the old windmills which were brought to Western Europe from Southwest Asia and North Africa by way of

Photo 11. Surface view of Khanats in Iran, East of Teheran

Photo 12. Dike construction in the Netherlands

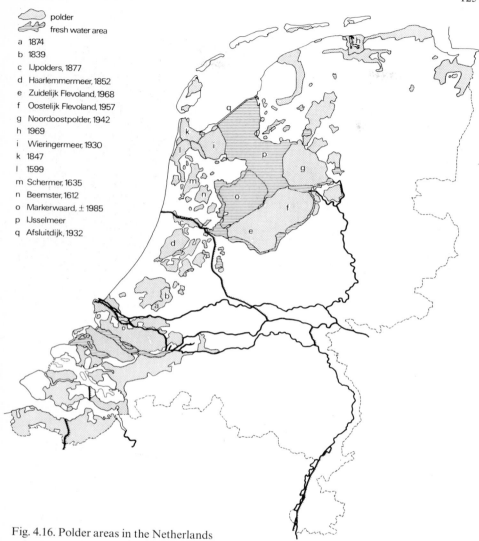

polder
fresh water area

a 1874
b 1839
c IJpolders, 1877
d Haarlemmermeer, 1852
e Zuidelijk Flevoland, 1968
f Oostelijk Flevoland, 1957
g Noordoostpolder, 1942
h 1969
i Wieringermeer, 1930
k 1847
l 1599
m Schermer, 1635
n Beemster, 1612
o Markerwaard, ± 1985
p IJsselmeer
q Afsluitdijk, 1932

Fig. 4.16. Polder areas in the Netherlands

Spain. They are in fact an essential part of the artifactial land resources, because they, or the more technically advanced pumping stations which are their successors, are indispensable for keeping the polders dry. The polders together with their dikes, waterways and windmills-pumping stations constitute a fully comprehensive land resource: the land itself with all its attributes for human land use. The polder areas of the Netherlands, constructed from the 15th century until today are shown in Fig. 4.16.

Part of a Dutch polder is shown in Photo 13. Dams and barrages in rivers are essential land resources in many countries; they serve both as a method of flood prevention, as in the case of large towns such as Baghdad (Iraq) and as a source of

Photo 13. View of a part of a polder in the Netherlands (Photo KLM Aerocarto B.V., The Hague)

water for irrigation and for urban and industrial uses. Some of the larger dams were constructed in the early years of the present century; the Ramadi barrage in the Euphrates River, northwest of Baghdad, is shown in Photo 14 as an example of an early construction. The lower Medjerda Dam in Tunisia is of more recent origin; it serves many purposes for water distribution in the lowland areas near the town of Tunis, in particular the irrigation in the Lower Medjerda Project. This dam is shown in Photo 15.

Modern dams fulfill other functions as well, e.g. they provide electricity and regulate stream flow for barge traffic. The direct impact of the use of rivers and canals on agricultural land use is shown for example by the extensive transport of sugar beets, directly after harvest, from the farms to large sugar factories. Nearly all the sugar beets produced in the Netherlands, i.e. enough to provide the total annual sugar consumption of a population of over 14 million, is transported by barges from farm to factory. Without barge transport, the feasibility of this crop in the Netherlands would probably be greatly reduced.

Roads and railroads can also be considered essential artifactial land resources. For example Roman and medieval roads even today fulfill functions in many rural areas of Europe. A modern example is the construction of railroads in Sumatra (Indonesia) by the Netherlands East Indies' Government at the beginning of this century. Immediately after the "pacification" of these areas the railroads were constructed in order to aid in their opening-up and development. In South Sumatra large plantations, mainly of Hevea rubber, were established along the railroad. Even today, the railroad is the main means of transport for products

Photo 14. The Ramadi barrage in Iraq

Photo 15. The Lower Medjerda dam in Tunisia

and materials. The railroad in this area is, therefore, an essential land resource for agricultural land use and for land development in general. Similar well-known examples exist in the United States and Canada. The construction of large transcontinental or national highways, e.g. through Central Brazil, has similar results.

Artifactial land resources have been constructed by mankind throughout the ages and are still being constructed today. Most of these must not only be constructed, but they must also be carefully maintained by human effort and organization. This fact might seem to constitute an essential difference between artifactial and natural land resources. The difference is, however, only partial and even gradual if one compares artifactial resources with soil and water resources, and is even less when they are compared with vegetation as a land resource.

4.4.2 Vegetation Resources

Vegetation must, to some extent, be considered a land resource. Vegetation is a land attribute insofar as it is "reasonably permanent or predictably cyclic". It may be natural, but it need not be so, as it may also be the "result of past or present human activity". There is no doubt that vegetation often "exerts a great influence on the present and future uses of the land by man" (see Para. 1.1). It might be reasoned, therefore, that all kinds of vegetation, including arable land uses which in general are reasonably permanent and more or less predictably cyclic, are land attributes. Whether they are always land resources needs to be considered.

A resource is "a means of supplying a want, stock that can be drawn on" (*Concise Oxford Dictionary*, 1972). In this sense, vegetation resulting from human inputs such as arable land and horticultural crops, although undoubtedly resources for mankind, cannot be called, "land resources". It is more difficult to draw a line between many kinds of forest plantations and between many types of grasslands; some of these are undoubtedly land resources, but other are not so much "stock that can be drawn on" as the result of continuous human activity.

In another sense, not all types of vegetation are "means of supplying a want" but act rather to inhibit the growth of certain crops, e.g. weeds growing among many arable and horticultural crops. Dense, natural or semi-natural vegetation which inhibits the clearing of lands for human land use is also in this sense, not a resource. It may be a resource in the sense that it may provide timber for construction; but at the same time, because it is being cleared, it is no longer reasonably permanent or predictably cyclic. Vegetation types which harbor pests, such as those kinds of woods and shrubs in Central Africa inhabited by the tsetse, *Glossina morsitans*, are certainly not resources for cattle breeding and for human land use in general.

Many types of vegetation are, however, important as land resources. These include:

a) natural forests producing useful timber or other forest products (lianas, caoutchouc, orchids etc.),

b) natural grazing lands in semi-arid areas (Integrated Surveys, 1967) but also in tundras and taigas (NELSON and CHAMBERS, 1969) and in Alpine areas,

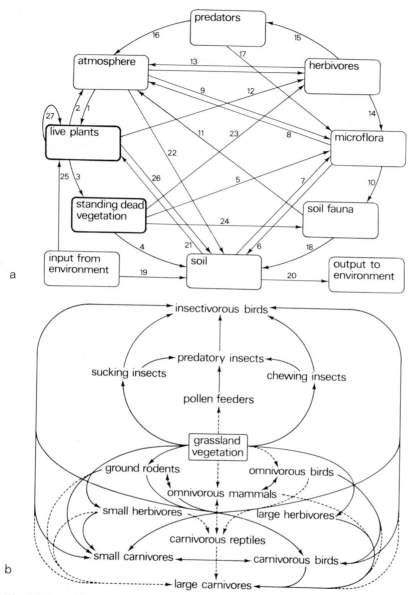

Fig. 4.17a and b. Models of Ecosystems. (After SCHULTZ and LEWIS. In: VAN DYNE et al., 1969)

c) natural and seminatural forests and grazing lands which, because of the particular nature of the land combined with centuries-old use in the same manner, have obtained a degree of permanency and a nearly stable position in the ecosystems of an area (grazing lands in many alpine areas below the forest boundary, grazing lands in peat marshes in the Netherlands),

d) natural or seminatural vegetation which conserves important species and acts, or may act as "gene-centers" for future plantbreeding,

e) natural or seminatural vegetation which, in some way or other, fulfills a specially useful ecological function, e.g. as areas of enhanced stability and variability in an otherwise monotonous area of intensive agriculture,

f) vegetation which serves several roles in different kinds of recreation, e.g., sheltering and visual roles.

In addition to terrestrial vegetation, one can also consider semi-terrestrial and aquatic types. No one type stands alone; each type is a part of a more or less developed ecosystem to which belong also many animal populations. In Fig. 4.17 (after VAN DYNE, et al., 1969) two diagrams of eco-systems are reproduced.

Because within the context of this book, no satisfactory treatment of vegetation and of ecosystems is possible, the reader is referred to the available literature. See e.g. VAN DYNE et al. (1969), EYRE (1970), NELSON and CHAMBERS (1969), MACAN and WORTHINGTON (1968), VICTOROV et al. (1964), Integrated Surveys (1967).

Chapter 5   Landscape Ecology and Land Conditions

5.1 General

Land resources—climate, geological formations, soils etc.—are natural phenomena and as such are interesting objects of study for the natural sciences. Each phenomenon is studied on a world-wide basis by a separate discipline, and every year new data on the composition and genesis of each of these land attributes are collected. Their interrelationships are also often found to be of considerable scientific interest, e.g. for the study of paleoclimates and of paleosols. The scientific data thus collected are eventually applied for land use purposes. The development of applied sciences depends heavily upon the support of the related "pure" sciences. Also, interdisciplinary problems can only be solved if the related monodisciplinary sciences are based upon sound principles.

Nevertheless, it is very useful to look at all land resources together from the viewpoint of land use. The accumulated knowledge from the different disciplines can be synthesized, and answers to the many questions on land use requirements may be found. This synthetical approach is called "*landscape ecology*", i.e. looking at the land, or at the landscape which is a natural arrangement of lands, in order to detect its influences on and interrelationships with the organisms—plants, animals and men—living on a particular tract of land or in a particular kind of landscape. One can do this in a general manner, taking into consideration the fact that all organisms need sources of foods, or nutrients, water and energy in a well-balanced manner. The survival of a given organism depends heavily on the kinds and qualities of foods, nutrients, water or energy which are available at a given place and time. These factors are studied in land resources surveys. In the surveys, land resources must be viewed both in terms of the natural and the applied sciences. The manner in which the information is combined depends on the nature of the lands under consideration as well as on the ecological relationships and the requirements of the organisms as viewed according to the envisaged land utilization types.

Land-use requirements constitute, therefore, an essential subject which must be studied in order to determine basic information on its beneficial application to land use. Few systematic studies have been made of these requirements. In a given region they are determined largely on the basis of local experience together with general ecological considerations or technical specifications. In particular the requirements of specific, important crops are difficult to find. Both "crop ecology" related to specific crops and "crop soil science" are so far relatively undeveloped. The available data are often of a restricted regional nature; more general data, often vague and generalized, are hidden in handbooks on specific crops which are not always available and which afford little or no possibility for comparisons among the requirements of different crops. Part of the problem lies in the ecological relationships themselves: it is impossible to give hard and fast quantitative data on the requirements of a specific crop with regard to a specific environmental factor, because the requirements and the influences depend on the interactions with other factors. Somewhat more clarity is essential for studying the implications of land conditions for land use.

Land management strongly influences the behavior of crops under given land conditions. This is the result of the fact that a cultural ecosystem is a dynamic complex involving crops and their treatment as well as the land conditions themselves. Crop requirements with regard to land conditions have close ties with the many kinds of land management. The responses of crops to different kinds of land management under various conditions must also, therefore, be discussed in this context. Land management has, however, a direct bearing on the land itself. Poor land management, even if it results in the production of good crops over a short period, may tend to increase land degradation. Some attention to land degradation, including agricultural land uses as well as, for comparison, non-agricultural land uses, is therefore appropriate at this stage.

Land conditions define the land resources in terms of answers to the land use requirements. These conditions have also been called land properties or, in those cases where special attention is paid to the limitative aspects of land attributes for land use, land limitations. Soil limitations and soil qualities are aspects of land limitations. Since land as a concept encompasses more than soil as a concept, land conditions embrace more than soil conditions. BEEK and BENNEMA (1972) introduced the concept of *Major Land Qualities* (see also BRINKMAN and SMYTH, 1973), which is extremely useful for obtaining a broader, and at the same time more specific, view of the land conditions.

Land conditions, which are related to the "reasonably permanent or predictably cyclic" attributes of the land, are, however, not always unchangeable. Land drainage and soil profiles may sometimes be changed by human technology to obtain more favorable conditions for land use requirements. Micro-relief may be sometimes considerably changed, e.g. to provide better land conditions for irrigation. In arid lands desalinization is a particularly effective means of improving land conditions. No paragraph on land conditions would be complete without an in-depth discussion of the possibilities for land improvement existing under different circumstances. As will be seen below, both the land conditions and the possibilities for their improvement, constitute essential diagnostic criteria in land evaluation.

To some extent, the determination of specific land conditions in a specific area for specific land utilization types in itself constitutes a means of land evaluation. A full system of land evaluation, including the establishment of land capability or land suitability classes, with or without quantitative data, requires a more elaborate procedure.

5.2 Landscape Ecology

Land is a very complex phenomenon. In a study of land for purposes of application to land use, investigations may be concentrated on those land resources which are the main variables in a given area. In many regions of the world, land resources are so closely related to soil and water resources that a careful study of these two variables provides sufficient information for land use. In other areas and for other land utilization types, the combined study of water resources and of vegetation types yields satisfactory results. Such a restricted choice of investigative methods should, however, be made only after considering their reliability and applicability. In other regions, no simple choice of a restricted number of disciplines is possible. A broader concept for land resources studies is therefore required. This concept is provided by landscape ecology.

The term "landscape ecology" was introduced in 1938 by the German geographer-biologist Carl Troll. It embraces two concepts which, both individually and in combination, arose from the efforts of scientists to reawaken an interest in the synthetical views of natural phenomena in our epoch of scientific specialization. "The concept of landscape ecology is born from a marriage of two scientific outlooks, the one geographical (landscape), the other biological (ecology)" (TROLL, in Integrated Surveys, 1966). The essence of landscape ecology is that it sees the land, as defined previously, first and foremost as the carrier of both natural and cultural ecosystems. Human ecology, which includes all of the many relations between man and the land, is specifically mentioned in this respect.

Landscape ecology considers the landscape, which is land seen as a natural phenomenon, as a whole and tries to describe qualitatively, and as much as possible quantitatively, the interrelationships among the many attributes themselves and with the ecosystems of which the land is a part. It provides a synthetical approach, based on sound analyses of the many parts as well as on careful study of the visible and invisible relationships. This approach can be described with a systems approach (CHORLEY and KENNEDY, 1971).

"A system is a structured set of objects or attributes. These objects and attributes consist of components or variables (i.e. phenomena which are free to assume variable magnitudes) that exhibit discernible relationships with one another and operate together as a complex whole, according to some observed pattern" (CHORLEY and KENNEDY, 1971). Ecosystems and landscapes are "open systems" in the sense that they are characterized by an exchange of both mass and energy with their surroundings. Ecosystems consist of plants, animals and their inanimate environment; human ecosystems represent the interlocking of social systems with ecosystems and as such are perhaps the structurally most complex systems imaginable.

In ecology, seen from the standpoint of biology which is a study of the relationships of organisms, there is a tendency to see the land, including relief, water and soil, as "the inanimate environment" of the organisms. For some purposes, this is an acceptable simplification. It neglects, however, the many interrelationships which exist among these attributes and the organisms. It also neglects the fact that landscapes, as carriers of ecosystems, are "control systems", i.e. they

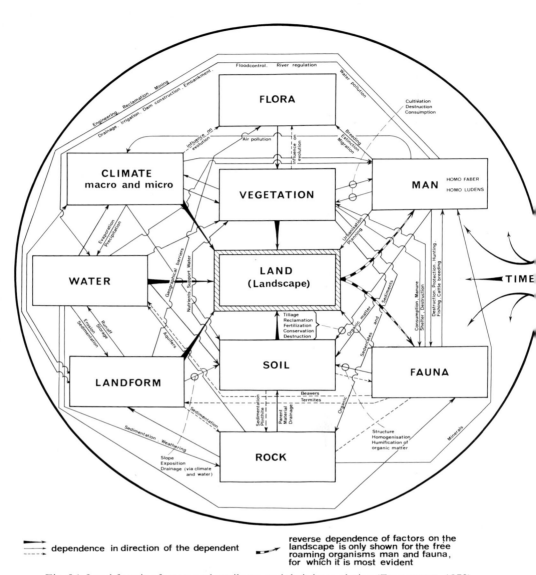

Fig. 5.1. Land-forming factors and attributes and their interrelation (ZONNEVELD, 1972)

are process-response systems in which the key components are controlled, or at least partly controlled, by some intelligence. This fact is of particular importance for land use, since its essence is that human intelligence controls many organisms and other variables for the benefit of mankind. The main objective of land use is to bring about the operation of particular "cultural ecosystems" in a manner determined by this intelligence. The landscape ecology of the cultural ecosystems is therefore of the utmost importance for land use. It is the study of the way in which different cultural ecosystems, also called "land utilization types", function within different landscapes, which are sets of living and inanimate attributes, with

Table 33. UNESCO Program on Man and the Biosphere (MAB); Scientific Content of the Program (UNESCO, 1971).

Project No. 1	Ecological effects of increasing human activities on tropical and subtropical forest ecosystems
Project No. 2	Ecological effects of different land uses and management practices on temperate and mediterranean forest landscapes
Project No. 3	Impact of human activities and land use practices on grazing lands: savanna, grassland (from temperate to arid areas), tundra
Project No. 4	Impact of human activities on the dynamics of arid and semi-arid zones' ecosystems. with particular attention to the effects of irrigation
Project No. 5	Ecological effects of human activities on the value and resources of lakes, marshes, rivers, deltas, estuaries and coastal zones
Project No. 6	Impact of human activities on mountain ecosystems
Project No. 7	Ecology and rational use of island ecosystems
Project No. 8	Conservation of natural areas and of the genetic material they contain
Project No. 9	Ecological assessment of pest management and fertilizer use on terrestrial and aquatic ecosystems
Project No. 10	Effects on man and his environment of major engineering works
Project No. 11	Ecological aspects of energy utilization in urban and industrial systems
Project No. 12	Interactions between environmental transformations and genetic and demographic changes
Project No. 13	Perception of environmental quality

different kinds and quantities of human controls, also called "land management" in its widest sense. Landscape ecology then may be defined as follows: "Landscape ecology is the study of the attributes of the land as objects and variables of ecosystems and of the processes which relate these objects and variables, including a special study of the key variables to be controlled by human intelligence".

Thus seen, landscape ecology provides the functional ties of the objects and processes of the different disciplines with each other and with the environment of plants, animals and men. It does not replace the individual disciplines, but it facilitates their functional integration, particularly for present and future uses of the land. Landscape ecology may itself be used as a basic discipline for "ecological land surveys" or "landscape ecological surveys". It may also be used in drawing network diagrams and for other means of clarifying interrelationships among the many resources and their use by men (see e.g. ZONNEVELD, 1972). A general diagram (after ZONNEVELD, 1972) is given in Fig. 5.1.

Good examples of the interrelations of ecology with different kinds of landscapes, as well as with human activities, are also found in the contents of the projects for the UNESCO program on Man and the Biosphere (MAB). These are listed in Table 33.

5.3 Land Resources Surveys

Monodisciplinary and Multidisciplinary Surveys

The survey of land resources includes the mapping and characterization of the kinds and quantities of land attributes as well as laboratory analyses to quantify specific characteristics. The monodisciplinary surveys of land resources are not treated in this book. They belong to the fields covered by related sciences (see Chapter 4). The relative merits of soil surveys and of ecological land surveys and the methodology of "Integrated Surveys of the Natural Environment" will, however, be discussed. Special mention must also be made of the impact of air-photo interpretation on the methodology of these surveys.

Are soil surveys always the best means for indicating the main ecological aspects of a landscape with regard to land use? In some cases the soils show, within a defined land area, only small differences, whereas other land attributes such as relief are sharply differentiated. A soil map of the area, even a physiographic soil map in which considerable attention is paid to landscape differences, may place too much emphasis on minor soil differentiae and not enough emphasis on locally more important land attributes such as relief, water and topoclimate (Fig. 5.2). On the other hand, a land area may show interesting soil differences, which, within a particular socioeconomic structure may be unimportant because only extensive grazing systems can be established (Integrated Surveys, 1967).

In still other cases interesting soil differences may have no operational importance because of the dominance of an extreme climate, either arid or cold, in the former case together with no availability of irrigation water and in the second, with no feasible heating facilities. In these and similar cases, the soil remains an important ecological factor, but the ecologically significant local differences are caused by other variables, e.g. relief (site, exposure to winds, rain, sun), altitude or water conditions. Also mutual influences of adjoining kinds of land use may sometimes be of particular interest (SCHREIBER, 1972). In terms of systems dynamics, the "key variables" of a certain tract of land are different in different regions.

These key variables depend on the kind of land and on the kinds of land utilization types which are relevant and foreseeable within an area. Climate, relief, water and soil conditions are always important ecological factors in any area, and other factors, such as geology, vegetation and artifactial elements may also be of considerable ecological importance for land use. The kinds and quantities of these factors should, therefore, always be determined in any survey of land resources. Special attention, however, should be given to those ecological factors which are determined to be "key variables".

Although it is impossible to give a general recipe for carrying out a land resources survey, some suggestions may be offered. The most comprehensive, and therefore at least in theory the best way of surveying land resources is undoubtedly the "integrated survey" which comprises a multidisciplinary inventory, producing in an integrated manner all possibly relevant data on the natural and human resources and constraints. In such a survey, all "single attributes" (ZONNEVELD, 1972), such as the ecological factors mentioned previously and a number of human factors are investigated in a manner which renders possible well-inte-

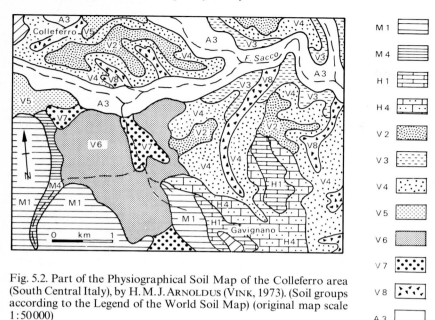

Fig. 5.2. Part of the Physiographical Soil Map of the Colleferro area (South Central Italy), by H.M.J.ARNOLDUS (VINK, 1973). (Soil groups according to the Legend of the World Soil Map) (original map scale 1:50000)

M = *Limestone Mountains*
    M 1 = Complex of lithosols and rendzinas, stony, fine-textured on steep slopes
    M 4 = Lithic rendzinas, fine-textured, on moderate slopes
H = *Hills of Schistose Sandstones*
    H 1 = Complex of sandy calcic regosols and of loamy calcic cambisols on steep slopes
    H 4 = Fine-textured chromic luvisols in colluvium with volcanic materials on gentle slopes
V = *Volcanic covers*
    V 2 = Complex of fine-textured lithosols and andosols on slightly convex plateaus
    V 3 = Complex of generally fine-textured lithosols and andosols on steep slopes
    V 4 = Complex of andosols and luvisols, medium- to fine-textured slopes
    V 5 = Complex of fine-textured luvisols and andosols on moderately steep convex slopes
    V 6 = Association of fine-textured mollic andosols and litho sols on moderately steep convex slopes
    V 7 = Complex of fine-textured andosols and luvisols in colluvium in concave depressions
    V 8 = Association of medium- to fine-textured andosols and gleysols in colluvium of valley bottoms
A = *Alluvium*
    A 3 = Association of fine-textured luvisols and cambisols in alluvium, well- to moderately well-drained

grated final results. Integration is promoted throughout the investigations by close teamwork and careful team management and by technical means such as the use of systematic interpretation of aerial photographs (REY et al., 1968). This approach may be supplemented by a more "holistic" land survey of the kind advocated by ZONNEVELD (1972) and schematically represented in Fig. 5.3, part A. Thus the single-attribute surveys provide sufficiently detailed information on those key variables which are of direct influence on land use and which may be

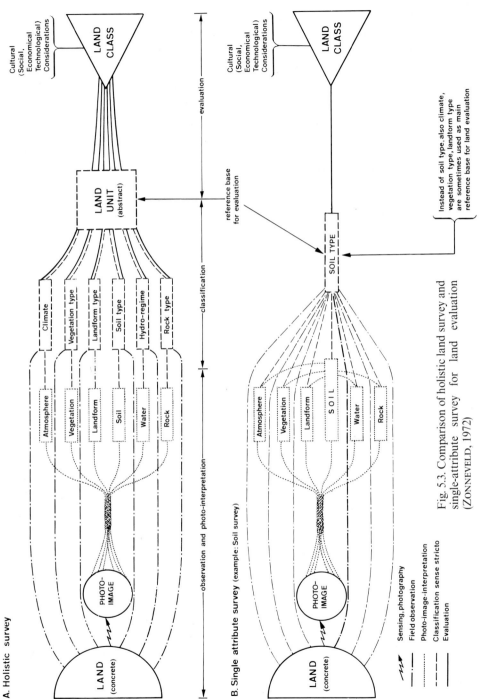

Fig. 5.3. Comparison of holistic land survey and single-attribute survey for land evaluation (ZONNEVELD, 1972)

essential for land improvement, whereas the holistic survey strengthens the knowledge of the landscape "as a whole", i.e. as an ecological complex with many interrelations among the many phenomena and processes.

Integrated Surveys and Ecological Land Surveys

An integrated survey is undoubtedly the best, because it provides all relevant information for land use planning which can be initially foreseen. Many projects for land use planning failed to give optimal results because of the lack of such comprehensive, varied information. On the other hand, it is impossible to carry out an integrated survey of a wide number of variables for each project. A more selective approach is therefore often necessary. If sufficient information on one or more aspects of the area exists, the integrated survey procedure as such may be

Table 34. Relations between planning and surveys (VINK, 1968)

Survey phase	Publishing scale of maps	Pilot projects	Planning stage	Decisions to be taken
		—	Formulating targets	
Preliminary investigations for operational outline budget	Sketch maps	—	Stock-taking and re-reformulating of targets	Choice of survey agencies; order 1st set of airphotos
Overall inventory of natural and human resources; indication of alternative devel. poss. and of priority	1:1000000 1: 250000 (sample areas + areas 1:50000)	maps plan	Drafting of alternative action programs; Plan pilot projects	Choice of survey disciplines and members 1st team
		execution	First outline of dev. plan	Choice of preferable developments and of priority areas; choice exec. agency pilot projects;
Semi-detailed surv. of selected areas	1:100000 to 1: 25000	execution		choices of survey disciplines and members 2nd team; order 2nd set of airphotos;
			Designing of plans 1st prior. dev. areas ("avant projects")	choice of first priority development areas
Detailed surveys of confirmed development areas; Technical design of projects, financial estimates	1:50000 to 1: 5000	evaluation	Second evaluation pilot projects; Implementation of confirmed projects	Confirmation of plans; choice of agencies for implementation and execution; choice of 3rd survey team and technical designing team

Execution of projects

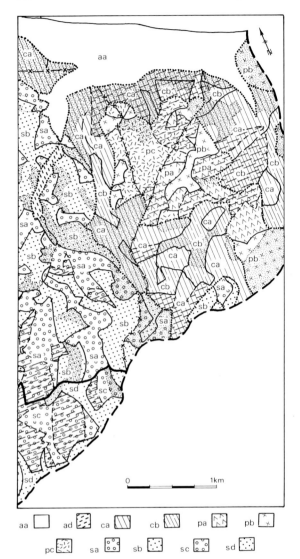

Fig. 5.4. Part of a landscape ecological map of the Montemignaio area (Central Italy) by W. Vos (VINK, 1973). (Original map scale 1:50000)

A: Alluvial landscape (less than 700 m altitude)
a)   alluvium of the Arno
a: alluvium of tributaries
C: Landscape of the clay-schists
ca: mainly accumulation (less than 700 m altitude)
cb: mainly denudation⎫
pa: and erosion   ⎬
     (less than 700 m altitude)⎭
P: Landscape of the Pietraforte (less than 700 m altitude) mainly accumulation
pl: mainly denudation/erosion
S: Landscape of the schistose sandstones
     — less than 700 m altitude:
sa: mainly accumulation
sb: mainly denudation/erosion
     — between 700 and 1000 m altitude:
sc: mainly accumulation
sd: mainly denudation/erosion
Special signs:
dashes: small local inclusions of accumulation (in denudative area) and of denudation (in accumulative areas)
points: severe erosion

streamlined, perhaps by means of a network diagram, in which the purpose of the survey and the kind of information needed are connected on the basis of existing knowledge, often supplemented by data from a reconnaissance of the area. In this manner, the investigations may be better directed and concentrated on the essential disciplines; however, some room should always be left for unforeseen needs, since no survey can be strictly directed on the basis of a network diagram. The essential feature of any resources survey is its investigation of unknown matter, and such investigations can always uncover new problems which must be solved for practical purposes of good land use planning.

    A greater efficiency may be obtained by careful consideration of the phases of land use planning and land development with regard to the kinds and detail of data which are wanted for each phase. Resources surveys and land-use planning are very interdependent. In Table 34, a general diagram of the phases and of the consequent map scales is given. This table should be read as a general outline; many parts of the procedure have an iterative nature, only part of which is indicated.

During the iterative process, as is shown in the table, a more precise choice of the survey disciplines in the different phases may be made. In this manner a high efficiency is reached without omitting the essential investigations with the appropriate amount of detail.

During the last years, for some purposes and within regions with typical characteristics, semi-detailed and detailed landscape ecological surveys, carried out by ecologists or geographers with a sufficiently extensive knowledge of the essential resources for land use in a given area, have been performed with some success. Examples are the surveys published by SCHREIBER et al. (1967), HAEBERLI (1971) and lately also by VINK (1973). Part of a map made under the guidance of the latter is reproduced in Fig. 5.4. In this map altitude and slope stability are the key variables for land use which form the main part of the map legend.

Various modifications of landscape ecological and single attribute maps (e.g. soil maps) are possible in order to obtain the essential information on the basic ecological factors and on the key variables of an area with not too much effort. As was pointed out in para. 2.3, modern survey techniques, such as the use of systematic interpretation of the stereo-images of aerial photographs, are also essential for this purpose. In some cases, an initial, general selection of large areas (on map scales of 1:500000 to 1:1 million) may be made in this manner with very little field work, provided that a certain amount of basic information on landscapes, soils and land use is available. A very good example, from Zaire, has been described by MARINET (1964).

The integrated surveys carried out by the Land Research Division of the Australian C.S.I.R.O. ("Commonwealth Scientific and Industrial Research Organisation) also provide an effective means for an initial land resources inventory of developing regions. These surveys are carried out by a limited survey team, usually consisting of a geomorphologist, a soil scientist and a vegetation expert. The team, after a careful and systematic interpretation of the aerial photographs of the area to be surveyed, carries out field work on sample localities during a limited period. For transport to the sample localities extensive use is made of helicopters, e.g. Eastern New Guinea. Land use maps, vegetation maps and other single attribute maps are produced around the central product of this work, which consists of a "Land Systems Map" in which a holistic inventory of land resources is represented. The maps, produced on scales between 1:250000 and 1:1 million, provide a good first inventory for studying the resources and constraints of the land for general land use planning and for deciding on the follow-up, by more detailed investigations, in parts of the area which appear promising for land development (CHRISTIAN and STEWART. In REY et al., 1968; HAANTJENS 1965, 1968; STEWART et al., 1968) (see Fig. 5.5).

A similar system, more detailed (maps on scales 1:50000 to 1:250000) and with more precise information for project planning, has been developed by MAHLER et al. (1970) in Iran. This system has been used for original surveys as well as

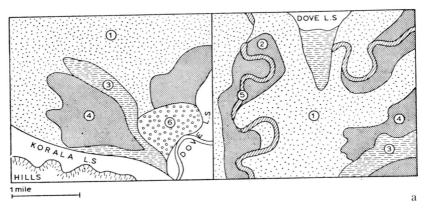

Altitude.—Just above sea level to 210 ft.

a

Land Units (19 Observations)

No.	Area (sq miles)	Land Form	Soil Group and Family	Vegetation	Land Class
1	90–110	**Prior meander tracts**	6, Ovessa dominant; 7, Safia subdominant; 7, Ubo minor	Tall alluvium forest	I, IId
2	25–35	**Terraced levees**	7, Safia dominant; 7, Ubo minor	Tall grassland and secondary forest	I, IId
3	18–28	**Back plains**	6, Ovessa	Irregular tall alluvium forest	IIIf
4	17–25	**Breakthrough splays**	7, Safia dominant; 7, Ubo minor	Tall grassland, *Timonius–Commersonia* scrub and secondary forest	I, IId
5	1–3	**Prior channels**	9, Obeia	*Pandanus* swamp woodland	VI–VIId,f
6	1–2	**High platform**	7, Embessa	Mid-height grassland	IIIs$_2$, VIs$_2$

Geology.—Recent alluvial silt overlying deltaic sand near coast and paludal clay near swamps; some alluvial gravel near Embessa.

Geomorphology.—Alluvial plains: mostly stable parts of prior Musa flood-plains. Prior meander tracts (1) up to 10 miles long and 3 miles wide have longitudinal gradients of between 1 in 500 and 1 in 1000. Down their centres prior channels (5) about 200 ft wide with steep banks 6–10 ft high are margined by terraced levees (2) ranging from 10–20 ft above the channel and 100–500 ft in width. At Embessa a high platform (6) at 190–210 ft has a gradient of 1 in 400: this and a lower platform at 100 ft are margined by prior breakthrough splays (4) up to 1 in 80 and closely channelled. The less stable portions of the land system consist mainly of channelled back plains (3) subject to occasional flooding.

Soils.—Stratified, generally silty alluvial soils, weakly acid to neutral near the surface, alkaline and calcereous in subsoil or deeper subsoil. Textures are mainly silty clay loam to silty clay over loamy fine sand to silty heavy clay (1), silty clay loam over sand to clay (2), and silty clay loam to silty heavy clay (3 and 4). The soils of the levees (2) and the breakthrough splays (4) and commonly also those of the meander tracts (1) have rather thick dark topsoils and are locally calcereous above 2 or 3 ft depth. The soils of the back plains (3) and most of those of the

meander tracts have poorly developed topsoils. Very gravelly or sandy soils with thick dark topsoil occupy the high platform (6). Strongly gleyed calcareous alkaline sands with thick dark clayey topsoils are found in the prior channels (5).

Drainage Status.—Land units 1–4 are well to imperfectly drained. The gravelly platform near Embessa (6) is excessively drained and the prior channels (5) are very poorly drained to swampy, with water-tables at 30 in. and above.

Vegetation.—Dominantly tall alluvium forest (1) with scattered high emergents up to 130–150 ft, occasionally 170 ft. The canopy, irregular, rather open to fairly dense, is at 115–130 ft. Lower storeys are irregular, generally rather dense. Palms, climbers, and buttresses are common. The imperfectly drained back plains (3) carry a poorer, slightly lower, and more irregular and open type of alluvium forest with abundant rattan and other palms. On the levee banks (2) and breakthrough splays (4) the original forest has mostly been replaced by tall grassland and secondary forest. Where burning of the grass has ceased, a rather dense scrub has developed which, given time and opportunity, may eventually revert to forest. Prior swampy Musa River channels (5) are covered with dense low small-crowned swamp woodland locally consisting of pure *Pandanus*. The high platform (6) supports mid-height grassland.

Fig. 5.5a. Legend see opposite page

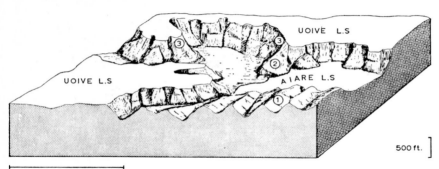

Altitude.—1000–1800 ft.

Relief.—250–600 ft.   b

No.	Area (sq miles)	Land Form	Soil Group and Family	Vegetation	Land Class
			Land Units (4 Observations)		
1	12–15	**Straight slopes 30–40°, and minor narrow crests**	6, Sisiworo, Kosi-wara; 8, Berudi; locally 18, ?Korua on narrow crests	Small-crowned hill forest; mid-slope forest and tall secondary forest and tall evergreen fan forest	VIIe,s₂, VIII
2	7–10	**Upper slopes, 40–60°**	Stony land; locally 14, Afore	Small-crowned hill forest; mid-slope forest	VIII
3	1–3	**Cliffs, 60–90°**	Stony land and rock outcrop	Small-crowned hill forest	

Geology.—Pliocene Mamama beds, flat-lying lacustrine mudstone, ash, and greywacke; overlain by andesitic ash and agglomerate, and capped by Pleistocene and Recent basalt lava flows. In the south, late Pleistocene fan-glomerate overlies the Mamama beds.

Geomorphology.—Hill ridges: of equilibrium type with shallow skeletal weathering. Predominant medium very steep straight slopes (1) either meeting in narrow sharp ridge crests (1) or leading up to medium straight precipitous upper slopes (2) and cliffs (3) up to 250 ft high.

Soils.—Very shallow undifferentiated dark brown acid to weakly acid loam to clay loam soils (1) and stony land (2,3). Locally rather shallow more weathered dark brown neutral soils; firm sandy clay to sandy clay loam (2) and very firm heavy clay with dark more friable clay topsoil approximately 10 in. thick (1). What appear to be truncated acid yellow-red clay soils occur locally in the south on narrow crests on fan deposits.

Drainage Status.—Excessively drained.

Vegetation.—Low and open hill forest, with bamboo often common, occurs in all land units, becoming very low and very open on precipitous slopes (3). To the east some deciduous trees come in. Some regrowth and secondary forest south of Toma and north of Biriri. Minor tall evergreen fan forest on gentle foot slopes of unit 1 near Bariji River.

Fig. 5.5a–c. Examples of three land systems from a CSIRO Land Systems Survey. (RUXTON et al., 1967). (a) Stable alluvial plains on coastal plain: MOMOIOGO LAND SYSTEM (175 sq miles). (b) Scarps and hill ridges adjacent to Bariji River gorge: BARIJI LAND SYSTEM (25·sq miles). (c) Hill ridges on basic-ultrabasic rocks in Sibium and Didana Ranges: FIOBOBO LAND SYSTEM (200 sq miles)

for obtaining comprehensive maps for land use planning, largely based on existing older maps, supplemented by air-photo-interpretation and additional field investigations. The way in which this system combines a sound theoretical background with a very pragmatic approach to the procuring of essential data on land conditions, makes it a promising method for use in many developing regions. It serves as an effective basis for the different stages of land evaluation.

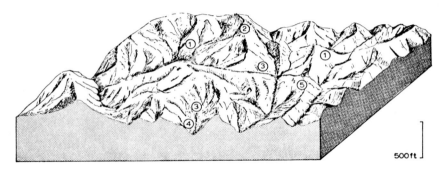

500 ft

1 mile   c

Altitude.—225–2500 ft.

Relief.—400–1000 ft.

No.	Area (sq miles)	Land Form	Soil Group and Family	Vegetation	Land Class
Land Units (11 Observations)				
1	160–170	**Straight slopes,** 30–45°	14, Didana; also 7, Avikaro; 6, Sisiworo	Small-crowned and very small-crowned hill forest; minor short grassland and scrub	VIIe,s_2, VIII
2	12–20	**Ridge crests,** 0–20°	11, Fiobobo; 8, Berudi	As unit 1; minor secondary forest	IVe,s_2,s_3, VIe,s_2
3	8–16	**Concave foot slopes,** 20–10°	14, Didana stony; stony land	Mixed deciduous hill forest	VIe,st
4	2–6	**Precipitous slopes and cliffs,** 50–90°	No data. Probably rock outcrop and lithosols	No data	VIII
5	2–4	**Broad crests,** 0–20°	17, Jare	Mid-slope forest	IIIe, VIe

Geology.—?Cretaceous Urere Metamorphic rocks, mostly hornfelsed basalt, and ?late Cretaceous or ?early Tertiary basic-ultrabasic plutonic rocks.

Geomorphology.—Hill ridges: of equilibrium type with relict weathering profiles on subaccordant crests between 1250 and 1400 ft near the Musa gorge; otherwise shallow skeletal and immature weathering. Predominant medium and long very steep straight slopes (1) meet in convex ridge crests (2) up to 100 ft wide and locally up to 600 ft wide (5) near the Musa gorge. Precipitous slopes and cliffs (4) up to 200 ft high occur adjacent to incised streams, whereas in the less-incised portions of the land system short moderate concave foot slopes (3) are common and are often boulder-mantled.

Soils.—Predominantly very shallow neutral to weakly acid soils: dark red-brown to brown gravelly clay (1) and stony clay to heavy clay (3), and un-differentiated clay soils (1). Deeper but still rather shallow weakly acid to neutral very firm to very plastic heavy clay soils with friable to firm clay

surface horizon, 6–12 in. thick, and commonly thick dark topsoil occur on many ridge crests (2) and have a thick mottled clayey C horizon. A few broad crests (6) are characterized by deep yellow-red to red weakly acid firm heavy clay soils.

Drainage Status.—Mostly excessively drained with generally well-drained foot slopes (3,4) and broad crests (6). Many crests (2) are imperfectly drained but also subject to rapid drying of the surface soil.

Vegetation.—Largely low small-crowned to very small-crowned thin-stemmed hill forest (1,2,4), very open on steepest slopes (4), locally scattered *Araucaria* and/or *Casuarina*, bamboo common. Poor and irregular mixed deciduous hill forest, with *Pometia* and *Anisoptera* common, on lower slopes bordering Musa valley (3), and here locally also small, occasionally large, areas of short grassland and scrub on steep slopes (1). Mid-slope forest to the north and north-east and locally elsewhere on deeper soils (5), *Anisoptera* common throughout.

Fig. 5.5 c. Legend see p. 143

5.4 Land Use Requirements

5.4.1 Cultural Ecosystems as Dynamic Complexes

Land Management

All agricultural land uses, and many other land utilization types as well, are in fact cultural ecosystems, i.e. open systems in which man tries to obtain his objectives by excercising human controls on the key variables within the ecosystems. As structured sets of phenomena and processes in nature, all ecosystems are dynamic complexes which are interrelated with other systems. Man can control this dynamism by careful management in the handling of his controls. On the other hand, the purpose of land use is to obtain social and economic benefits for the people who use the land. Land use is based on the available land resources and must be adapted to these resources as well as to human requirements by means of many tools—mechanical, chemical and biological—combined into management systems. Agricultural land use, furthermore, always involves the growth of specific crops and/or the breeding of specific kinds of animals. In some cases, systems of extraction of natural products (wild rubber, medicinal herbs, game cropping) may be considered agricultural land use in its widest sense.

Because of the complex nature of land use, which includes ecological and technological as well as economic and social aspects, it is difficult to find a good approach for studying it. Land utilization types, treated in Chapter 3, provide a basis for discussing some of the technological and socioeconomic aspects. Mention was also made in Chapter 1 of anthropological and institutional aspects. The crucial points which directly link the land with its use have still to be treated. These include the particular requirements of specific crops, animals and management systems and the particular resources and constraints which determine in what manner and to which degree these requirements can be met on a specific tract of land. The latter are here called "land conditions" or often "land qualities" (BEEK and BENNEMA, 1972; see also BRINKMAN and SMYTH, 1973).

Relations between Land Use Requirements and Land Management

Neither land use requirements nor specific crop requirements are absolute data: both may be modified by different systems of land management. Similarly, land conditions are often not completely fixed, but may be modified by systems of management, e.g. the application of water and/or of fertilizers, or by methods of land improvement, e.g. leaching of salts, deep plowing of soils, removal of hardpans. Our knowledge of these modifications, both of a recurrent and of a nonrecurrent, nearly permanently effective nature, although rapidly expanding, is still far from complete. Some land management systems, e.g. with minimum tillage, have only been investigated during the last few years and only under certain land conditions (see e.g. BLEVINS, 1970; BLEVINS et al., 1971).

Land improvement has booked many successes in improving land conditions in many regions of the world, but the appropriate methods of drainage and leaching, e.g. of the Mesopotamian soils of Iraq, for drain-spacing as well as for the use of tiledrainage or open drains, are still under discussion. Additional methods, either of adapting land management or land conditions or both, may be found in the near future. It is clear, however, that the interaction between these two main factors of land use is by no means clear under all circumstances. A further complication is the fact that the interactions among the factors which make up the land conditions lead to different kinds of solutions in land management and improvement.

Lack of water for plant growth may be caused either by the climate alone, or by the soil alone, or by soil and relief together, or by soil and climate together. Finding a remedy depends heavily on which aspects of the over-all land condition, "lack of water" are the causes. It also depends on the other aspects of the land, i.e. on the availability of water and on the relief as well as on the feasibility of several kinds of irrigation within one or more land utilization types. "Lack of nutrients" also shows very varied aspects. In humid temperate climates, and often also in irrigated areas, the application of manure and fertilizers is a relatively simple remedy. But even in humid temperate climates, there are instances where availability of nutrients is seriously hampered by lack of water in certain tracts of land. Both irrigation and the application of fertilizers may cause deleterious side-effects on adjoining, and sometimes even on rather distant, tracts of land.

Leaching of salts from arid lands without a proper overall system of drainage may cause increased salinity by seepage on adjoining lands. Large applications of nitrogen fertilizers may cause excesses of nitrogen in adjoining waters and in the lands influenced by them (see e.g. THOMAS, 1972; RUSSELL et al., 1972). The effect of soil erosion on adjoining lands, both by increased erosion on previously stable lands and by silting-over of lands and silting-up of reservoirs, has been known for many decades. Therefore, not only the interactions within a given tract of land but also the interactions between tracts have to be seriously considered.

Land degradation is often the result of insufficient consideration of the actual land conditions in relation to the cultural ecosystems which are, or have been, carried by the land. It may also be caused by outside influences, often unforeseen or simply neglected, on natural or seminatural ecosystems. All reasonably permanent, agricultural and other, land uses must therefore be seen also as potential causes of land degradation. If insufficient care is taken in adapting land uses, through land management and/or land improvement, to the natural and cultural ecosystems, degradation may result not only on the tract itself but on physically related lands. Tracts of land may be physically related because they are adjoining or because they are connected through transport media: air and water. It is therefore proper that a discussion of land degradation should precede treatment of land conditions themselves. The latter are among the most significant data for land evaluation (see also RAUSCHKOLB, 1971).

5.4.2 Crop Requirements

Crop Ecology

Not as much is known about the requirements of specific crops under relevant land utilization types as might be assumed from the present level of agricultural

Table 35. Consumptive use of water. Areas of different crops and consumptive use of water in Mesilla Valley Area, New Mexico, and Texas, as estimated by integration method, using different units, 1936 (ISRAELSEN and HANSEN, 1962)

Land classification	1936 area, acres	Consumptive use[a]	
		unit, feet[b]	annual acre-feet
	(a)	(c)	(ca)
Irrigated crops			
Alfalfa and clover	17077	4.0	68308
Cotton	54513	2.5	136282
Native hay and irrigated pasture	216	2.3	497
Miscellaneous crops	11117	2.0	22234
Entire irrigated area	82923	2.74	227321
Natural vegetation			
Grass	2733	2,3	6286
Brush	6733	2.5	17332
Trees-Bosque	3532	5.0	17660
Entire area	13198	3.13	41278
Miscellaneous			
Temporarily out of cropping	5569	1.5	8354
Towns	1523	2.0	3046
Water surfaces, pooled, river, and canals	4081	4.5	18364
Bare lands, roads, etc.	3124	0.7	2187
Total (entire area)	110418	2.72	300550

[a] ca = the product of unit consumptive use in feet (c) times area in acres (a).
[b] = 305 mm.

science. Perhaps the best known, more or less world-wide, requirements include some for temperature and day-length. One might also include the sensitivity of some crops to frost action, often even of short duration (night frosts). Less definite data exist for "altitude requirements" of certain crops in the equatorial regions, such as cinchona and tea. On the island of Java, cinchona is preferably grown above an altitude of 1500 m and never below 1000 m. Tea is grown preferably above 800 m and never below 250 m. Other crops, such as sugar cane, Hevea rubber and cocoa, are preferably grown below 400 m altitude, but exceptions exist; on very good soils and under a favorable climatic regime, cocoa may be grown up to 700 m altitude in some parts of Indonesia. Some observations on the growth of the olive tree in Italy have recently been made by MANCINI (1973). Some general facts about drought influences are relatively well known. Cotton is grown only in climates with a relatively long dry period, as are other crops such as varieties of coffee and sisal. For other crops, of which Hevea rubber is a good example, even an almost negligible yearly incidence of drought causes a lesser growth and decreased yield. Occasionally, some crop requirements are at least partly determined by the relative vigor of the growth of the crop in comparison with the vigor of its most common diseases.

Table 36. Soil requirements of different crops

Crop	Water requirement	Water tolerance (= air requirement)	Drought tolerance	clay/loam texture requirement
rice	high	high	low	medium
maize	low/medium	low	medium/high	low
tapioca (*Manihot sp.*)	medium	low	medium	medium
sisal	medium	medium[a]	medium	medium
rubber	high	high	low	high
coffee	medium	low	medium	low
cocoa	medium	low	medium	medium
tea	high	medium	low	low
cinchona	high	medium	low	low
teak	medium	low	medium	medium
tobacco	medium	low	medium	low
date palm	medium	low	medium	low
citrus	med,um	low	medium	medium
wheat	low/medium	low	medium	high
barley	low/medium	low	medium/high	low
oats	medium	high	low	low
rye	low	low	low/medium	low
potatoes	medium/high	medium/high	low	low
mangolds	high	high	low	low
sugar beet	high	medium	low	medium
peas (*Pisum sp.*)	medium	low	medium	medium
beans (*Vicia sp.*)	medium	low/medium[a]	low[a]	medium[a]
flax	medium	low	low	medium
cherry	medium/low	low	medium	low
apple	medium/high	low	low/medium	medium
pear	high	medium	low	low/medium

[a] To some extent depending on the variety planted.

In his *Ecologie Agricole*, PAPADAKIS (1938) includes many valuable data on crop ecology. He recognizes three main groups of crops: (1) winter crops, (2) crops of the warm summers, (3) crops of the cool summers. In the first group, which contains many small cereal crops (wheat, barley, oats, rye), special emphasis is given to wheat, leguminous crops and flax. Included in the second group, which is characterized by crops which have almost no resistance to frost, are the large cereals (maize, sorghum, millet). Rice, which properly belongs to this ecological group, is not treated, perhaps because of the complications provided by the many kinds of irrigated rice. To this group also belong such crops as "leguminous summer crops": *Phaseolus sp.*, *Vigna sp.*, and soybean; cotton is also a typical member of this group. Typical members of the third group are sugarbeet and potato. In this original book, PAPADAKIS included information on climatic requirements (see also Chapter 4) and on soil and water requirements. In a later publication PAPADAKIS (1966) classified the crops more particularly with regard to their climatic requirements. Many valuable data on the ecology of cereal growing in Europe have been published in the *Agroecological Atlas of Cereal Growing in Europe* (BROEKHUIZEN et al., 1969).

Soil structure requirement	Heavy texture tolerance	Calcium requirement	Acidity requirement	Acidity tolerance	Salinity tolerance
low	high	low	low	high	low/medium
medium	low	low	low	low	low/medium
medium	medium	medium	low	medium	low
low[a]	high[a]	medium	low	medium	medium
low	high	low	medium	medium	low
high	low	medium	low	low	low
high	low	medium	low	low	low
high	low	low	high	high	low
high	low	medium	low	medium	low
medium	high	high	low	low	low
high	low	medium	low	low	low
high	low	high	low	?	high
high	medium[a]	high	low	medium	low/medium[a]
high	medium/high	high	low	low	medium
low	medium	low	low	medium	high
low	high	low	low	high	low
low	high	low	low	high	medium
high	low	low	high	high	low
medium	high	low	low	high	medium
high	high	medium	low	medium	medium/high
high	medium	medium	low	low	low[a]
medium[a]	medium/high	medium[a]	low	low	low[a]
high	low	medium	low	low	low
medium	low/medium	low	low	medium	low
high	low	medium	low	low	low
high	medium	medium	low	low	low

Water requirements of crops grown in arid regions are important, because they determine the quantities of irrigation water needed. Some data have been mentioned previously (Table 4). Relative requirements for forest crops in the Netherlands have also been cited (Table 28). ISRAELSEN and HANSEN (1962) cited data on the consumptive use of water by crops, natural vegetation and miscellaneous land uses in New Mexico (Table 35; 1 foot = approx. 305 mm, 1 acre = 0.405 ha). Thus far, no general list of water requirements of crops in the different parts of the world exists, although some data from different parts of the world have recently been summarized (Field Book, 1972).

Soil Requirements of Crops

Specific information on soil requirements of crops is difficult to find and often vague, partly because crop specialists often tend to neglect studying the soils and soil scientists tend to neglect studying the crops. Soil information in crop handbooks is therefore often vague, and in books on soil science information on the requirements of specific crops is often completely lacking. A good review of the requirements of cocoa has been given by SMYTH (1966). As was recently noted at a

Table 37. General indications on the salt tolerance of plants (Field Book, 1972)

Species (common name)	$EC_e \times 10^3$ Millimhos/cm at 25° for yield decreases of		
	10%	25%	50%
A. Forage Crops			
Cynodon dactylon (Bermudagrass)[a]	13	16	18
Agropyron elongatum (tall wheat grass)	11	15	18
Agropyron desertorum (crested wheat grass)	6	11	18
Festuca arundinacea (tall fescue)	7	10.5	14.5
Hordeum vulgare (barley, hay)[b]	8	11	13.5
Lolium perenne (perennial rye grass)	8	10	13
Phalaris tuberosa var. *stenoptera* (Harding grass)	8	10	13
Lotus corniculatus var. *tennuifolius* (birdsfoot trefoil)	6	8	10
Elymus triticoides (beardless wild rye)	4	7	11
Medicago sativa (alfalfa)	3	5	8
Dactylis glomerata (orchard grass)	2.5	4.5	8
Alopecurus pratensis (meadow foxtail)	2	3.5	6.5
Trifolium hybridum and *Trifolium pratense* (alsike and red clovers)	2	2.5	4
B. Field Crops			
Hordeum vulgare (barley grain)[b]	12	16	18
Beta vulgaris (sugar beet)[c]	10	13	16
Gossypium hirsutum (cotton)	10	12	16
Carthamus tinctorius (safflower)	8	11	12
Triticum vulgare (wheat)[b]	7	10	14
Sorghum vulgare (sorghum)	6	9	12
Soja max (soy bean)	5.5	7	9
Sesbania macrocarpa (sesbania)[b]	4	5.5	9
Saccharum officinarum (sugar cane)	3	5	8.5
Oryza sativa (rice, paddy)	5	6	8
Zea mays (corn)	5	6	7
Vicia faba (broadbean)	3.5	4.5	6.5
Linum usitatissimum (flax)	3	4.5	6.5
Phaseolus vulgaris (field bean)	1.5	2	3.5
C. Vegetable Crops			
Beta vulgaris[c]	8	10	12
Spinacia oleracea (spinach)	5.5	7	8
Lycopersicum esculentum (tomato)	4	6.5	8
Brassica oleracea var. *italica* (broccoli)	4	6	8
Brassica oleracea var. *capitata* (cabbage)	2.5	4	7
Solanum tuberosum (potato)	2.5	4	6
Zea mays (sweet corn)	2.5	4	6
Ipomoea batatas (sweet potato)	2.5	3.5	6
Lactuca sativa (lettuce)	2	3	5
Capsicum frutescens (bell pepper)	2	3	5

[a] Average for different varieties. Suwannee and coastal Bermuda grasses are about 20% more tolerant, and common and Green field are about 20% less tolerant, than the average. For most crops varietal differences are relatively insignificant.

[b] Less tolerant during seedling stage. Salinity at this stage should not exceed 4 or 5 mmho/cm, EC_e.

[c] Sensitive during germination. Salinity should not exceed 3 mmho/cm during germination.

Table 37. (continued)

Species (common name)	$EC_e \times 10^3$ Millimhos/cm at 25° for yield decreases of		
	10%	25%	50%
Allium cepa (onion)	2	3.5	4
Daucus carota (carrots)	1.5	2.5	4
Phaseolus vulgaris (green bean)	1.5	2	3.5

D. Fruit Crops

Because woody plants are susceptible to chloride and sodium toxicity, specific salt effects as well as general salt effects must be considered. The following data are applicable when rootstocks are employed that do not accumulate Na or Cl rapidly, or when these ions do not predominate in the substrate.

These values are not so well established as those in the previous tables, and only the levels corresponding to about 10 to 20 per cent decreases in yield are indicated.

Species (common name)	$EC_e \times 10^3$ millimhos/cm 10–20% yield decreases
Phoenix dactylifera (date)	8
Punica granatum (pomegranate)	
Ficus carica (fig)	4–6 (estimated)
Olea Europaea (olive)	
Vitis spp (grape)	4
Cucumis melo (muskmelon)	3.5
Citrus paradisi (grapefruit)	3.5
Citrus sinensis (orange)	3
Citrus limonia (lemon)	2.5
Pyrus Malus (apple)	
Pyrus communis (pear)	
Pyrus armeniaca (apricot)	
Prunus domestica (plums, prunes)	all about 2.5
Prunus Amygdalus (almond)	
Prunus Persica (peach)	
Rubus spp (blackberry, boysenberry)	2.5
Rubus idaeus (red raspberry)	1.5
Poraea americana (avocado)	2
Fragaria spp (strawberry)	1.5

meeting of experts (BRINKMAN and SMYTH, 1973), "ecological requirements of individual crops and of land utilization types (should) be systematically studied". It is indeed possible that the soil data-processing programs of FAO and of other national and international agencies could be of assistance in this comprehensive work.

Apart from the book of PAPADAKIS (1938) EDELMAN (1941) provides valuable information on the "Soil Science of Crops", particularly of crops grown in the equatorial regions. He derived his information mainly from pre-war publications in Indonesia (at the time: the Netherlands East Indies). This publication contains a large amount of experimental data and of general experience on the cultivation of several crops, mainly on the islands of Java and Sumatra. The following crops are discussed: rice, sugar cane, tobacco, coffee, tea, rubber, cinchona, oil palm, sisal, sweet potatoes, coconut palm as well as the planted forest crop of teak. DE SMET (1962) gives a brief summary of requirements of some common arable crops in the Netherlands.

The complete assemblage of the existing knowledge is a task in itself. It is therefore outside the scope of this book even to make an attempt. From the present author's experience, supported by data from the preceding literature, some information on the soil requirements of some crops can, however, be given. This information is based primarily on experience in three different countries: Indonesia, Iraq and the Netherlands. This experience, which in general is descriptive and comparative rather than quantitative, is given in Table 36. It is comparable to the information on forest crops in the Netherlands given by VAN LYNDEN (1967) and mentioned in Para. 4.3.2 (see also Field Book, 1972). Only some of the more permanent soil conditions are indicated. Salinity tolerance is indicated separately in Table 37.

Less permanent conditions, such as the availability of nutrients, depend heavily on the land utilization type: in highly "industrial" land utilization types, most nutrient deficiencies can be corrected with fertilizers. In more "traditional" types, the nutrient status of the soils is important for all crops, albeit specific crops have different requirements with regard to both total quantities and ratios of the different nutrients (VINK, 1963). These differences are partly due to the different kinds of consumptive use: fruitbearing plants (e.g. cocoa), usually need more potassium whereas plants whose products are derived from vegetative growth (tea, rubber, cinchona) need relatively more nitrogen, given a certain kind of soil. There is of course no doubt that the quantities of manures and fertilizers applied are also strongly influenced by the soil conditions. Information on nutrient requirements of plants is given in Table 38. A review of trace element problems in Europe was made by RYAN et al. (1967).

5.4.3 Land Management Requirements

Animal Requirements

This paragraph emphasizes animal requirements within a given land utilization type. The degree to which animal requirements are related to the land conditions depends heavily on the intensity of the land utilization type and on the actual requirements of the management of the farm. Actual animal requirements, not directly related to management procedures, do exist, i.e. availability of particular nutrients or an excess of toxic elements. An example of the former is the incidence of selenium-deficiency for sheep in certain parts of New Zealand (LEAMY, 1966). In addition to specific soil requirements for the growth of pastoral vegetation and for their nutrient contents, specific land requirements, e.g. not-too-steep slopes for grazing, need for drinking water, also exist. The latter is closely connected with

Table 38. Plant nutrient elements in kg contained in different yields of crops (Field Book, 1972)

Crop	Yield kg per ha	Nutrients in kg per crop yield					
		N	P	K	Ca	Mg	S
Maize	3 800	106	39	78	6	6	5
Oats	1 800	34	7	9	2	3	4
Wheat	2 000	56	22	34	10	4	4
Rice (paddy)	5 300	92	19	119	24	12	—
Rice grain	3 200	70	7.5	10.8	—	—	—
straw	5 500	21	2.6	48.1	—	—	—
total	8 700	91	10.1	58.9	—	—	—
Soybeans	1 700	140	45	67	5	5	4
Groundnuts	1 500	105	6.6	34.9	19.2	12.8	
Potatoes	20 200	140	39	190	3	7	6
Sweet potatoes	15 000	70	8.8	91.3			
Cassave	25 000	161	17.2	112.9	44.0	18.5	
Sugar beets, roots	35 000	145	45	195.0	68	42	18
leaves	23 000						
Sugar cane	25 000	30	20	60			
Cotton seed	1 100						
lint	600	73	28	56	8	6	3
Alfalfa	6 700	157	39	151	136	17	18
Red clover	4 500	90	22	78	68	17	7
Hay (mixed)	5 000	85	35	90	48	21	15
Tomatoes	22 300	112	39	196	17	20	22
Cabbage	33 600	112	28	121	49	11	78
Tobacco	1 700	90	22	129	67	10	4
Coffee (fresh berries)	5 000	35	3	35			
Oil palm (bunches)	15 000	90	8.8	10	2.1		
Coconut (nut)	1 500	13	1.8	10	4.2		

Data from: V. IGNATIEFF and H. J. PAGE; Efficient use of fertilizers 1968, and other sources. The average nutrient content of crops in percentage can be found as follows: For instance 70 kg N per 3200 kg rice is equivalent to 2.19 kg N per 100 kg of grain or 2.19% N; 21 kg per 5500 kg straw is eq. to 0.38 kg N per 100 kg of straw or 0.38% N.

farm management procedures within a specific land utilization type. A good study of grazing capacity of lands in Ireland has recently been made by LEE and DIAMOND (1972).

Land Management Constraints

Land management requirements, which include farm management requirements, can be but poorly described in general terms. The easiest manner is often to indicate the limitations to management which are imposed as constraints on a specific land utilization type by certain land conditions. Some general indications and some specific cases can, however, be given.

Distinct differences exist among land management requirements of several main groups of land utilization types: a) pastoral types, b) arable land types, c) types with perennial crops, d) irrigated types. These broad groups can be even further differentiated into range-grazing pastoral types and barn-feeding kinds of pastoral land use, and into irrigated agriculture with gravity irrigation and sprinkler- or trickle-irrigation, respectively. In range-grazing the availability of drinking water at many points, dispersed over the range, is a major consideration for land management (e.g. to avoid local overgrazing), but slopes may be fairly steep as long as the cattle can graze on them without hazards of erosion. In types with barn-fed cattle, water poses much less of a problem, but the slopes have a certain maximum imposed by the mechanical harvesting methods of the fodder. In gravity irrigation, only fields with nearly flat surfaces and smooth and gentle slopes can be used, whereas in sprinkler- and trickle-irrigation much steeper slopes, provided they have sufficiently permeable soils, can be used.

Farm Mechanization

There is also a difference between comparable land uses with or without extensive farm mechanization. Highly mechanized, industrial systems of agriculture need a land pattern with homogeneous surfaces to facilitate efficient land use, whereas in smaller, traditional types of land use this requirement is much less important. Mechanization of tillage, of course, raises specific soil conservation problems, which are also closely related to the climate, the land forms and the soils. Mechanization of the application of pesticides poses different problems. In lands with dissected relief, the use of aerial applications poses great problems, but the use of motor-sprayers and motor-dusters also involves consideration of several factors, i.e., the movement of vehicles to and through the plantations, e.g. of tea or rubber, as well as the local climatic conditions: air-convection of sprays and dusts. Mechanization of harvests involves different problems which depend primarily on the kind of crop to be harvested. Root crops cannot be harvested from too heavy soils, peas for canning are harvested with machines which allow only for a certain maximum clay content of the soils. The more complicated systems of mechanized harvesting can only be carried out on flat to nearly flat or gently sloping surfaces.

Mechanization of the transportation of harvested products from field to farm is often a major consideration. Flat or gently sloping areas are undoubtedly the easiest and the cheapest in this respect. The marginal conditions of relief and soils, in the engineering sense (construction and maintenance of roads and bridges) are to some extent determined by the bulk and the value of the product to be transported. Rather valuable products such as tea, coffee or cocoa can be transported feasibly over much larger distances, and over much more dissected terrain to the processing plant than fairly cheap products such as sisal or rubber.

The requirements for mechanized rice cultivation in Surinam have been studied in somewhat more detail. Pons (1972) gives the following information on the requirements for crop growth and farm management:

"Organic matter content in the topsoil should not be high and there should be no peat layers in or on the soil. The latter would cause difficulties during puddling or irrigation; the former may cause unwanted temporary nutrient imbalance. Both would decrease bearing capacities.

"Permeability should be medium, especially of the subsoil. With high permeabilities too much water is lost to the subsoil and maintenance of water levels in adjoining plots under different irrigation management is difficult or impossible. Low permeabilities would cause difficulties for plant growth, even for rice, difficulties in irrigation management during the different stages of rice growth and harvest, and difficulties during plowing and seedbed preparation.

"Structural stability should be as high as possible. A low stability of the soil structure would cause impermeability of the top soil, resulting in damage to the rice plant by toxic compounds. High structural stability maintains permeability of the top soil during irrigation and prevents migration of fine soil components to the subsoil which would clog the pores below the plow layer and would make the subsoil impermeable.

"Chemical conditions for plant growth should be adequate. The soil reaction should be neither too low nor too high; sufficient availability of nutrients is needed; and salinity should not exceed a certain level."

Obtaining Information on Requirements

In most cases, the requirements of a specific land utilization type are taken for granted and are only stated implicitly in the discussions on land conditions, land qualities or land suitability. Experimental results on the responses of certain crops to certain kinds of management on specific soils may in fact be used to derive more quantitative information on the requirements. The development of a more systematic approach to land use requirements would, however, provide a great advantage for critical studies on the subject.

Once a certain type of land use is sufficiently well known to the investigator, the drafting of its land management requirements is often a rather simple matter of common sense combined with a systematic approach. This is certainly true in all cases where conditions are relatively favorable or where clear differences can be seen among various kinds of natural land resources and their constraints. The difficulty lies in the marginal cases, i.e., whether a certain tract of land, given certain over-all conditions, still meets the requirements of a certain land utilization type or not. In each given case, the complex economic, ecological and technological inter-relationships indicated in the foregoing paragraphs come into play. It is therefore often very difficult to give general rules or to provide general criteria.

The problem of land use requirements, which will repeatedly appear in the rest of this book, has no easy solution. Local and regional solutions, and the circumstances under which they were found, will have to be carefully studied and compared in order to systematize our knowledge and experience in this field.

5.4.4 Crop Responses to Management: Land Productivity

Given a certain climate, farm management, particularly the management of the land and of the crops themselves, is the most decisive influence on plant production. The scope of this book does not allow for a complete treatment of this subject matter, as is understandable in view of the whole libraries and several many-volume textbooks that have been written about this field. Moreover, the

yearly output of publications on the techniques of plant and animal production
by research institutions around the world is so large that even a review of the
output in a single year would fill a good-sized book. Of more concern for us are
the direct relations between the land resources and the responses of crops to
different kinds and quantities of management.

Relations between Land Conditions and Crop Responses

Several authors, foremost among whom is CH. E. KELLOGG (1961), have mentioned that, particularly in the highly industrialized land utilization types, the

Table 39. Effects of the applications of chemical fertilizers (N, P, and
K in optimal quantities for each kind of soil) for tea growing on
three different soils in Java (Indonesia), (VINK, 1963a)

Soil	Yield without fertilizers (kg/ha)	Percentage yield increase with optimal fertilizers	Yield increase in kg/ha
1	2000	60%	1200
2	1400	70%	1000
3	1000	50%	500

Table 40. Relative data on the effectiveness of complete mineral fertilizers (NPK) on
different soils of the USSR (TYURIN and SOKOLOV, 1958)

Soils	Yield relationships			Yield increases	
	unferti-lized	NPK 0.45 cwt/ hectare	NPK 1.2 cwt/ hectare	NPK 0.45 cwt/ha	NPK 1.2 cwt/ha
Podzolic loams	100	150	212	50	112
Gray forest loams	105	150	210	45	110
Degraded and leached chernozems	118	152	231	34	113
Thick chernozems	150	163	214	13	64
Common chernozems	143	164	218	21	75
Precaucasian chernozems	103	137	152	34	49

Table 41. Yield-ratings of hop monoculture; experiments
1944–1948 (RID, 1958)

	Quantity of fertilizers applied			Yields
	N	P	K	1944–1948
Brownearth	100	100	100	100
Pseudogley soil	154	122	158	116

different responses to management of crops grown on different soils form perhaps the most crucial aspect of the natural variability of soils. Several examples of this were given in an earlier publication (VINK, 1963a), one of them being reproduced in Table 39 (see also VAN DAM, 1973). Similar results can be found in a number of other publications. Some interesting data published by TYURIN and SOKOLOV (1958) are given in Table 40. Results on hop-production and some interesting data from pot experiments with several different soils are given in Table 41 and 42. In Tables 43 to 48 (cited from JACKS, 1967) data on nutrient uptake and crop yields in different soils are demonstrated.

Table 42. Results of fertilizer experiments on some different soils in Germany as found in a pot experiment over a period of twenty years (DÖRR, 1958)

| | Yield-ratings | | |
	mineral fertilizers	stable manure	straw + nitrogen
Browned rendzina Mesotrophic brown-earth	100	100	100
Brownearth with moderate base saturation	91	87	88
Brownearth with "pseudogley"	87	82	83
Rendzina in "Muschelkalk"	87	80	82
Pelosol (litholic soil, clay)	85	78	83

Table 43. Soil types and total mineral status of plants by development phases (% of dry matter) in the USSR (TSERLING et al. in JACKS et al., 1967)

| Plant | Phases | Soil type | Mineral status plant | | |
			N	P_2O_2	K_2O
Winter wheat	Tillering	Derno-podzolic	3.0–4.4	0.7–1.4	4.0–6.5
		Chernozem	3.7–4.5	0.9–1.0	3.4–5.9
	Embryo ear formation	Derno-podzolic	1.2–2.0	0.5–1.2	2.8–4.5
		Chernozem	1.4–2.1	0.5–0.8	2.2–2.4
Winter rye	Heading stage	Derno-podzolic	0.8–1.4	0.4–0.6	2.1–2.4
		Chernozem	0.8–1.5	0.4–0.6	2.1–2.6
	Ripening	Derno-podzolic	0.6–0.9	0.4–0.6	1.0–1.2
		Chenozem	0.7–1.3	0.4–0.5	0.8–1.3
Spring barley	Tillering	Derno-podzolic	3.6–4.3	0.7–1.0	5.4–6.0
		Chernozem	3.4–3.6	1.1–1.2	4.1–4.4
	Embryo ear formation	Derno-podzolic	1.1–1.4	0.6–0.7	2.3–2.4
		Chernozem	1.2–1.3	0.6–0.7	1.7–2.1
	Ripening	Derno-podzolic	0.8–1.1	0.4	1.1–1.4
		Chernozem	1.0–1.1	0.6–0.7	1.0–1.3

Table 44. Data of biological productivity of farm crops in the USSR. (PERSHINA. In JACKS et al., 1967)

Profile section	Soil	Crop	Annual litterfall contribution of soil, cent/ha				Litterfall contribution %		
			Total of dry biomass, cent/ha	above ground mass	roots	total	Litter-fall % of biomass	above-ground mass	roots
19	Light chestnut heavy loamy	Summer wheat Saratov 29	62	8	4	12	19	66	34
20	Dark chestnut heavy loamy	Summer wheat Eritr. 841	80	17	5	22	28	70	30
20	Dark chestnut heavy loamy	Maize VIR-42	11	23	15	38	34	60	40
19	Light chestnut heavy loamy	Maize VIR-42	68	8	10	18	26	44	56

Table 45. Productivity (wheat q/ha) of sub-group profiles in Saskatchewan (Each value is the average of 10 experiments for the years 1958–63 inclusive) (RENNIE and CLAYTON. In: JACKS et al., 1967)

| Treatment | Sub-group profile | | | | |
| | Chernozemic order | | | Humic eluviated gleysol | (P = 0.05) |
	Calcareous	Orthic	Eluviated		
Check	13.4 ± 6.6[b]	15.8 ± 6.8	14.2 ± 7.2	16.2 ± 7.5	1.2
Inc. I[a]	3.0 ± 2.7	4.6 ± 2.9	5.2 ± 2.7	6.7 ± 1.5	0.5
Inc. II	3.1 ± 3.0	6.0 ± 2.9	5.6 ± 3.1	9.9 ± 2.5	0.4

[a] Increase in yield over check for $NH_4H_2PO_4$ applied at 19.7, and II 19.4 kg P/ha.
[b] Standard deviation.

Table 46. Yield of wheat (q/ha) grown on four sub-group profile types in Saskatchewan (RENNIE and CLAYTON. In: JACKS et al., 1967)

| Soil association | Year | Treatment | Sub-group profile | | | |
| | | | Chernozemic order | | | Humic eluviated gleysol |
			Calcareous	Orthic	Eluviated	
Weyburn	1960	Check	18.9	18.2	15.7	26.1
		Fert.[a]	24.8	22.2	25.9	34.7
	1962	Check	6.4	8.2	5.4	7.5
		Fert.[a]	9.2	10.0	8.1	12.1
Oxbow	1958	Check	10.6	20.6	11.9	6.9
		Fert.[a]	16.6	30.4	21.8	10.2
	1960	Check	20.0	33.4	26.1	16.4
		Fert.[a]	24.8	36.6	31.8	22.8

[a] 9.7 kg P/ha as $NH_4H_2PO_4$.

Table 47. Effect of selected physical factors on wheat yields in Saskatchewan (RENNIE and CLAYTON. In: JACKS et al., 1967)

Factors	Maximum effects (q/ha)
I Zonal Climate and Soil	6.9
II Soil Texture	5.5
III Kind of profile	4.4
IV Topography	1.8

Table 48. Relationship between yield and the moisture profile for four sub-group profile types in Saskatchewan (Average values for all treatments for the 1960–63 period) (RENNIE and CLAYTON. In: JACKS et al., 1967)

Sub-group profile		cm of available water				
		120-cm profile (spring)	120-cm profile plus p.p.tn.	Water used by crop	Yield q/ha	E.T.R.[+]
Cherno-zemic Order	Calcareous	6.68	20.68	21.77	14.6	1490
	Orthic	7.80	21.72	21.51	17.2	1250
	Eluviated	11.30	25.30	23.62	17.6	1340
	Humic Eluviated Gleysol	12.65	26.85	25.98	19.3	1350
	L.S.D. (P=0.05)	0.91	—	1.15	1.1	70

Table 49. Net benefit (expressed as percentage of the expected gross income) from drainage improvement in certain soil classes in the Netherlands (A Priority Scheme, 1960)

Soil class	Winter groundwater level below surface	
	0–20 cm	20–40 cm
Marine clay	25	10
River clay	20	5
Peaty soils	25	0
Sandy soils	20	0

Responses of crops to land management involve many different factors. In the older investigations, after fertilizer applications, attention was paid to the drainage and irrigation. Data on these factors were sometimes derived from experiments, but often only one kind of soil was investigated and therefore no statements on the differences of responses on different lands could be made. Comparative data on responses to drainage and irrigation are often derived from empirical and comparative investigations; for this reason, they are often expressed in a less quantitative manner. Nevertheless, they are of significance for land use. Information on the effect of drainage in the Netherlands (A Priority Scheme, 1960) and of irrigation in New Zealand (LEAMY, 1962) is given respectively in Tables 49 and 50. The results of experiments on soil productivity of German soils with different water conditions were published by ARENS, KRÄMER and LANGNER (1958), see also SCHLICHTING and SCHWERTMANN (1972). Some data on crop responses to desalinization are given in Fig. 5.6 and Table 51.

Table 50. Characteristics of selected soils from each climate zone, their rating under dryland and irrigation farming, and the potential benefit of irrigation to them (LEAMY, 1962)

Soil name and classification	Characteristics affecting land use	Dryland suitability for agriculture		Irrigation suitability for agriculture		Potential benefit of irrigation	Climate
		Index	Rating	Index	Rating		
Waenga fine sandy loam. Very weakly developed	Deep, fine textured, very slight soluble salt accumulation, high nutrient status, moderately well drained	28	low	71	high	very high	Semiarid
Molyneux very shallow loamy sand. Weakly developed *Sitic* soil	Very shallow, coarse textured, low nutrient status, subject to wind erosion	10	very low	22	low	low	Semiarid
Pigburn silt loam. Very weakly developed *Pallic* soil	Deep, fine textured, no subsoil impediments; high nutrient status, moderately well drained	52	moderate	86	very high	high	Subhumid
Queenberry very shallow sandy loam. Weakly developed CO-*Pallic Fulvic* soil	Very shallow, coarse textured, low nutrient status, subject to wind erosion	14	very low	24	low	low	Subhumid
Maungawera silt loam. Very weakly developed *Fulvic* soil	Deep, fine textured, high nutrient status, moderately well drained, no subsoil impediments	69	high	87	very high	low	Subhumid to humid
Dublin very shallow fine sandy loam. Weakly developed *Fulvic* soil	Very shallow, very low nutrient status, subject to wind erosion, very uneven microrelief	15	very low	19	very low	very low	Subhumid to humid

Table 51. Relation between electrical conductivity, Cl⁻ and Na⁺ and yield of Berseem clover (ELGABALY. In: Salinity Seminar, 1971)

Salinity conditions	Depth	E.C. × 10^3 mmhos/cm	Cl⁻	Na⁺	Cutting	Yield dry weight g/cm²
Saline	1st foot	9.4	87.0	70.8	1st	39.8
throughout	2nd foot	8.2	78.0	67.0	2nd	163.7
	3rd foot	8.4	86.3	56.7	3rd	154.7
						358.2
Saline in 2nd	1st foot	3.5	34.9	25.5	1st	136.7
and 3rd feet	2nd foot	7.6	83.9	54.5	2nd	244.6
	3rd foot	7.7	85.3	64.6	3rd	228.3
						609.6
Saline in	1st foot	1.4	13.5	13.8	1st	228.7
3rd foot	2nd foot	5.7	33.8	53.1	2nd	317.5
	3rd foot	6.9	66.0	65.0	3rd	282.0
						828.2
Non saline	1st foot	1.4	5.3	11.5	1st	225.2
	2nd foot	2.2	11.4	20.5	2nd	274.9
	3rd foot	2.1	5.1	18.9	3rd	443.5
						943.6

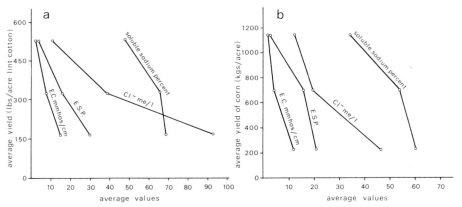

Fig. 5.6a and b. Effects of EC, ESP, Cl⁻, and SSP on yields of cotton (a) and corn (b) (ELGABALY. In: Salinity Seminar, 1971)

Variability of Crop Responses

Crop responses to management are in general discussed as average figures. Their variability is, however, often characteristic of differences in responses to different soils and of the resulting differences in optimum management. This variability, measured over a number of years, gives an indication of the risk run with a certain crop on a certain soil due to the normal variability of the local climate. It also is

Table 52. Yield variations of rye on 7 soil types in the Netherlands during three consecutive years (after VINK, 1963a)

Percentages of yields considered good (more than 3200 kg per ha per year), normal (2500 to 3200 kg/ha/year) and poor (less than 2500/kg/year)

Soil type	good	normal	poor
Q = deeply humic loamy sand	27	57	16
B = deeply humic sand	6	71	23
H = podzol in sand (excessively drained)	8	37	55
M = podzol in sand (well drained)	13	66	21
L = hydromorphic soil in sand (poorly drained)	33	50	17
A = acid brown soil in loamy sand (well drained)	29	47	24
S = regosol in sand (excessively drained)	3	42	55

influenced by the sensitivity differences of the different soils to the manner in which and the time at which a farmer executes his operations. No farmer can know what weather conditions will prevail two or more days after his operations. For example, a soil with a low structural stability may be strongly influenced by the incidence of rain within a week after tillage. Some soils, therefore, are very variable, which makes them climatically hazardous (e.g. due to low water retention) and often also very sensitive to land management operations (e.g. due to low structural stability). In Table 52 (after VINK, 1963a) the variability of arable land soils in a sandy area of the Netherlands is given; these figures result from trial harvests in large numbers during the years 1950 to 1952, which showed a lower climatic variability than is normal in this region.

Even from these figures, one can see a considerable difference in variability in the different soils with such a relatively insensitive crop as rye. Due to the great yield hazards on such soil types as H and S, the crop responses to management are only satisfactory in less than 50% of the cases, which results in less intensive management on these soil types for most farms.

Soil Productivity

The study of the responses to management of different crops in different soils has been for many years the object of attention of many persons and institutions in the United States. Responses to management are often, in fact, the most directly applicable characteristics of soils in well-established, relatively stable industrial systems of land use. The U.S. Soil Survey has included tables in its County Soil Survey Reports, indicating the productivity of soils under two or more management classes. An example is given in Table 53.

KELLOGG (1961) describes "soil productivity" as "that quality of a soil that summarizes its potential for producing specified plants or sequences of plants under defined sets of management practices. It is measured in terms of outputs in relation to inputs for a specific kind of soil under physically defined systems of management". It is therefore a physical soil condition which is largely dependent on the response of the plants to different soil management operations. Some of the earliest quantitative work on soil productivity was carried out by R. T. ODELL and

Table 53. Some data on yields of corn and wheat under different management conditions in La Porte County, Indiana, USA (after ULRICH et al., 1944); management classes A and B

Soil mapping units	Yields of corn (100 = 50 bushels) management class		Yields of wheat (100 = 25 bushels) management class	
	A	B	A	B
Toledo silty clay, dr.	90	100	80	100
Carlisle muck, drained	40	100	—	—
Griffin Loam (pr. and dr.)	80	90	40	60
Hanna loam (drained)	50	80	50	80
Willvale loam (drained)	40	70	40	80
Tracy loam, eroded phase	10	40	30	50

his co-workers (RUST and ODELL, 1957). In the same years, some interesting publications summarizing soil productivity in several parts of the U.S.A. appeared (SHRADER et al., 1960; AANDAHL et al., 1965; BARTELLI et al., 1966). Some general considerations on the interpretation of "soil characteristics important in soil management" were published by KRANTZ (1957). In the latter publication, the following thoughts are expressed (see also AANDAHL, 1957): during the first decades of the soil survey, great emphasis was placed upon the native fertility level of the soil; productivity ratings, based on the soil's native ability to produce, were developed. With the increasing application of soil management and technology, crop yield potentials were greatly increased by fertilization and other improved practices, but in particular by irrigation of the desert soils of the Western United States. A better knowledge of the response to management became, therefore, highly desirable. In the later decades, farmers have learned to aim at the highest economic yield-potential by applying the best-known combination of management practices; on many soils, several alternative combinations have been found to be applicable. This approach had also a marked influence on the study of the soil components and the soil characteristics themselves, leading to investigations on the nature of clay-minerals, to better determinations of the stability of soil structures and to more thorough investigations on the nature of the subsoil. The latter were stimulated particularly by the large land-levelling operations carried out for the establishment of irrigation projects. Subsequently, investigations on soil salinity and on the quality of irrigation water were carried out.

More or less parallel to this, soil conservation experts and institutions carried out research on land management in relation to soil erodibility. The work carried out by several research workers at the experiment station of Coshocton (Ohio) provides a good example of this work (HARROLD, 1962). Here, the emphasis was on increased soil conservation rather than on optimalizing economic yields, but in their practical applications in most parts of the United States, the two schools of thought were applied jointly.

During the last years, new economic developments as well as new developments in science and technology have led to many kinds of investigations in soil and crop management. The research on "no-tillage farming" is cited here as a typical example. Table 54 contains data on these investigations. It was also found

Table 54. A comparison of corn yields on six different soils using no-tillage vs. conventional tillage methods during 1969 (BLEVINS et al., 1971)

Soil	Soil texture	Soil slope	Parent material	Corn yield bu./Ac.	
				No-tillage	conventional
Crider	silt loam	3%	loess over limestone	143	128
Donerail[a]	silt loam	3%	phosphatic limestone	136	117
Faywood	silty clay loam	7%	limestone	132	133
Grenada	silt loam	2%	loess over acid sandstone and shale	104	104
Loradale[a]	silt loam	6%	phosphatic limestone	130	110
Lowell	silt loam	8%	limestone	149	132
			Average	132	121

[a] Data from S. H. PHILLIPS' experimental plots in Woodford and Fayette Counties.

that under specified conditions in Kentucky on Donerail silt loam, "no-tillage treatments had higher volumetric moisture contents to a depth of 60 cm during most of the growing season" for a corn crop (BLEVINS et al., 1971).

The advances of agricultural science, often combined with and sometimes induced by changes in economic conditions, have in other parts of the world also produced a large number of interesting data on responses of crops grown in many different soils to new kinds of management. Of particular importance are investigations on grassland management (WIELING, 1971) and on the mechanisms and effects of different kinds of tillage, including minimum-tillage and zero-tillage (KUIPERS et al., 1970; KOUWENHOVEN and TERPSTRA, 1972). The responses of crops in different soils to irrigation with relatively saline water have become important for many arid and semi-arid countries, such as Tunisia; investigations of this situation, under the aegis of the United Nations Development Program (UNDP) and largely sponsored by UNESCO, have led to some very interesting results (UNESCO/UNDP, 1070; VAN'T LEVEN and HADDAD, 1967). Recently, a very interesting book has been published, showing results from Israel (YARON, DANFORS and VAADIA, 1973); in this book, special emphasis is given to consumptive use of crops, to the timing of irrigation and to the three main irrigation systems: flood (basin or furrow) irrigation, sprinkler irrigation and trickle irrigation.

Special Crops

The responses of horticultural crops to soil and land management have for a long time merited special attention, mainly because these crops, often grown for their quality, need special care. This care can often be applied economically because of the relatively high prices of the harvested products. In Table 55 (after VAN DAM, 1967) some production costs of several horticultural crops in the Netherlands are demonstrated (see also VAN DAM, 1973). Extra care may also lead to earlier maturity which in itself often results in higher market prices. Special investigations have been carried out on several crops in Belgium and the Netherlands, e.g.

on asparagus (VAN NERUM and PALASTHY, 1966; VAN DAM, 1967, 1973; REIJMER-
INK, 1973). Studies of other crops such as apples (BAEYENS et al., 1964; VAN DAM,
1973) and strawberries (VAN DER BOON, 1967) have provided interesting data.
Data on root development of asparagus, which shows a high correlation with
yields, on shallow- and deep-reworked soils in the Netherlands are given in
Table 56. Extensive investigations have been carried out on the land management
for hothouse tomatoes, data on the influence of ground-water levels on the times
of ripening and on the yields of hothouse tomatoes being given in Table 57. This
crop exemplifies the fact that one must consider the complete management of the

Table 55. Some data on production costs of horticultural crops in the Netherlands
(after VAN DAM, 1967)

Crop	Production cost in Hfl./ha (in 1964)
Carnations in hothouse	—f 200000.—
Crop-sequence of Cucumbers and Lettuce in heavily heated hothouses	—f 150000.—
Crop-sequence of Tomatoes and Lettuce in heavily heated hothouses	—f 120000.—
Hyacinths (Bulbfields)	—f 30000.—
Apples	—f 8000.—
Asparagus	—f 5000.—
Brussels Sprouts	—f 4000.—

Table 56. Rooting of asparagus in shallow- and deep-reworked
soils (REIJMERINK, 1973)

Soil	Number of lateral roots	
	shallow-reworked	deep-reworked
Brown plaggept	1699	1783
Psamment	1819	1170
Aquod	1455	1329

N.B. Deep reworking together with subsoil manuring may give
other results; experiments are still in progress.

Table 57. Influence of groundwater level on the "earliness" of
the harvest and on the total yields of hothouse tomatoes,
1960/1964 (VAN DAM, 1967)

Lowest groundwater-level in cm[a] below surface	Number of experimental plots			
	early	late	high yields	low yields
less than 80 (129)	69	60	67	62
80–120 (166)	78	88	86	80
more than 120 (45)	23	22	17	28

[a] Between brackets the total number of plots in each group
respectively.

ecological systems in order to obtain the best results, i.e. a good yield at an early date. Careful manipulation of soil and hothouse climate together with the groundwater conditions provides several alternative solutions, provided that the soil conditions within a hothouse are homogeneous, so that a certain set of operations may be used for the whole (VAN DAM, 1967, 1973).

In an earlier publication (VINK, 1968) and in Para. 3.2, an example was given of the fact that also in other land utilization types, a change in one aspect of crop management may affect crop and soil management as a whole, e.g. tea growing in Java (Indonesia). Tea had been grown on plantations in Jave since the last decades of the 19th century. Several relatively advanced techniques had been introduced in the management system. Around 1950 the "blisterblight" fungus disease (Exobasidium vexans) was transported by aircraft from India where it had always been endemic without doing great damage owing to the local climate. This fungus produces blisters on leaves and young shoots and in this manner may prevent all growth of the tea bushes. At the time of introduction of the disease in Java, the wages for plantation labor also increased considerably. These two factors produced changes which could only be managed by introducing a whole set of technological advances which only then were becoming available on an operational scale: chemicals and implements. The shade trees had to be cut to change the microclimate, thus making it less favorable for the development of the fungus on young leaves and shoots; this led to the need for application of more nitrogen fertilizers and more insecticides to combat the other serious pest of tea growing: the tea-fly (Helopeltis sp.). Soil response to these operations differed considerably: on the best soils results were excellent, so that the increased yields paid for all new operations and still left an extra margin of profits, but on some of the poorer soils, tea growing deteriorated rapidly. Areas with excellent soils, but with strongly dissected relief had to be taken out of production because of difficulties in transportation and in access for combating pests. Studies of soils and relief had to be made for planning more dense plantation road systems. Detailed climatic and topoclimatic studies were undertaken (sunshine hours, precipitation frequence, wind direction) for planning accurate and efficient procedures for pest control and crop management. Tea factories had to be adapted to curing the different kinds of leaves, produced by the different harvesting systems (shorter picking rounds) which had to be introduced, in order to continue to fulfill the requirements of the export markets. Technical skills of the managers and of all their personnel at various grades had to be increased.

Theoretical Considerations

In recent years, a new stimulus to better theoretical considerations on crop and land management has been given by the work of C.T. DE WIT and his co-workers (DE WIT, 1966; VAN ITTERSUM, 1971; see also Para. 1.3). These scientists calculate the potential yields of different crops on the basis of the photosynthetic process, which is the determining process for crop growth and yields. Photosynthesis is, in its potential, determined by amount of sun-energy which reaches the plants. On a world scale, this amount is a function of the geographic latitude. On this basis VAN ITTERSUM (1971) calculated the potential yields of three rice varieties. Although these production figures have thus far seldom been realized, the order of magnitude has been obtained under special conditions at the Indian Rice Research Institute: 23 tons per hectare per year in continuous cropping experiments. The value of these calculations for judging conditions of crop ecology, including land resources and soil and crop management, lies in the fact that more definite normative figures for the theoretically reachable level are being obtained. Limitations for a specific variety at a given geographic latitude lie partly in management and partly in land conditions, but also in their mutual interaction and in their interaction with socio-economic conditions in the widest sense. Research in this area remains as difficult as ever, but at least more precise information concerning the goal to be reached or at least approximated, has been obtained.

5.4.5 Land Degradation

A Comprehensive Approach

In 1971, for the preparation of the United Nations Conference on the Human Environment, held at Stockholm in 1972, the Food and Agricultural Organization of the United Nations (FAO) published a paper on land degradation (RAUSCHKOLB, 1971). The approach used in this paper covers a conglomerate of subjects which have thus far been treated under separate names such as "soil erosion", "soil conservation", "soil salinization" and "soil pollution". The comprehensive approach is advantageous because it clears the way for a manysided discussion on all aspects related to misuse of the land. It does not invalidate the older approaches, particularly the "soil conservation" approach introduced by H. H. BENNETT and extensively described in his well-known book (BENNETT, 1939). In fact, soil conservation is as urgent today as it was 35 years ago (see also HUDSON, 1971). However, the interactions among all land uses, rural as well as urban, can be viewed more comprehensively if they are grouped together as land degradation. Agricultural land use is influenced by and has influence upon other land uses. The interactions in both directions are considered of special importance today.

Land degradation, as discussed by RAUSCHKOLB (1971), consists of the following:
— Category I: erosion and sedimentation, salts and alkali, organic waste and infectious organisms;
— Category II: industrial inorganic wastes, pesticides, radioactivity and heavy metals;
— Category III: fertilizers and detergents.

These categories, according to RAUSCHKOLB, indicate differences in order of magnitude of the kinds of degradation as well as priorities for their handling. According to this line of thought, "the causes of land degradation of the first category will require immediate application of available technology and the development of new technology to prevent degradation reaching a state of emergency". The causes of land degradation in the second category would "represent a lower order of magnitude in importance because of their lesser extent, intensity or rate of increase". Category III would then contain "those causes of degradation which are of lowest priority". They would "constitute no widespread immediate hazards to soil" nor would there be "numerous isolated areas requiring attention".

To understand these statements, one should see them in their proper perspective. The intention of this first inventory on short notice, was to provide an overall view of the world situation. Furthermore, and very understandably, the problems of the developing regions of the world were emphasized. Since these regions cover at least half of the world's land surface, there is much to be said for such an approach in a broad first inventory. As was stated by Dr. EDOUARD SAOUMA in his foreword to the publication, it is also thought "to be of value in the general field of land development", which is undoubtedly true. The problems caused in developing regions by those elements contained in Categories II and III are of less direct impact on the standard of living and on the way of life of these regions. Speakers from developing regions have expressed to an audience from the industrialized world the fact, that "they would be glad to accept some more pollution if concurrently they would receive the high standards of living of the industrialized world".

The FAO publication furthermore looks at these matters from the viewpoint of "what happens to the soil". From this viewpoint, the first category mentioned contains undoubtedly the most serious and widespread causes of land degradation. In another FAO publication (RUSSELL, et al., 1972), the "effects of intensive fertilizer use on the human environment" are thoroughly discussed from a different viewpoint, i.e., the effects of agricultural land use on the human environment as a whole. The combination of these two different points of view is possible and very necessary. Agricultural land use shows many interactions, physicochemical as well as socio-economic, with other human activities. With increasing development and industrialization, these interactions are steadily growing, and their fundamental importance must be recognized.

The Impact of Land Degradation

The impact of processes of land degradation may be measured with different yardsticks. One can use the purely scientific one, by means of which the processes caused by human activity are compared with the processes which could have been active without any human interference. Using absolute norms of this kind, it would be found that all human land use causes some degradation, be it only the changes in humus content and in the activity of soil organisms even in dense tropical plantations with shade trees which are to some extent comparable to the primeval forest. Even in most forests under some kind of management, the fact that the dead wood is taken away changes the ecosystem and would, therefore, constitute a type of degradation. On the other hand, the normal, so-called "geological" processes of erosion and denudation, in many arid regions as well as in areas with inherently unstable geological formations, would not be land degradation by human influence, and would, therefore, not be properly included under land degradation *sensu strictu* if the purely scientific approach were used.

Photo 16. Landscape in the sandy region of the Netherlands (Photo Stichting voor Bodem-kartering, Wageningen, no. R 25-114)

Given the fact that without land use in its proper sense, only some millions of human beings would be able to live on the whole earth, it is clear that other yardsticks have to be used. Any yardstick used must, to a certain extent, be of normative nature, and it may be that in different regions, with different land resources and different human conditions, different yardsticks have to be applied. One should then be able to answer the following questions:

(1) Does a given process constitute land degradation in the sense that, by its action, the productive capacity of the lands on which it is acting, either directly or indirectly, is thereby decreased for present and future uses?

(2) Does the process act upon the land in a manner which is not only discernible, but which has a significant impact in a quantitative sense?

(3) Does the process act in a manner which, without constituting land degradation in the normal, terrestrial, sense, has an impact on the environment of man or of other organisms, which is considered degrading in a quantitative sense?

(4) Can the process itself, or at least its quantitative impact, be impeded or in any other way lessened by human means, including the means of non-use of certain tracts of land?

(5) Must the process, even though it can be impeded or lessened, be accepted on certain tracts of land because of serious socio-economic reasons?

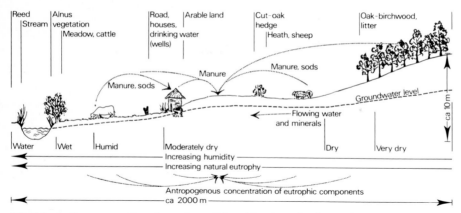

5.7. Schematic cross section through traditional land use in the sandy areas of the Netherlands

There are many clear cases, particularly in Category I of land degradation, in which at least the first two questions can be answered in the affirmative with the use of normal diagnostic criteria from soil science and physical geography. There are also several examples in past and present land use, in which land degradation was caused by projects or activities which were meant to be purely constructive.

An example from the past is the well-known system of "old arable land soils" or *Plaggenboden* (Plaggepts) in the sandy regions of northwestern Europe (see Photo 16). This system, which was started in the early Middle Ages and continued until the beginning of this century, has often been cited as an example of the build-up of soils by man. The system is schematically shown in Fig. 5.7. The manure of cattle and sheep, mainly derived from grazing on the outlying pastures and moors, was dropped in the barns and sheep pens, where it was mixed with organic matter from the topsoils of these same outlying areas. This mixture was spread upon the arable lands near the farms, and thus a continuous arable system could be maintained even on very poor sandy soils. The application of this system over nearly a thousand years caused the development of very deep humose topsoils (between 50 cm and 120 cm thick) on the arable lands: the *Plaggenboden* of northwest Germany, Belgium and the Netherlands. Quite rightly, these soils are described as exemplifying the fact that man can make soils which have a higher productivity than was possible in nature (EDELMAN, 1950; EDELMAN et al., 1958). It is often forgotten, however, that for this build-up of soils on a rather restricted area, a much larger surface area was depleted of organic matter and of the substances of the topsoil. Depending on the natural land resources, surfaces of between 10 and 40 times as large were used for grazing and for the cutting of the topsoil, which as sod was brought to the barns and shippons (traditional sheep-barns) for mixing with the droppings. This depletion can still be seen in several sandy regions of the Netherlands.

Other cases related to the drainage and reclamation of lands can also be shown. Drainage projects have often proved beneficial to land use on the wetter lands. It has often not been realized, however, that the drainage of wet lands may

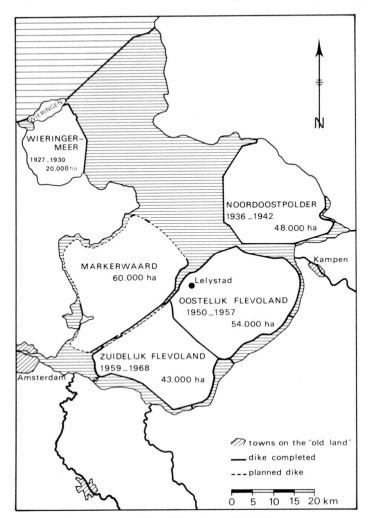

Fig. 5.8. The IJsselmeerpolders ("Zuyderzee Works")

also cause excessive drainage of the surrounding, originally dry lands. Thus areas with originally good grazing lands have been transformed into dry arable lands or at least into grazing lands of a poorer quality than was originally the case. Land reclamation projects in the Netherlands have shown similar influences if insufficient attention was paid to the underground hydrology (see Para. 4.3.2). The Zuyderzee Works are a good example (Fig. 5.8).

These Works consist of a "closing dyke" across the old Zuyderzee, now called "IJsselmeer", and of five large polders, with a total surface area of over 200000 hectares. For the diking and drainage of each polder a period of approximately ten years is needed. The first polder, *Wieringermeer*, was reclaimed around 1930; the lands adjoining this polder were mainly polders with a good system of water management, so that no particular hydrological difficulties were encountered. The second polder, the *Noordoostpolder* (northeastern polder) was drained around 1941 and here, after World War II, it was found that the adjoining older lands showed considerable symptoms of drought due to subsoil drainage towards the new polder (VEENENBOS, 1950); this situation had to be corrected insofar as possible, depending on the nature of the soils, by subsoil irrigation, an expensive and not always satisfactory tool.

To prevent the occurrence of similar processes upon reclamation of the newer polders *(Oost Flevoland, Zuid Flevoland)*, extensive investigations on the geo-hydrology and on the effects on soil productivity of drying-out were carried out (VOLKER et al., 1969). These led to accurate calculations of ground-water flow and seepage (see Fig. 4.14) and numerous data on the relative production values of different soils with different ground-water levels (Table 58). The project was then reshaped so that bordering lakes would prevent excessive seepage from and drying-out of, adjoining lands. Nevertheless, some effects, particularly, on non-agricultural lands, are now observed (see also Para.4.3.2). One of the nature reserves, the *Naardermeer* near Amsterdam, has, probably because of the draining of the Zuid Flevoland Polder, shown a change in water conditions which will turn parts of its reed marshes into wetland forests. Processes of a similar nature which induce soil salinity were mentioned in Para.4.3.1.

The second question, whether a process has a significant impact rather than only a discernible one, may seem superfluous in some cases. Still, processes such as soil leaching (transport of ions and colloids to an illuvial horizon in the subsoil) are sometimes the subject of discussions. These discussions are, however, seldom relevant because the processes of soil formation are of such a long duration that they have no impact within the relevant and foreseeable future, of three to five generations. The natural processes of soil formation, therefore, cannot be considered to constitute a type of land degradation. If, however, a soil is leached by rain water which, through industrial agents or otherwise, has a continuously low pH value (= high acidity) of for example, pH 4.5 to 2.5, the result may well be a kind of land degradation on certain soils, often the poorer. The intention of the question then is that the extent of the effect should be quantitated by investigations on the particular kinds of soils and lands.

An activity not mentioned in the FAO publication (RAUSCHKOLB, 1971), probably because our Question 2 in this regard is not answered in the affirmative on a world scale, is land degradation by mining activities. On a world scale, mining is carried out only on negligible surface areas. The destruction of lands by different kinds of open-pit mining (coal, lignite, gravel and other road construction materials) may, however, lead locally to serious land degradation. Subsoil mining on a large scale and even the exploitation of oil and natural gas may also locally lead to land degradation, e.g. by subsidence causing serious regional drainage problems.

Often not enough systematic attention has been paid in the past to our Questions 3, 4, and 5. The influence of agricultural land use on the degradation of aquatic ecosystems has only recently been brought to the attention of the general public. The influence of the use of fertilizers and pesticides (RUSSELL et al., 1972)

Table 58. Relative value of the productivity of grouped types of soil in the Veluwe border area of the IJsselmeer at varying summer ground water levels (VOLKER et al., 1969)

Soils	Summer ground water levels in cm below surface															
	30	40	50	60	70	80	90	100	120	140	160	180	200	220	240	260
Arable land 1949																
Sand: humus layer 40–50 cm	—	—	—	—	—	—	100	99	95	88	80	73	68	65	64	64
Sand: humus layer 70–80 cm	—	—	—	—	—	100	100	100	100	99	98	96	93	91	91	91
Arable land 1950–1951																
Sand: humus layer 40–50 cm	—	—	—	—	—	—	—	—	100	99	96	92	87	84	83	82
Sand: humus layer 70–80 cm	—	—	—	—	—	—	—	—	100	100	100	98	96	94	93	93
Grassland 1949																
Humous sandy soil	—	95	98	100	100	100	99	96	85	73	64	58	56	55	—	—
Peat	—	110	110	108	104	98	92	87	79	73	70	68	63	68	—	—
Clay on peat: clay layer 20–40 cm	—	127	130	120	104	87	75	67	60	60	60	60	60	60	—	—
Clay on peat: clay layer 40–60 cm	—	123	130	127	118	110	104	99	95	95	95	95	95	95	—	—
Clay on peat: clay layer >60 cm	—	119	125	128	130	130	130	130	130	130	130	130	130	130	—	—
Grassland 1950–1951																
Humous sandy soil	83	89	94	97	99	100	100	100	98	93	90	90	90	—	—	—
Peat	90	95	99	102	104	105	105	104	102	96	92	92	92	—	—	—
Clay on peat: clay layer 20–40 cm	102	120	128	125	115	105	96	90	87	87	87	87	87	—	—	—
Clay on peat: clay layer 40–60 cm	102	114	121	123	122	119	117	115	114	114	114	114	114	—	—	—
Clay on peat: clay layer >60 cm	92	98	105	110	114	118	121	124	127	128	128	128	128	—	—	—

also requires our attention in this respect. Much good investigative work is still needed to indicate on which lands, and with which kinds of management the dangers really exist. Sufficient data have thus far been collected to demonstrate that this is a very real problem which must be faced right now in all regions of the world where large quantities of industrial chemicals are being used. It is understandable that, as a cause of direct land degradation, the first FAO publication places these matters in its lowest category of priorities. In many industrialized regions, however, the problem is actually very urgent.

In relation to Question 4, whether a process can be impeded by human means, again in many cases, particularly in regard to soil conservation, little or no doubt exists. Any means to be applied must however be not only technically but also socio-economically applicable. Intensive systems of terracing, e.g. in paddy cultivation in Ceylon or Java or in vineyards in some Mediterranean areas, can only be maintained or established in certain land utilization types. Some cover crops, such as those used in Hevea and oil palm plantations, cannot be used in other kinds of tropical agriculture. There is very little room for generalization in this field. Only after careful study of the land resources and of the relevant and foreseeable land utilization types, can decisions on the feasibility of land conservation be made. The fact that in many land utilization types the best means of soil conservation is a good stand of the crop, is often neglected. Soil conservation is, therefore, easiest on those lands where crop growth and the response of the crop to the normal management operations are high (see also VINK, 1963a). This is the reverse side of the soil conservation maxim which reads in the obverse "to use a soil according to its capabilities and to treat it according to its needs". The crop should be grown in a soil which is sufficiently suitable to provide all of the elements needed for good development of the plants, and the "system plant-soil" should be treated according to its needs to make good growth possible. For this, a good system of land evaluation is the essential prerequisite (see Chapter 6).

The last question, whether a degradation process, even though it can be impeded, should be accepted for serious socio-economic reasons, is a very difficult one. In its simple form, this may mean that a certain amount of soil erosion in an area has to be accepted, at least for a while, because the use of adequate soil conservation measures is not feasible for the farmers (BALL et al., 1957). Land development and soil conservation projects cost time and money, and these are not always readily available, while the schooling of farmers in better methods of land use is often a process of even longer duration. The change from one degrading crop to another more appropriate one may be retarded because of marketing problems. Finally, everywhere in the world a certain amount of land degradation has to be accepted because of the growth of populations and the extension of urban areas. The waste products, at least partly unavoidable, have to be put somewhere, which may often cause land degradation, at least in limited areas. A careful study of land resources followed by land evaluation in the light of the natural and human resources and constraints, must give the best, or the least deleterious, solution in each area.

In regard to environmental pollution, WIENER (1972) mentioned three interacting "geometries": the resources geometry, the demand geometry and the pollution geometry. Each is a subsystem of the whole, which could be called the "model of the human environment". In a similar manner, the term "degradation geometry" could be substituted for "pollution geometry", thus making this approach valid for the subject of this paragraph. WIENER also points to four different levels in the "demand geometry" of human beings:

"Level One   — The metabolism of the body and mind of the individual;
Level Two   — The physical habitat of the individual and his close family, his home;
Level Three — The communal habitat—the vital services supplied within the community framework;
Level Four — The wider environment, as we generally consider it in the developed world".

In this hierarchy of viewpoints, no man can expect attention to be given to a higher level unless the demands at the lower levels are reasonably satisfied. Land degradation is therefore very much dependent on land productivity in relation to population density and standard of living.

Causes of Land Degradation

Land degradation is often, and has been in the past, caused by insufficiently balanced land use resulting from the establishment of land utilization types which are, or were, insufficiently adapted to the land resources of an area. Although a

Photo 17. Inland dunes, badlands in the Netherlands, often originally caused by disruptions of land use (today treasured as nature reserves) (Photo Mrs. E. BOOY, Natuurmonumenten, Amsterdam)

certain amount of adaptation of the land is possible by land improvement, definite limits are imposed by the natural constraints of the land as well as by the limits of technology and of feasibility. Land degradation often also results from insufficient correlation among the different land utilization types, agricultural and urban, within an area. Their interactions, caused by direct physical proximity as well as by landscape ecological processes (e.g. surface water, subsurface water, air transport) and human actions (transport systems), have to be studied to prevent otherwise unforeseeable kinds of degradation. Only a careful attuning of the various land utilization types within a region to the ecological conditions, in their widest sense, and to each other, may yield acceptable solutions (McHARG, 1969).

Land degradation has also been caused in the past by the sudden disruption of originally stable land utilization types. The *Wüstungen* in parts of central and northwestern Europe, often caused by epidemics and wars in the late Middle Ages, are still today often badlands, permanently unsuitable for any kind of agricultural use (Photo 17). Any land utilization type to be established should, in so far as possible, be established only after a thorough study of its internal stability as well as of its external stability in the foreseeable future. A good example of a modern evaluation study which covers many of the relevant factors in a given area is provided by the "Environmental Evaluation System for Water Resource Planning" of the U.S.Bureau of Reclamation (DEE et al., 1972, 1973). Similar studies, using these and other methods of evaluation, are of significance for preventing land degradation and environmental pollution by future land use.

5.4.6 Requirements of Non-Agricultural Land Utilization Types

The requirements of non-agricultural land utilization types are only briefly mentioned in this text. It is, however, deemed necessary to make some reference to them because of their ever-growing interactions with agricultural land use. The typically urban and industrial types compete with agricultural land use for locations and for transportion facilities. Transportation facilities for urban and industrial use, however, often prove to be also of great benefit for agriculture. Urban concentrations compete with the nearby horticultural enterprises for land, while at the same time the development of horticulture is stimulated by the nearness of markets for easily perishable products. Industrial wastes, including radioactive materials, are one of the causes of land degradation cited in an above-mentioned paper (RAUSCHKOLB, 1971). Urban wastes, and some industrial wastes, if properly processed, may provide animal fodder or manure for agricultural land use. The water needs of urban and industrial land uses are, particularly in arid regions but also in highly industrialized regions, often competitive with the agricultural needs. On the other hand, the energy needs, often provided by energy produced with water (construction of dams), may make a multipurpose project feasible where a single agricultural irrigation project is not. In some cases, lands which are unsuitable for agriculture, e.g. too rocky or too dry, may be used for urban and industrial development, but in areas with a strong relief, competition for the flatter parts of an area is a common phenomenon.

There are a number of physical requirements for urban and industrial land uses which are, in general, more a matter of degree than of absolute requirements. It is easier and cheaper to build on soils with a good bearing capacity or on good hard rock, but the situation of the city of Amsterdam shows that large towns may also be built on very weak peat, provided that somewhere underneath a formation with a sufficient bearing capacity is found; the latter may be at a depth of ten or more meters. For very high buildings, a greater bearing capacity is needed than for low ones. Whether a particular kind of building can be constructed at a particular location is today mainly a matter of feasibility, i.e. comparison between inputs (investments + maintenance and operation) and outputs ("yields" in terms of economic production or of human comfort and satisfaction). The advances in building technology in Amsterdam from the Middle Ages until today also clearly show, however, the importance of advancing construction techniques on the thick peat deposits (more than 10 m). Extreme cases of altitude or strongly dissected relief may be considered as absolute limitations for larger urban or industrial uses. Severe natural instability of slopes, often occurring in rocks consisting predominantly of shales, is perhaps the most serious limiting factor in certain areas (FLAWN, 1970; BARTELLI et al., 1966; McHARG, 1969).

The relation of non-agricultural rural land uses to agricultural land use is, in general, more direct. It is therefore worthwhile considering these and their requirements. Although it is difficult to give an exhaustive list of these land uses, they may be grouped in the following main categories:

(1) engineering uses such as air fields, traffic ways, highways, dikes and embankments, waterways, community development and light industries, sources for materials;

(2) recreational uses such as holiday-bungalows (vacation homes), campsites, picnic and play areas, athletic fields, golf links, recreational roads, paths and trails;

(3) wildlife and nature conservation.

Engineering Constructions and Community Development

There is a complete set of literature on the relations between engineering constructions and the land (see e.g. TSCHEBOTARIOFF, 1953), in general called "soil mechanics" and "engineering soil science". As indicated in Para.4.3.1, engineering soil science is a separate science, not to be confused with the "agricultural soil science" or "pedology" which is referred to in this book. In a previous publication (VINK in REY et al., 1968), we mentioned that soils in the sense of engineering are "the unconsolidated materials to be used (in some manner) in engineering construction". The soil types of the airfield classification system, often also used for other engineering purposes, are given in Table 59 (CASAGRANDE cited by TSCHEBOTARIOFF, 1953). These provide a general idea of the criteria used for determining the requirements of engineering constructions. Many quantitative determinations and a large number of formulas for arriving at sound construction principles have been developed for this science (CAPPER et al., 1971). Other methods of "terrain evaluation" (STEWART et al., 1968) are based on relatively specific knowledge of the engineering requirements of the land. HAANTJENS (1968) gives a list of "land

Table 59. The soil types of the air-field classification (ARTHUR CASAGRANDE) system and their identification[a]

Major divisions	Soil groups and typical names	Group symbol	General identifications (on disturbed samples)[b] — Dry strength[b]	Other pertinent examinations	Observations and tests relating to material in place	Principal classification tests (on disturbed samples)
Coarse grained soils	**Gravel and gravelly soils** — Well-graded gravel and gravel-sand mixtures, little or no fines	GW	None			Mechanical analysis
	Well-graded gravel-sand mixtures with excellent clay binder	GC	Medium		Dry unit weight void ratio	Mechanical analysis, liquid and plastic limits on binder
	Poorly graded gravel and gravel-sand mixtures, little or no fines	GP	None		Degree of compaction	Mechanical analysis
	Gravel with fine silty gravel, clayey gravel, poorly graded gravel-sand-clay mixtures	GF	Very slight to high	Graduation Grain shape	Cementation Stratification and drainage characteristics	Mechanical analysis liquid and plastic limits on binder, if applicable
	sands and sandy soils — Well-graded sands and gravelly sands, little or no fines	SW	None	Examination of binder wet and dry	Ground-water conditions	Mechanical analysis
	Well-graded sand with excellent clay binder	SC	Medium to high	Durability of grains	Traffic tests	Mechanical analysis, liquid and plastic limits on binder
	Poorly graded sands, little or no fines	SP	None		Large-scale load tests	Mechanical analysis
	Sands with fines, silty sands, clayey sands, poorly graded sand-clay-mixtures	SF	Very slight to high		California bearing-ratio tests	Mechanical analysis, liquid and plastic limits on binder, if applicable

[a] From ARTHUR CASAGRANDE cited by TSCHEBOTARIOFF (1953).
[b] For binder, fraction passing United States Standard mesh No. 40.

Table 59. (continued)

Major divisions	Soil groups and typical names	Group symbol	General identifications (on disturbed samples)		Observations and tests relating to material in place	Principal classification tests (on disturbed samples)
			Dry strength[b]	Other pertinent examinations		
Fine-grained soils containing little or no coarse-grained material — Fine-grained sands having low to medium compressibility; liquid limit < 50	Silts (inorganic) and very fine sands rock flour, silty or clayey fine sands with slight plasticity	ML	Very light to medium	Shaking test and plasticity	Dry unit weight water content and void ratio	Mechanical analysis, liquid and plastic limits, if applicable
	Clays (inorganic) of low to medium plasticity, sandy clays, silty clays, lean clays	CL	Medium to high	Examination in plastic range	Consistency, undisturbed and remoulded	Liquid and plastic limits
	Organic silts and organic silt-clays of low plasticity	OL	Slight to medium	Examination in plastic range, odour, colour	Stratification, roof holes, and fissures	Liquid and plastic limits from natural condition and after oven drying
Fine-grained soils having high compressibility; liquid limit > 50	Micaceous or diatomaceous fine sandy and silty soils, elastic silts	MH	Very slight to medium	Shaking test and plasticity	Drainage and ground water conditions. Traffic tests	Mechanical analysis, liquid and plastic limits, if applicable
	Clays (inorganic) of high plasticity, fat clays	CH	High to very high	Examination in plastic range	Large-scale load tests	Liquid and plastic limits
	Organic clays of medium to high plasticity	OH	Medium to high	Examination in plastic range, odour, colour	California bearing-ratio tests. Compression tests	Liquid and plastic limits from natural condition and after oven drying
Fibrous organic soils with very high compressibility	Peat and other highly organic swamp soils	Pt	Readily identified			Consistency, texture and natural water content

[a] From ARTHUR CASAGRANDE cited by TSCHEBOTARIOFF (1953).
[b] For binder, fraction passing United States Standard mesh No. 40.

Table 60. Significant land attributes for engineering (HAANTJENS, 1968)

(i) *Geology.* The information presented concerns mainly general data on lithology and in some cases on structure. Any information on the presence of hard gravel is given. Geology is essentially a week link in the survey procedure in New Guinea, because it is difficult to make many observations of fresh rock, due to considerable weathering, and because differences in lithology are commonly poorly reflected in the photo patterns, again probably due to weathering. Wherever possible, the data are augmented by information derived from preceeding geological surveys.

(ii) *Land forms.* Data are presented on the following parameters and characteristics:

1. Altitude, indicated by six hypsometric classes, from 0–250 ft to 4500–6000 ft. The proportion of each land system occurring within various hypsometric classes is given.

2. Relief, indicated by seven classes ranging from nil (< 20 ft, but spelled out further, if possible) to very high (> 1500) and by the maximum and minimum relief.

3. Slope steepness, indicated by eight classes from level ($0° 30'$) to cliffed ($> 72°$), the level slope class being subdivided into four gradient classes. Most classes are expressed in degrees and percent as well as in gradients.

4. Slope index, a weighted summation for each land system of slopes in different classes of steepness, ranging from 0 (100% slopes $< 10°$) to 100 (100% slopes $> 30°$).

5. Slope form, qualitatively described by such terms as straight, convex, benched, hummocky, etc. Observations on slope form, particularly the assessment of the degree and nature of slumping, contribute to the evaluation of *slope stability.*

6. Crest width, indicated by 5 width classes ranging from knife-edged (< 15 ft) to very broad (> 500 ft).

7. Crest form, quantitatively indicated by such terms as even, stepped, peaked, accordant, rounded, flat, etc.

8. Crest pattern, qualitatively described by such terms as long, short, straight, parallel, radial, branching, where necessary with a remark on any dominant direction.

9. Ridge crest density, qualitatively indicated by such terms as very fine, coarse, etc. This is supported by semi-quantitative information in the form of a stream pattern plan.

10. Size of land form, indicated qualitatively, or in yards for the diameter of rounded areas, and for the width, sometimes also length, of elongated areas, and in feet for the height of scarps and terrace edges.

(iii) *Streams and drainage.* Information is presented on the following characteristics:

1. Stream pattern and density, shown on a plan drawn from an aerial photograph. This is done only for land systems with noticeable relief, because small streams can neither be seen nor infered in forested plains. Whether or not a valley or gully actually contains a stream, can often not be seen on the air photos, requiring somewhat arbitrary decisions based on field experience.

2. Stream gradient, expressed in the same classes as slope steepness.

3. Width of stream bed, indicated as a range in yards, or qualitatively as very narrow, etc. for small streams.

4. Stream bed characteristics, indicated qualitatively by such terms as bouldery, gravelly, sandy, muddy, and mentioning any available information on rock bars, rapids and waterfalls.

5. Stream banks, indicated as either cut into rock or into alluvium. In the latter case, their height above residual flow level and their steepness is indicated.

6. Residual stream flow, qualitatively characterized by such terms as very shallow and rapid, sluggish, or tidal, etc. The probable water depth in feet of sluggish streams is tentatively indicated. Permanency of flow is the rule in New Guinea, but where climatic records and run-off relationships suggest intermittent flow in certain streams, this is mentioned.

7. River flooding, rated for areas of land adjacent to streams, according to frequency, seasonality and potential damaging nature of floods. Estimates are of necessity based on circumstantial evidence, derived from local residents, as well as from soil, vegetation and land form features.

Table 60. (continued)

8. Inundation, rated according to duration and depth. This is distinguished from river flooding by long duration, lack of flow, and flow manner.

9. Drainage status of land, expressed in five classes from well drained to swampy. The semi-quantitative rating is based on depth and severity of gleying in the soil, wetness characteristics in the vegetation, and water tables observed.

10. Surface run-off characteristics, very qualitatively assessed in relation to through-drainage on the basis of slope steepness and estimates of soil and rock permeability; see also Section V (b) (iii).

(iv) *Weathering and soils.* The following characteristics mentioned in the report are of possible significance to engineers.

1. Drainage status, already discussed in the previous section.

2. Permeability, qualitatively assessed in five classes from very rapid to very slow. The estimates are based largely on field determinations of texture, consistency and structure.

3. Soil texture properties. Several kinds of data are available. Textures according to the USDA system of particle size distribution and texture nomenclature, and based on field estimates, are given in the soil descriptions. Liquid limit and plastic limit determinations on representative samples, mostly from a depth between $1/2$ to $2\frac{1}{2}$ ft were carried out by the soil mechanics laboratory of the Public Works Department, Port Moresby. On the basis of these data the soils were given the appropriate designations according to the Unified Soil Classification system. Linear shrinkage was also determined on the samples and all soils tentatively placed in eight shrinkage classes, from negligible (< 1) to extremely high (> 20).

4. Engineering soil depth. This term has been applied, in contrast to agricultural soil depth, to indicate the depth to any underlying consolidated material. It is estimated in five depth classes from very shallow (< 2 ft) to very deep (> 15 ft). Consolidated rock is defined as being too hard to be penetrated by a hand auger or spade. Such rock may still be weathered, and engineering soil depth therefore provides only a very crude guide as to the depth at which fresh rock may be encountered.

5. Engineering soil depth index, a weighted summation for each land system of different soil depth classes, ranging from 0 (100% very shallow soils) to 100 (100% very deep soils).

6. Degree of weathering and soil development. This characteristic is only of indirect significance to engineers. It is used in assessing soil depth beyond the normal augering limit of 6 ft. On erosional hill slopes, it is used together with information on slope form [see Section IV (a) (ii)], and vegetation characteristics in qualitatively assessing the degree of *slope stability.*

(v) *Vegetation.* The engineer's main interest in vegetation would appear to be the relative ease of its removal. Visibility, for instance as affecting the need for path clearing for line surveying, can also be of some importance. Only a first attempt has been made to assess vegetation for these purposes, by tabulating for all forest types such data as number of large (> 5 ft girth) trees per acre, canopy density, presence of lianes, development of buttress roots, height and density of shrub layer, visibility at eye level. Data on timber species and volumes, as assessed by the survey, can be of value to engineers, if local construction materials are to be used.

---

attributes estimated or measured, which are significant for civil engineering". These include: (1) geology, (2) land forms (subdivided into ten different aspects), (3) streams and drainage (subdivided into ten different aspects), (4) weathering and soils (six different aspects), (5) vegetation. His very instructive list, reproduced in Table 60, was made for the conditions of Australian New Guinea, but it is very useful for other countries and circumstances.

Table 61. Dimensions, loading rates and physical conditions of three soil disposal systems for septic tank effluent (BOUMA, 1971)

Type of soil, position of the bed in the soil, and level of surface of ponded effluent	Age of system	Loading rate		Soil moisture tension		Estimated flow from bottom + sidewalls (L/d)	Calculated flow (bottom only)	
		L/d	L/m²	Below bed	At sides		From perc. rate (L/d)	From Ksat (double tube) (L/d)
1. Plainfield loamy sand bed: 20–80 cm Effluent: 40 cm	10 years	±2400	±28	20 mbars	23 mbars	±2500	1392000	261000
2. Saybrook silt loam bed: 60–90 cm (In IIC: stony sandy loam till) Effluent: 70 cm	12 years	320	13	80 mbars	60 mbars	± 280	288000	19000
After two weeks of seration followed by induced ponding		800	33	50 mbars	40 mbars	± 800	288000	19000
3. Ontonagon clay bed: 90–135 cm Effluent: 110 cm	4 months	± 720	±65	6 mbars	6 mbars	± 16	255	22.5

Explanation of abbreviations: L = liters, d = day. Indicated depths in Column 1, are those below the soil surface.

In New Zealand, useful work has been done on the correlation between pedo-logical soil classification and engineering data requirements (NORTHEY, 1966). The best general source for the United States is the previously mentioned book by BARTELLI et al. (1966). A large amount of useful information from the U.S. is also obtained in the newer County Soil Survey Reports (ABMEYER and CAMPBELL, 1970; CALHOUN and WOOD, 1969; GRICE et al., 1971; RASMUSSEN, 1971).

Many of the requirements for community development are similar to those for engineering (houses, roads) or for recreational facilities (sports fields, lawns); some are similar to those of horticulture (flower-growing, tree plantations). A special aspect of community development is the requirements for sewage systems. In general, some kind of septic tank system is needed, and here special problems, depending on the land contitions, arise. BOUMA et al., (1972; see also BOUMA, 1971) conducted special studies on this subject in Wisconsin. They found that seepage from the tanks should be continuous, but not too quick, to prevent on the one hand the clogging-up of the system and on the other hand the infiltration of insufficiently purified water into the hydraulic system. A few relevant data are produced in Table 61.

Recreation

Many kinds of recreation are closely interrelated with agricultural land use. Al-though various modifications occur, this is just as true in a sparsely populated country like Canada as in a densely populated country like the Netherlands. A review of recreational land uses was given in Para. 3.4. Because these include many different kinds of land use, no general list of requirements can be made. Many sports fields require lands with little or no relief and rather permeable soils

Table 62. Example of the SCS system for the determination of "potentials" of an area for water sports (after EDMINSTER, 1966, cited by VAN LIER, 1972)

Area properties	Multiplier number	Rating number	Score
Climate	1	7	7
Scenery	1	9	9
Water areas			
existing[a]	4	10	40
inland sites[a]	3	2	6
Population of people			
size and distribution	2	7	14
age and occupation	1	5	5
Proximity and access			
proximity to urban centres	1	10	10
Totals	13		S_{act} 91

$S_{max} = 13 \times 10 = 130 \qquad S_{act} = 91$

Suitability $= 100 \times \dfrac{91}{130} = 70\%$

[a] Possible limiting factors.

which are not too easily spoiled by the treading of many feet during the whole or most of a year. Similar requirements exist for playgrounds and camping grounds, though in these areas a certain, not too excessive relief is usually found to be beneficial. For "general open-air recreation" (walking, hiking etc.), considerable variability in the land is highly appreciated. KIEMSTEDT (1967) mentioned several factors: (a) forest and water-borders, (b) reliefenergy, (c) kinds of land use (which may be agricultural), and (d) climate. VAN LIER (1972) presented quantitative data, based partly on the methodology of the U.S. Soil Conservation Service; some of his figures are given in Table 62 to 65 (partly after EDMINSTER, 1966).

Table 63. Results of the application of the adapted SCS system for the Drunense Duinen area (after SEGERS, cited by VAN LIER, 1972)

Type of outdoor recreation	Maximum score	Actual score	Suitability (%)
1. Sports and Playing	165	124	75
2. Picnicking	185	134.5	72
3. Camping (shelter, caravan)	190	127.5	67
4. Staying in recreational lodges	205	138	67
5. Walking for pleasure	180	132.5	74
6. Bicycling	165	119.5	72

Table 64. Physiographic subdivision for outdoor recreation potentials (after VAN WIJK, cited by VAN LIER, 1972)

Climate	— macroclimate (clouds, temperature, etc.)
	— microclimate
Landscape	— high vegetation (hedges, woods, trees, etc.)
	— relief
	— parcellation
	— open water
	— built-up area
	— flora and fauna
	— invisible elements (groundwater, soil, etc.)

Table 65. Soil and hydrological conditions required for playgrounds and woods (after VAN WIJK and VAN DEN HURK, cited by VAN LIER, 1972)

Intended use	Profile	Hydrology	Special requirements
Playgrounds	upper layer 0.50 to 0.60 m with a good permeability and a well-bearing top layer	water-table > 0.30 m below surface	top layer "clean", non-slippery, not too hard or too soft; a small degree of relief is permitted
Woods with different kinds of decidous trees	upper layer 0.50 to 0.60 m mostly mineral without sharp boundaries	water-table > 0.40 m below surface	moist, fairly humic upper layer; no severe fluctuation of water table; pH-KCl over 4.5 to 5.0

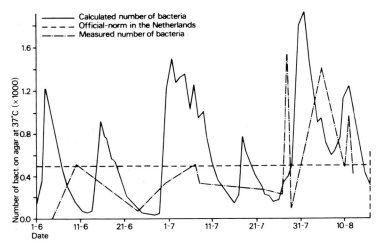

Fig. 5.9. Measured and calculated number of bacteria in the pool of the inland beach "Loofles" (the Netherlands) during 1968. (After VAN LIER, 1970, cited by VAN LIER, 1972)

Another important aspect is the number of people which a recreational object on a particular tract of land can accomodate per day or per year. The fact that different kinds of land in Canada are judged in this respect is evident from the way in which the suitability of the different lands for the different recreational land utilization types is handled (Dept. Reg. Econ. Exp., 1969; see also Para. 3.4.) In the latter publication, the various land utilization types for outdoor recreation are described, and some information on their requirements is given. An explicit list of the physical requirements has, however, not yet been published. Land use requirements can often be read from the way in which the land attributes are considered to limit such a use. An example from Canada is cited in Table 66. The overcrowded inland waters which are situated near urban areas and which are used in summer for bathing are a special example. The bacterial content of the water is an essential aspect of their use. A graph from a pool in the Netherlands is given as an example in Fig. 5.9.

Criteria for Requirements and Limitations

Requirements of land uses as well as the limitations imposed by the land sometimes show several gradations. There is, for example, a large range of qualities of different lands between lands which are "absolutely unsuitable" for a certain use and lands which are perfect for the use. In land utilization types in which rather high investments are feasible, the adaptation of the land to the requirements of a particular use provides good possibilities. Such is often the case with athletics fields, where very high investments per unit surface area can be applied. In Fig. 5.10 the suitability for playgrounds after investments of various sizes is given for an area near Amsterdam.

	0	1	2	3	4	5	6
Water quality		moderate —— weed patches ——→ —— Murky water ——→ (no pollution)		—— extensive weeds ——→ —— aquatic nuisances ——→ (no health hazard)		—— pollution (degree of limitation depends on prevalence and hazard)	
				—— cool water ——→ —— cold water ——→ (limits swimming) (limits bathing)		—— v. cold water (precludes use)	
Miscellaneous		—— beach exposed ——→ (limitation depends on prevalence of condition)					
Special hazards				—— dangerous slopes, current or undertows ——→ (severity of limitation depends on prevalence of condition)			
Beach gradients (general conditions)		less than 8% 1%	10% 12%	15% ‖ more than 15%		not a B	
Beach materials (comfort and hazard factor)		pebbles over pea-size firm till	—— cobbles —— (depending on comfort factor) gravel	smooth bed rock	boulder-pavement rough sharp bed rock unsorted rocks		
			unstable dunes				
Development area		numerous boulders	poor soil cover only 50% of required area	extensive rockiness minimal development area available	boulder pavement		
Access problems	slight	moderate		severe		v. severe	
	0	1	2	3	4	5	6

Instructions for use:

1. Ascertain approximate value for individual limitations.
2. Total values for all limitations: value 2 — downgrade 1 class
   value 4 — downgrade 2 classes
   value 6 — downgrade 3 classes
   value8 — downgrade 4 classes
   value 8 + — look for other features.

3. These are general guide lines. Do not deduct full points where limitations overlap (e.g. exposed) beach and very cold water; aquatic nuisances and extensive weeds).
4. Presence of other recreation features may overcome a degree of limitation.

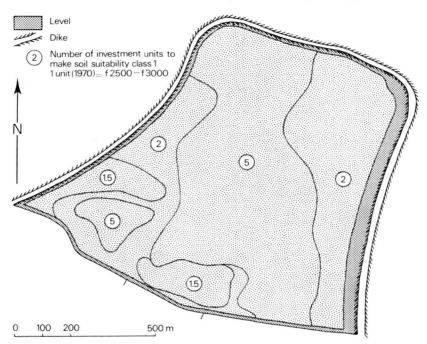

Fig. 5.10. Investment for drainage and soil improvement measures to ensure a suitability class 1 for playgrounds in the future recreation project Twiskepolder near Amsterdam. (After Van Wijk and Van den Hurk, 1971, cited by Van Lier, 1972)

In his book "Design with Nature", McHarg (1969) makes valuable contributions to the solution of the multiple land use problem. His approach is based on the different requirements of the different kinds of land use with regard to the physiography, i.e. the land conditions. Table 67 contains his ranking criteria of the landscape ecological factors for multiple land use on Staten Island (U.S.A.). This approach is very sound; the use of ranking criteria is often the method to objictify an evaluation in which a certain degree of subjective judgement is unavoidable. In Table 68 the compatibility of land uses according to McHarg is demonstrated; it includes many important contributions to the problem of multiple land use, although perhaps some of the subjective judgements in this table may not be valid under all circumstances. This approach to compatibility can also be adapted to local circumstances; McHarg's table was used for regional planning of the Potomac River Basin (U.S.A.). Finally, Fig. 5.11 and 5.12 contain two examples of the results of multiple land use planning according to the design of McHarg, as applied to two landscapes of the Potomac River Basin. The plan is based largely on the compatibilities cited in Table 68 and on the relative suitabilities of the different land units to the different kinds of land use. This part of McHarg's approach goes right through landscape ecology and land use requirements into the stage of design and planning. The principles involved, basically the adaptation of the land uses to the natural land requirements as well as to each other and to

Table 67. Ranking criteria of the landscape ecological factors for multiple land use on Staten Island (USA) after McHARG, 1969).

— ranking order left to right: × = high importance
      / = less importance
— ranking order right to left: ● = high importance
      = = less importance

C: Conservation; P: Passive recreation; A: active recreation;
R: Residential development; I: Commercial and industrial development.

Ecological factor	Ranking criteria	I	II	III	IV	V	C	P	A	R	I
Climate											
Air pollution	Incidence max→min	High	Medium	Low		Lowest	=	=	●	●	
Tidal inundation	Incidence max→min	Highest Recorded	Highest Projected			Above Flood-Line			=		●
Geology											
Features of unique, scientific and educational value	Scarcity max→min	1 Ancient Lakebeds 2 Drainage Outles	1 Terminal Moraine 2 Limit of Glaciation 3 Boulder Trail	Serpentine Hill	Palisades Outlier	1 Beach 2 Buried Valleys 3 Clay Pits 4 Gravel Pits	×	×		●	×
Foundation conditions	Compressive strength max→min	1 Serpentine 2 Diabase	Shale	Cretaceous Sediments	Filled Marsh	Marsh and Swamp			/	×	×
Physiography											
Features of unique, scientific and educational value	Scarcity max→min	Hummocks and Kettleholes within the Terminal Moraine	Palisades Outlier	Moraine Scarps and lakes along the Bay Shore	Breaks in Serpentine Ridge		×	×		●	
Land features of scenic value	Distinctive most→least	Serpentine Ridge and Promontories	Beach	1 Escarpments 2 Enclosed Valleys	1 Berms 2 Promontories 3 Hummocks	Undifferentiated	×	×	/	×	
Water features of scenic value	Distinctive most→least	Bay	Lake	1 Pond 2 Streams	Marsh		×	×	/		
Riparian lands of water features	Vulnerability most→least	Marsh	1 Stream 2 Ponds	Lake	Bay	1 The Narrows 2 Kill Van Kull 3 Arthur Kill	×		●	●	
Beaches along the bay	Vulnerability most→least	Moraine Scarps	Coves	Sand Beach		1 The Narrows 2 Kill Van Kull 3 Arthur Kill	×		/	●	=

Phenomena rank

Value for land use

Table 67 (continued)

Ecological factor	Ranking criteria	I	II	III	IV	V	C	P	A	R	I
		Phenomena rank					Value for land use				
Surface drainage	Proportion of surface water to land area most → least	Marsh and swamp	Areas of constricted drainage	Dense stream/swale network	Intermediate stream/swale network	Sparse stream/swale network	/	/	●	●	●
Slope	Gradient high → low	Over 25%	25–10%	10–5%	5–2½%	2½–0%			●	●	●
Hydrology											
Marine Commercial Craft	Navigable channels deepest → shallowest	The Narrows	Kill Van Kull	Arthur Kill	Fresh Kill	Raritan Bay	/	/			×
Pleasure Craft	Free expanse of water largest → smallest	Raritan Bay	Fresh Kill	The Narrows	Arthur Kill	Kill Van Kull	/	×	×		
Fresh water											
Active recreation (swimming, paddling, model-boat sailing, etc.)	Expanse of water largest → Smallest	Silver Lake	1 Clove Lake 2 Grassmere Lake 3 Ohrbach Lake 4 Arbutus Lake 5 Wolfes Pond	Other ponds	Streams		/	×	×		
Stream-side recreation (fishing, trails, etc.)	Scenic most → least	Nonurbanized perennial streams	Nonurbanized intermittent streams	Semiurbanized streams	Urbanized streams		×	×	/		/
Watersheds for stream quality protection	Scenic streams most → least	Nonurbanized perennial streams	Nonurbanized intermittent streams	Semiurbanized streams	Urbanized streams		×	×			
Aquifers	Yield highest → lowest	Buried valleys		Cretaceous Sediments		Crystalline *rocks*	×				
	highest → lowest			Sediments		rocks					
Aquifer recharge zones	Important aquifers most → least	Buried valleys		Cretaceous Sediments		Crystalline rocks	×			●	
Pedology											
Soil drainage	Permeability as indicated by the height of water table most → least	Excellent-good	Good-fair	Fair-poor	Poor	Nil	=	×	×	×	×

Table 67 (continued)

| Ecological factor | Ranking criteria | Phenomena rank | | | | | Value for land use | | | | |
		I	II	III	IV	V	C	P	A	R	I
Foundation conditions	Compressive strength and stability most → least	Gravelly to stony, sandy loams	Gravelly sand or silt loams	Gravelly sandy to fine sandy loam	1 Sand loam 2 Gravel 3 Beach sands	1 Alluvium 2 Swamp Muck 3 Tidal marshlands 4 Made land	×		/	×	×
Erosion	Susceptibility most → least	Steep slopes over 10%	Any slope on gravelly sandy to fine sandy loam	Modern slopes (2½–10%) on 1 Gravelly sand or silt loam 2 Gravelly to stony sandy loams	Slopes (0–2½%) on gravelly sand or silt loams	Other soils	×	●	●	●	●
Vegetation											
Existing forest	Quality best → poorest	Excellent	Good	Poor	Disturbed	None	×	×			●
Forest type	Scarcity most → least	1 Lowland 2 Upland dry	Marsh	Upland	Upland moist	Absence	×	×		●	
Existing marshes	Quality best → poorest	Good	Fair		Poor (filled)	None	×	×	||	||	||
Wildlife											
Existing habitats	Scarcity most → least	Intertidal	Water-related	Field and forest	Urban	Marine	×	×	||		
Intertidal species	Environmental quality based on intensity of shore activity least → most activity	1	2	3	4	5	×	×	||		
Water-associated species	environmental quality based on the degree of urbanization non → fully urbanized	1	2	3	4	5	×	×	/		
Field and forest species	Forest Quality best → poorest	1	2	3	3	5	×	×	||	||	

Table 67 (continued)

Ecological factor	Ranking criteria	Phenomena rank					Value for land use				
		I	II	III	IV	V	C	P	A	R	I
Urban-related species	Presence of trees abundant → absent	1		2		3					
Land use Features of unique, educational, and historical value	Importance most → least	Richmond Town	1 Amboy Road 2 Tottenville Conference	Area with abundance of landmarks	Area with sparseness of landmarks	Area with absence of landmarks	×	×	×	×	/
Features of scenic value	Distinctive most → least	The Verazzano Bridge	Ocean Lines Channel	Manhattan Ferry	1 The Goethals Bridge 2 The Outerbridge crossing 3 The Bayonne Bridge	Absence	×	×	×	×	/
Existing and Potential recreation resources	Availability most → least	1 Existing public open space 2 Existing Institutions	Potential nonurbanized recreation areas	Potential urbanized recreation areas	Vacant land (with low recreation potential)	Urbanized areas	×	×	×		/

The western hills,covered
in forest,offer the best
recreation in this region.

Relatively steep slopes,
unsuitable row crops,are
often admirable for orchards.

Urbanization is best
located as nodes on
shale ridges.This land
has a low agriculture
value but is highly
scenic and preferable
for settlement.

The Valley permits intensive crop agriculture on
productive limestone soils.

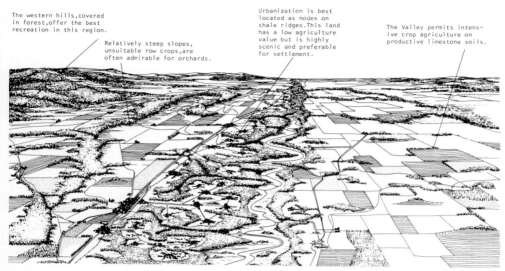

Fig. 5.11. The Great Valley of the Potomac River Basin. (After McHARG, 1969)

Plateaus and flat ridges
on the crystalline base
provide the best opportunity
for urbanization in this
region.

Some crop land,pasture,
forests and limited high
quality sites for urbanization
are appropriate to the
quartzite band.

Limestone and dolomite
valley over an aquifer
provide the highest
agricultural value.

Gentle slopes of the
crystalline upland
contain high quality
agricultural land in
flood plains and valleys.

The entire area represents
an attractive pastoral
landscape with many historic
places and buildings.

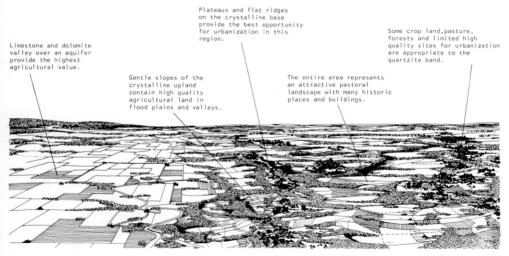

Fig. 5.12. The Piedmont Area of the Potomac River Basin. (After McHARG, 1969)

the human demand pattern, is very valuable. The land evaluation phase (see Chapter 6) is, however, short-circuited in a manner which is not acceptable in many cases. Only in areas where the demand geometry and the resources geometry are clearly differentiated and show a quantitative resemblance, at least with regard to the order of magnitude of the demands and the corresponding resources, may such an approach be justifiable. In most areas of the world, particularly in those areas with the most crucial land use problems, these patterns may

Table 68.

- O Incompatible
- – Low compatibility
- = Medium compatibility
- X Full compatibility

- O Incompatible
- – Low compatibility
- = Medium compatibility
- X Full compatibility

- O Bad
- – Poor
- = Fair
- X Good

INTERCOMPATIBILITY OF LAND USES

		URBAN	SUBURBAN RESIDENTIAL	INDUSTRIAL	INSTITUTIONAL	MINING: shaft-mined coal	active opencast coal	abandoned coal spoil	QUARRYING: stone and limestone	sand and gravel	VACATION SETTLEMENT	AGRICULTURE: row crops	arable	livestock	FORESTRY: even-stand softwood	uneven-stand softwood	hardwood	RECREATION: saltwater oriented	freshwater oriented	wilderness	general recreation	cultural recreation	driving for pleasure	WATER MANAGEMENT: reservoir	watershed management
URBAN		X																							
SUBURBAN RESIDENTIAL		=	X																						
INDUSTRIA		X	O	X																					
INSTITUTIONAL		–	X	O	X																				
MINING	shaft-mined coal	O	O	X	O	X																			
	active opencast coal	O	O	X	O		X																		
	abandoned coal spoil	O	–	X	=			X																	
QUARRYING	stone and limestone	O	O	X	O				X																
	sand and gravel	O	O	X	–					X															
VACATION SETTLEMENT		O	O	O	=	O	O	X	O	O	X														
AGRICULTURE	row crops	O	=	=	=	=	O	O	O	O	O	X													
	arable	O	=	–	=	=	O	–	O	O	–	X	X												
	livestock	O	=	–	X	=	O	=	O	O	=	X	X	X											
FORESTRY	even-stand softwood	O	O	O	–	=	O	X	O	O	–	O	–	–	X										
	uneven-stand softwood	O	–	O	=	=	O	X	O	O	X	O	O	O		X									
	hardwood	O	–	O	=	=	O	=	O	O	X	O	O	=		X	X								
RECREATION	saltwater oriented	–		O	X		O			O	X							X							
	freshwater oriented	–	X	O	X	O	O	X	O	X	X	–	=	=	=	X	X		X						
	wilderness	O	O	O	–	–	O	X	O	O	–	O	O	–	–	X	X	X	X	X					
	general recreation	X	X	–	X	–	O	X	O	=	X	–	–	=	–	X	X	X	X	X	X				
	cultural recreation	X	=	O	X	O	O		O	O	–	–	=	=	–	X	X	X	X	X	X	X			
	driving for pleasure	O	O	O	=	O	O	=	O	–	=	–	X	X	–	X	X	X	X	X	X	X	X		
WATER MANAGEMENT	reservoir	–	–	=	X	O	O	=	O	O	X	O	–	–	–	X	X		X	X	X	=	X	X	
	watershed management	O	O	O	=	O	O	X	O	O	=	O	–	–	O	X	X		X	X	X	=	X	X	X

NATURAL DETERMINANTS / CONSEQUENCES

		SLOPE	0–5 %	15–25 %	over 25 %	VEHICULAR ACCESSIBILITY	SOILS: gravels	sands	loams	silts	AQUIFER RECHARGE AREAS	WATER SUPPLY DEPENDABILITY	CLIMATE: fog susceptibility	temperature extremes	CONSEQUENCES: AIR POLLUTION	WATER POLLUTION	STREAM SEDIMENTATION	FLOOD AND DROUGHT CONTROL	SOIL EROSION
URBAN		X	=	–	O	X					O	X	–	O	O	O	O	O	O
SUBURBAN RESIDENTIAL		X	X	=	–	=					–	X	–	–	=	–	O	O	O
INDUSTRIA		X	–	O	O	X					O	X	=	–	O	O	–	O	–
INSTITUTIONAL		X	X	=	–	=					=	=	–	–	X	=	=	=	=
MINING	shaft-mined coal	–	=	X	=	X					O	X	X	X	X	–	–	X	–
	active opencast coal	–	X	X	–	X					O	X	X	X	X	O	O	–	O
	abandoned coal spoil	X	X	=	O	O					O	O	X	X	X	=	=	=	–
QUARRYING	stone and limestone	–	X	X	O	X					X	O	X	X	X	X	=	=	=
	sand and gravel	X	X	–	O	X	X				X	=	X	X	O	X	=	=	=
VACATION SETTLEMENT		X	X	X	=	–					=	–	X	=	=	=	–	–	–
AGRICULTURE	row crops	X	=	O	O	X	O	X	X	X	O	X	X	O	X	O	O	=	O
	arable	X	=	–	O	X	O	–	X	=	=	=	X	–	X	=	–	–	–
	livestock	X	X	X	=	=	–	=	X	X	X	–	X	=	X	=	=	=	=
FORESTRY	even-stand softwood	X	X	=	–	=	X	X	X	X	X	O	X	=	X	X	–	=	–
	uneven-stand softwood	X	X	X	X	–	=	X	X	X	X	O	X	X	X	X	X	X	X
	hardwood	X	X	X	X	–	=	=	X	X	X	O	X	X	X	X	X	X	X
RECREATION	saltwater oriented					=						X	X	X	X	X			
	freshwater oriented					=					X	X	X	X	X	X			
	wilderness					O					X	O	X	X	X	X	X	X	X
	general recreation					=					X	O	X	X	X	X	X	X	
	cultural recreation					X					X	–	X	X	X	X	X	=	X
	driving for pleasure										X	O	X	X	X	X			
WATER MANAGEMENT	reservoir	O	O	=	X	O				O	X	X	X	X	X	X		X	
	watershed management					O		X	X	X	X		X	X	X	X	X	X	

show great differences in areas such as overpopulation, unbalanced growth of essential land uses or restricted resources patterns. For social and economic reasons, the largescale migration of populations, or the large-scale change of land use patterns is often not feasible. Only a more careful land evaluation, taking into account the many natural, technological, economic and social aspects of all land utilization types, can lead to a justified planning of land use. McHarg's basic principles remain valuable, however, even in these cases.

Wildlife and Nature Conservation

In the well-known Land Use Capability Classification the U.S. Soil Conservation Service made a gesture of historical importance through its recognition of class VIII—suitable only for wildlife and nature conservation. This was the first time that agriculture categorically recognized that certain lands would be better used for purposes other than economic production. The attitude taken was also correct: since agriculture wants to do its best to produce as much as possible to satisfy human needs, only those lands which cannot contribute to this goal by reasonable means are left out of production. The happy instance that there is also a need, at the time not always officially recognized, for the conservation of natural habitats and of natural variability, provided a suitable alternative use. The increased standards of living in the industrialized world, to which soil conservation and modernized agriculture have made major contributions, provided more leisure time and more money for those forms of recreation which are dependent on the natural habitats, such as hunting. At the same time, the developing world increasingly used its natural habitats for touristic purposes of several kinds and for well-controlled game cropping (see e.g. BROWN, 1967). Nature conservation for more general outdoor recreation also became of greater importance, while at the same time the interest of agriculture in "marginal lands" for economic production started to decrease.

The land requirements of wildlife and nature conservation have tended, during the last few years, to show a more positive tendency. The activities of the Canada Land Inventory are a good example. In this inventory, a separate "Land Capability Classification for Wildlife" is made (McCORMACK, 1971; PERRET, 1969). This system emphasizes two kinds of wildlife which are of special importance in Canada: ungulates and waterfowl. These two groups of animals clearly have different requirements. The particular physical characteristics considered are: parent material, soil profile, depth, moisture, fertility, landform, climatic factors and vegetation. For waterfowl the main requirements are: lands with a wide variety and abundance of good habitat elements, such as fertile soils with good water-holding characteristics, and a topography which is well suited to the formation of wetlands. The predominant water areas required are both shallow and deep permanent marshes and deep, open bodies of water with well-developed marsh edges. For ungulates, the main requirements are a wide variety and abundance of food plants and of other habitat elements. The limitations of an area can also be described with different degrees of seriousness which, as described above, is, in actual practice, often just as illustrative as the description of the use requirements.

Vegetation experts, occasionally together with soil scientists (WIESLANDER and STORIE, 1953), have for some decades made many investigations on the relations between vegetation types and their habitats. Their intention has often been to gain purely scientific knowledge on the ecology of vegetation types, but in many cases practical applications for forestry or for grassland management were also definitely expected and obtained (EYRE, 1970; NELSON and CHAMBERS, 1969; VAN DYNE et al., 1969; MACAN and WORTHINGTON, 1968; VIKTOROV et al., 1964; also important publications of a more limited scope such as DE BOER, 1958; ZONNEVELD, 1966; TADMOR, ORSHAN and RAWITZ, 1962; MARTIN, 1956; DE LANGE and SMIT, 1971).

The comparison between the requirements of wildlife and nature conservation, on the one hand, and of agricultural and other more man-induced land uses was rarely, if ever, made. In the last few years, "ecology" has attained such worldwide attention, that at least some attempt should be made to start the proceedings for such a comparison. Several guidelines can be suggested for this purpose. The main hypothesis is that an ecosystem with great diversity tends to be stable, whereas an ecosystem with low diversity tends towards instability (VAN

LEEUWEN, 1966; VAN DER MAAREL and LEERTOUWER, 1967; WESTHOFF, 1970, 1971). For agricultural production, man creates monotonous systems with poor stability over homogeneous surfaces, whereas the greatest natural diversity is found along "gradient lines" or "gradient zones" where, within a short distance, the habitat factors show many variations. In other words: homogeneous surfaces meet better the requirements of agricultural production, whereas the requirements of natural diversity are met in heterogeneous zones which are often found bordering these surfaces. Homogeneity may be caused entirely by the more permanent factors of the land such as: relief, soils and hydrology, but it may also be induced by human influences on vegetation and on soils and hydrology. There is, therefore, a difference between the fundamental requirements of the two land use types: agriculture and "natural" vegetations, which may help in evaluating the land for these purposes. On the other hand, some requirements may also be met by man-made changes or by human management.

5.5 Land Conditions

5.5.1 Land Qualities

Definitions

Land qualities, or "land conditions", constitute the expression of the way in which the land can meet the requirements of the different kinds of land use. The natural and man-made land attributes, or groups of correlating attributes, must be regarded in terms of "land qualities" in order to derive from them the proper answers concerning the possibilities and constraints of land use and land management. BEEK and BENNEMA (1972) introduced "major land qualities" as a concept in land evaluation, after KELLOGG (1961) and VINK (1960) had for some time been using the narrower concept of "soil qualities" in soil survey interpretation. KELLOGG (1961) writes: "... we appraise separate soil qualities, which we should think of as limited interpretations based upon inferences from soil characteristics. Productivity, fertility, tilth and erodibility are examples. In actual practice soil drainage, as a soil condition, is mainly an interpretation. These terms have been used so long that some regard them as soil characteristics. *But they are not.* They cannot be seen or measured directly. We can only appraise them indirectly by inference from soil characteristics, from plant growth, and from the effects of practices on soil stability". It is clear from this and other texts that soil qualities are directly related to the practical requirements of different kinds of land use. They are based on combinations of soil characteristics which have an interrelated influence on a specific aspect of use (see also SCHEFFER and LIEBEROTH, 1957).

Land qualities are defined along similar lines. The definition in the "Background Document of the FAO Consultation on Land Evaluation" (BRINKMAN and SMYTH, 1973) reads as follows: "A single land quality is a complex attribute of land which, when used as a diagnostic criterion, acts in a manner clearly distinct from the actions of most other land qualities in its influence on the suitability of land for a specific kind of land use. The expression of each land quality is determined by a set of interacting single (or compound) land characteristics having different weights in different environment depending on the values of all characteristics in the set". In the ensuing discussion (BRINKMAN and SMYTH, 1973), the following points were brought to light: Land qualities are land conditions which determine the degree to which a certain tract of land can be put to a certain use. Examples of land qualities relevant to plant production are:

"— ecological conditions such as availability of water for plant growth, availability of oxygen for root growth, availability of radiation (for the assimilation functions)",

"— conditions influencing management such as possibilities for mechanization, resistance to soil erosion",

"— conditions related to improvement possibilities such as response to fertilizers, possibilities for irrigation".

"A major land quality can be defined as a land condition or land characteristic which has a direct bearing on a basic requirement of the use, or in other words, which answers a basic demand of the use ... Land characteristics such as texture, soil depth, and precipitation are determinants for the level of available water, but are not major land qualities". Major land qualities have also been called (BEEK and BENNEMA, 1972): "major ecological conditions, including phyto-ecological, bio- or zoo-ecological, human-ecological and agro-ecological conditions" i.e. conditions related, respectively, to the requirements of plant growth, animal growth (and health) and well-being of human beings; agro-ecological conditions are related to management practices in agriculture, or to rural ecological conditions in their broadest sense.

The following groups of major land qualities for agricultural land use are mentioned in the "Background Document" (BRINKMAN and SMYTH, 1973):

(1) major land qualities related to plant growth,
(2) major land qualities specifically related to animal growth,
(3) major land qualities related to natural product extraction,
(4) major land qualities related to practices in plant production, in animal production or in extractions.

The complete list of the qualities themselves is given in Table 69.

Other groups of major land qualities might be determined, e.g. with relation to non-agricultural land uses. Some examples could be:

— major land qualities related to agricultural settlements and light industries,
— major land qualities related te recreation,
— major land qualities related to wildlife and nature conservation.

A separate kind of land use, which requires special treatment, is irrigated agricultural use. Many of the land qualities related to the latter are basically indicated in the preceding four groups, particularly in Groups 1 and 4. With a view to the special, often very intricate, ecological relationships existing in irrigated agriculture, a special paragraph is devoted to this subject (Para. 5.5.4.).

Table 69. Major land qualities related to agricultural land use (BRINKMAN and SMYTH, 1973) (see also Table 95)

1. *Major land qualities related to plant growth*

    — availability of water
    — availability of nutrients
    — availability of oxgen for root growth
    — availability of foothold for roots
    — conditions for germination (seed bed c.a.)
    — salinization and/or alkalinization
    — soil toxicity of extreme acidity
    — pests and diseases related to the land
    — flooding hazard
    — temperature regime (including incidence of frosts)
    — radiation energy and photoperiod
    — wind and storm as affecting plant growth
    — hail and snow as affecting plant growth
    — air humidity as affecting plant growth
    — drying periods for ripening of crops and at harvest time

2. *Major land qualities specifically related to animal growth*

    — hardships due to climate
    — endemic pests and diseases
    — nutritive value of grazing land
    — toxicity of grazing land
    — resistance to degradation of vegetation
    — resistance to soil erosion under grazing conditions
    — availability of drinking water
    — accessibility of the terrain

3. *Major land qualities related to natural products extraction*
    — presence of valuable wood species
    — presence of medicinal plants and/or other vegetation extraction products
    — presence of fruits
    — presence of game for meat and/or hides
    — accessibility of the terrain

4. *Major land qualities related to practices in plant production, in animal production or in extractions*

    — possibilities of mechanization
    — resistance towards erosion
    — freedom in the layout of a farm plan or a development scheme, including the freedom to select the shape and the size of fields
    — trafficability from farm to land
    — vegetation cover in terms of favorable or unfavorable effects for cropping

Relations to Land Management

Not all land qualities can be modified by man, and many of them can only be modified to a certain extent. Still, their improvement is one of the main contributions of technology to an increased standard of living in most parts of the world. For purposes of improvement, the individual properties of which a land quality consists must be rated in relation to the ecological impact of the quality as a whole as well as to the improvement measures which can be made. Land improvement, therefore, also warrants special treatment (see Para. 5.5.3).

The impact of a land quality on a particular kind of land use may sometimes be measured, but must often be rated by other means. In most cases only single or compound land properties, forming part of a larger land quality concept, can be measured. These measurements may either be directed towards obtaining general information on the way a particular factor affects, for instance, plant growth, in a manner related to the detection of "natural laws", or they may deal with the impact of a particular property under specified land conditions. Some examples, related to soil management, were given in Para. 5.4.4. The many agricultural experiments and soil-chemical as well as soil-physical investigations which have been carried out around the world during the last century, starting with JUSTUS VON LIEBIG, fall under the first approach—investigating general trends. The latter approach, investigations under welldefined land conditions, is more recent. In the U.S.A. and in a few other countries, it is common practice to define the soil type in which an experiment is carried out. In many parts of the world, however, this tradition does not exist, and thus unwarranted gereralizations are not uncommon.

General trends may also be investigated by experiments under "idealized" conditions, e.g. pot experiments. These, and others including many kinds of laboratory investigations, are essential to our knowledge of the soil properties which form a large part of the ecological land conditions. Their proper combination and use under given land conditions are however a problem. Idealized conditions per definition do not occur in nature. The use of data from idealized circumstances is therefore often difficult to apply in actual practice. In the following, some examples of the measurement and of the rating of land properties as part of land qualities, or ecological land conditions, are given.

Measurement and Rating of Land Properties

The major land quality of "availability of water" can be approximated by the following kinds of measurements: precipitation, ground water (VAN HEESEN, 1970) and water retention capacity of the soil. These measurements, combined and compared with the ecological requirements of a given crop at the different stages of its development, indicate with sufficient accuracy the degree in which this major land quality is present in a particular case; if necessary, water balance calculations at different seasons can be made for larger land units.

The major land quality of "availability of nutrients" (for plant growth) has for a long time been the main concern of soil chemists. Measurement of the availability of different nutrients, although methodological problems exist, can be sufficiently ascertained by several quantitative procedures: laboratory determinations, pot experiments and field investigations.

The "availability of oxygen for plant roots" is the proper term for indicating what is more often called "excess water". Water in itself is never in excess, but when overabundant it drives the air from the soil pores. This land quality is therefore usually measured by determining the degree of "excessive wetness", which determines in many cases also the "availability of foothold for plants"; the latter is however also often determined by soil depth and by the porosity and structure of the subsoil.

The "conditions for germination" are determined by the availability of water at the time of sowing and by the structure of the topsoil. The latter depends in most cases on the stability of the soil structure in relation to tillage operations. These may be determined by laboratory experiments, but actual practical experience is also of considerable importance.

There is abundant literature on the influence of salinization and alkalinization of soils in relation to plant growth (Salinity Laboratory Staff, 1954; Salinity Seminar, 1971; UNESCO/UNDP, 1970). The determination of this quality is one of the main concerns in judging actual and potential land uses and possible improvements in arid and semi-arid regions.

In the same manner, many determinations—biological, agronomical, meteorological, chemical and physical—as well as systematized practical experience based on comparative investigations exist for many parts of the world. The actual problem is, however, to combine the available knowledge at a given time for a given region with its specific land conditions. It is then usually found that enough is known about the extreme circumstances occurring in a region, e.g. steep lands with very shallow soils on the one hand, versus well-drained, flat lands with deep soils on the other hand, but that the problems arise in deciding on the grades of the different qualities for the mediocre lands. In most regions, these lands cover two thirds or more or the surface area. Usually, one finds that much less precise information exists for the determination of the ecological conditions of these lands than is needed, and that much more variability exists in the ecological conditions of these lands than was dreamed of before a land resources inventory was made.

Determination of these ecological conditions of the mediocre lands is the most essential part of resources investigations for land use. A somewhat better availability of water may make possible the cultivation of a crop which is in high demand. A somewhat greater permeability may make desalinization possible and thereby lead to considerable land improvements. A less steep slope may permit the mechanization of agriculture under certain systems of management. To investigate extensively each separate kind of land to determine these qualities would be too expensive and would last many years. It is therefore necessary to systematize the work and to select for quantitative investigations of high cost and long duration only those kinds of land which (1) have been judged to be sufficiently representative of at least some of the main ecological conditions, and (2) are either promising enough so that experiments will also provide directly applicable information for future management, or are of a marginal nature but show promise which, if fulfilled, would open up relatively large surface areas for future use.

The investigations leading to this selection usually themselves lead to better knowledge of the ecological land conditions. They consist primarily of a relative grading of the different attributes in relation to either present or future land use or both. They are carried out on the basis of the land resources maps by comparing the data provided by these with the land use requirements (see Para. 5.4) and with observations on land use in the region itself as well as in comparable regions with similar land resources. Some examples are presented in the following.

Table 70. Examples of Agricultural Land Ratings for New Guinea land resources surveys (HAANTJENS, 1965)

a) *Altitude (l) Ratings*[a]

Altitude	0–2000	2000–3500	3500–5500	5500–8000	8000–10000	10000–12000	>12000
l rating	0	1	2	3	4	5	6

Note

In excessively cloudy and wet climates ratings of zones between 3500 and 8000 ff should be made one higher.

[a] Largely as a measure of climate: decreasing temperature (particularly at night), increasing wetness, but probably also involving such factors as radiation, CO_2-pressure. Rainfall distribution could also have been used as a land characteristic, but data are too few for it to be consistently listed. In a crude form it is used in determining land suitability from soil depth and available soil moisture.

b) *Erodibility (e) Ratings*

Slope steep- ness	0°–0°35′ 0–1%	0°35′–2° 1–3.5%	2°–6° 3.5–10%	6°–10° 10–17%	10°–17° 17–30%	17°–30° 30–56%	30°–45° 56–100%	>45° >100%
Slope stability	S U	S U	S U	S U	S U	S U	S U	S U
l rating	0 0	0 1	1 2	2 3	3 4	4 5	5 6	6 6

Notes

1. At this stage no quantitative assessment of slope stability can be given. It should be assessed jointly by the team from soil characteristics and land form and vegetation. Soil features that may point to instability are shallowness and poor horizon differentiation in the soil, absence or poor development of A horizon, coarse textured surface horizons overlying relatively slowly permeable subsoils. Land form indications of instability include evidence of slumping, soil creep, terracettes, gullying sheet wash.
2. Slopes below 17° should be considered stable unless there is clear evidence to the contrary. Slopes above 17° should be considered unstable unless there is clear evidence to the contrary.

c) *Flood (f) Ratings*

Flood number	0	3	4, 5, 6	7, 8, 9	10, 11, 12	13, 14, 15
f rating	0	1	2	3	4	5

Flood numbers are arrived at in the following way:
Allocate 3 points for rate flooding (once in 6–12 years)
6 points for common flooding (once in 1–5 years)
9 points for frequent flooding (twice per year or more often)
2 points for unseasonal flooding (flood free season less than 4 months)
2 points for damaging flooding (considerable sedimentation and/or scouring)
1 point for deep flodding (deeper than 1 ft.)
1 point for long flooding (water remains on land more than 6–15 days)
(where flooding lasts longer than 15 days it should be considered as inundation)

Table 70. (continued)

d) *Determining w Rating on Sites Affected by Rainwater Gleying (Topsoils)*

Degree of gleying	Weak			Moderate			Strong		
Vegetation	G	M	P	G	M	P	G	M	P
Gleying stops at									
< 6 in.	0	0	0	0	0	1	0	1	2
6–10 in.	0	0	1	0	1	2	1	2	2
11–20 in.	0	1	2	1	2	2	1	2	3
21–40 in.	1	2	2	1	2	3	2	3	3
> 40 in.	1	2	3	2	3	3	2	3	4

Use table only if non-gleyed topsoil is <6 in. thick. If it is thicker all w ratings in top three rows should be decreased by one unit, if possible, and the bottom two rows should be treated according to Table 6 A. Lf gleyed horizons are <3.5 in. thick in top three rows or <6.5 in. thick in bottom two rows, they should *not* be considered, unless there are strong vegetation indications of poor drainage.

e) *Salinity (c) Ratings*

Salinity Class	Non-saline	Weakly saline	Saline	Strongly saline
Conductivity (millimhos/cm)	<4	4–8	8–15	>15
< rating	0	1	2	3

Note
These ratings apply to wholly saline soils as well as those with a saline B or C horizon above 2 ft. Soils with saline horizons between 2 and 4 ft. should have ratings 1 unit lower and soils with saline horizons between 4 and 6 ft. 2 units lower.

For Australian New Guinea, the Australian C.S.I.R.O. (Commonwealth Scientific and Industrial Research Organisation) developed a system for assessing the agricultural land characteristics on the basis of their land resources surveys (see also Para. 5.3) (HAANTJENS, 1965). The following land attributes are taken into account: (1) altitude (largely as a measure of climate), (e) erodibility, (s) stoniness and cobbliness, (r) rockiness, (f) flash floods, (i) inundation, (w) drainage, (p) permeability, (d) soil depth, (m) available soil waterstorage capacity, (t) topsoil consistency, (a) soil reaction, (c) salinity, and (n) nutrient status. For each of these properties, scales of ratings have been constructed. Some examples of these ratings are shown in Table 70. It is clear from these ratings that, insofar as possible, well-defined quantitative data on land properties are used. Some of these data may be used to assess the ratings of the major land qualities described previously. The ratings themselves are used by CSIRO to compute directly estimates on land suitability; broad climatic data not used in the basic ratings are also introduced. Vegetation, which is not rated as a land property, is however used as an indicator, e.g. of wetness of the lands. The system, which is well developed and clearly presented, may, with suitable adaptations as to the kind and nature of land

Table 71. Standard mapping symbols for land classification surveys, Bureau of Reclamation, (1967)

Basic land classes and subclasses	**Profile note abbreviations**

Basic land classes and subclasses

Arable
Class 1   — 1
Class 1R — 1R
Class 2   — 2s, 2t, 2sd, 2td, 2std

Tentatively Nonarable
Class 5
   Pending investigation — 5s, 5t, 5d, 5st, 5sd, 5td, 5std
   Pending reclamation — 5(1), 5(2s), 5(2t), etc.
      Project drainage 5d(1), 5d(2s), 5d(2t), etc.
      Similar outclasses for flooding 5f
   Pending investigation or reclamation
      Isolated 5l(1), 5f(2s), 5i(2t), etc.
      Similar subclasses for High 5h and Low 5l

Nonarable
Class 6 — 6s, 6t, 6d, 6st, 6sd, 6td, 6std
   Isolated 6l(1), 6t(2s), 6i(2i), etc.
   Similar subclasses for High 6h and Low 6l

Informative appraisals

Land use
Prc — Paddy rice, cleared
Prp — Paddy rice, partially cleared
C   — Cultivated diversified
Ngl — Native grassland
Cf   — Closed forest
Mof — Mixed-open forest
Lof — Low-open forest
W   — Lakes, ponds, and reservoirs
Eb   — Bamboo and brush-covered flood plains
Ws   — Swamps
M   — Villages and towns
         ROW — right-of-way

Productivity
1, 2, or 6 denoting land class level of factor

Land development
1,2, or 6 denoting ranges in project land development costs
(excluding Project drainage which will be separately
estimated). Land development does not influence land class.

Land Drainability
X   — good
Y   — Restricted
Z   — Poor or negligible

Additional appraisals
      Soils
k   — shallow depth to coarse sand, gravel or pisolite
b   — shallow depth to relatively impervious substrata
v   — very coarse texture (sands, loamy sands)
l   — moderately coarse texture (sandy loams, loams)
m   — moderately fine texture (silt loams, clay loams)
H   — very fine textures (clays)

Topography
g   — Slope
u   — Surface
j   — Irrigation pattern
c   — Brush or tree cover
r   — Rock cover

Drainage
f   — Surface drainage — flooding
w   — Subsurface drainage — water table
o   — Drainage outlet

Note: These appraisals may be defined further by use of subscript
       numerals, such as k_1, k_2 and k_3 indicating ranges of depth.

Profile note abbreviations

Soil texture
   st   — stones and stony
   k   — cobbles and cobbly
   g   — gravel and gravelly
   vcos — very coarse sand
   s   — sand
   fs   — fine sand
   vfs — very fine sand
   lcos — loamy coarse sand
   ls   — loamy sand
   lfs — loamy fine sand
   cosl — coarse sandy loam
   sl   — sandy loam
   fsl — fine sandy loam
   vfsl — very fine sandy loam
   l   — loam
   si   — silt
   sil — silt loam
   scl — sandy clay loam
   cl   — clay loam
   sicl — silty clay loam
   sc   — sandy clay
   sic — silty clay
   c   — clay

Soil structure, type
   gr   — granular
   cr   — crumb
   pl   — platy
   pr   — primatic
   cpr — columnar
   abk — angular blocky
   sbk — subangular blocky

Consistence
Dry: Lo — loose, noncoherent
       so — weakly coherent
       sh — slightly hard
       h — hard
       vh — very hard
       eh — extremely hard

Moist: Lo — loose, noncoherent
       vfr — very friable
       fr — friable
       fi — firm
       vfi — very firm
       efi — extremely firm

Wet: so — nonsticky
       ss — slightly sticky
       s — sticky
       vs — very sticky

Plasticity
       po — nonplastic
       ps — slightly plastic
       p   — plastic
       vp — very plastic

Cementatiom
       cw — weakly cemented
       cs — strongly cemented
       ci — indurated

Moisture Retentivity
       P_{15} — 15-bar pressure

Exchange Acidity
       NEA — neutral salt
       EXAL — exchangable aluminium
       BEA — buffered salt

Table 71. (continued)

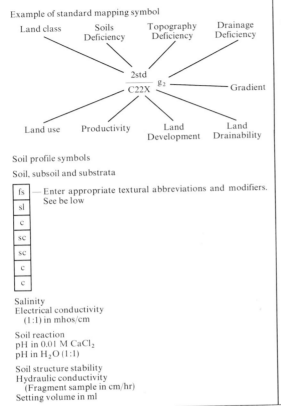

Example of standard mapping symbol

Land class   Soils   Topography   Drainage
              Deficiency   Deficiency   Deficiency

                    2std
                    C22X   g₂
                                          Gradient

Land use   Productivity   Land   Land
                            Development   Drainability

Soil profile symbols

Soil, subsoil and substrata

fs	— Enter appropriate textural abbreviations and modifiers.
sl	See be low
c	
sc	
sc	
c	
c	

Salinity
Electrical conductivity
    (1:1) in mhos/cm

Soil reaction
pH in 0.01 M CaCl₂
pH in H₂O (1:1)

Soil structure stability
Hydraulic conductivity
    (Fragment sample in cm/hr)
Setting volume in ml

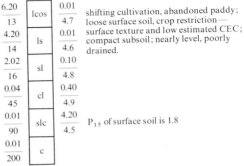

Example of standard profile note
(Profile represents 3-meter depth)

6.20 / 13	lcos	0.01 / 4.7	shifting cultivation, abandoned paddy; loose surface soil, crop restriction —
4.20 / 14	ls	0.01 / 4.6	surface texture and low estimated CEC; compact subsoil; nearly level, poorly
2.02 / 16	sl	0.10 / 4.8	drained.
0.04 / 45	cl	0.40 / 4.9	
0.01 / 90	slc	4.20 / 4.5	P₁₅ of surface soil is 1.8
0.01 / 200	c		

Explanation: 0.01, 0.01, 0.10, 0.40, 4.20 are EC (1:1);
                4.7, 4.6, 4.8, 4.9, 4.5 are pH in CaCl₂

                13, 14, 16, 45, 90 and 200 are settling volume;
                9 is profile number

The essential components of the above notation include: location of sampling, crop or over cover and condition; surface, slope and/or land development requirements. Deep profile notes will also include soil, and substrata data of each significant moisture retentivity at 15 bars, exchange acidity, etc.

characteristics, be used for different lands under different climatic and cultural conditions.

The Iran Manual of Multipurpose Land Classification (MAHLER et al., 1970) gives guide lines for the assessment of land potentialities for several relevant land utilization types in Iran. The way in which the different land attributes are rated is, however, comparable to the Australian system. Separate ratings are given for dry farming and for irrigated agriculture respectively, as well as for range grazing types and for forestry. The land properties are handled as "land limitations", but this makes no essential difference (see also Para. 5.5.2).

A large amount of excellent work on the ecological and economic properties of the land has been done since the early 1930's by the United States Bureau of Reclamation. This work is based on "land classification surveys" and is used primarily to compute as accurately as possible the "payment capacity" to be expected from various lands under irrigation. The system, essentially developed for the semi-arid and arid areas of the U.S.A., has since also been applied in many developing regions in other countries (MALETIC and HUTCHINGS, 1967; MALETIC, 1966; Bureau of Reclamation, 1953, 1967). A few of the essential aspects of the

Table 72. Land classification specifications detailed land classification sample project Colorado (Bureau of Reclamation, 1953)

Land Characteristics	Class 1 — Arable	Class 2 — Arable	Class 3 — Arable	Class 4P — Limited Arable	Class 6 — Nonarable
Soils					
Texture	Sandy loam to friable clay loam.	Loamy sand to very permeable clay.	Loamy sand to permeable clay.	Gravelly loamy sand to clay.	Includes lands which do not meet the minimum requirements for the other land classes and are not suitable for irrigation. They include: lands with very shallow or stony soils, impermeable subsoils, excessive concentrations of salt, pH above 9.0 and more than 15% exchangeable sodium, shallow depth to lime hardpan, low available moisture capacity; rough hummocky and severely channel-dissected bottom-lands, large dunes, overflow and runoff channels not susceptible of fill and other correction and use; timbered bottomlands, permanent waste and sump areas; short steep slopes between terraces and step slopes bordering valley lands; small isolated or high arable tracts not susceptible to delivery of irrigation water so far as the proposed plan is concerned; and other obviously non-arable areas, such as small bodies of arable land lying within large bodies of non-arable land when these would obviously not make usable fields.
Depth: To sand, gravel or cobble	36" plus—good free working soil of fine sandy loam or finer; or 42" of sandy loam	24" plus—good free working soil of fine sandy loam or finer; or 30" of sandy loam to loamy sand.	18" plus—good free working soil of fine sandy loam or finer; or 24" of coarser-textured soil.	6" plus good rooting soil; 12" of loamy sand.	
To shale, raw soil from shale, impervious clay or loam	60" plus; or 54" with minimum of 6" of gravel overlying impervious material or sandy loam throughout.	48" plus; or 42" with minimum of 6" of gravel overlying impervious material or loamy sand throughout.	42" plus; or 42" with minimum of 6" of gravel overlying impervious material or loamy sand throughout.	36" plus; or 30" with minimum of 6" of gravel overlying impervious material or loamy sand throughout.	
To penetrable lime zone	18" with 60" penetrable.	14" with 48" penetrable.	10" with 36" penetrable.	8" with 24" penetrable.	
Alkalinity of soil paste	pH less than 9.0 unless soil is calcareous, total salts are low. Negligible exchangeable sodium.	pH 9.0 or less unless soil is calcareous, total sands are low. Negligible exchangeable sodium.	pH 9.0 or less unless soil is calcareous, total salts are low. Negligible exchangeable sodium.	pH less than 9.0. Less than 15% exchangeable sodium.	
Salinity	Total salts not to exceed 0.2%, or conductivity of saturation extract 4 mmhos/cm. or less. May be higher in open permeable soils and under good drainage conditions.	Total salts not to exceed 0.5%, or conductivity of saturation extract 8 mmhos/cm. or less. May be higher in open permeable soils and under good drainage conditions.	Total salts not to exceed 0.5%, or conductivity of saturation extract 8 mmhos/cm. or less. May be higher in open permeable soils and under good drainage conditions.	Total sands may slightly exceed 0.5% under conditions permitting periodic leaching by flooding.	
Topography					
Slope	0.1 to 2.0% in general gradient	Less than 5% in general gradient.	Less than 8% in general gradient.	Flat or depressional to 20% on smooth slopes.	
Size and shape	400 feet minimum run. 8 acres minimum size.	300 feet minimum run. 5 acres minimum size.	150 feet minimum run. 2 acres minimum size.	Tracts not less than 2 acres in size; not more than 30 acres associated with arable land in 160-acre farm units.	

Table 72. (continued)

Land Characteristics	Class 1 — Arable	Class 2 — Arable	Class 3 — Arable	Class 4P — Limited Arable	Class 6 — Nonarable
Topography					
Surface	No restrictions; or less than 135 cubic yards excavation per acre. Less than 0.2' average cut and fill.	Moderate restrictions; or less than 400 cubic yards excavation per acre. Less than 0.5' average cut and fill.	Appreciable restrictions and may require sprinkler irrigation; or less than 800 cubic yards excavation per acre. Less than 1' average cut and fill.	Smooth to hummocky, but even enough to permit gravity irrigation. Little or no levelling anticipated.	
Cover:					
Brush (over 6') Trees (6" to 15" diameter)	50% or less cover. 7 trees or less per acre.	100% cover or less. 20 trees or less per acre.	100% cover or less. 40 trees or less per acre.	50% or less cover. 7 trees or less per acre.	
Stone and cobble	8 cubic yards or less per acre.	25 cubic yards or less per acre.	50 cubic yards or less per acre.	Insufficient to interfere with grazing or mowing.	
Drainage					
Outlets: Surface	Less than 45' of shallow surface drains required per acre.	Less than 160' of shallow surface drains required per acre.	Less than 330' of shallow surface drains required per acre.	No artifical drainage anticipated, except such improvements as may be required for developement of adjacent better arable lands.	
Subsurface	No specific farm subsurface drainage required.	No specific farm subsurface drainage required.	Less than 115' of open or 230' of tile subsurface drains of average 6' depth per acre; spacing not less than 375' for open or 190' for tile drains on uniform areas. Pumped or inverted wells permissible at comparable cost.		

Notes:　Rights-of-way are delineated as "R.O.W." rather than Class 6. The include state and national highways, county and other community roads, railroads, main or project canals, laterals, drains or waste ditches but not farm laterals. Townsites, schools and other similar permanents installations are indicated by Bureau symbols.

Recommended _____　　　Approved _____

　　　　Project engineer　　　　　　　　　　Regional Director

Date　　　　　　　　　　　　　　　　　Date

procedures used are shown in Tables 71 and 72. The classes indicated are directly related to the feasibility of irrigation under the prevailing circumstances. They may be read in the context of this paragraph as indicating the grades of the various land properties (see also Para. 5.5.4) and Chapter 6). One must, however, view the system used by the Bureau of Reclamation with a critical eye, particularly with regard to the direct manner in which land resources surveys, ecological appraisal of land conditions and economic feasibility classification are combined. This approach may be advantageous for a project in which all circumstances have been studied in detail, but may cause difficulties if extrapolated to other projects without sufficient adaptation to socio-economic and ecological conditions. There is no doubt, however, that the U.S.B.R. system provides many essential contributions to the problem of the appraisal of ecological land conditions.

Parametric Methods

A useful contribution to this field was the introduction of "parametric methods" into land evaluation. One of the earliest methods was devised by R. Earl STORIE (1950, 1954). The "Storie-index" for lands has long been one of the highlights in a very difficult period with regard to land evaluation. The Storie-index is a simple formula:

A = soil profile, B = soil texture, C = slope and D = various attributes, depending on the nature of the land. The result is expressed in a percentage of the best arable land of California. Similar indexes have been made for grazing and forest lands. The Storie-index was made mainly for taxation purposes, as was another system which involves the grading of a number of land attributes, but in this case with the use of tables—the German *Bodenschätzung* (see e.g. TASCHEN-MACHER, 1954). An example from this system is shown in Table 73.

The parametric approach to ecological land conditions has been developed lately by a number of French and Belgian scientists, of whom J. RIQUIER has made the most important contributions. His studies are based on investigations of the influence of different land characteristics on crop growth and agricultural production (RIQUIER and BRAMAO, 1964; RIQUIER et al., 1970; RIQUIER, 1971). RIQUIER's method leads to a careful consideration of the different properties and their interactions; hopefully, it may finally lead to the elaboration of completely quantiative ecological production models. In Nigeria, the following soil characteristics were used to determine productivity: H. soil moisture content, D. drainage, P. effective soil depth, T. texture and structure of the A-horizon, N. base status, S. soluble salts content, O. organic matter of the A1-horizon, A. mineral exchange capacity and nature of clay, M. reserves of alterable minerals in the B-horizon.

The consideration and, where possible, compuation of major land qualities, or major ecological land conditions, and their components are valuable for a better understanding of the ecological production systems of land use. More complete knowledge may lead to a better adaptation of land management practices for agricultural production and for other rural land uses. The application of various kinds of minor and major land improvements can also be more systematically

Table 73. Example of the „Bodenschätzung", "Ackerschätzungsrahmen" (estimates for arable land)

Bodenart (Type of soil)	Ent-stehung[a] (Compo-sition)	"Zustandsstufe"[b]						
		1	2	3	4	5	6	7
S	D		41–34	33–27	26–21	20–16	15–12	11– 7
(sand)	Al		44–37	36–30	29–24	23–16	18–14	13– 9
Sl (S/lS)	D		51–43	42–35	34–28	27–22	21–17	16–11
(slightly	Al		53–46	45–38	37–31	30–24	23–19	18–13
loamy sand)	V			42–36	35–29	28–23	22–18	17–12
lS	D	68–60	59–51	50–44	43–37	36–30	29–23	22–16
(loamy sand)	Lö	71–63	62–54	53–46	45–39	38–32	31–25	24–18
	Al	71–63	62–54	53–46	45–39	38–32	31–25	24–18
	V			50–44	43–37	36–30	29–24	23–17
	Vg				40–34	33–27	26–20	19–12
SL	D	75–68	67–60	59–52	51–45	44–38	37–31	30–23
(lS/sL)	Lö	81–73	72–64	63–55	54–47	46–40	39–33	32–25
	Al	80–72	71–63	62–55	54–47	46–40	39–33	32–25
	V	75–68	67–60	59–52	51–44	43–37	36–30	29–22
	Vg				47–40	39–32	31–24	23–16
sL	D	84–76	75–68	67–60	59–53	52–26	45–39	38–30
(sandy loam)	Lö	92–83	83–74	73–65	64–56	55–48	47–41	40–32
	Al	90–81	80–72	71–64	63–56	55–48	47–41	40–32
	V	85–77	76–68	67–59	58–51	50–44	43–36	35–27
	Vg				54–45	44–36	35–27	26–18
L	D	90–82	81–74	73–66	65–58	57–50	49–43	42–34
(loam)	Lö	100–92	91–83	82–74	73–65	64–56	55–46	45–36
	Al	100–90	89–80	79–71	70–62	61–54	53–45	44–35
	V	91–83	82–74	73–65	64–56	55–47	46–39	38–30
	Vg				60–51	50–41	40–30	29–19
LT	D	87–79	78–70	69–62	61–54	53–46	45–38	37–28
(loamy clay)	Al	91–83	82–74	73–65	64–57	56–49	48–40	39–29
	V	87–79	78–70	69–61	60–52	51–43	42–34	33–24
	Vg				57–48	47–38	37–28	27–17
T	D			63–56	55–48	47–40	39–30	29–18
(clay)	Al		74–66	65–58	57–50	49–41	40–31	30–18
	V			62–54	53–45	44–36	35–26	25–14
	Vg				50–42	41–33	32–24	23–14
Mo				45–37	36–29	28–22	21–16	15–10
(peat)								

Parent rock

[a] D = diluvial deposits, Al = alluvial deposits, Lö = loess deposits, V = residual soil, Vg = stony residual soils.

[b] "Zustandsstufe" = some indication about the natural fertility connected with the process of soil formation.

considered on the basis of this knowledge. Finally, as will be discussed in Chapter 6, the study of land qualities is an essential factor in the development of more complicated systems of land evaluation.

5.5.2 Land Limitations

The use of land limitations is a different way of expressing the land conditions or land qualities discussed in the preceding paragraph. If land qualities are ranked on positive scale, leading from the lowest rating of the poorest ecological conditions to the highest rating of the best, then the use of limitations provides the reverse, or negative scale, detracting from the best possible conditions towards the poorest, which have the strongest and the largest amount of limitations. Thus, the difference lies only in the approach, not in the essentials of the methods.

A good system of using land limitations has been developed in Portugal (CARDOSO, 1963). It is based on the soil survey of Portugal with added special observations on land resources. A Land Classification Manual has been developed which facilitates application of the system to all land units of the survey. For each of these units (soil families) tables have been developed which indicate the main limitations and their influence on plant production. The system is periodically adapted and revised according to new data from agricultural experiments and from practical experience. An example is given in Table 74.

Table 74. Example of a land limitations table for the soil and land use survey of Portugal (Serviço de Reconhecimento, 1963)

Soil family: parahydromorphic brown mediterranean soils on sandstones or argillaceous conglomerates, (symbol Pag).

Average characteristics:
Nature of the soil: $N = 3$
Effective depth: $E = 1$ to 4
Risks of erosion: $Er = 3$
Water deficiency: $Ha = 3$ or 2
Excess water: $Hd = 2$ to 4

Classification (Use capability classes according to combinations of D (slope) and E (effective depth (A is best, E is poorest).

Pag	E 1	E 2	E 3	E 4
D−1	Ch or Dh	Ch or Dh	Ch or Dh	Dh
D−2	Cs	Cs or Ds	Cs or Ds	Ds
D−3	Ce	De	De	Ee
D−4	De	Ee	Ee	Ee
D−5	Ee	Ee	Ee	Ee
D−6	Ee	Ee	Ee	Ee

The land attributes used in the Portuguese system include (SALGUEIRO et al., 1964):

N   — Nature of the soil (a holistic characteristic of the soil: texture, structure, porosity, nutrient content etc.),
E   — Effective depth (more than 45 cm to 35 to 25 to less than 25 cm),
Er   — Erodibility of soil (slight, moderate, great),
D   — Slope (0–2–5–9–16–25% and more),
Re   — Risks of erosion (Er + D) (five classes),
     — Previous erosion (gullies), where necessary,
Ha   — Water deficiency of soil (five classes),
Hd   — Excess of water in soil (five classes),
Hi   — Flooding and inundation (four classes),
P   — Stoniness (five classes),
R   — Rock outcrops (five classes),
S   — Toxic salts (four classes).

During the last few years, a system of land limitations has also been made by the Soil Survey of Scotland (HESLOP and BOWN, 1969) in which the following "defects" of the land are especially considered:

(1) Soil limitations:
     — drainage defects (ground water logging, peaty layer),
     — root zone defects (e.g. stoniness),
(2) Site limitations:
     — topographic limitations (steep slopes, rocky areas, soil pattern),
     — climatic limitations (see also Para. 4.2.1 and BIRSE et al., 1970).

The limitations approach has some advantages under conditions where quantitative knowledge of the land resources and ecological land conditions or of the land utilization types and their requirements is scarce. Limitations can be used to provide a first, approximative orientation about the ecological land conditions, based on general principles derived from landscape ecological knowledge, always present once a survey is made, combined with general knowledge of ecological requirements and common sense. It is therefore a useful tool for the first phases of planning and for establishing more precise methods to obtain knowledge about ecological land conditions. Land (or soil)-limitations maps can provide enough general knowledge about agro-ecological conditions and are easier to read for the non-specialist than are the resources maps, however essential, on which they are based. Examples of a soil map and of the derived soil limitations map are given in Fig. 5.13.

5.5.3 Land Improvement

Gradual Improvement by Management Practices

Although in many cases man has to adapt his land uses to the prevailing land conditions, there are also methods which enable him to adapt land conditions, to a greater or lesser extent, to the requirements of certain land utilization types. A number of these belong to the management procedures utilized throughout the year: adaptations of tillage and harvest procedures, of the chemical compositions of fertilizers, of the cover crops which are grown to prevent soil erosion and to

Fig. 5.13a and b. Examples of part of a Soil Map from the Agro Pontino (Central Italy) and of its derived soil limitations map (made by Miss M. DESSING, Amsterdam, 1971).
(a) *Soil map:* (Soil groups according to the legend of the World Soil Map). D = Regosols and phaeozems in dunesand, L 1 = Eutric fluvisols in lagoonal sand, S1, S21, S22, S23 = Ochric planosols in loam of the coastal ridges, S33, S34 = Chromic luvisols in sandy loam of the coastal ridges, S42 = Complex of phaeozems and histosols of the interridge depressions, with variable extures, M11 = Complex of luvisols and fluvisols in sandy clay loam of the colluvial depressions, M31/33 = Planosols in sandy clay loam, very well developed, of the highest marine terrace ("Latina level", 16 to 26 m above sea level), M32 = Gleyic luvisols in sandy clayloam of the "Latina level", M4 = Complex of planosols and fluvisols in sandy clay loam on slopes of the marine terraces, V1 = Chromic vertisols in the depression of the Pontine Marshes (3–14 m above sea level).
(b) *Soil Limitations Map:*
1 = Soils with only slight limitations for agriculture
2 = Soils with several light limitations for agriculture
3 = Soils with some severe and light limitations for agriculture
4 = Soils with several severe limitations for agriculture
5 = Soils with many severe limitations for agriculture (not shown in this part of the map)

improve soil structure. These land management procedures are in general handled and seen as annual practices, primarily directed towards ensuring a good crop during the particular year. Often, however, they have more lasting effects, which can lead to land improvement, i.e. to enhancement of the ecological land conditions or land qualities with regard to certain crops or certain land uses. On the other hand, some management practices may also lead to a worsening of land conditions; even if they do not lead to erosion or comparable processes, too high doses of chemical fertilizer may lead to toxicity effects, e.g. too high potassium content of soils and plants can cause serious toxic effects in cattle.

The gradual improvement of land conditions by good management practices is often more important than is realized in the design of land use projects. Under humid temperate and tropical conditions particularly, experience has shown that soil structure and organic matter content may be very much improved and that certain nutrients, e.g. phosphates and in some cases potassium, may be considerably enhanced. Gradual improvement of saline or alkaline soils is not in itself impossible; it is, however, too complicated, particularly with regard to systematic drainage, to be a practical proposition for long-term improvements. Gradual construction of terraces using small-tillage equipment is not at all impossible (see e.g. BENNETT, 1939), but it is often done in one or two operations and not as a continuous part of farm management practices. Soil amendments such as lime and gypsum are also sometimes given by repeated applications.

Land Improvement by Non-recurrent Practices

Land improvement is in general not carried out by recurrent practices, but by non-recurrent operations, the effect of which is expected to last for a number of years. Some land resources (climate, geology, relief, soils, water, vegetation, artificial resources; see Chapter 4) may, under certain conditions, be influenced by human technology to lead to better ecological land conditions for specified kinds of land use. The ecological land conditions involved are found in Group 1 of the list of major land qualities (see Table 69, p. 198), but examples of improvements of major land qualities from the other groups also exist.

Perhaps the most common improvement in the world is the enhancement of the availability of water by some kind of irrigation system. Water availability can be enhanced by causing an increase of the total amount available or by adapting the time of availability to the water requirements of specific crops during specific periods of their development (see Para. 5. 5.4.). Availability of oxygen for root growth, by systematic drainage and by the prevention of inundations, is also a common practice (LUTHIN et al., 1957; VAN WIJK et al., 1966). Many landscape-ecological and soil-physical, as well as engineering problems are involved in land drainage. In larger projects the administrative and institutional aspects are also of paramount importance (HELLINGA, 1960).

Land drainage is an essential prerequisite for desalinization and dealkalinization, as well as for most systems of irrigation, particularly those with gravity irrigation and those which utilize water with a relatively high salt content. Improvement of land conditions in old irrigation areas, particularly in the semi-arid and arid zones of the world, is often primarily a matter of improving or even establishing good drainage systems.

Drainage may furthermore considerably enhance the availability of nutrients as well as the foothold for roots. In humid equatorial areas this is often even the case on steep hills with moderately permeable soils. We have seen major improvements in the growth of Hevea rubber and tea on plantations with moderate slopes, in parts of Indonesia, by the establishment of carefully constructed drainage systems along the slopes. Drainage—as well as irrigation systems—is advocated for tea plantations in Northeast India (GRICE, 1971; BISWAS and SANYAL, 1971). Drainage systems, if properly constructed and maintained, may also decrease the erodibility of some tracts of land. Conditions for germination may be indirectly improved by drainage because of the ensuing improvements in soil structure.

As was pointed out previously, drainage of lowlying areas may cause excessive dryness of soils in higher areas; in the devising of drainage systems, one must therefore consider not only the landscape ecology of the tracts to be drained, but also of tracts which, because of their hydrological proximity, might be adversely influenced by the project. Drainage may also adversely affect the availability of drinking water for cattle; if the water table is only lowered by 50 to 150 cm, relatively simple mechanical means, including "self-help apparatus" for the cattle, may be used to overcome this problem, but in any case attention must be paid to this consequence (see also HAGAN et al., 1967).

Changes of relief are usually changes of microrelief, leading either to land levelling for irrigation, sometimes for drainage and sometimes for special land uses (athletics fields) or to increase of microrelief by terracing systems. These operations are in general carried out to enhance major land qualities (availability of water, availability of oxygen for root growth, possibility of mechanization, resistance towards erosion) but, unless carefully carried out, may lead to changes in the soil profile which may adversely affect plant growth; if the humous topsoil is removed, deleterious effects can certainly be expected.

Apart from the construction of fully climatized hothouses, climatic hardships can only partially be corrected by land improvement. The planting of hedges against adverse winds is a well known and often effective means for improving the land for some crops, e.g. orchards. Locally, other means are used, e.g. the digging of ditches in depressions for the prevention of night frosts on slopes. Sometimes also recurrent management practices, e.g. planting in furrows against arid winds, are used.

The prevention, or at least combating, of plant pests and diseases related to the land, can sometimes be locally met by land improvement operations. One example is the addition of sulfur powder to soils to increase their acidity, e.g. for tea plantations on volcanic soils; it prevents the development of a rootfungus which otherwise would be catastrophic for tea grown in some of these soils. Drainage is sometimes also a good means for preventing serious incidence of root-fungi. Other diseases related to the land must be controlled by management practices, e.g. potatodiseases in the Netherlands are controlled by not planting potatoes more often than once every three years on the same tract of land. In this case, the practice is even regulated and enforced by national law. The destruction of host vegetations over large tracts of land may sometimes be the best means of controlling certain pests or diseases. The "sleeping sickness" of cattle (*Glossina morsitans* c.a.) in some parts of Africa, e.g. Rwanda and Zambia, is sometimes controlled by the destruction of certain vegetation types in which the flies nestle and feed (BUIJCKS et al., 1966; VERBOOM, 1965). In theory at least, some vegetation may harbor predators of plant pests; there is as yet little exact information about the possible effects of this situation, but more research in this field is essential for the near future.

Accessibility of the terrain as such can usually not be changed. Accessibility is primarily a function of the natural relief and of soil and water conditions. But the construction of roads and bridges contributes artifactial elements to the land which can to some extent correct the natural situation. The construction of tunnels through mountains, for the transport by road and railroad as well as by pipelines, may be said to belong to land improvement for agricultural and other land uses.

Soil improvement comprises the improvement of the soil itself for one or more land uses, i.e. the improvement of conditions for plant growth, e.g. by mixing soil horizons of different textures, by bringing calcareous subsoils on top of acid soils, by destroying hardpans which obstruct root growth and impede water movement. Soil improvement may also be used to increase the resistance of soil and vegetation on grazing lands, i.e. to make peaty lands better trafficable by cattle and machines (grass mowers), and similarly, to increase the quality and capacity of recreational lands such as athletic fields and playgrounds. To achieve this purpose, peaty lands, and sometimes also clayey and loamy soils, are overlaid with a cover of sand.

Land Improvement as an Investment

Land improvement may thus be seen from the purely ecological and technological sides. It is, however, also essential to look at land improvement as an investment, or as a combination of economical and technological activities undertaken in order to arrive at a desired ecological effect. Such an approach has been very efficiently carried out in Iran (MAHLER et al., 1970) and has since been accepted as

Table 75. General definitions of initial input requirements for land improvement in Iran (MAHLER et al., 1970)

Level	Technical difficulty	Cost	Example
"A" Low	Low, may require some technical advisory services to the landowner	Low, can in general be borne by the landowner	Stone clearing, simple land preparation work, simple levelling
"B" Moderate	Moderate, requires important technical advisory services to the landowner	Moderate, can be borne by the landowner with credit facilities	Simple grading, moderate anti-erosion work. Widely spaced open drains.
"C" High	High, needs to be entrusted to specialists both for planning and execution.	High, requires government funds or long-term credit facilities to the landowner	Tile drainage, terracing, simple land reclamation work
"D" Very high	Usually also requires use of special equipment	Very high, requires large goverment funds, subsidies might also be required	Complex land reclamation work

Table 76. Definitions of land improvement requirements in terms of land improvement works (MAHLER et al., 1970)

Level	Grading	Artificial drainage	Initial salt leaching	Stone picking	Others
Low	(g)	(d)	(l)	(sp)	(Small letter)
Moderate	g	d	l	sp	Small letter
High	G	D	L	SP	Capital Letter
Very high	*G*	*D*	*L*	*SP*	*Capital letter*

Table 77. Example of an improvement table for land qualities under two land utilization types, with low and high recurrent inputs, respectively (BEEK and BENNEMA, 1972)

Input requirements for improvement and maintenance of the land qualities (levels O—A—B—C—D—E) correspond with the horizontal columns. The land utilization types of this example are: dry farming of annual crops (O—A—B) and irrigated annual crop farming (C—D—E).

Grades of relevant land qualities

Levels of input requirements		availability nutrients	availability water	absence risk erosion	absence risk salinization	availability oxygen	availability conditions for mechanization	freedom lay-out of scheme	yield potential
(Natural land conditions)	O	3	4	2	2	3	2	1	5
	A	2	4	1	2	2	1	1	4
	B	2	4	1	2	2	1	1	4
	C	1	2	2	4	3	2	1	3
	D	1	1	1	3	2	1	1	2
	E	1	1	1	1	1	1	1	1

n.h. yield potential scale: 1 = very high
2 = high
3 = medium
4 = low
5 = very low

Explanation:

Input level O   No inputs for improvement—corresponds with severely yield-reducing land qualities are availability of water, availability of nutrients and availability of oxygen.

Input level A   The nutrient availability can be improved to a high grade with fertilizer use, and the availability of oxygen during the growing season can be improved one grade through simple drainage practices. The yields also improve from a very low (5) to a low level (4), which may however be interesting because of the low inputs required.

Input level B   Is not relevant for dry farming because the availability of capital is insufficient to improve the land qualities more than input level A, and the yield potential remains low. This input level could therefore be omitted from the final report of the land evaluation study.

Input level C   Corresponds with a low cost irrigation system, which can considerably improve the availability of water; however, pump capacity is not strong enough for a year-round optimal water supply (grade 2 available water). Furthermore the restricted use of irrigation water increases the risk of salinization to grade 4. The drainage problems increase (available oxygen grade 3) and cannot be controlled at this input level. As a consequence the possibilities of mechanization decrease (grade 2) and the increased risk of salinization is aggrevated by the deficient drainage conditions. Yield potential is estimated at level 3 (medium); however, this level may not be sustainable due to the progressive salinization. It may be concluded that input level C is not recommended for practical implementation, and should, like level B, be excluded from the final report.

Input level D   Can guarantee year-round optimal availability of water; however, the drainage conditions cannot be satisfactorily improved, which results in a medium risk of salinization (grade 3), yield potential is high but may not be sustained.

Input level E   Is similar to level D; however, there is more capital available for recurring costs, which for the land under consideration is required for an adequate constant control of drainage (available oxygen) and the related salinization risk. The high recurring costs are compensated by the higher yield potential at a sustained level.

                 The over-all conclusion of the evaluation of this land unit is that dry farming at level A and irrigation farming at input level E are the most indicated from the point of view of land management, land conservation, and sustained production.

It will be noticed from this example that the improvement of one land quality may influence another quality, e.g. irrigation may influence the possibilities of mechanization, the risk of salinization, and the availability of oxygen. In such a case the affected land qualities need to be re-evaluated.

part of an international program (BRINKMAN and SMYTH, 1973). The general definitions of initial input requirement levels of the Iranian system are given in Table 75; this system is used mainly for reconnaissance surveys (scale 1:250000) when data are not sufficient to specify the type and importance of the land improvement works. For detailed and semi-detailed surveys (1:50000 and larger scales), rating scales for the kinds of land improvement used in Iran are given for the same four levels (Table 76).

A more general system, directly related to some major land qualities, has been developed by BEEK and BENNEMA (1972). These authors propose five different input levels for improvement and maintenance:

A. Low initial input requirements
B. Medium initial input requirements
C. High initial input requirements
D. Very high initial input requirements with normal recurring costs
E. Very high initial input requirements with high recurring costs.

They have in addition adapted the original table of MAHLER et al., including specifications in terms of U.S. dollars; the latter is only meant as an illustration, probably mainly based on experience in Latin America. The data from BEEK and BENNEMA (1972) are given in Tables 77–79.

Regional studies of the improvement of certain lands for relevant and foreseeable land utilization types are found in many countries. Perhaps the most general approach, for a large country, is given by TYURIN et al. (1965), who describe the applications of soil surveys for land improvement in the shape of "Soil-Meliorative Maps". Other interesting examples are described by OLBERTZ and SCHWARZ (1966), GAESE et al. (1971) and DE SMET (1969).

The special problems of saline soils and their improvement have been described by many authors, only a very few of whom are mentioned here (JANITZKY, 1957; Salinity Laboratory Staff, 1954; KOVDA and EGOROV, 1964; DIELEMAN et al., 1963; HULSBOS and BOUMANS, 1960; Salinity Seminar, 1971; KOVFA et al., 1973). Some of these problems will also be touched upon in the discussion on irrigation. For some examples see Table 80.

Table 78. Example of the improvement levels of MAHLER et al. (1970) applied by BEEK and BENNEMA (1972)

Level	Total cost per hectare	Examples	Technical implications for execution
A Low	Less than US$ 50, costs borne by farmer with occasional credit facilities	Special crop management Simple soil management Fertilizers in modest quantities, contour cultivation	May require some technical advisory service to the farmer
B Medium	US$ 50–100 cost borne by farmer with short term credit facilities	Intensive soil management (liming, soil amendments), simple engineering (land smoothing), ridge terraces, widely spaced open surface drains	Requires important advisory services to the farmer
C High	US$ 100–200 requires long term credit facilities	Land grading, broad based terraces, mole drainage	Specialized engineering work, contractor services often with special equipment
D and E Very high	More than US$ 200, long term credit facilities often through regional development projects often through regional development projects with a national priority	Reclamation work land levelling for irrigation, bench terraces, tile drainage, deep tile drainage, deep plowing	Execution is beyond on farm development and implies regional planning and development

Table 79. Land improvement practices by engineering (**a**) and management (**b**) (BEEK and BENNEMA, 1972)

(a)

Land improvement Practices: Soil/water engineering	Produce — Mixed farming	Forestry	Cult. grasslands	Natural grasslands	Perennial crops	Semiannual crops	Annual crops	Capital inputs — Development B medium	Development C high	Development D very high	Recurring normal	Recurring high	Farm power — four wheel	two wheel	animal	hand	Employment high	Employment medium	Employment low	Farm size	Technical knowhow — high	medium	low
Land smoothing	×					×	×	×			×		×	×	×			×	×	any	×	×	
Land grading	×		×		×	×	×		×		×	×	×						×	any	×	×	
Land levelling	×				×	×	×		×	×	×		×						×	any	×	×	
Deep plowing	×				×		×			×	×		×						×	any	×		
Deep plowing "sanding"							×			×	×		×						×	any	×		
Subsoiling	×		×		×	×	×	×			×		×	×	×		×	×	×	any	×	×	
Ridge terraces	×				×	×	×	×			×		×	×	×		×	×	×	any	×	×	
Broad base terraces	×			×	×	×		×	×		×		×	×	×		×	×		any	×	×	
Bench terraces	×			×	×	×		×			×		×	×	×		×	×		any	×	×	
Broad channel terraces	×		×				×		×		×			×	×	×	×	×	×	any	×	×	
Level terraces	×		×		×	×	×	×			×		×	×	×	×	×	×	×	any	×	×	
Ridge construction	×			×	×	×	×		×		×		×			×		×	×	any	×		
Contour banks	×		×		×	×	×	×			×		×		×	×	×	×	×	any	×		
Dam construction	×	×	×	×	×	×	×			×	×	×	×		×	×	×	×	×	any	×	×	×
Dike construction		×		×						×	×	×	×						×	any	×	×	×
Bedding	×	×	×		×	×	×	×			×		×			×	×	×	×	any	×	×	×
Surface drain construction	×		×	×	×	×	×	×			×		×			×	×	×	×	any	×	×	×
Diversion channel construction	×		×		×	×	×	×			×		×			×		×	×	any	×	×	
Canal construction	×		×		×	×	×		×		×		×			×			×	any	×		
Ditch lining			×						×		×		×			×		×	×	any	×	×	
Mole drain installation	×			×	×	×	×		×		×		×					×		any	×		
Tile drain installation	×				×	×	×			×	×		×				×	×		any	×	×	
Brush clearing					×	×					×		×	×		×	×		×	any	×	×	
Jungle clearing		×							×		×					×			×	any	×	×	×
Pioneering (stump removal and controlled burning)							×			×	×					×			×	any	×		
Stone removal	×				×	×	×				×		×			×	×	×	×	any	×		
Rock blasting	×				×	×			×			×	×				×		×	any	×	×	
Gully control	×		×	×	×	×	×		×		×		×			×	×	×	×	any	×	×	×
Mechanical windbreaks						×	×	×	×					×	×	×		×	×	any	×	×	

Table 79 (continued)

(b)

Land improvement practices: Soil management		Chemical fertilizers	Liming	Soil conditioners	Minimum tillage	Soil cover with dead material	Dune stabilization	Soil fumigation	Ditch plowing
Most affected land qualities		n	n	es	s	w	e	d	o In
Produce	Annual crops	×	×	×	×			×	×
	Semiannual crops	×	×		×			×	×
	Perennial crops	×	×		×	×		×	×
	Natural grasslands	×	×						
	Cult. grassland	×	×			×			×
	Forestry	×	×						
	Mixed farming	×	×	×	×			×	×
Capital inputs — Development	A low	×	×		×	×		×	
	B medium			×					×
	C high								
	D very high						×		
Capital inputs — Recurring	normal	×	×		×	×	×	×	×
	high			×					
Farm power	hand	×	×	×	×	×	×		
	animal	×	×	×	×	×	×		
	two wheel	×	×	×	×	×	×		
	four wheel	×	×	×	×	×	×	×	×
Employment	low	×	×	×	×	×	×	×	×
	medium	×	×	×	×	×	×		
	high	×	×	×		×	×		
Farm size	small	×	×	×				×	×
	medium	×	×			×	×	×	×
	large	×	×			×		×	
Technical knowhow level	low					×			
	medium	×	×			×	×	×	×
	high	×	×	×		×	×	×	×

5.5.4 Irrigation

What is irrigation? Is it the supply of water to a crop on a recurrent seasonal basis? Or is it a permanent land improvement which changes the ecological land conditions, a non-recurrent investment? Or is it soil improvement in the strictest sense, because it changes the characteristics of the soil profile, sometimes even, in a taxonomical sense, at a very high level (Soil Order)? Irrigation may be one or more of these together and often all in combination. It is one of the oldest means

Table 80. Land improvement by leaching of salts in Iraq (EL-DUJAILI and ISHMAIL in: Salinity Seminar, 1971

(a) Salts and ESP as affected by leaching at Dujailah

| Description | Depth of soil layer in cm | | | | | | | |
| | 0–30 | | 30–60 | | 60–100 | | 100–150 | |
	ECe	ESP	ECe	ESP	ECe	ESP	ECe	ESP
Before leaching	106.0	34.0	37.0	38.0	34.0	44.0	36.0	44.0
After 12 days leaching, 15 cm[a] drainage	6.5	15.0	13.5	33.0	—	—	—	—
After 42 days leaching, 52 cm drainage	3.0	8.0	2.6	23.0	—	—	—	—
After 69 days leaching and 84 days cropping	2.6	7.0	2.2	21.0	7.5	38.0	24.0	43.0
After 69 days leaching and 93 days cropping	3.8	5.5	2.0	20.0	—	—	—	—
After 69 days leaching and 3 cropping seasons	3.6	4.2	3.9	10.0	8.1	19.0	16.0	21.0

[a] 15 cm Drainage indicates that during the period specified a water depth of 15 cm is discharged by the field drains.

(b) Drainage discharge (Dujailah experiment)

| Type of drain | Leaching | | 1956/57 winter crop | | 1957 summer crop | |
	mm/day	dr/irr	mm/day	dr/irr	mm/day	dr/irr
Tile drains 25 m spacing with 1.2 m depth	12	53%	1.2	47%	1.2	12%
Open drain 150 m spacing and 2 m depth	2.0	14%	0.9	36%	0.9	13%

Table 80 (continued)

(c) Effect of fertilizers, salinity and crop sequence on yield (kg/ha) — Greater Mussaiab Project

Studied crop	Preceding crop	Year	Salinity ECe mmhos/cm		Fertilizer treatment					
			0–30 cm	30–60 cm	O	N	NK	PK	NP	NPK
					Yield in kg/ha					
Wheat	cotton	64	1.2–3.8	1.3–3.7	96	276	672	240	1088	924
	fallow	63	2.3–3.3	2.1–4.2	1296	1398	1580	1200	1564	1932
	sesame	64	2.5–5.0	2.3–5.5	108	676	1020	384	1232	1260
	green gram	66	2.2–3.0	2.6–3.6	288	744	700	448	844	780
	sweet clover	65	1.0–2.7	1.3–2.6	1500	2200	2700	1900	3448	2868
Cotton	berseem	63	1.3–4.9	1.7–5.5	608	720	912	688	828	1008
	leaching	62	1.5–2.1	1.0–2.3	240	284	544	244	376	524
Sesame	—	64	1.3–3.2	1.8–4.2	136	280	264	140	344	300

d) Effect of fertilization of leached soil on yield — Hawijah experiment

EC mmhos/cm		Rice yield kg/ha		Green gram kg/ha	
0–30 cm	30–60 cm	Not fert.	Fert.	Not fert.	Fert.
0.62	0.70	440	632	544	672

e) Average wheat yield in 1957/58 in kg/ha (Dujailah) after leaching

No fertilizer	40 kg/ha of N	80 kg/ha of N	80 kg/ha of N + 32 kg P_2O_5/ha
800	1400	1760	2720

f) Barley yield in relation to water table in Annana in 1956/1957

Average depth of water table in cm below surface	Barley yield in kg/ha
50	648
65	952
100	1552
110	1300
148	1748
156	2856

of enhancing land productivity as well as one of the oldest causes of land degradation. Irrigated agriculture, with all its land utilization types, is practiced on more than 160 million hectares (400 million acres; ISRAELSEN and HANSEN, 1962). Figures for a number of countries in different parts of the world are given in Table 81.

Table 81. Some data on irrigated surface areas in 26 countries situated in different parts of
the world (Israelsen and Hansen, 1962).
Irrigated areas of each of the countries in which more than one million acres are irrigated
shown in thousands of acres

Country	Total area	Area cultivated annually	Irrigated	Percentage of cultivated land that is irrigated
1 Afghanistan	160 000	22 267	8 645	39
2 Argentina	686 528	75 000	2 500	3
3 Australia	1 903 732	21 000	1 600	8
4 Burma	167 545	20 000	1 300	6
5 Chile	183 294	13 620	3 367	25
6 China	2 458 646	267 640	131 820	48
7 Egypt	247 166	6 604	6 604	100
8 France	136 102	78 219	6 178	8
9 India	782 003	318 000	63 630	20
10 Indonesia	470 954	35 000 [a]	11 115	32
11 Iran	401 958	—	5 000	—
12 Iraq	110 080	—	8 150	—
13 Italy	74 478	54 856	5 190	9
14 Japan	91 320	15 055	8 307	55
15 Korea (South)	23 953	4 790	1 610	34
16 Mexico	486 639	57 700	5 330	9
17 Netherlands	8 224	—	2 528	—
18 Pakistan	233 432	52 376	27 000	52
19 Peru	328 998	39 500	3 212	8
20 Philippines	74 085	16 245	1 242	8
21 Sudan	619 200	17 537	3 500	20
22 Taiwan	8 887	2 160	1 337	62
23 Thailand	128 095	13 400	3 264	24
24 Union So. Africa	302 310	19 027	1 350	7
25 U.S.A.	2 322 016	340 998	33 022	10
26 U.S.S.R.	5 503 857	—	16 062	—
Total	17 473 502	1 499 994	362 863	Avg. 26.64

[a] Arable area.

Possibilities and Problems

In the ecological as well as in the technical and economic sense, irrigation provides many possibilities and causes many problems. It always demands a relatively high level of technical know-how, which to some extent has been present for
many centuries and sometimes for several millenia, in traditional systems of land
use (Mesopotamia, Ceylon, India, Indonesia). In its traditional as well as in its
modern and advanced forms, irrigation demands specific operations for maintenance and management, often involving not only technical know-how and manual dexterity, but also perseverance as well as institutional and social organization and political stability.

To some extent, irrigation and drainage are always linked together. The fact
that this is not so in some of the large, very old traditional systems makes their

modernization much more difficult. What determines the need for drainage in irrigated agriculture and how can we make the most efficient use of our very scarce water resources? Which water resources can be used under which conditions of climate and of land? To what degree can calculations of the water balance of lands and crops and the traditional measurements of soil permeability and of other physical soil characteristics provide us with sufficient information for irrigated land use? Only very few of these questions can be discussed at all, and none of them thoroughly, in a general book on land use. Regional and local conditions vary considerably, and the experiences gained in different areas vary accordingly. A careful comparative study of land conditions and of the corresponding techniques and experiences in the different irrigated land utilization types would be of great benefit to world agriculture; too much is still left to individual experience supported by a few elementary quantitative formulae. The gaps existing between soil physics and soil technology as well as those between soil technological science and soil technological practice are still very wide. They are caused mainly by the fact that the actual variations in land conditions are often too great to be put in simple formulae. Elaborate model experiments together with the above mentioned comparative studies are needed to fill these gaps (see KOVDA et al., 1973).

Irrigation Purposes

Irrigation is practiced basically because a particular crop needs more available water than is provided under the prevailing land conditions. These may be (1) an absolute lack of the total quantity of water needed during its growing period, (2) a lack of water during specific periods of its vegetative development, or (3) a lack of water during periodically recurring years of excessive drought. The quantity of water needed is mainly a function of the consumptive use of the crop during its vegetative phases. Usage differs widely among the many crops on which irrigation is practiced. In some cases, however, although the real lack of water is not very great, the land user prefers to provide easily available water by irrigation for better growth or higher productivity. It is not possible to give a complete list of all the crops in the world which are grown with irrigation. Only some of the very common examples may be mentioned:
— rice (in all countries between the equator and the warm temperate, mediterranean zones: from Java to the Po Valley in Italy);
— wheat (mainly in arid regions);
— barley (mainly in arid regions);
— cotton;
— sugar cane;
— pastures and fodder crops;
— orchards of various kinds (citrus, date palm, olive, almond) and other fruit crops such as cocoa (in some areas of Latin America);
— maize, soybeans, tobacco;
— many horticultural crops (lettuce, tomatoes, carrots, etc.).
    A much longer, more systematic list would probably show that nearly all agricultural and horticultural crops are grown with irrigation somewhere in the world (see also Yearbook of Agriculture, 1957, 1958; BISWAS and SANYAL, 1971;

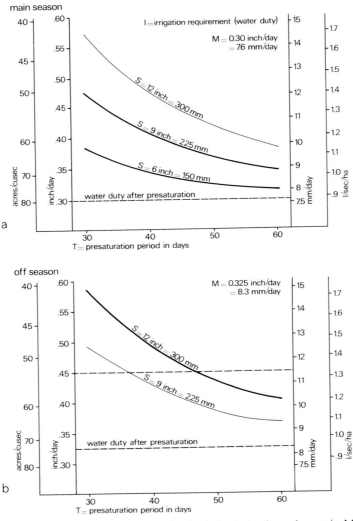

Fig. 5.14. Water requirements for lowland rice irrigation schemes in Malaya (VAN DE GOOR and ZIJLSTRA, 1968)

KOVDA et al., 1973). Several data indicating the water requirements of the principal crops in the Baghdad area (Iraq) are given in Table 4 (p. 52). These are the requirements under desert-climate conditions (mean annual precipitation between 100 and 150 mm). The requirements of crops depend, in their order of magnitude, mainly on the nature of the crop itself; the actual figures for a given climate are also influenced by the general circumstances of evapo-transpiration as calculated e.g. with Penman's formula (ISRAELSEN and HANSEN, 1962). For highly productive new varieties, such as the so-called "green revolution" varieties of rice and wheat, consumptive use is also related to the high yield-capacity of these varieties. The general rule, that highly productive varieties need optimum ecological conditions, plays a particularly great role in the field of water consumption (see also YARON et al., 1973).

A fair example of irrigation requirements under equatorial lowland conditions in Malaysia is described by VAN DE GOOR and ZIJLSTRA (1968). In this system, water requirements are determined by four main factors:
(a) water for evapo-transpiration,
(b) water for percolation,
(c) water for establishing a water layer in the field,
(d) water for saturation of the soil.

Under the conditions of flooded rice fields, the evapo-transpiration rate is always at the maximum possible under the prevailing climatic conditions, i.e. the potential evapo-transpiration rate. Water loss by percolation is determined by the local land conditions; this differs from irrigation under arid conditions, where in general a minimum percolation is needed to prevent salinization. There is no conclusive evidence on the thickness of the water layer needed on an irrigated rice field; a moderate water depth of between 5 and 10 cm seems to be satisfactory. For saturation of the soil approximately 15 cm (5 to 6 inches) of water is required. Furthermore, as in any irrigation scheme, water loss during distribution in the canals is unavoidable; under the Malaysian conditions, with smallsize holdings, the loss is estimated at 50% of the net requirement in the fields, which means an average irrigation efficiency of 66% from the water supplied at the main "prise d'eau". In Fig. 5.14, the water requirements during and after the pre-saturation period are given for the main season and for the off-season.

Many methods, techniques and materials exist for applying irrigation water to the fields. Their application depends partly on the source of water: (a) flowing open water (rivers), (b) stagnant water (reservoirs), (c) subsoil water (wells). Flowing water leads in most cases to gravity irrigation, i.e. the flow of water by its own gravity along a natural or artificial gradient, towards the fields, where it is used either for basin irrigation or for furrow irrigation. Since ancient times water wheels (operated by men or animals) and other simple mechanical devices have also been used (see Fig. 5.15).

Today in many cases, particularly for small irrigation schemes and for individual holdings, the use of pumps (engine-operated, often with gasoline) is common.

The application of water from stagnant sources depends on the size of the scheme and on the kinds of crop to which the water is applied. One often finds in any scheme that even though the main system is worked by gravity, pumps are used locally for application to individual holdings or even to more highly situated parts of a project. The use of water from wells nearly always implies some source for lifting the water to the surface. Well water has been drawn since ancient times e.g. by animal-drawn water wheels (see Photo 18) and is today drawn by various pumps. Artesian water, coming to the surface under natural pressure occasionally can be used but it is only rarely available in quantities suitable for irrigation. The transport of water to the fields by the ancient system of "khanats" or "khareez" was discussed in Para. 4.4.1 (p. 123) (see also SOUSA, 1969).

The importance of the construction of dams and reservoirs for the establishment of irrigation schemes is sufficiently understood. In many cases, the construc-

The Sumerian

" Dalia "

The Assyrian

" Dalia "

Fig. 5.15. Example of Sumerian and Assyrian Water-lift Methods, the "Dalia" (SOUSA, 1969)

The "Dalia" is a primitive water hoist which had been used by the Sumerians, Babylonians and Assyrians and is still used at present in the Basrah district to lift water. It is called "Dalia" and is very similar to the "Shaduf" of Ancient Egypt which is still in use there today. Water is lifted in a leather bucket or any other kind of pail of any make. This bucket is supported by a rope tied at the upper end to a bar, which in turn is supported by a horizontal pole resting on two up-rights, and is weighted at its free end usually with a lump of clay. The rope tied to the bucket is pulled downwards by a man standing at the edge of the water until the bucket is pressed beneath the surface of the water and fills. It is now lifted up, the weight at the end of the swinging pole assisting its upwards move, until level with the irrigation channel, when it is emptied, and the whole process is repeated. A "Dalia" is seldom employed to lift water more than about six feet.

The oldest representation of the Iraqi "Dalia" is depicted on an archaic Sumerian seal as shown in the upper reproduction. Here we have a tree with fruit, perhaps a fig tree in which case it is the oldest known case of the fig tree in art, and a nude human figure picking the fruit. Another scene on the right side of the imprint represents another nude figure using the "Dalia" in raising water with a bucket.

An improved "Dalia" is exhibited on another imprint depicted on the wall of the palace of Sennacherib at Niniveh as reproduced in the lower figure. Here we notice that the bar holding the bucket at one end is supported by a brickwork base instead of a horizontal pole. The weighted end of the pole is also bent to form a sort of a handle to help raising and lowering it. Two "Dalias" are noticed in the Assyrian design, one of which raises the water to a streamlet then relifting it by a second double "Dalia" to another streamlet at a higher level. This procedure is still applied today in a similar case by erecting two pumps for raising the water twice to a high level (see: A. PATERSON "Palace of Senacherib, Plate 32 33; G. CONTENAU "Every day Life in Babylonia and Assyria", 1914, pp. 43–44).

tion costs for large dams are too high to be carried by irrigation schemes alone. Multipurpose dams, combining the use of water power for electricity with the construction of navigable waterways and with irrigation, are often the rule. Photos 14 and 15 (p. 127) show dams which are used mainly for irrigation schemes and for flood prevention in the downstream areas. The construction of dams in

Photo 18. Animal-drawn water wheel in a date palm orchard in Iraq

Photo 19. Embankment of the Euphrates river in the Ramadi project, Iraq

lowland areas often also necessitates the construction of embankments both above and below the dam site to prevent unwanted flooding of the adjoining lands (see Photo 19).

Irrigation Methods

The modern application systems of irrigation consists mainly of the following (see e.g. YARON et al., 1973).
(a) gravity irrigation,
(b) sprinkler irrigation,
(c) trickle irrigation,
(d) subsurface irrigation.

The requirements of these methods with regard to the land conditions differ in many aspects. Gravity irrigation requires sufficient gradients for its flow and fields sufficiently level and in some manner embanked for its application to the crops. Sprinkler irrigation and trickle irrigation are less dependent on the relief, but need investments and recurrent costs in pumps and other apparatus. Subsurface irrigation requires level fields with sufficiently permeable soils; it is practiced for instance in some sandy soils in the Zuyderzee polder area of the Netherlands and for providing water to athletics fields on sandy soils. Subsurface irrigation has no evaporation losses apart from those of the crop which it supplies, but seepage losses may occur.

Gravity irrigation tends to have more losses on the way from intake to the field, whereas sprinkler irrigation may have considerable losses due to wind drift and evaporation during application. Trickle irrigation, developed during the last years in orchards in Israel, is particularly useful for application to orchards on rather permeable soils; the water is applied at low pressure from plastic tubes laid along the rows of trees at intervals of one or a few meters.

The establishment of a permanent gravity irrigation scheme is a major land improvement, but it requires continuous management and maintenance and good over-all organization. Subsurface irrigation schemes have to some extent the same requirements, although they can often be more easily carried out on small individual holdings. Sprinkler irrigation and trickle irrigation need very few permanent land improvements. On the other hand, desalinization and desalkalinization of soils is usually carried out by gravity irrigation.

Gravity irrigation is better applicable with relatively saline water, because less damage to the foliage of the crops can result. With sprinkler irrigation and trickle irrigation, one has better control over the amount of water applied at a particular time; they offer a somewhat higher efficiency, at least if properly managed in schemes which are not too large. MOHRMANN (1959) advocates the use of sprinkler irrigation as supplemental irrigation in the humid tropics; he indicates that it is useful for crops such as beans and potatoes which are grown during the dry season and for some perennial crops. Supplemental sprinkler irrigation is often applied to pasture and field crops, even in humid temperate climates such as those which prevail in the Netherlands. It may have great possibilities in semi-arid

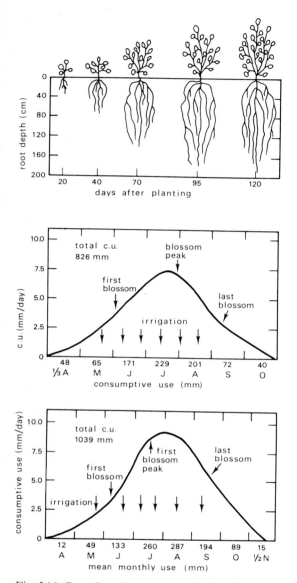

Fig. 5.16. Growth and evapo-transpiration of cotton (BIELORAI. In: YARON et al., 1973)

regions with winter rains, where it can be used to obtain maximum yields of wheat and of other winter crops grown in these areas (see e.g. VINK, 1970b). As MOHR-MANN (1959) states, in some projects a combination, in one valley, of gravity irrigation on flat lowlands and sprinkler irrigation on the adjoining higher land may well be more effective than a necessarily expensive project to cover also the high areas with gravity irrigation. For the same purpose, on suitable crops, trickle irrigation may now be used. MOHRMANN mentions the following advantages of sprinkler irrigation over gravity irrigation:

— fewer requirements as to the topography of the land,
— no need for levelling, which is costly and may destroy essential soil characteristics,
— less sensitive to erosion,
— most economic use of the available water,
— very valuable for newly sown fields,
— very mobile and flexible for use on young plantations,
— may be labor-saving if permanent installations are established,
— better aeration of the soil,
— may give a higher fertilizer efficiency.

On the other hand he notes the following disadvantages of sprinkler irrigation:

— high operating costs,
— high initial cost which has to be amortized over a short period (10 to 15 years),
— poor distribution of the water if high winds occur,
— delicate operations when moving lines and sprinklers in a still wet crop, over wet soil,
— need for skilled staff for operations and maintenance,
— diseases and pests may be enhanced by the high air humidity during sprinkling,
— sprinkling when the sun is high may cause burning of foliage.

The frequency of applications of irrigation is a function of both the needs of the crop and the land conditions, e.g. the water retention capacity of the soils and the rooting depth allowed by soil conditions. In Fig. 5.16 and Table 82 (from YARON et al., 1973) information is given on the response of cotton to different irrigation treatments.

Investigations into the suitability of land conditions for irrigated land use have been made since ancient times, with many different methods. Particularly well known is the U.S.-Bureau of Reclamation system, which was referred to in preceding paragraphs (Bureau of Reclamation, 1953, 1967; MALETIC, 1966; MALETIC and HUTCHINGS, 1967). Very interesting work was done at an early

Table 82. Mean values of consumptive use, yield and water use efficiency of cotton in a three-year experiment in the Negev (Israel) (cited after AMIR and BIELORAI, from YARON et al., 1973)[a]

Treat-ment	Date of irri-gation after planting (days)	Consump-tive use, mm	Water applied mm	Yield, kg/ha		Rela-tive yield %	Water use efficiency, kg cotton/ mm water
				seed cotton	Lint		
1	—	237	—	1880	760	39	0.79
2	70	348	110	2770	1120	58	0.80
3	70, 92	445	208	3830	1500	80	0.86
4	70, 92, 104	535	298	4750	1870	100	0.89
5	67, 88, 109 125	610	373	4800	1860	100	0.79

[a] Date of planting – April 20. There was a 10% variation in seed cotton yield between years. The results indicated that maximum yield was achieved with three irrigations per season.

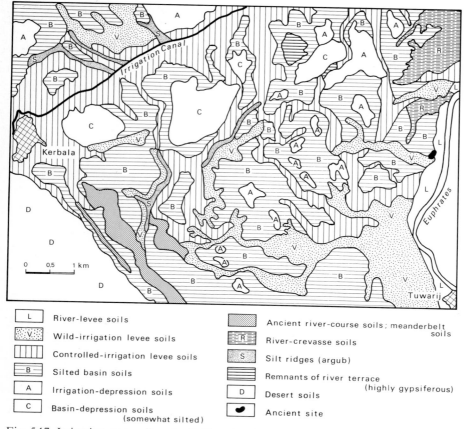

Fig. 5.17. Irrigation as a soil and relief-forming factor in the Lower Mesopotamian Plain. Simplified soil map of the Euphrates-delta plain between KERBALA and TUWARIJ showing the distribution of soil units physiographically distinguishable (SCHILSTRA, 1962)

date by JEWITT and his co-workers in the Gezira Scheme of Sudan (see e.g. ADDISON, 1961) and by DURAND (1956) in North Africa. Excellent work from Pakistan is available in mimeographed reports; the work from the latter country as well as from several other countries is referred to in a recent publication (Salinity Seminar, 1971).

Dangers of Land Degradation

The main dangers of land degradation which may be provoked by irrigation are:
(b) erosion and landslides,
(b) salinization,
(c) waterlogging,
(d) sedimentation.

Table 83. Average texture of the uppermost part of the irrigation cover (0–60 cm) in Mesopotamia in direction downstream (DELVER, 1962)

Area	Euphrates deposits			Tigris deposits		
	s	si	c	s	si	c
Middle Tigris left bank				16.3	50.6	33.1
Yusufiya	15.3	50.0	34.7			
Yusufiya (200–300 cm)	15.6	50.6	33.8			
Latifiyah	17.3	47.1	35.6			
Diwaniya	15.7	50.3	34.0			
Rumaitha	14.8	50.0	35.2			
Rumaitha (200–300 cm)	15.1	50.5	34.4			
Shatra	14.5	54.4	31.1			
East Ghyrraf[a]	10.3	56.3	33.4			
Dujaila				11.0	—	—
Ali Gharbi				11.6	59.3	29.1

[a] This area has been sedimented by both rivers.

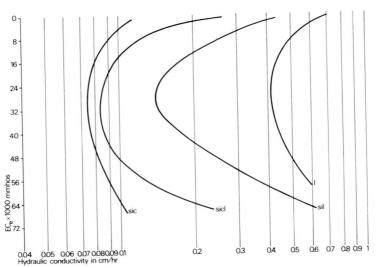

Fig. 5.18. The relation between hydraulic conductivity (determined after 20 hrs percolation) and ECe for soils with different textures at Rumaitha, Iraq (DELVER, 1962)

Good examples of the first three are found in the literature already referred to (see e.g. FLAWN, 1970; Salinity Seminar, 1971; KOVDA et al., 1973). The danger of sedimentation is less generally recognized. Still, it is a serious problem in some regions, notably in Mesopotamia (VINK, 1970b). The original hypothesis that irrigation sediments were very beneficial to agricultural productivity has been completely reversed, at least for many parts of this region. The large sediment loads carried by the Twin Rivers, Euphrates and Tigris, result in continuous silt problems in the irrigation canals and in the deposition of a poorly structured soil cover which is one meter or more thick and which has a low permeability (see Fig. 5.17 and Table 83).

These conditions cause great troubles in preventing the salinization and in improving the desalinization of these lands. The low topsoil permeabilities (see Fig. 5.18), combined with the presence of saline ground waters, provide problems for agricultural land use in this region which are much greater than was originally thought. The great difficulty in maintaining good water transport in the continuously silting irrigation canals enhances these difficulties even further.

Chapter 6   Land Evaluation

6.1 General

Definitions

Land use is a set of biological and technological human activities, engaged in for economic and social purposes. These activities are directed towards the management and improvement of land resources. Land resources as such are phenomena of nature which are described in strictly scientific terms; they give no indication themselves of how they could or should be used. Land qualities, or ecological land conditions, are used as a means for indicating the direct relations between the land as an ecological complex and the biological and technological activities of land use. A land quality is a "complex attribute of land which acts in a manner clearly distinct from the actions of most other land qualities in its influence on the suitability of land for a specific kind of land use". The land qualities may therefore be used as diagnostic criteria for land suitability, but they do not themselves indicate a suitability (BRINKMAN and SMYTH, 1973). Land qualities are extremely useful in indicating how a land, with given natural (resources) characteristics, could be used in a given land utilization type. They do not, however, indicate whether one land utilization type would be better suited to a particular kind of land than another. Land qualities are also essential for indicating improvement needs of lands, but they do not indicate whether a particular improvement would be suitable for execution within any relevant and foreseeable land utilization types.

For the purpose of judging "land suitability", both for land use and for land improvement, a systematic land evaluation is necessary. Land evaluation is "the process of collating and interpreting basic inventories of soil, vegetation, climate and other aspects of land in order to identify and make a first comparison of promising land use alternatives in simple socio-economic terms" (BRINKMAN and SMYTH, 1973). Land evaluation therefore bridges the gap between the physical, biological and technological means of land use and its social and economic purposes. Land evaluation is not economics, but neither is it a purely physical discipline; it is the utilization of social and economic parameters in evaluating physical data. The actual characteristics and behavior patterns exhibited by the social and economic data used for this purpose lie within the sphere of the investigations carried out by the social scientists and economists; likewise, the physical data are, or at least should be, used as parameters for social and economic evaluations.

This definition of land evaluation is narrower than that used by STEWART et al. (1968), who state that "terrain evaluation", which is a purely physical evaluation, often used for military purposes, belongs to land evaluation. Terrain evaluation, in the commonly used sense, however, is combined with land conditions which are land qualities; it is not concerned with the socioeconomic aspects of land use. Neither are the purely engineering evaluations of land conditions, although transport economics, particularly in developing regions, can be very important; in general, however, these aspects are considered at another level or in another phase of a project (see e.g. Integrated Surveys, 1968). Agricultural land use is always carried out in enterprises which are units for economic production under given social conditons; the consideration of economic and social parameters, i.e. of "quantities (considered) constant in case considered, but varying in different cases" (Concise Oxford Dictionary) is essential in land evaluation for agricultural purposes. It is left to the economic and social sciences to study the true values of these parameters and their variations as well as the laws and trends which can be discerned in their evolution.

Land suitability is "the fitness of a given tract of land for a defined use; differences in the degree of suitability are determined by the relationship, actual or anticipated, between benefits and required inputs associated with the use on the tract in question" (BRINKMAN and SMYTH, 1973). In its most quantitative form, land suitability is expressed in economic terms of inputs and outputs, or in its results as net income or, especially in developing regions, as standard of living of the farming population. In non-agricultural rural land uses, e.g. in recreation, the economic results are of less direct importance, and economic inputs often have to be compared with social values; the test of suitability, which in ecconomic enterprises can be compared with a desired income or standard of living, must, in the latter cases, be compared with the input per social category, e.g. the number of urban people using a recreation facility, which the relevant administrative bodies are willing to spend (see also VINK, 1960, 1967).

Land evaluation is, however, often carried out in relative terms, partly because insufficient quantitative information is available, and partly as a first approximation in a complicated iterative procedure (see Para.6.5). This is often called "land suitability classification" of which the definition reads (BRINKMAN and SMYTH, 1973): "Land suitability classification is an appraisal and grouping (or the process of appraisal and grouping) of specific tracts (of land) in terms of their relative land suitability for a defined use".

Land evaluation may be involved more or less directly with the actual market values of soils, e.g. for taxation or for credit facilities (STORIE, 1950, 1954; TASCHENMACHER, 1954; FOUND, 1971), but this is often not the case. Market values of soils are first and foremost determined by local or regional supply and demand. The same kinds of land may have very different market values in nearby regions, and, under given local conditions, very different soils may be bought and sold for the same price. Land suitability is the expression of the physical and ecological potential of a land based upon certain social and economic assumptions; the market value may well be the result of very different assumptions and very different potential land uses, e.g. influenced by the proximity of urban concentrations.

Assumptions Used in Land Evaluation

The assumptions used in land evaluation are concerned with the nature and processes of the relevant and foreseeable *land utilization types*. The fact that a land utilization type is considered relevant is in itself an assumption; alternative sets of land suitabilities may be made for different land utilization types, and these may be added to if other types are foreseen. The nature of the assumptions has to do with the economic and social conditions in their widest sense and with the level of technical know-how of the farmers (see als VINK, 1963a). These assumptions, and the kinds of land utilization types, must be clearly indicated in any land suitability classification.

The assumptions may be concerned not only with the kind of land use which is relevant on the tract of land itself, but also with outside effects if certain sets of management practices are assumed. This situation may occur e.g. when a certain amount of soil erosion, which is considered unavoidable, may also lead to pollution of waters by fertilizers and by sediment. A comparable situation is caused by drainage or irrigation of lands, as a result of which excessive drainage and water-logging or salinization, respectively, occur in adjoining lands (see Para. 5.4.5 and 5.5.4). In some cases in which the destruction of vegetation or the use of pesticides must perhaps be taken into account, a quantitative approach might be made possible by assuming a certain "social cost" inherent in a specific land utilization type. Whether this social cost, which may or may not be expressed in economic terms, is permissible depends on the responsible authorities; the presence of such a cost should, however, be indicated in a suitable form when discussing specific cases of land suitability for specific land utilization types (see e.g. DEE et al., 1972, 1973). It is difficult to decide today whether a predicted future scarcity of essential minerals, such as fossil fuels and basic materials for fertilizers (P,K) should already be taken into account. The problem should, however, be noted so that it can be acted upon if necessary.

Land evaluation, using sets of assumptions which are of value only during a specific period, is always relatively ephemeral. Changing social and economic conditions, or technological developments, including the introduction of new varieties of crops, may lead to different suitabilities of the land. The basic land resources are much more permanent. These can only be changed by large projects of major land improvements or by catastrophic natural processes: volcanic eruptions, earthquakes or floods. In general, therefore, land resources data and land resources maps are the only reliable bases for predictions and interpretations of land qualities and land suitabilities. Basic land resources maps can always be reinterpreted for practical use with new assumptions or under new conditions.

Land suitability can be interpreted from land resources maps using two main sets of assumptions about land conditions:

(a) *Actual land suitability*, i.e. "the suitability of land units for the use in question in their present condition—without major land improvements",

(b) *Potential land suitability*, i.e. "the suitability of land units for the use in question at some future date after major land improvements have been effected where necessary" (BRINKMAN and SMYTH, 1973).

The latter may be done with or without consideration of repayment costs, or amortization, of major capital inputs which are required for the effectuation of the major land improvements. In both kinds of suitability classifications, the recurrent annual expenditures inherent in each land utilization type must be considered. Major land improvements are improvements of the kind discussed in Para. 5.5.3.

Some Examples

There is no essential difference between "land suitability" and "land use capability". The latter term has been used for many years in the system of the U.S. Soil Conservation Service (BENNETT, 1939; HUDSON, 1971) and has been modified and adapted in many countries, with or without the use of the original "eight classes". The only difference, mainly theoretical, lies in the fact that the definition of land use capability presupposes *per se* the "retention of the integrity of the soil", whereas in land suitability, although any judgement must be made with a view to the longevity of the land utilization type, the actual relation to soil erosion is left to the management practices belonging to the land utilization type. A practical difference in approach lies in the fact that separate "land use capability surveys" existed originally in the U.S.A., and still exist there as well as elsewhere. But these surveys, if executed in a scientifically correct and practically useful manner, are in fact a kind of landscape ecological survey. They provide the basic resources data in such a manner that the land use capability can be easily interpreted from a given set of normative data. The technological and socio-economic assumptions of the land use capability surveys have not always been clearly indicated. In fact, it was not until 1958, more than 20 years after the system was first used, that the assumptions used in the U.S.A. were published by KLINGEBIEL (1958). These assumptions point to the kinds of highly industrialized land utilization types which are common in the United States. In other circumstances, other assumptions have to be, and often are taken into account, but their consideration has not always been clearly elucidated.

The Land Classification of the U.S. Bureau of Reclamation (1953, 1967) is also a system which leads to the evaluation of land suitabilities in a manner similar to that used in the present text. The use of this system, in particular for irrigated land utilization types, has led to a special treatment of some of the relevant problems, some of which have been taken over for international use (BRINKMAN and SMYTH, 1973).

The Cornell System of Economic Land Classification (CONKLIN, 1957; Yearbook of Agriculture, 1958) covers a field which, although showing a large overlap with the land evaluation discussed in the present text, has some other characteristics. Its emphasis is more on the classification of the land utilization types in an economic sense, and it is less concerned with the actual and potential suitabilities of the land as derived from the basic land resources.

Soil survey interpretation (BARTELLI et al., 1966; VINK, 1963a) is in general a kind of land evaluation. Depending on the kind of interpretation which is made from the soil maps, it provides information about land qualities or land suitabilities. Soil survey interpretation as such is most useful in all regions where the soils are the main key variables in the cultural ecosystems; in areas where other land attributes are more important, soil maps and their interpretations are only satisfactory if the essential land attributes have been satisfactorily mapped, e.g. as soil phases.

Land evaluation is an essential tool in land use planning. It is assigned the indispensable task of translating the data on land resources into terms and categories which can be understood and used by all those concerned with land management, land improvement and land development. The process of integrating land evaluation and land use planning is, however, much more complicated than is often realized. This is partly due to the fact that it is only recently that the complicated nature of the planning processes themselves has become clearer (DROR, 1971; HAYES, 1969; FOUND, 1971). The different steps and procedures in land evaluation itself are also only gradually being developed (VINK, 1963a; BEEK and BENNEMA, 1972; BRINKMAN and SMYTH, 1973; see also Para. 4.3.1 and 5.3).

6.2 Actual Land Suitability and Soil Suitability

Actual Land Suitability

Actual land suitability is an indication of the possibility of using the land within a particular land utilization type without the application of land improvements which require major capital investments. It is, in cases in which land improvement projects are considered, also called "suitability without the project". It is by no means equivalent to present land use, since substantial improvements in land use are often possible without major, non-recurrent, capital investments in the land.

Actual land suitability may differ from present land use in various aspects and from different causes.

(a) Within the existing land utilization type, the introduction of new crops or of new varieties of existing crops is often possible.

(b) Within the existing land utilization type, better methods of crop and land management may be applicable.

(c) Within the existing land utilization type, a simple reallotment of fields of adjoining farms may facilitate the growing of crops or the use of lands for pastures (see Fig. 6.1).

(d) There are often one or more land utilization types applicable to the lands considered, but which have thus far not been realized, either because they are completely unknown to the region or because the know-how of the farmers is thus far insufficient for their application.

(e) The lands are not used at all, but could be used by simple clearing operations.

The causes which have led to the situation that actual suitability is not realized in present land use are various and often complicated. Their solution is therefore often difficult and may be more complex than is the case by realizing some kinds of potential suitability. Still, as land resources are generally fragile, the development of land use without major changes of the land conditions can make major contributions to world development while avoiding some of the unfavorable side-effects which often accompany "land development" (with major land improvement works) in its full sense (MAHLER, 1972).

Some of the more important causes for this "lag" between present use and actual suitability are the following.

Political instability always has been, and today still is, a cause for present land use lagging behind actual land suitability. This instability may be both external, between countries, and internal, within one country. The effect of the first case is that the farmers tend to take a conservative view of developments; it makes it difficult for them to make investments in such things as fertilizers, new tools and buildings. Internal instability prevents the setting up of sound administrative bodies, such as agricultural extension services and trustworthy credit facilities for the development of agriculture.

Changes in the over-all economic structure, which influence market prices of inputs as well as of outputs, may make existing land use obsolete without its being realized either by the farmers or, often, even by advisory and administrative agencies. The traditional approach to agriculture has in itself certain advantages: sudden changes in agricultural land use cause disruptions which may result in grave hazards for the agricultural population as well as for its lands, and therefore for a country. Nevertheless it has to be realized that particularly during this century, many changes in economic structures have brought about very important changes in land suitability, and that this is by no means at an end.

An example is provided by the suitability of soils in the Netherlands for flax (VINK, 1962). Before 1914, flax was grown to a considerable extent on the loamy Pleistocene sands ("coversands") of this country. Nearly every village in the sufficiently loamy areas had its own flax for household use, and some of the large textile industry centers in the eastern and southern parts of the country were partly based on this crop. After 1914, the arrival of cotton from other parts of the world (America, Egypt) and probably also the rising wages of farm labor, led to the disappearance of this crop within a few years. Today, nobody would dream of growing flax in the Netherlands outside the area of the very rich young marine polders.

The disappearance of flax occurred within a very few years. Ostensibly, substitutes for its place within the land utilization type could easily be found. But this is not always the case. Many postwar (after 1945) changes have seriously affected the feasibility, and therefore the suitability, of growing crops on certain lands, both in a positive and in a negative sense. The reasons are often political changes or changes in economic policy of governments and of international bodies. A good example of the latter is the changes which are brought about by the European Common Market in the economic structure of agriculture in the participating countries. The general rise, and growing scarcity, of agricultural labor in these countries, due to the enormous increase in industrialization, are basic factors in this process.

In this context it is difficult to determine when an economic change, either in prices of outputs or of inputs, can be considered to affect land suitability. Land suitability is used for middle and long term predictions for the planning of agri-

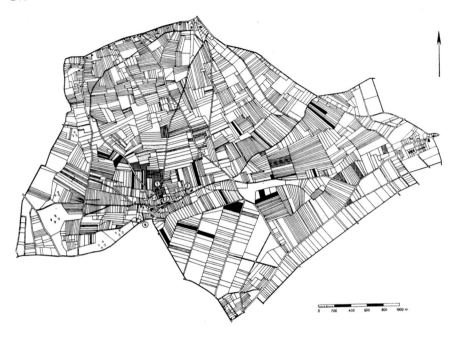

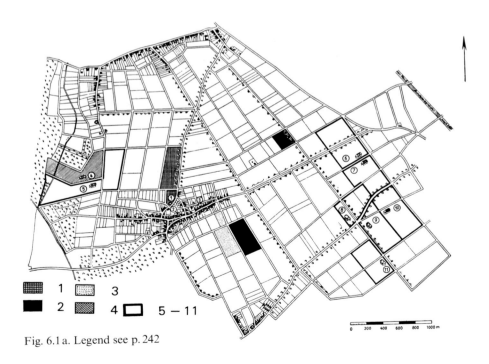

Fig. 6.1a. Legend see p. 242

Fig. 6.1b. Legend see p. 242

cultural land use. It should not, therefore, be affected by incidental, even if large, changes in economic relations. Land suitability can be said to be influenced only by the instigation of actual structural economic changes; whether land suitability is affected is a matter for consultation between land suitability experts and economists in each separate case.

Economic, Social and Technological Conditions; Changes in Suitability

Considerations of the economic aspects of actual land suitability are also occasionally influenced by what actually constitutes "actual land suitability". This determination is of particular importance for areas which are situated at a considerable distance from potential markets. The main cause for certain crops not being grown in such an area may be the distance itself, often combined with a poor transportation system and a poorly developed commercial organization. It may then well be that, for a particular crop in a particular land utilization type, e.g. coffee or cocoa or tobacco in medium-sized holdings, the internal situation of the region is such that no major improvement works are needed. The internal, actual land suitability, which is comparable to the thus far more often used "soil suitability", may then be very good for some of the lands of the area, provided that prices are assumed which would only be attained locally after improvements were made in the transportation and marketing systems. Because resources surveys in these areas, and their dependent land suitability ratings, are often made precisely for judging the feasibility of road and railway development, the *internal actual land suitability* of an area is often the more important feature for practical use. Still, the *external actual land suitability*, i.e. the land suitability without major

---

Legend to Fig. 6.1a and b. Examples of land reallotment projects (JACOBY, 1961)
(a) Strasberg, German Federal Republic*

1. Before reallotment				2. After reallotment			
Village farms				Outside farms			
Number of fields		area		Number of fields		area	
old	new	old	new	old	new	old	new
19	2	18.7	17.3	14.6	1	9.8	16
21	2	15.8	15.1				
15	2	11.0	11.0				

(b) Cloondeash (Co. Mayo), Eire*

1. Before reallotment		2. After reallotment
	Number of fields	
	old	new
	42	1
	21	1
	30	2

* The numbers 1, 2, 3 etc. refer to the fields of individual farms nos. 1, 2, 3 etc. before and after reallotment.

improvement works, e.g. road systems, outside the area proper, may be such that, for the time being, the crops under consideration cannot be grown with any reasonable profit, or with a sufficient standard of living for the local population. The internal actual land suitability is then an *external potential land suitability*, i.e. only realizable after the construction of roads and related works. For the area itself, this may be solved by taking suitable, and often alternative, economic assumptions with regard to the prices of inputs and outputs in the area itself. If a larger region, of which the area forms a part, is considered, the situation may become more difficult because distances to markets of lands, each of which have the same internal actual land suitability, may be very different. In the case of a land suitability rating, which is based on the physical resources of the land, the economic parameters have to be fixed, and economic "zoning" is not easily applicable. The "internal actual land suitability" of the larger region, which comprises the "external land suitabilities" of different areas within the region, will therefore have to be based on the relative suitabilities of the physical resources without correction for economic assumptions, or alternative economic assumptions for the different circumstances which may prevail will have to be made. The final solution can then only be reached after careful integration of the "land suitability" and "economic planning" stages; this is a fair example of how often land evaluation and land use planning must proceed together.

Social, cultural and institutional structures often also cause present land use to lag behind actual land suitability. It is not true that these structures are always inherent in the land utilization type and that therefore the land utilization type has to be changed before other changes can come about. The land utilization type is primarily concerned with internal farm organization; over all social and institutional conditions, and perhaps occasionally other cultural aspects of rural life, may be different for the same land utilization type. Typical examples are found in tropical and in arid regions, but similar situations are also not uncommon in the industrialized countries with temperate climates.

In Central Cameroun, the normal land utilization type is a combination of shifting cultivation and cocoa-growing. As far as the actual land suitability goes, the lands used under this system could be much extended. Similar situations in other countries, with either cocoa or coffee as a cash crop, point also to this possibility. Ten years ago, however, according to information obtained from the local experts on agricultural extension, this was not possible because of the patriarchal family system, in which only the oldest man of the family could own and manage the land. The younger men were not allowed to settle themselves and their families in otherwise suitable lands.

In Central Rwanda, lands that were suitable for the agricultural land utilization type practiced by the farmers of the Bahutu tribe were only partly occupied. The Bahutu farmers feared that the lands would be claimed again by members of the Watussi tribe, who were the original feudal lords, but recently abolished as such by the revolution of 1960.

In Iraq and in several of the Arab countries in the arid zone until one or two decades ago the land was owned mainly by land owners who possessed very large tracts of land on which the farmers were tenants (WARRINER, 1962). The tenancy system led to under-use of the lands in many cases. Agrarian reform has shifted the trend toward a use which better approximates to actual land suitability; there is a danger now, however, that too intensive uses without proper adaptations such as drainage, may lead to land degradation by increasing salinity. In this area, a final answer will be to realize a potential land suitability with major improvements consisting in particular of desalinization and drainage and often including modernization of the existing irrigation systems.

In the Netherlands and in many other countries of western Europe, large shifts in actual land suitability have occurred during this century. The first took place with the introduction of chemical fertilizers, modern agricultural machinery (with tractors instead of horses) and modern pesticides and weed-killers. This shift, which often took half a century to be realized on any single farm, in fact amounted to a change in land utilization type. The actual land suitability for this new type was, under pre-Common Market conditions and with relatively low wages, leading to a trend of a higher suitability for the poorer soils; this often included the dry sandy soils, provided that sprinkler irrigation could be applied.

Changes of actual land suitability, concurrent with changes from one land utilization type to another, are the rule rather than the exception. This is very clear if actual land suitabilities for uses with and without sprinkler irrigation are considered, respectively. Developments in the Netherlands since the late 1950's have led to a shift of the actual land suitability in what still has to be considered the same land utilization type: family holdings, largely mechanized and with full use of fertilizers and pesticides, generally with "mixed farming" of arable land and pastures. Actual land suitability, in particular for arable land, is now often lower than was the case some decades ago. Social circumstances prevent a rapid adaptation of present land use to the new situation, although recent trends point towards its gradual realization.

Actual land suitability is therefore not a completely fixed datum; it develops with technological and economic developments and with the development of agricultural research and its applications. It has to be assessed for particular land utilization types under particular conditions, together with certain assumptions for a middleterm period of about 10 years. It then has to be critically considered and if necessary revised according to changed conditions, often with some changes in the economic and other assumptions. The degree to which the revision will be needed depends partly also on the manner in which the original suitability assessment was expressed. If this was done in absolute terms of yields of specific crops, revision may be necessary fairly often. If it was done in terms of the total number of crops, or of the crop range of the potential rotation on arable lands, the likelihood exists that much less revision is necessary (see e.g. VINK and VAN ZUILEN, 1967): soils with good possibilities for many crops will always remain good soils, whereas soils with suitabilities for only a limited number of crops will always retain some limitations.

Several examples of changes in actual land suitability which were due to changes in technology or to those in agricultural research and its applications, were mentioned above. Additional information on the gap between present land use and actual land suitability caused by differences in agricultural practices can, however, be given. Some changes are due to the infestation by pests which were not originally endemic in an area; an example from the growth of tea in Java was described in Para. 5.4.5: due to the arrival of the "blisterblight" fungus disease on the leaves, actual land suitability shifted towards those lands where tea can be grown without shade trees.

The Lag between Agricultural Research and Its Applications

Differences between actual land suitability and present land use may also occur because a lag between agricultural research and its application, often based on the local difficulties in applying research knowledge which was found to be well applicable elsewhere. This lag may be the result of:

(a) Mistakes made in assessing the actual land suitability: this can occur either if the land utilization type under consideration has not been sufficiently investigated, or if the assumptions based on economic and social conditions have been different from the actual situation.

(b) Gaps between agricultural research and agricultural extension.

(c) Agricultural advice for the existing land utilization type being inapplicable because of social or economic constraints or because of inapplicability of knowledge and experience gained elsewhere.

(d) Lack of agricultural research data directed towards the land conditions prevailing in a country or region.

Mistakes in the assessment of actual land suitability should of course be avoided as much as possible. But the study of land utilization types and their inherent constraints is not always easily done in the relatively short time which is usually available for the production of land resources maps and the land suitabilitiy assessments based upon them. Cooperation between resources experts and agronomists, including plant production experts and farm management specialists, is urgently required; experience has proved, however, that it is not always easy to achieve this (see also Para. 6.5).

Gaps between agricultural research and agricultural extension may cause situations in which a large amount of knowledge is available at central research institutions, but not sufficiently available to the farmers. This situation is fairly common, not only in typical developing regions. The build-up of a competent agricultural extension staff of various grades, who have on the one hand a sufficiently up-to-date knowledge of scientific achievements and who on the other hand have an intimate day-to-day knowledge of the problems and constraints on the farms under the land conditions of their region, is a very difficult job. In many developing regions, the difficulties are aggravated by the lack of suitable personnel of the intermediate grades—graduates with B.Sc. degrees in agronomy and higher-class technicians. This lack of personnel often exists in two senses: an absolute lack in the country as a whole, and a lack of interest among the people of these categories, and of their wives, to live under often fairly primitive rural conditions. The latter reason, but often also the former, has proved to be a great handicap for land development in other fields such as the establishment of projects and the maintenance and operation of the projects once they are established.

Another essential aspect of efficient agricultural extension is the need for the farmers to have sufficient knowledge so that they can absorb the extension services offered to them. The establishment of rural agricultural schools, sufficiently spread over the country and at a level which is appropriate for farmers' sons with a normal intelligence and with about six years of basic school education, is one of the most essential means of bridging the gap between present land use and actual land suitability. Different extension techniques exist which may be used to reach the farmers themselves; an important one is the establishment of local fields in which agricultural techniques and crops are demonstrated under representative land conditions.

It is not uncommon that agricultural advice is found to be inapplicable in a region because of social or economic constraints. Agricultural research is in many aspects concerned with applied biology and with agricultural engineering. It has to be applied, however, on farms which are primarily economic production units within a special social context—of families and of larger social units. The traditional methods, particularly of tillage and of harvesting, have often for many centuries played a role in this social context. Some of the age-old systems of irrigated rice cultivation are good examples (see e.g. G. J. VINK, 1941), but similar situations occur in other land utilization types as well (DE SCHLIPPE, 1956; TOSI in Integrated Surveys, 1966; VAN DUSSELDORP, 1967; GALJART, 1968). Social conditions can act as a serious constraint for bridging the gap between the existing land use and the land use which would be possible, even without any major investments. The lack of suitable credit facilities tends to enhance these constraints. Agricultural extension is just as much a matter of economics and sociology as it is of the relatively simple application of modern techniques and the introduction of new varieties of crops.

One means of improving present land use is the transfer of knowledge and experience from the same or similar land utilization types in other regions, countries, or continents. This approach is often very useful, because the actual results of many years of farming experience may be directly transfered without the need for expensive experiments, always necessarily of rather long duration. But the applicability of this knowledge should be regarded not only in the light of the comparability of socio-economic conditions, but also in the light of the comparability of the prevailing climate and land conditions. The failure of good information to be applied under other conditions is often due to insufficient comparison of the land conditions. In particular, foreign experts often fail to regard the constraints to land use inherent in the differences of land conditions. Many completely sterile discussions are kept going in different countries because the experiences and experimental data relate to different land conditions. A systematic transfer of knowledge and experience is possible (VINK, 1963a), provided that use is made of the available scientific means, which include the classification on a world-wide scale of climates and soils; it is for the latter that world-wide systems of soil classification, in particular the Legend of the Soil Map of the World and the U.S. Soil Taxonomy (see Para. 4.3.1), are essential. No over-all system for comparing land attributes and land conditions on a world-wide basis exists as yet; even regional systems, such as the C.S.I.R.O. land systems approach, have not thus far produced classifications which are useful for the transfer of knowledge and experience. The use of suitable climatic classifications, together with one of the more general systems of soil classification, and added to by other knowledge of land conditions, has to fill the gap. This requires a certain knowledge of the terminology and relative importance of these classifications. The production of the Soil Map of the World itself, which is now in progress, as well as of land conditions maps based on the former, will undoubtedly provide a better general basis for the transfer of knowledge and experience. The scale of the map, 1:5 million, will however not be sufficient to make it applicable for detailed predictions on land use (FAO/UNESCO, 1971).

In many countries there is a large body of agricultural research data, very few of which are actually applied in practical agriculture. One might even say that this situation has become a world problem. One cause of this situation is a matter of philosophy, but there are also matters of personal career and of financial support to research involved.

The nineteenth century was the age of development of the natural sciences; general laws of behavior of organic and inorganic bodies were found to be applicable in many different ways. This development continues today, and without the discernment of general laws and of more or less generally applicable stochastic trends, no modern science and no applied sciences would be possible. But generalizations tend to lose contact with reality in cases where many complex interrelations exist. This is often the case in land use, of which the complex ecological and economic interrelations have been touched upon in the foregoing chapters. Applications of fertilizers, or of other land management operations, are always tested under specific land conditions, i.e. those of the experimental field or farm on which the general agricultural research is carried out. These land conditions are never fully representative of all the land conditions of an area or a country which the experiments have to serve; unless the experiments are supplemented by trials under other land conditions, the application of the results in practical agriculture may not be carried out with the modifications suitable for specific land conditions. Furthermore, the economic feasibility of the application of experimental data, as well as the way in which a particular operation can be wedged in among other labor requirements on a farm, must be determined: the entire organization of farm management may be affected by the introduction of fairly simple innovations. The use of pilot farms, selected on the basis of their representativeness for land conditions and for socio-economic conditions and run as economic enterprises, is therefore essential.

Matters of personal career are not often touched upon in formal literature. But in many parts of the world the personal considerations of individual scientists have a great influence on the kinds of research which are being carried out. This situation is very understandable, because scientists are often judged by the number of their publications which have appeared in recognized international journals and also sometimes by the number of international publications in which they have been refered to. The result is often publication of information which at least has the pretense of being of general interest rather than of applicability in a given area. This approach could at least partly be used also for studying the responses to management and the productivity under different land conditions, provided that in each publication a sufficiently clear description and classification of the land attributes were given. But even in such a case, problems can occur because the average agronomist does not have sufficiently detailed knowledge of soil classification and land classification, whereas often the help of competent scientists in these fields is either not requested or not offered.

The preceding personal causes are also strengthened by the way in which agricultural research is often organized and financed. It is easier to organize and finance one large institute for agricultural research than to establish a larger number of relatively small research institutes which are representative of regional land conditions. The large central institute is necessary in any case, because a central research line for general problems not directly connected with regional problems is needed; it is often forgotten, however, that the application of the data from a general institute has to pass through the phases of regional and local experimental fields, experimental farms and pilot farms.

Even if a certain number of local experiments are carried out, the danger still exists that the land conditions of these experiments will not be representative of the major land conditions prevailing in the area concerned. Field officers responsible for the establishment and maintenance of experiments prefer to select good farms and good soils for their experiments. Often there is a high correlation between what a field officer considers to be a good farm and the best land conditions in an area: it is easier to be a good farmer on a good soil than to be judged as such on a soil with several limitations. Farmers on more productive soils earn higher incomes, have often therefore received a better education, and have more time and money, or land to spend for purposes which are not directly productive, such as experiments. A field officer furthermore wants to be sure that the crops in his experiment show at least a decent stand, which is also more easily accomplished by establishing the experiment on good soils.

The gaps between present land use and actual land suitability are therefore much less easily overcome than is often thought. Systematic experiments covering all representative land conditions are impossible or at least not feasible under most circumstances in any country. It is therefore of the highest importance to utilize as much as possible the available knowledge and experience from elsewhere as well as from within the region, by systematic transfer of knowledge and experience and by systematizing the existing farmers' knowledge and experimental data from within the region. The actual experiments or pilot projects to be carried out may then be reduced to "bench mark" conditions and to those conditions in which the gap between present land use and actual land suitability is estimated to be the greatest. These experiments should furthermore be carried out in such a manner that the influence of more than one variable on land use can be discerned (FERRARI in JACKS et al., 1967).

Soil Suitability

One must distinguish between "actual land suitability" and "soil suitability". This distinction derives from the different definitions of "land" and "soil", respectively (see Paras. 1.1 and 4.3.1). "Land" is a wider concept than "soil" and, ultimately, tracts of land tend to represent "unique tracts of the earth's surface" (BRINKMAN and SMYTH, 1973). "Soil" is a narrower concept in the sense that it does not include the human and social implications involved in the term "land"; it is wider in the sense that identical soils may be recognized in very different parts of the world and under completely different land use conditions. Also, "soil" in the sense of the definition used here (Para. 4.3.1) embraces a large enough part of the "natural science" aspects of "land", that, if duly considered under given conditions of climate and hydrology, "soil suitability" contains the most essential basic aspects of "actual land suitability".

"Soil suitability" is defined as: "physical suitability of soil and climate for production of a specific crop or group or sequence of crops, or for other defined uses or benefits, within a specified socio-economic context but not considering economic factors specific to areas of land". Parallels used in different countries are "land capability" and "vocation du sol" (BRINKMAN and SMYTH, 1973). It has also been indicated (Para. 1.3) that water and soils "are the main resources with which land use is continuously concerned". It was mentioned previously that "water and soils are, on the one hand, the stable resources on which all land use must be based; on the other hand they can, to some extent, depending also on their position with regard to the other resources of a given region, be manipulated and adapted to man's requirements". One should not wonder, therefore, at the fact that investigations of soil suitability are found useful for many purposes of land suitability predictions (see e.g. BARTELLI et al., 1966; VINK, 1963a; VINK and VAN ZUILEN, 1967, 1974).

Soil suitability comes close to what we termed previously, "internal actual land suitability". Soil suitability is concerned with the direct usefulness of soils for a particular purpose, under specified socio-economic conditions and with certain assumptions as to the generalized, over-all land conditions. The difference between soil suitability and internal actual land suitability lies in these assumptions. Soil suitability generalizes in some way or other the conditions of artifactial land resources and sometimes of other land resources which are not directly connected with the soils themselves. A good example can be taken from the General Soil Suitability Map of the Netherlands on scale 1:200000 (VINK and VAN ZUILEN, 1967, 1974), in which the following assumptions were made:

"1. The evaluation of the suitability was carried out under the economic and technical situation of agriculture prevailing in the Netherlands about 1960. As soon as the economic circumstances or the technical possibilities would change appreciably, a revision of the map will be necessary.

2. With a view to this situation the yardstick has been a rough estimate of what a good farmer can achieve under good conditions of parcellation and accessibility. In view of the great differences in water management of comparable soils in different parts of the country, an effort has been made to establish as a standard the most favorable water management prevailing in sufficiently large areas within each soil unit. For the latter it was found to be necessary in some cases to use within one soil unit two different standards in different parts of the country.

3. The classification supplies an ordinal arrangement only in so far as it indicates the range of use capabilities existing within the types of management current in the Netherlands about 1960 in arable land and grassland farming.

4. The numbering and the description of the classes do not indicate the financial value nor the suitability for improvement of the soils.

5. Owing to the small scale of the map an appreciable variation in the suitability for agriculture can be found within the soil units and consequently within the land classes. This has been taken into account as much as possible in the descriptions of the classes. This means among other things that the map must be regarded as a whole and that separate use of the individual sheets or parts of these is not recommended."

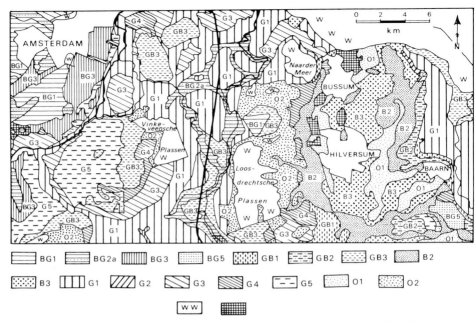

Fig. 6.2. Part of the General Soil Suitability Map for Arable Land and Grassland of the Netherlands, scale 1:200000 (VINK and VAN ZUILEN, 1967, 1974). N. B. The full legend of the national map is given; those of the classes which do not occur on the cut-out have been put between brackets.

▦ = not classified   ww = water

Legend of the General Soil Suitability Map of the Netherlands, scale 1:200000.

Major Class BG: ARABLE LAND AND GRASSLAND SOILS
Soils generally suited to arable land and usually also to grassland.

BG 1:   Arable land and grassland soils of wide suitability; generally, if well drained, very well suited to most arable crops, with good to very good yields and a high yield security, locally slightly drought-susceptible; with good water management well suited to grassland, but partly with summer-depression, very good fodder quality.

BG 2:   Arable land and grassland soils of wide suitability; if well drained generally well suited to most arable crops but with limitations for some crops and/or lower yield security; generally well suited to grassland, but with more or less strong summer depression, very good fodder quality.

BG 2a: with limitations caused by chemical and/or physical properties (clay content, structure, potash fixation, lime deficiency, luxuriancy).

(BG 2b: with limitations caused by slope and/or age of the soils).

BG 3:   Arable land and grassland soils of fairly limited suitability; generally, with adequate water management, well suited and locally very well suited to a limited crop rotation with wheat as principal cereal crop, locally however less favorable or even unsuitable; moderately to well suited to grassland – the wetter parts late in spring – sometimes with a more or less strong summer depression, good to very good fodder quality.

(BG 4:   Arable land and grassland soils of limited suitability; well to very well suited to an extensive rotation with rye as principal cereal crop, locally also to some commercial crops – the wetter parts however are hazardous for winter crops; moderately to well and locally very well suited to grassland, good fodder quality).

BG 5:   Arable land and grassland soils of very limited suitability; generally well suited to rye, oats and mangolds – the more loamy and/or clayey or humose parts are also more or less suited to sugar beet and/or wheat; more or less suited to permanent grassland.

(BG 6:   Arable land and grassland complex of strongly varying suitability; soils varying considerably over short distances: the best parts are equivalent to those of class BG2; considerable areas however poorly suited to arable land and grassland are also included).

(BG 7:   Arable land and grassland complex of limited suitability; soils with a suitability varying considerably over short distances: the dryer parts are generally well suited to rye, oats potatoes, locally also to mangolds, and poorly suited to grassland; the wetter parts are poorly suited to arable land but well suited to grassland with a good gross production and a slight summer depression, well suited to grazing, moderate to good fodder quality).

Major Class GB: GRASSLAND AND ARABLE LAND SOILS

Soils generally suited to grassland and in many cases also to arable land.

GB 1:   Grassland and arable land soils of fairly limited suitability; productive grassland soils – the driest parts with a slight summer depression, the wettest parts late in spring, locally too wet for grassland – well suited to grazing, good fodder quality; the well drained loamy or clayey parts are well to very well suited to an extensive rotation with rye as principal cereal crop, in some cases to a limited rotation with wheat as principal cereal crop and locally also to some commercial crops, the other soils are partly too wet and/or too heavy for arable lands.

GB 2:   Grassland and arable land soils of limited suitability; grassland soils with a good gross production, but often late in spring, locally poorly suited to grazing (too wet), moderate fodder quality; generally more or less suited to an extensive rotation with rye as principal cereal crop, but partly too hazardous for winter crops – the wetter parts are unsuitable for arable land.

GB 3:   Grassland and arable land complex of limited suitability; soils of strongly varying quality when under grass – the best parts have a good gross production, are late in spring, but without summer depression, the driest parts have a low gross production with a strong summer depression, the wettest parts are too wet for grassland, – moderate to good fodder quality; the soils have in some parts a limited suitability, but are in general too heavy and/or too wet and/or too peaty for arable land.

Major Class B: ARABLE LAND SOILS

(B 1:   Arable land soils of limited suitability; only suited to drought resistant and/or early crops, locally suited to a few commercial crops; at most moderately suited to permanent grassland (low gross production)).

B 2:   Arable land soils of very limited suitability; generally well suited to rye, oats and potatoes and in the wetter or more moisture-retaining areas also to mangolds.

B 3:   Arable land soils of extremely limited suitability; generally at most moderately suited to rye, oats and potatoes.

Major Class C: GRASSLAND SOILS

G 1:   Firm sensitive grassland soils; with a good gross production, but very sensitive to a good water management, sometimes late in spring, with a sufficiently firm sod, good fodder quality.

G 2:   Firm late grassland soils; with a good gross production, often late in spring, sometimes with a more or less strong summer depression, firm sod, moderate to good fodder quality.

G 3:   Soft sensitive grassland soils; with a good gross production, very sensitive to a good water management, usually late in spring, having a very sensitive sod under poor management, strongly varying fodder quality.

G 4:   Grassland soils of varying suitability; generally with a good gross production – the driest parts with a summer depression, the wetter parts late in spring and sometimes with of a sod – moderate to good fodder quality.

G 5:   Grassland soils of moderate suitability; generally with a moderate gross production – locally too wet or too dry – moderate fodder quality.

Major Class O: UNSUITABLE SOÌLS

Soils predominantly poorly suited to arable land and to grassland.

O 1:   Predominantly too dry soils.

O 2:   Predominantly too wet soils.

	1	2	3	4
3) suitability of use after improve-ment (Based on the new soil types, after improvement; by way of simplification, these are not given in this table.)	suitable for most crops with good yields	suitable for most crops with good yields	suitability dependent on methods of improve-ment applied; if hardpan is fully removed and humus-status restored, suitable for most crops	not suitable for agriculture
2) suitability of improvement	no improvement necessary, but humus-status should be watched	to be improved with relatively simple methods breaking of hardpan and im-provement of humus-status	to be improved, but only with compli-cated methods	not suitable for improvement
1) present suitability of use	suitable for most crops with good yields	only suitable for the less exacting crops, but these also with lower yields	only moderately suitable for a few crops with poor yields	not suitable for agriculture
soil classification	Oxisols, moderate-ly weathered with-out hardpan	Oxisols, heavily weathered with slight hardpan	Oxisols, heavily weathered and eroded, with thick hardpan	Oxisols, severely eroded, pre-domin-antly consisting of lateritic hard-pan

schematic profiles

humic soil material
weathered soil material
hardpan
slightly weathered soil material

depth in cm

Fig. 6.3. Suitability of use and suitability of improvement; schematized example (VINK, 1963a). [3 is based on the new soil types, after improvement (cf. Fig. 2). By way of simplification, these are not given in this table]

An example from this map, with the complete legend, is shown in Fig. 6.2.

The important assumptions, which represent the point at which internal actual land suitability and soil suitability diverge, are indicated in "assumption 2". Here some assumptions have been made to standardize certain land conditions which are not refered to in the assessment of soil suitability: (a) accessibility of the fields, and (b) water management conditions. Both accessibility and water management conditions are land conditions. The degree to which they can be accurately depicted on a general landscape ecological map is still being determined, but in areas where they are sufficiently "permanent or predictably cyclic", they are land attributes, which is the case in most areas of the Netherlands. The water management conditions have even been indicated as a "soil phase" on the Soil Map (scale 1:50000) of the Netherlands, which is the successor to the soil map on scale 1:200000 on which the above-mentioned soil suitability map was based. On the latter, water management conditions were only partly indicated, which was in keeping with the generalized nature of the soil map.

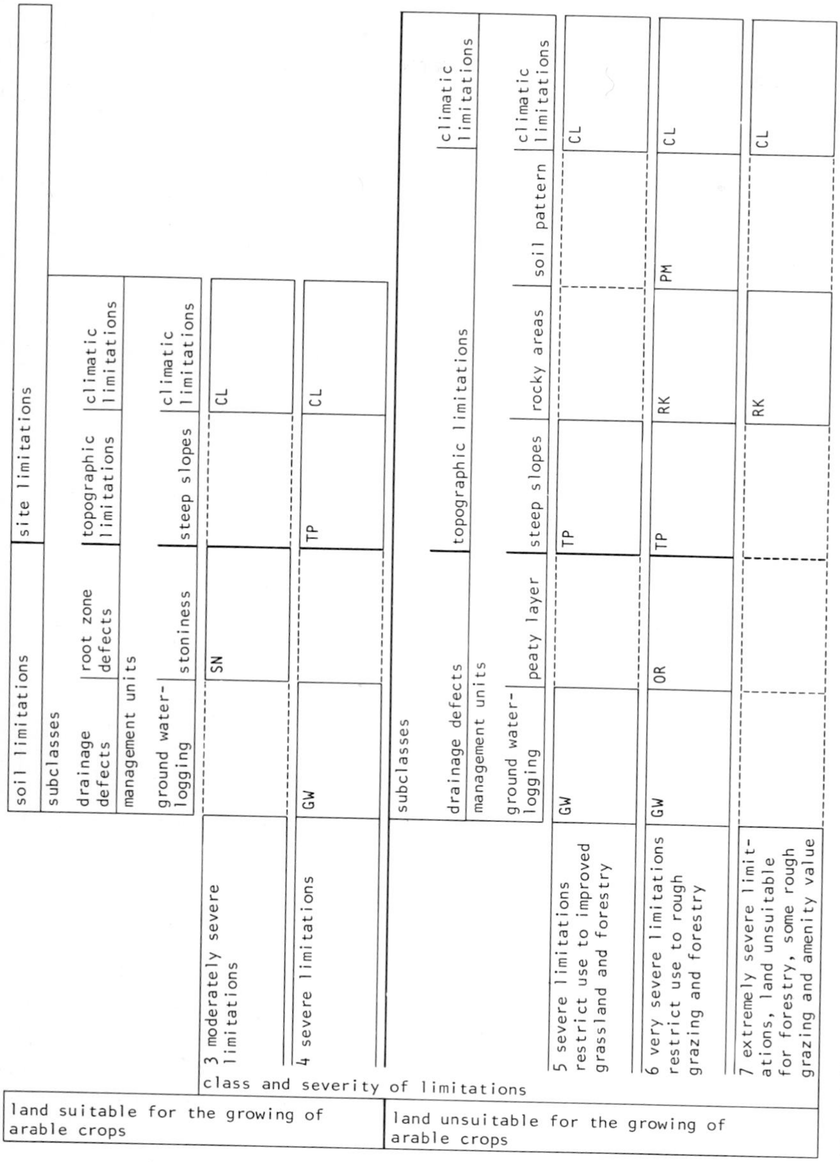

Fig. 6.4. Legend of the Land Use Capability Map of Candacraig and Glenbuchat, (HESLOP and BOWN, 1969)

Soil suitability maps must, therefore, provide normalized assumptions, not only for the socio-economic conditions (see above, assumption 1.) and for the land utilization types (assumption 3.), but also for certain land conditions which are not included in a normal soil survey (assumption 2.). This requirement is a disadvantage in so far as the directly applicable socio-economic conditions of land use are concerned, but it is a distinct advantage with regard to the "natural science aspect" of the interpretation of soil surveys. It bases the predictions of a soil suitability map as much as possible on the really permanent land attributes and leaves open their applicability for predictions under various assumptions, often not only on land use suitability but also on land improvement suitability, i.e. the suitability of soils and lands for permanent improvements, which properly belong to the field of potential land suitability (see Para.6.3). For an example see Fig.6.3.

Soil suitability maps have been made in many parts of the world. They have become essential documents in most development projects and in many projects for town and country planning, in developing as well as in industrialized regions. A good example of a soil suitability map, or as it is called, land use capability map, on a detailed scale (1:25000) has been produced from an area in Scotland by HESLOP and BROWN (1969). It is interesting to note that some typical land attributes which are not normally noted on a soil map or on a soil survey interpretation map, have been indicated on this map, notably the "climatic limitations"; the legend of this map is reproduced in Fig.6.4.

6.3 Potential Land Suitability

The Use of Major Land Improvements

Potential land suitability "relates the suitability of land units for the use in question at some future date after "major improvements" have been effected where necessary, suitability being assessed in terms of expected future benefits in relation to future recurrent and minor capital expenditure" (BRINKMAN and SMYTH, 1973). "Major improvements" in the sense of this definition are "substantial non-recurrent inputs in land improvement which can rarely be financed or executed by the individual farmer and which will effect a very significant and reasonably permanent change (i.e. lasting in excess of about ten years) in the characteristics of the land" (BRINKMAN and SMYTH, 1973). In the cited text, which is the most important general reference for international use, an additional distinction is made between "potential land suitability classification *without* amortisation of major capital inputs" and "potential land suitability classification *with* amortisation of major capital inputs". This distinction is sometimes very useful in actual land use planning, where large investments are considered, but for the general problems of suitability it is of less importance.

Land improvements were discussed in Para.5.5.3, where it was shown that they may be classified in four or five levels according to the order of magnitude of the investments and the way in which the improvement has to be executed: by farmers, with or without outside assistance, and in relatively complicated projects, respectively. The improvements mentioned in Table 76 (p. 215) and Table 78 (p. 217) under level "A = low" can in general, therefore, not be considered as major land improvements in the sense of the present paragraph, but there is no absolute rule to give for this. If the land utilization type belongs to a form of socialized agriculture, either a collective farm or a state farm for example, or if in any other manner the farm size and system of tenure lead to large units with a sufficiently strong economic background, e.g. certain types of company-owned plantations or haciendas, several kinds of major land improvements, such as the establishment of permanent irrigated agriculture, may well be within the possibilities of the "individual" farm (see e.g. Para. 3.3, Table 5, p. 54). The determination of whether a certain land improvement is to be considered a major improvement in the sense of this paragraph therefore depends also on the land utilization type to which it is going to be applied.

Major land improvements can be so termed in the sense that they bring about a change in land characteristics and in land conditions. These changes must be, at least, of a reasonably long duration, for which in the previously mentioned definition a minimum period of 10 years or more is quoted. Most land improvements involve microrelief, soils and water conditions, but some may also be related to the vegetation, such as the clearing of primeval forest or of other very dense vegetation types which need at least some decades for their regrowth. Occasionally these improvements lead to the establishment of important artifactial land attributes, such as large irrigation structures, polders, embankments. In the case of soil improvements, such as changes in the soil profile, no artifactial elements are introduced in the landscape, but the soils themselves have become largely man-made ("Arents" according to the U.S. Soil Taxonomy).

Road Systems and Reallotments

Some discussion is possible on whether the construction of road systems or of major transport roads and the reallotment of fields belong to land improvement. The definition of "land" (Para. 1.1) includes "the results of past and present human activity, to the extent that these attributes exert a significant influence on present and future uses of the land by man". As all land attributes have to be "reasonably stable or predictably cyclic", the simple reallotment of fields, with no more than the shifting of fences or of boundary stones is, materially speaking, too ephemeral to be included in land improvement. If, however, this reallotment is accompanied by a considerable change in the systems of roads and canals, as is very often the case in the polder areas of the Netherlands, there is a good case for including these in "major land improvements" as (1) they are certainly of a great stability and (2) certainly exert a significant influence on present and future uses of the land by man (BIJKERK et al., 1970).

In the preceding paragraph we discussed the importance of roads (highways, railroads) for actual land suitability. We decided there that a separation should be made between external and internal actual land suitability. This has been done on the assumption that major roads, generally with ballast beds and paved surfaces, have to be seen as land attributes. Here also, no general opinion exists as yet whether roads are to be considered as land attributes. If the definition of "land" is read as has been done above, there is no doubt that roads of a "reasonably permanent" character must be seen as belonging to the land, since they certainly affect the present and future uses of the land by man.

Changes in land attributes and in the resulting land conditions may be improvements within one land utilization type, but they may constitute or induce

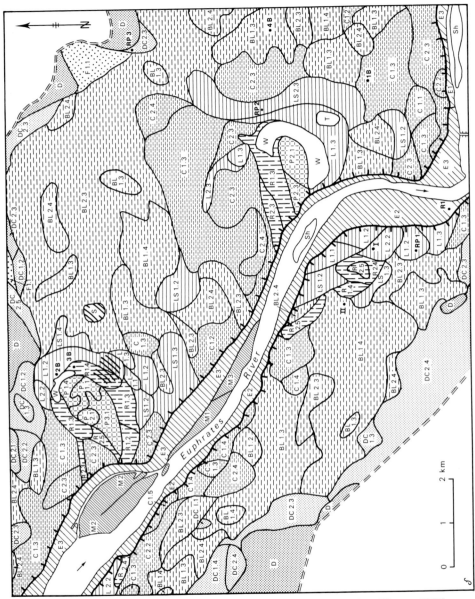

Fig. 6.5. Semi-detailed soil map of the Central part of the Ramadi project (YAHIA, 1971)

land degradation within other land utilization types. The construction of major
highways in saline or alkaline plains may result in land degradation, particularly
in arid lands, because the natural drainage systems may be disturbed if no special
measures are taken to guard against it. Increased salinization of the land around
the major highways is a very serious phenomenon, resulting from insufficient

correlation of the services of road construction and land reclamation. Degrada-
tive effects of a different nature often result from the establishment of roads in
unstable hilly lands; this is particularly serious in many lands where shale pre-
dominates in the geological formations or where the shale is interbedded with
sandstone. The resultant land degradation, repeated occurrence of landslides,
damages both the purpose for which the road was built and the land use in the
area around the road. Changes in drainage conditions have been mentioned in
Para. 5.4.5 as being often deleterious to agricultural land use in adjoining lands as
well as to nature reserves and other land uses with "ecological" purposes.

Examples from Iraq and from the Netherlands

Fig. 6.5 to 6.9 contain an example of a land development project with land improvements which is being carried out in the Ramadi area (Middle Euphrates
Valley) of Iraq (after YAHIA, 1971). In Fig. 6.5, a part of the basic soil map is given.
This is a physiographical soil map in the sense described in Para. 4.3.1. The main
soil map units are the "Ismus" ("Iraq soil mapping units") which are similar to soil
series, and have in fact been called "soil series" in the past; in view of the newer
soil classification systems, however, this is not supportable, since most of them
contain important taxonomic divergences. Their soil profile characteristics, which
are only partially indicated in Fig. 6.9, were extensively discussed in the original
publication (YAHIA, 1971). Table 84 contains some soil qualities, representative of
land qualities or ecological land conditions. Fig. 6.6a and 6.6b indicate soil salinity and soil drainability respectively and are also indicative of land qualities. In
Fig. 6.7a and b the "present land use capability map", indicating actual land

Table 84. Soil qualities related to drainage of the Ramadi area (YAHIA, 1971)

Physiographical unit and symbol	Perme-ability	Internal drainage	External drainage	Present soil dr.	Potential soil dr.
River levee L	rapid	rapid	rapid	good	very good
Silted low river levee LS	moderately rapid	rapid	rapid	medium	good
River crevasse C	moderate, mo. rapid	medium, slow	slow, medium	medium, poor	good to medium
River basin BL	moderate, mo. slow	medium, slow	slow, medium	medium, poor	good to medium
Point bar P	rapid	rapid	rapid	good	very good
River bed R	rapid	rapid medium	slow, medium	medium, poor	good
Desert colluvium DS (upper parts)	rapid	rapid	rapid	good	very good
Do, (lower parts)	moderate mo. slow	medium, slow	slow, medium	medium, poor	good to medium
Fans F	rapid	rapid	rapid	very good	very good

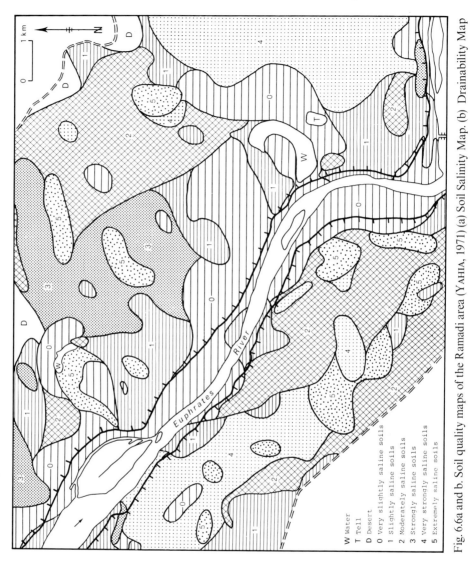

W Water
T Tell
D Desert
0 Very slightly saline soils
1 Slightly saline soils
2 Moderately saline soils
3 Strongly saline soils
4 Very strongly saline soils
5 Extremely saline soils

Fig. 6.6a and b. Soil quality maps of the Ramadi area (YAHIA, 1971) (a) Soil Salinity Map. (b) Drainability Map

suitability, and the "potential land use capability map", indicating potential land suitability after establishment of a project including desalinization, drainage and improved irrigation, are shown. The assumptions and legends of these maps are given in Tables 85 and 86, respectively. Finally, Fig. 6.8 contains the project layout. The treatment of these matters in the Ramadi project clearly reflects a very modern and efficient approach to land improvement and land development.

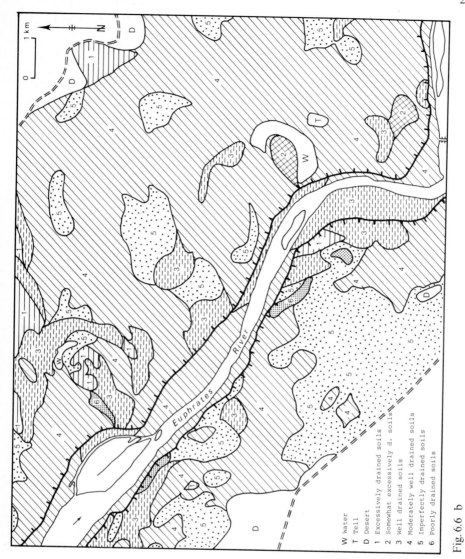

W Water
T Tell
D Desert
1 Excessively drained soils
2 Somewhat excessively d. soils
3 Well drained soils
4 Moderately well drained soils
5 Imperfectly drained soils
6 Poorly drained soils

Fig. 6.6 b

The "Peat Reclamation Colonies" in the Netherlands also represent some very interesting examples of major land improvement which lead to different potential land suitabilities. These are areas of undulating Pleistocene "coversands" (wind-blown deposits) in which podzols and related soils were formed and which during the Middle and Late Holocene were covered by peat growth of some meters thickness (DE SMET, 1969). From the 16th century onwards this peat was systemat-

Table 85. Present land use capability (actual land suitability) in the Ramadi area (Iraq) (after YAHIA, 1971)

a) Assumptions

1   The capability classification is in the first place based on the influence of permanent characteristics and qualities of the soils e.g. soil texture, type of clay mineral, depth of soil profile, permeability, topography and position, internal and external drainage depicted on the soil map; this is therefore the first basic map for the land classification.

2   Salinity of the soil under present conditions is also of major importance, although it cannot be considered a permanent soil quality because it increases with time, see Fig. 6.7; the soil salinity map is the second basic map for this land classification.

3   Salinity of the ground water also affects the overlying soils. Thus it is an important limiting factor under present soil conditions. The ground water salinity map is the third basic map for this land classification.

4   Land is classified according to the continuing hydrological conditions of the area that affect its use; under present conditions this includes the prevailing, rather primitive, irrigation system. These conditions are reflected on the drainability map which is the fourth basic map for the land classification.

5   The socio-economic conditions of the farmers in the studied area have no significant influence towards improvement of the present capability classification. The use of fertilizers or of other improvement measures cannot be expected in the near future.

6   In the area studied, the desert land under the semi-arid climate (± 100 mm rainfall) is considered non-arable. Its position requires difficult and expensive engineering practices to provide irrigation water. These requirements are impossible in the light of the present economic conditions of the farmers and even in the future.

7   In the Ramadi area data on response of soils and crops to management are lacking; therefore the different soils studied are placed into present capability classes mostly by field observations made during the soil survey and by interpretation of the soil characteristics and qualities related to use and management. Some data about the crop adaptability and productivity are transfered from the results of the experimental farms established on the alluvial soils of the Euphrates and Tigris flood plains.

b) Classification

Class 1.   Arable, lands that are highly suitable for irrigation farming, being capable of producing sustained high yields of a wide range of climatically adapted crops at reasonable cost.

Suitable crops: vegetables, field crops, green manure, cereals and orchards.

Class 2.   Arable, lands of moderate suitability for irrigation farming, being measurably lower than class 1 in productive capacity, adapted to a somewhat narrower range of crops, more expensive to prepare for irrigation or more costly to farm.

Subclass 2 sa: good soils with some limitations due to salinity only.
Suitable crops: good and medium salt tolerance vegetables, cotton, green manure, cereals, and date palm.

Subclass 2 s: deficiencies due to slight salt concentrations and moderately heavy-textured subsoils.
Suitable crops: vegetables, field crops, green manure, cereals and date palm.

Subclass 2 d: deficiencies due to moderately good or imperfect drainage.
Suitable crops: vegetables, field crops, green manure and cereals.

Subclass 2 t: deficiencies due to topographical characteristics.
Suitable crops: Green manure and cereals.

Table 85 (continued)

Subclass 2 dt:	deficiencies due to the topographical and drainage conditions.
Suitable crops:	green manure.
Class 3:	Arable; lands that are suitable for irrigated farming but with more distinct restrictions owing to more extreme deficiencies in the soil or drainage conditions than described for class 2-land.
Subclass 3 s:	deficiencies due to moderate salt concentrations and moderately good drainage or slightly inferior soils, fairly good yields.
Suitable crops:	green manure and cereals.
Subclass 3 sd:	deficiencies due to high salt concentrations, and imperfect of poor drainage, or inferior soils.
Suitable crops:	barley and rice.
Subclass 3 sdt:	deficiencies due to high salt concentrations, imperfect of poor drainage and topography.
Suitable crops:	barley and rice.
Class 4.	Limited arable; lands are included in this class only after special economic and engineering studies have shown them to be irrigable.
Subclass 4 sd:	deficiencies due to very high salt concentrations and imperfect or poor drainage; very inferior soils.
Suitable crops:	rice.
Subclass 4 l:	deficiencies due to position allowing periodic flooding, requiring an engineering and economic determination for flood control.
Suitable crops:	4 l (2s), summer vegetables, green manure and cereals.
	4 l (2d), do,
	4 l (2sd), do,
	4 l (3s), do.
Class 5.	Non-arable; lands non-arable under present conditions but possibly arable after reclamation of the area.
Subclass 5 t/l:	non arable because of position requiring engineering practices.
Class 6.	Non-arable; lands non-arable under both existing and future conditions within the Ramadi Project plan.

ically dug in order to obtain turfs for household fuel; this activity continued in some small areas of the Netherlands until a few years ago, when the very last remnants were put under nature conservancy restrictions. In adjoining areas of Western Germany and in comparable peat districts of Ireland similar operations are still being carried out. In Fig.6.10, a series of diagrams of the operations carried out in the Netherlands are given. Fig.6.11 contains a schematic cross section of a part of the landscape, indicating the differences in relief and the soils resulting from the uncovering of the original Pleistocene sands, with remnants of the peat cover. In Table 87 the actual land suitability classes are indicated, with information on possible improvements; no indications are given in the original publication on the final suitability (potential land suitability) to be obtained. These may be considered to result finally in a fairly uniform suitability of a level higher than that of Class 3 (the best class in the given system), but they also depend on the kind of land utilization type which is assumed to be the best under potential conditions.

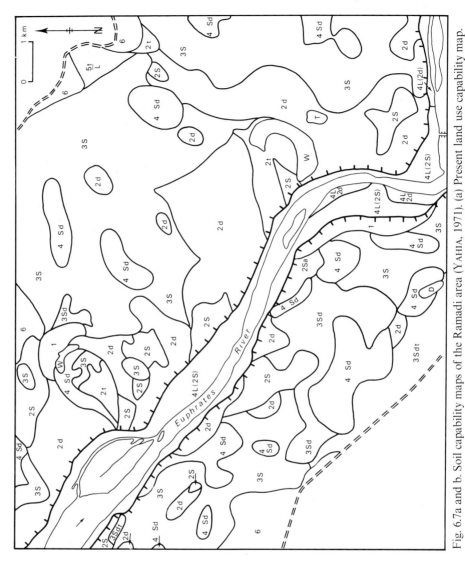

Fig. 6.7a and b. Soil capability maps of the Ramadi area (YAHIA, 1971). (a) Present land use capability map.
(b) Potential land use capability map

    The primary purpose of the original land reclamation was that of fuel exploi-
tation. But the influence of the municipal authorities of the town of Groningen, in
particular, led to the execution, during the 16th to 19th centuries, of what was in
fact a dual-purpose project: fuel + land improvement. This project resulted in
very much improved land for an agricultural land utilization type. An arable land
type in which potatoes were, and to some extent still are, the most important crop

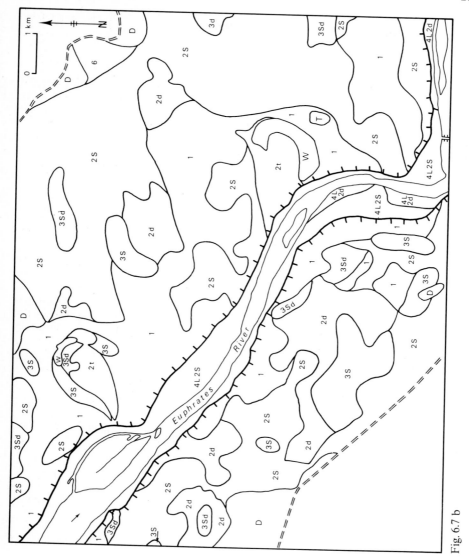

Fig. 6.7 b

was established in the 19th century. The development of this land use type was also made possible because of the systematic application, with help of the municipal authorities, of town refuse and of night soil. The coming of chemical fertilizers made increased yields possible, particularly of potatoes, the yield of which increased to 50 tons per hectare per crop. The quality of these potatoes was not sufficient for human consumption, which led to the establishment of factories

Table 86. Potential land use capability (potential land suitability) in the Ramadi area (Iraq) (after YAHIA, 1971)

a) Assumptions

1   The permanent soil characteristics and qualities which were mentioned before.

2   Leaching of the excess soluble salts and exchangeable sodium is possible in general, but with restrictions on certain soils; no deterioration of the soil structure would occur.

3   Resalinization of the lower parts of the river basin soils having strongly or extremely saline ground water is considered as a permanent limiting factor (see below).

4   Construction of a new irrigation system (see Fig. 6.8) will provide in all parts of the area adequate water supply for all crops under intensive agricultural use with increased percentage of cultivated area both in winter (66–100%) and summer (to 25–40%).

5   Construction of the drainage system also will improve the internal drainage of the soils and as a consequence a high crop production can be achieved.

6   The fertility of the soils can be increased by using fertilizers and proper crop rotation, so that high yields could be obtained. For this the agricultural extension services will have to assist by increasing the knowledge and the efficiency of the farmers.

7   Some cooperative societies have already been established in the area and some more are being created; the principal goal of these as declared by the farmers themselves is to provide all possible measures required for improving soils and crop management and economic conditions on their farms.

9   Local differences related to road facilities, size and shape of the land classes and their location within the area studied, and differences in skill or resources of the farmers are not considered for this classification as they do not reflect differences of the basic resources of the area.

b) Classification

Class 1.	Arable.
Suitable crops:	vegetables, field crops, green manure, cereals and orchards.
Class 2.	Arable.
Subclass 2s:	deficiencies due to slight salt concentrations and moderately heavy-textured subsoils.
Suitable crops:	vegetables, field crops, green manure, cereals and date palms.
Subclass 2d:	deficiencies due to moderately good or imperfect drainage.
Suitable crops:	vegetables, field crops, green manure, and cereals.
Subclass 2t:	deficiencies due to the topographical conditions, in so far as not levelled within the scope of the project.
Suitable crops:	green manure and cereals.
Class 3.	Arable.
Subclass 3s:	deficiencies due to moderate salt concentrations and moderately good drainage or slightly inferior soils, fairly good yields.
Suitable crops:	green manure, cereals and rice.
Subclass 3sd:	deficiencies due to high salt concentration and imperfect or poor drainage, or inferior soils.
Suitable crops:	cereals and rice.
Class 4.	Limited arable.
Subclass 4sd:	deficiencies due to very high salt concentrations and imperfect or poor drainage, very inferior soils (not represented in map).
Suitable crops:	rice.
Subclass 4l:	deficiencies due to position allowing periodic flooding, requiring an engineering and economic determination for flood control measures.

Table 86 (continued)

Suitable crops: summer vegetables and crops, green manure and cereals.
                  41 (2d), summer vegetables and crops, green manure and cereals.
                  41 (2sd), do,
                  41 (3s), do,
Class 6.   Non-arable

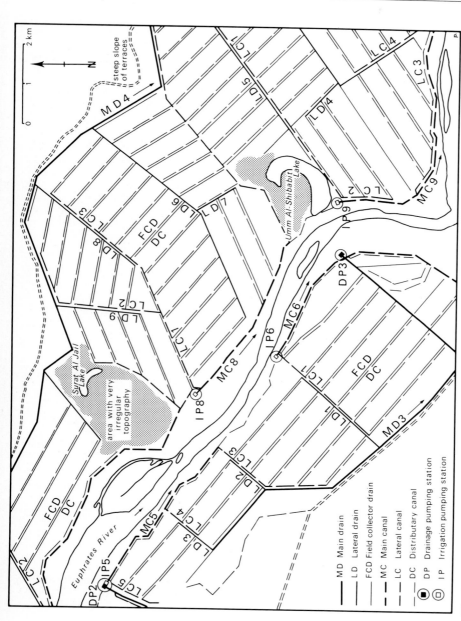

Fig. 6.8. Layout of drainage and irrigation system of the middle part of the Ramadi Project (AL RAWAFED, 1968, cited by YAHIA, 1971)

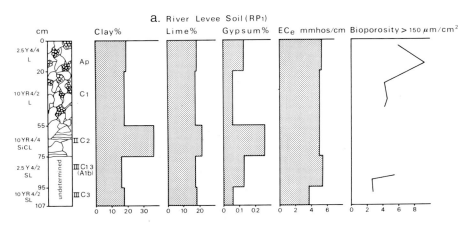

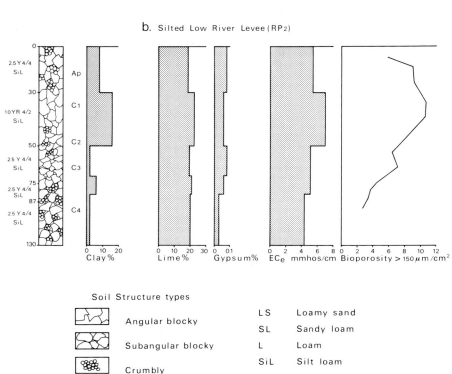

Fig. 6.9 a–e. Trends of soil structure, clay, lime and gypsum contents, salinity and distribution of the biopores in the investigated soils in the Ramadi area, Iraq (YAHIA, 1971)

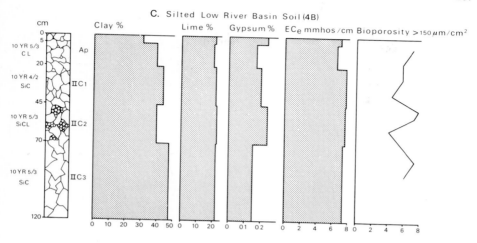

c. Silted Low River Basin Soil (4B)

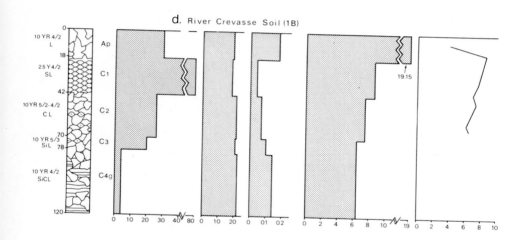

d. River Crevasse Soil (1B)

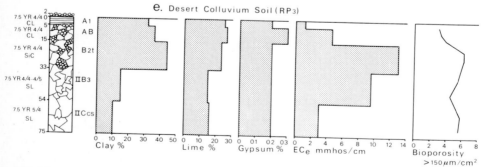

e. Desert Colluvium Soil (RP3)

Fig. 6.9 c–e

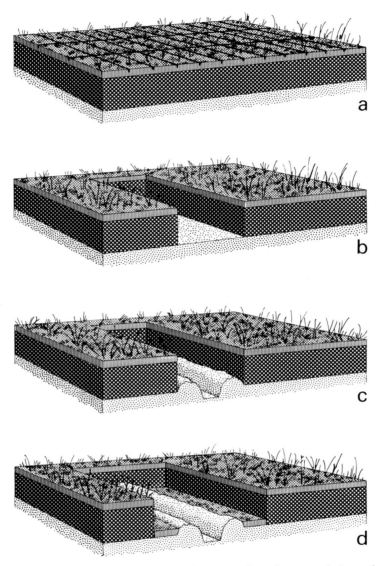

Fig. 6.10a–h. Diagrams showing the excavation of peat and the reclamation of the pit bottoms (DE SMET, 1969)

producing different carbohydrate products. The continuous cultivation of the arable lands caused however a gradual disappearance by oxidation of the originally present peat-remnants in the topsoil; this situation necessitated the instigation of modern land improvements. These improvements must, of course, also be geared to modern requirements of homogeneity of larger fields, concurrent with mechanization of the agriculture. Specific requirements for other land utilization

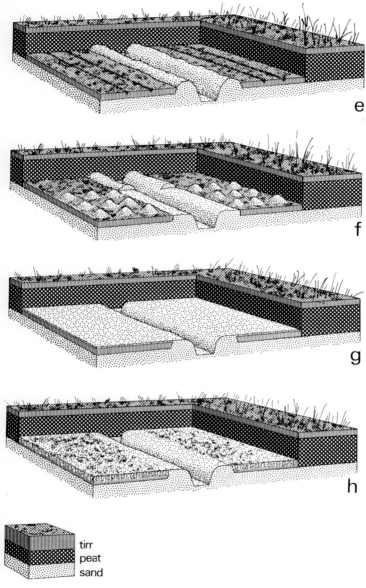

tirr
peat
sand

Fig. 6.10 e–h

types which are now being established in the area, such as mixed farming with grass leys of long duration and various kinds of horticulture must now also be met. Potential land suitability, and the improvements leading toward it, must also, therefore, be considered for land utilization types other than those originally present in the area.

Table 87. Soil suitability classes and ways of improving the soil (DE SMET, 1969)

Soil improvement	Suitability class				
	1	2	3	4	5
lowering the ground level	●				
raising the ground level			●	●	●
mixing sand into the plow-layer			●	●	●
breaking up and working of laminar peat (e.g. subsoiling)	●	●	●	●	●
breaking up ortstein (e.g. subsoiling)	●	●	●		
breaking and turning up ortstein	●	●	●		
breaking and removing of loamy pans				●	
breaking up and removing laminar peat and other unfavorable layers and turning up sand (e.g. deep plowing)	●	●	●	●	●
raising and lowering adjacent dry and wet soils, respectively (levelling)	●		●		●

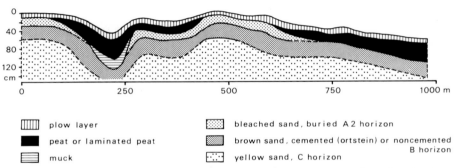

Fig. 6.11. Schematic profile across a typical part of the old peat reclamation landscape (DE SMET, 1969)

Differences between Actual and Potential Land Suitability; Economics of Water Use

Quantitative information on the differences between actual and potential land suitability is only available for a relatively small number of cases, as proper project evaluations after execution of major land improvements do not abound in the world (see e.g. HAYES, 1969). Some indicative examples may, however, be given.

In some horticultural areas in the Netherlands, land improvement produced remarkable results. Some results obtained by the application of a sand cover on polder soils are indicated in Table 88, which is based on calculations from basic experimental data (HIDDING, 1967). Apart from the application of a sand cover, mixing of the topsoil with subsoil layers of poorer quality was tried, but this procedure yielded less satisfactory results.

Table 88. Calculated revenues for ten-year rotations (2 × tulips, 2 × iris, 1 × gladioli, 3 × potatoes and 2 × headed cabbage) with various soil improvements (HIDDING, 1967)

Thickness of sandcover (cm)	Mixing depth (cm)	%age coarse sand	Mean Annual Revenues (Hfl/ha/year)
0	45	0	Hfl 11200.—
0	30	0	Hfl 11610.—
5	45	10	Hfl 11190.—
10	45	15	Hfl 11880.—
5	30	20	Hfl 12210.—
10	30	27	Hfl 12370.—
15	45	31	Hfl 12000.—
15	30	43	Hfl 12360.—

Mechanized application of the sand costs approximately Hfl. 1000.— per ha. An application of enough coarse sand gives a lowering of the annual (recurrent) costs in the order of Hfl. 500.— per ha, because full mechanisation of harvest becomes possible. Some interesting data on the actual cost of land improvements, e.g. drainage and liming, are also found in the report on West Donegal, Eire (An Forais Taluntais, 1969).

Table 89. Time required to reach potential in relation to land conditions on grazing lands in Ireland (LEE and DIAMOND, 1972)

County	Soil No.	% dry	Potential (L.U./100 acres) 43 lb N/acre	206 lb N/acre	Growth rate % 1958–67	Time (years) to reach potential from 1971 43 lb N/acre	206 lb N/acre
Meath	24	85	86	108	3.8	7	13
Cork	9	92	92	115	3.7	13	20
Wexford	Clonroche series (Nth)	100	89	111	3.8	12	19
Limerick	Elton series	100	89	111	2.3	19	29
Galway	23	100	86	108	2.9	20	30
Cavan	15	40	72	84	2.4	27	34
Leitrim	17	0	55	—	1.3	41	—
Clare	13	0	63	—	1.2	54	—
Limerick	13	0	63	—	0.0	—	—

On permanent grazing lands there is a possibility that land improvement may be achieved by continuous applications of chemical fertilizers. These influence the composition of the grassland vegetation in such a manner that the "vegetation" attribute of the land is changed for a long period. To arrive at this improvement itself may also take many years. Recent investigations in Ireland have produced some interesting results in this respect (Table 89 after LEE and DIAMOND, 1972).

The U.S. Bureau of Reclamation has always paid a considerable amount of attention to the relation between physical land factors, including major improvements such as irrigation projects, and the farmers' incomes. This system is based on a number of principles, which have been explained by MALETIC (1966):

1. The prediction principle, which "states that the classes in the system must express the soil-water-crop interactions expected to prevail under the new moisture regimen resulting from irrigation".

2. The economic correlation principle which "states that in a particular project setting the physical factors of soil, topography, and drainage are functionally related to an economic value".

3. The principle of permanent and changeable factors, which "states that the changes in land arising from irrigation development impose a need to identify characteristics that will remain without major change and those which will be significantly altered".

4. The arability-irrigability principle, which "states that the selection of lands for irrigation proceeds through an initial step in which land areas of sufficient productivity to warrant consideration for irrigation are identified and that there is superimposed upon this determination the selection of lands to be specifically included in the plan of development".

All these principles are clearly related to the prediction of potential land suitability, in this case particularly for irrigable land. In another publication (MALETIC and BARTHOLOMEW, 1966), the relationship between different climates and incomes in the Western U.S.A. were put into model calculations. Fig. 6.12 shows the relative productivity of irrigation in the different soil-climate zones of this region. The evaluation of potential land suitability in the USBR system is in general related to the "repayment capacity" of the lands after irrigation. This relationship can be represented in a three dimensional graph, such as that reproduced in Fig. 6.13 (MALETIC, 1970). Payment, or repayment, capacity of irrigated lands may be calculated in farm budgets; this has been done by NIELSEN (1963) for two different kinds of soils representing: A. good lands, and B. moderately good lands (Table 90) (see also VINK, 1960, 1963a; Para. 6.5). Similar calculations have been made by SELDON and WALKER (1968) for irrigated rice in Thailand.

In Pakistan, the economics of water use were investigated for the irrigated plains (ASHRAF ALI, BRINKMAN and RAFIQ, 1972). Irrigation is here partly carried out from canals and partly from tube wells. The costs of the water are measured in

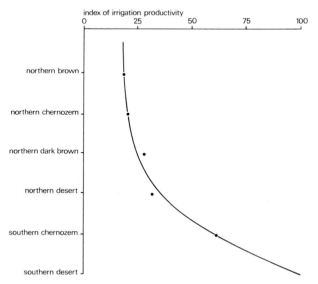

Fig. 6.12. Regression model showing relationship between the Great Soil Groups and the Index of Irrigation Productivity in the Western U.S.A. (MALETIC and BARTHOLOMEW, 1966)

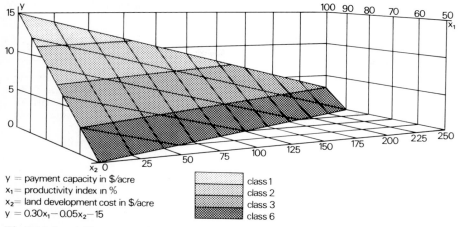

y = payment capacity in $/acre
x₁= productivity index in %
x₂= land development cost in $/acre
$y = 0.30x_1 - 0.05x_2 - 15$

class 1
class 2
class 3
class 6

Fig. 6.13. Land Class-Payment Capacity surface. (After: MALETIC, 1970)

Table 90. Budgets of two different kinds of lands under typical farming, and their repayment capacities (NIELSEN, 1963)

	Budget A	Budget B
Tentative land class	1	3s
Productive capacity index	100	70
Size of farm		
Total acres	320	320
Irrigable acres	100	100
Man days of labor	364	359
Total farm investment (exclusive of land development)	$ 63 200	$ 59 600
Gross farm income	17005	14 244
Total farm expenses	10 801	10 201
Net farm income	$ 6 204	$ 4 043
Return to investment	632	596
Return to labor and management	4037	2812
Total payment capacity	1 535	635
Payment capacity per irrigable acre	15.35	6.35

Budget A represents lands which in the soil scientist's judgment are of the best quality, in the area of study, from the standpoint of crop adaptability and yield potential. These lands are assigned a productive capacity index of 100 and are adopted as the basis for comparison in evaluating other lands to be classified. According to our budget analysis, these lands have a total payment capacity of $ 15.35 per irrigable acre for paying project and private development costs when organized into a typical 320 acre farm with 100 acres irrigable.

Budget B represents lands which the soil scientist judges to have only 70 per cent of the productive capacity of the lands represented by Budget A. This budget shows a total of $ 6.35 per irrigable acre available.

Table 91. Simplified cropping patterns under irrigation by climate and land capability subclass (ASHRAF ALI et al., 1972). All intensities 150% [a].

	I		IIw		IIs sandy		IIs clayey		IIa	
Subhumid	special [b]	10	fodders	5	fodders	5	fodders	5	fodders	5
	fodders [b]	5	Basmati	70	gr. nuts	50	Basmati	95	maize	50
	maize	40	maize	25	maize	20	wheat	45	Basmati	20
	Basmati	20	wheat	45	wheat	70			wheat	70
	wheat	60								
Main [c] semi-arid	special	10	fodders	5	fodders	5	fodders	5	fodders	5
	fodders	5	maize	50	gr. nuts	50	Basmati	90/70	cotton	30
	cotton	40	cotton	20	cotton	20	wheat	45/70	Basmati	20
	maize	20	wheat	70	wheat	70			maize	20
	wheat	60							wheat	70
Dry semi-arid	special	10	fodders	5	fodders	5	fodders	5	fodders	5
	fodders	5	cotton	50	cotton	40	IRRI	40	cotton	50
	cotton	50	maize	20	gr. nuts	30	cotton	30	IRRI	20
	maize	10	wheat	50	gram	40	wheat	70	wheat	70
	wheat	40	gram	20	wheat	30				
	gram	20							fodders	5
Main arid [d]	special	10	fodders	5	fodders	5	fodders	5	cotton	50
	fodders	5	cotton	70	cotton	60	cotton	40	IRRI	20
	cotton	60	gram	50	gr. nuts	10	IRRI	30	wheat	70
	gram	40	wheat	20	gram	50	wheat	50		
	wheat	20			wheat	20	gram	20		

[a] Intensities 100 per cent in kharif, 50 in rabi on very wet land, and in areas with good ground water and clayey, wet, or saline-alkali soils; 75 per cent in kharif and 75 in rabi in other casses.
[b] Special includes perennial and annual crops with a very high value per acre. Percentages given for special and fodders apply both in kharif and rabi, and should be doubled for calculation of intensity.

Pakistan rupees per acre-foot of water; these are, for canal water, Rs. 5 per acre-foot in kharif (summer) and Rs. 10 per acre-foot in rabi (winter), and for tube well water, Rs. 25 wherever fresh ground water is available. In areas with saline ground water, canal remodelling and drainage are necessary to increase kharif supplies, and storage plus drainage, to increase rabi supplies; these improvements cost approximately Rs. 50 per acre-foot and between Rs. 90 and Rs. 120 per acre-foot, respectively. In Table 91 the cropping patterns for different land classes in different climatic regions and different land classes are given. Table 92 shows the irrigation water use of these cropping patterns and the net value of the cropping patterns in terms of irrigation water, indicative of their payment capacity. The authors indicate that with modern management, i.e. with a modernized land utilization type, Land Classes I and II allow economical use of irrigation water (canal water) costing up to approximately Rs. 50 per acre-foot in kharif and up to Rs. 90 to 120 in rabi and that this would give marginal returns of Class III land, whereas the use of this water on Class IV lands would be highly uneconomical. The tube well water could be used economically, where available, on lands of

Table 91 (continued)

IIIw		IIIs		IIIa		IVw		IVs		IVa	
fodders	5	fodders	5	Basmati	100	—		gr. nuts	100	Basmati	100
Basmati	75	gr. nuts	95	wheat	50	—		wheat	50	wheat	50
maize	20	wheat	45								
wheat	45										
fodders	5	fodders	5	Basmati	100/75	—		gr. nuts	100	Basmati	100/75
Basmati	75/50	gr. nuts	95	wheat	50/75	—		wheat	50	wheat	50/75
maize	20	wheat	45								
wheat	45/70										
fodders	5	fodders	5	IRRI	75	—		gr. nuts	75	IRRI	75
IRRI	70	gr. nuts	70	wheat	75	—		gram	75	wheat	75
wheat	70	gram	70								
fodders	5	fodders	5	IRRI	75	IRRI	100	gr. nuts	75	IRRI	75
IRRI	70	gr. nuts	70	wheat	75	wheat	50	gram	75	wheat	75
wheat	70	gram	70								

[c] Double figures refer to land in fresh and saline ground water areas respectively.
[d] Excludes coastal arid and frost-free arid climates, roughly from Hyderabad south.

Classes I, II, and III but would be marginal or uneconomical on Class IV lands, even with modern management. Under more traditional land utilization, only the lands of Class I and Class II could be economically irrigated. Theoretically, only the water of the present canal system could be used economically on Class IV lands, but this is in most cases already used more effectively on better lands (see also Fig. 6.14). Therefore, if the existing canal systems are taken as land attributes, the actual land suitability on Class III lands is somewhat higher than the potential land suitability on Class IV lands. It is interesting to note that therefore land improvements are more feasible on the better lands than on the poorer lands.

This aspect is very important in land improvement and in potential land suitability. If one disregards the quantitative aspects of potential land suitability and of the land improvements leading to this, one gains the impression that improvement of the poorest lands would produce the best results. This is very understandable, since the impression of "causing crops to be grown where nothing could be sown beforehand" would, in a purely qualitative way, produce this effect. It is also understandable from a social standpoint, as ostensibly the opening up of the poorest lands would provide new stimuli for development to the poorest areas of a country. Finally, the improvement of the poorest lands is a much more intriguing technical challenge than the relatively clear-cut increase of already fairly productive lands (see also FOUND, 1971).

Table 92. Irrigation water use and cropping patterns in the Plains of Pakistan (ASHRAF ALI et al., 1972)

a) Irrigation water use[a] of cropping patterns by climate and land capability subclass.

Climate	AF[b] per acre CCA, in kharif and in rabi										
	land cap. subclass										
	I	IIw	IIs sandy	IIs clayey	IIa	IIIw	IIIs	IIIa	IVw	IVs	IVa
Subhumid											
kharif	...2.8	4.5	2.6	5.0	2.7	4.6	3.5	5.0	—	5.0	5.0
rabi	...1.5	1.0	1.5	1.0	1.5	1.0	1.0	1.0	—	1.5	1.0
Main semi-arid[c]											
kharif	...2.4	2.3	2.6	5.0/3.7	2.7	4.6/3.3	3.5	5.0/3.8	—	5.0	5.0/3.8
rabi	...1.5	1.5	1.5	1.0/1.5	1.5	1.0/1.5	1.5	1.0/1.5	—	1.5	1.0/1.5
Dry semi-arid											
kharif	...3.0	2.9	3.0	3.6	3.3	4.1	3.0	4.1	—	4.2	4.1
rabi	...1.7	1.7	1.4	1.9	1.9	1.9	1.1	1.9	—	1.3	1.9
Main arid											
kharif	...3.4	3.4	3.4	3.9	3.7	4.5	3.4	4.5	6.0	4.5	4.5
rabi	...1.6	1.5	1.5	1.9	2.2	2.2	1.2	2.1	1.4	1.5	2.1

b) Net value[d] of cropping patterns in terms of irrigation water use by climate and land capability subclass under modern management.

Climate	Rs per AF in kharif and rabi										
	land cap. subclass										
	I	IIw	IIs sandy	IIs clayey	IIa	IIIw	IIIs	IIIa	IVw	IVs	IVa
Subhumid											
kharif	...136	94	97	95	94	66	68	62	—	27	14
rabi	...235	193	161	193	185	128	105	110	—	11	−42
Main semi-arid											
kharif	...158	103	94	95	109	66	68	62	—	27	14
rabi	...235	195	161	194	185	128	105	110	—	11	−12
Dry semi-arid											
kharif	...148	109	96	104	121	64	59	60	—	25	11
rabi	...203	156	183	153	145	100	180	86	—	91	−21
Main arid											
kharif	...167	140	113	120	135	72	52	70	29	22	21
rabi	...213	152	182	103	81	50	202	36	−54	105	−39

[a] Under-watering (a traditional practice to spread available water over more land) has not been considered in this study. It may have short-term advantages only under traditional management in subhumid and semi-arid areas. Under modern management this practice is expected to be uneconomical due to the higher fixed production costs (*e.g.* for fertilizers) and the necessity to use part of the water on less productive land. In addition, under-watering gradually increases salinity.
[b] At watercourse head.
[c] Double figures refer to land in fresh and saline ground water areas respectively.
[d] Not counting water cost.

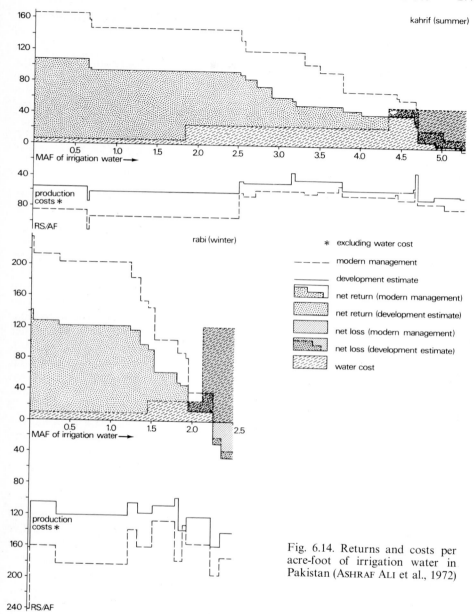

Fig. 6.14. Returns and costs per acre-foot of irrigation water in Pakistan (ASHRAF ALI et al., 1972)

Some interesting quantitative data on the feasibility of irrigation in tea plantations have been given by BISWAS and SANYAL (1971).

Generalizations are particularly dangerous with regard to land conditions. There is no doubt that there exist in the world large areas of potentially excellent lands which are now only poorly productive, because one factor, for example, high salinity, limits all other aspects. In such a case, it is possible to improve these lands with a very poor actual land suitability to reach a high, and sometimes even very high, potential land suitability. Even then, however, when compared with conditions within a certain region, these soils often are not the poorest soils if their other characteristics are considered. A good example is a comparison of the "river levees soils" of Iraq with the "river basin soils" of the same country (see Fig. 6.5 to 6.9, p. 256/267). There exist in several areas of Iraq basin soils with a lower salinity than levee soils in some other parts. Still, improvement of the rather permeable and easily cultivable soils of the river levees, which also offer much better possibilities for root development, is more feasible than that of the heavy, poorly permeable, heavy clay soils with vertic characteristics which predominate in the basins.

Improvements Seen as Investments

For irrigation projects, this situation is even more clearly expressed if the limited water resources are taken into account. In most arid and semi-arid regions, but also in many other areas where irrigation is practiced on a large scale, water is even more limited than soils. It is therefore necessary to consider carefully how the most efficient use can be made of the scarce water resources (see also Para. 4.3.2). But in all other cases, financial limitations exist. These financial limitations are of great importance both on a national scale and on the individual farms themselves. National investments have to be carefully measured, whether they are from truly national sources or have been obtained through loans from international or other agencies. On a national scale, it is absolutely essential that the investments in land improvement be of the highest efficiency, as even then they must compete with investments in other economic activities such as industries and transport. A careful consideration of the ultimate "payment capacity" of land development projects, whether irrigated or not, is therefore a national necessity; this can only be done if land resources are carefully investigated and the actual and potential land suitabilities, based on investigations of land resources and land conditions, are measured with quantitative considerations if necessary approximative, of their relative efficiencies.

Perhaps even more important is the weighing of the ultimate efficiency of land improvements within the farm budget. The aim of land improvement is land development, and the intention is finally to create good possibilities for a higher standard of living for the rural populations. This means that the farms must not only have a certain "payment capacity" in terms of irrigation water or of other duties to be paid on land improvement, but that they must first and foremost obtain a higher net income if recurrent inputs and outputs on the farm, including the necessary operations for management and maintenance of land improvements, are considered. If this goal is not achieved, a land improvement project may give a satisfactory impression in a purely technical sense, but it does not really contribute to land development. In the long run, projects of the latter kind deteriorate and either tend toward the development of other means of earning a living for the local populations, e.g. chicken raising or pig breeding instead of arable land farming, or they run down because insufficient funds for their operation and maintenance are made available.

In some cases, land improvement projects are carried out for social or political reasons. The right of governments to do so is indubitable. This kind of project may even be essential if seen from the standpoint of general national development. The approach to these projects should, however, also include the necessary calculations on "payment capacity", based on careful considerations of the land resources, and other financial measures should be taken to avoid too heavy duties on the project itself.

In such cases, the matter of amortization of the major capital investments in land improvement plays a very important role. It was touched upon in the first pages of this section, where, according to the new international system of land evaluation (BRINKMAN and SMYTH, 1973), it has even been utilized as the distinguishing factor between two categories of potential land suitability. In a general system of land evaluation, this usage seems to put too much emphasis on the matter. Whether amortization of the major, non-recurrent, capital investments in land improvement is considered in a land evaluation is partly a matter of expediency. Quite often, the cost of these investments is not yet known and cannot even be sufficiently approximated at the first stage in which an approximative land evaluation has to be made. Furthermore, these first phases of land evaluation often are not sufficiently quantitative for calculations on amortization cost to contribute to the decisions. The purpose of the first evaluations is to provide a general view of the surface area which could be improved, as related to the total surface area, and of the location, in particular in the case of irrigation projects, of possible dam sites and of the main topographic conditions. At this stage, the eventual positions of the sites for major engineering works are often not yet known (e.g. dams and major canals), and therefore their cost cannot be approximated.

As planning and evaluation gradually proceed together, however, (see also Para. 6.5) the situation becomes clearer. At a certain moment the decision must be made, on the basis of the available resources and their possible improvements, on how to proceed in the final stages of a project. At this point, further assumptions on economic parameters must be made, and the amortization cost of the land improvements and of other kinds of major investments must be decided upon, at least as to their order of magnitude. In some countries, the order of magnitude of the ratio between development cost to be amortized and non-amortized is a more or less fixed percentage. In the Netherlands approximately 70% of the cost of rural reconstruction projects is directly amortized by the Government as a part of the national budget for the current year. The other 30% has to be paid as an annuity by the land owners. In addition, the land owners have to pay the fixed general rates for operations and maintenance whereas the land users, tenants or owners, have to pay the annual cost of maintenance and operations on the farms. Many other solutions to this problem can be envisaged; it is undoubtedly of advantage if a definite national policy exists for these aspects of land improvement.

Ecological Impact of Land Improvements

In the future, the effect of land improvements will have to be measured, more than thus far, not only by the economic and social expediency of the measures to be taken, but also by their ecological impact. In the previous chapters, references have been made to this problem. The development of suitable criteria for this key problem is now being undertaken by several agencies, e.g. the International Bank for Reconstruction and Development (I.B.R.D., often called the "World Bank") and its associated agencies in Washington D.C. Additional reference to ecological considerations will be made in the following chapter.

6.4 Land Evaluation Classifications

A New International System

The previous text contains repeated reference to the new international system of land evaluation (BRINKMAN and SMYTH, 1973). This system also includes a new proposal for land classification, based on the system of evaluation developed at the FAO Consultation (Wageningen, 1972), at which this evaluation system was discussed. In Table 93 the essential aspects of this classification are shown (BRINKMAN and SMYTH, 1973). It has been arranged at a number of levels, each of which has its own significance.

Table 93. Categories and groupings of the new international system of land suitability classification (BRINKMAN and SMYTH, 1973)

Category	Order	Class	Subclass	Unit [a]
Number of groupings	three	unlimited	unlimited	unlimited
Groupings	1. Suitable — 1.1 / 1.2 / etc.	1.2w / 1.2t / 1.2wt / etc.	1.2w (1) / 1.2w (2) / 1.2w (3) / etc.	
	2. Conditionally suitable — 2.1 / 2.2 / etc.	2.1At / 2.1Bt / etc.		
	3. Unsuitable — 3.1 / 3.2 / etc.			

[a] Land Suitability Unit.

Unclassified land: Land of undetermined suitability for the defined use has no place in the classification until such time as its suitability can be determined. Such land will be shown as a blank on maps and in interpretative tables or by the letters NC—not classified. In practice, a land utilization type which is considered relevant to a survey area may be clearly irrelevant to certain land units within the area. To avoid possible confusion, the letters NR—not relevant—could be used in place of a classification of these particular units. The letters NR could also be applied to interpretative combinations which are irrelevant in that they are not meaningful. For example, no meaningful classification of the *actual suitability* of land can be made for a use which cannot be introduced without major land improvement.

The "Order" of the land suitability classification is of the highest significance. Here, the decision must be made whether a particular tract of land is suitable or not for a particular land utilization type. Suitable land is defined as "land on which (sustained) use for the defined purpose in the defined manner is expected to yield benefits that will justify required recurrent inputs without unacceptable risk to land resources on the site or in adjacent areas". Whether "sustained" use is always a prerequisite or not is in some cases debatable. As was discussed in the section on "Land Degradation", occasionally a certain amount of degradation is unavoidable under a given land utilization type, because of social conditions or because the ensuing enrichment of good bottom lands outweighs the degradation of some poor hill lands; the approach of "sustained use" is, however, undoubtedly to be recommended in more than 99% of the cases (see also Para. 5.4.5).

The more important aspects of the definition of "Order 1" are the normative approaches which are inherent in this system. The "defined purpose" and the "defined manner" refer to the way in which land utilization types must be indicated. This subject, which was discussed in Chapter 3, is of the highest importance for land evaluation classification. Without a careful description of the land utilization types for which the classification is developed, no real indications for land use can be given. In this respect too many mistakes have been made in the past, partly because resources surveyors, in particular soil surveyors, did not give enough time or attention to this subject or because farm management experts or farm economists either were not available or did not cooperate in the project. The essential information on plant production and farm management of certain land utilization types has to be gathered, although the amount of detail may depend on the circumstances of the project. This is also reflected in Table 94, in which some suggestions for the legends of land suitability maps, based on the New International System, are given.

A second normative approach, which is in fact the crucial part of the system, is found in the fact that the land use on lands of Order 1 is "expected to yield benefits that will justify required recurrent inputs". This is very clear: suitability is determined by the net result of outputs minus inputs on a recurrent, usually annual, basis. These are first and foremost benefits for the individual farmer, whether on a traditional farm of 1 hectare, or on a state farm or collective farm of more than 5000 hectares. Farming is an economic activity which must produce positive net results; otherwise the activity must be stopped. Given certain economic conditions and a certain land utilization type, it is the land resources which determine whether the net results will be positive or not. To be classified in Order 1, lands must have the essential prerequisite that, under the given conditions, they can produce positive results. If, for social or political reasons, or for reasons of national economy, positive results must be obtained even though to a first approximation, the land would not belong to Order 1, then the land utilization type, or the economic conditions, have to be changed or, if feasible, the land conditions must be improved. In the latter case, the potential land suitability has to be considered, and under certain conditions it might well be positive even though the actual land suitability were negative. Some information on how this can be handled and indicated is given in Table 94. Land evaluation hinges on the crucial decision of whether net results are positive or not. This decision,

Table 94. Use of the New International Land Suitability Classification in Map Legends (Brinkman and Smyth, 1973)

The map legend might take the following form:

Actual suitability classification

	Land utilization types		
	A	B	C
1	1.1	1.3	1.2
2	1.2	2.1H	1.2
3	1.3	3.1	1.3
4	1.2		
etc.			

In some cases both Actual and Potential suitability classifications could be combined in a single tabular legend by dividing each "cell" linking land units and utilization types, e.g.:

Actual suitability class

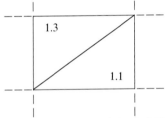

Potential suitability class (with amortization of capital inputs)

It is undesirable to present a Potential suitability classification without amortization of capital inputs unless a specification in broad classes of required major improvements is also shown. This can be achieved by dividing each "cell" into three to indicate the classification of required major improvement between the Actual and Potential suitability classifications. This division into three will also clarify relationships in the case of a Potential suitability classification "with amortization of capital inputs".

Actual suitability class

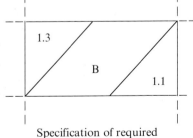

Potential suitability class with or without amortization of major capital inputs

Specification of required major capital inputs

If only a single kind of evaluation of a single use is being presented, the separate mapping units, instead of being numbered, could show either the Actual suitability classification, or the Potential suitability classification plus specification of required major capital inputs.

according to the system discussed here, has to be made in a clear manner. Making it is unavoidable, but the criteria on which it can be based leave a large number of questions which are not always easily answered. In the ideal case, exact quantitative data, based on farm budgets, should be presented (see Tables 90 to 92 and Fig. 6.13 and 6.14). In many cases, however, approximative estimates, based on systematic transfer of knowledge and experience with due consideration of the land conditions, have to serve (see also Para. 6.5 and VINK, 1963 a). The crucial decision—"positive or not"—also implies that a sufficiently high standard of living for the farming population can be assured. It is often easier to determine, by comparative investigations, the general level of the standard of living, than to ascertain the exact analytical data of farm budgets. Because national economic planning, based on multi-year plans, often is also centered on standards of living in terms of annual incomes per family, this approach may be suitable for the land evaluation as well as for the applications of land evaluation within a national context.

The land use defined must also meet the requirement that it is "without unacceptable risk to land resources on the site or in adjacent areas". This refers to land degradation in its widest sense, including soil conservation as well as the larger issues of environmental management. Some reference was made to this in Para. 5.4.5 on Land Degradation. In fact, the normative "ecological" criteria are rapidly becoming as important as the economic and social criteria. Some of the implications of this are more extensively indicated in Chapter 7.

If the net results are not positive, an acceptable level of the standard of living included, the lands must be classified as belonging to Order 3, "Unsuitable Land", of which the definition reads: "Land having characteristics which appear to preclude its (sustained) use for the defined purpose in the defined manner or which would create production, upkeep and/or conservation problems, requiring a level of recurrent inputs unacceptable at the time of the interpretation". The definition clearly shows the effort which has gone into its careful wording. The latter is very necessary because, in accordance with what was indicated previously, the decision on whether a tract of land belongs to Order 1 or to Order 3 is a crucial one. The wording of the definition of Order 3 leaves open the possibility that some doubtful cases which are initially classified as belonging to Order 3, may eventually prove to be of sufficient suitability. Thus, in keeping with a general rule in land evaluation, i.e., that a rather conservative view of the suitability of lands is usually more justified than a too optimistic one, extremely doubtful cases can be classified in Order 3.

As is clear from Table 94 (p. 281), the system is applicable to both the actual and the potential land suitability classifications. The major, non-recurrent land improvements have been classified according to the Iranian system, which was described in Para. 5.5.3 (see in particular Tables 75 to 78, p. 214 to 217). The fact that these improvements are not the only possible ones should be noted. Many major improvements are possible in agriculture which can be considered major improvements in land use e.g., improvements in plant varieties, in animal stock, in cultivation methods and tools, or the use of chemical fertilizers or even of simple household refuse. These methods, particularly in many tropical land utilization types, often constitute much more important improvements for land use than

Table 95. Major land qualities and their symbols to be used in the subclasses of the new international land suitability classification (mainly after BEEK and BENNEMA, 1972)

1. Major land qualities related to plant growth (symbol)
— availability of water (w)
— availability of nutrients (n)
— availability of oxygen for root growth (o)
— availability of foothold for roots (Fh)
— conditions for germination (seed bed c.a.)
— salinization and/or alkalinization (Sa)
— soil toxicity or extreme acidity (To)
— pests and diseases related to the land (d)
— flooding hazard (In)
— temperature regime (including incidence of frosts) (t)
— radiation energy and photoperiod (r)
— wind and storm as affecting plant growth (Cw)
— hail and snow as affecting plant growth (h)
— air humidity as affecting plant growth (Ah)
— drying periods for ripening of crops and at harvest time (Hs)

2. Major land qualities specifically related to animal growth
— hardships due to climate (Ch)
— endemic pests and diseases (De)
— nutritive value of grazing land (Ng)
— toxicity of grazing land (Pt)
— resistance to degradation of vegetation (Vd)
— resistance to soil erosion under grazing conditions (Eg)
— availability of drinking water (Wd)
— accessibility of the terrain (Ta)

3. Major land qualities related to natural product extraction
— presence of valuable wood species (Tf)
— presence of medicinal plants and/or vegetation extraction products (Pm)
— presence of fruits (f)
— presence of game for meat and/or hides (g)
— accessibility of the terrain (Tb)

4. Major land qualities related to practices in plant production, in animal production or in extractions
— possibilities of mechanization (m)
— resistance towards erosion (e)
— freedom in the layout of a farm plan or a developed scheme, including the freedom to select the shape and the size of fields (Lo)
— trafficability from farm to land (Tr)
— vegetation cover in terms of favorable or unfavorable effects for cropping (Ve)

would be obtained from major land improvements. The difference lies in the fact that all the other improvements in agriculture involve less investment in the land and more in the crops, which cannot be considered as "reasonably permanent or predictably cyclic" attributes of the land. The "other major agricultural improvements" which are not "major land improvements" have a different place in the farm budget, e.g. with regard to their amortization; they do not lead to the formation of artifactial land attributes, as is the case in general with "major land improvements". Improvements in agriculture which are not major land improvements belong to that part of land use which is defined in the land utilization type (see Chapter 3).

The Orders are subdivided into Classes, Subclasses and Land Suitability Units (see Tables 93 and 94, pp. 280 and 281). The number of these subdivisions is unlimited, so that the particular conditions of a region, of greater or smaller surface area, may be reflected in their sequence. It is proposed that Class 1.1 would comprise the best lands of Order 1, i.e., the best lands of the region under consideration, and that the following numbers should reflect land of decreasing suitability. In Order 3, usually only 2 classes are recognized: 3.1 "at present unsuitable but possibly to be made suitable by land improvements or by kinds of land use at present not acceptable", and 3.2 "unsuitable" where limitations are so severe that no future use in the defined manner can be foreseen.

The subclasses would best be used to indicate the limitations or the land qualities which are the main constraints for land use in the defined manner. This may be done by a simple system, such as the one in use by the U.S. Soil Conservation Service (w = water, s = soil, e = erosion hazard, etc.) or by a more elaborate one based on the land qualities, such as has been proposed by BEEK and BENNEMA (1972) and is indicated in Table 95.

The sets of symbols used in Table 95 were chosen because of their mnemotecnic value, i.e. they may be easily remembered because of their association with the terminology referred to. Other sets of symbols could be used, e.g. in which the position in the system would be clearer, such as P1 to P15 (P = plant growth) for the first group of major land qualities, A1 to 8 for the second group, N1 to 5 for the third group and M (= management) 1 to 5 for the fourth group. With other groups of major land qualities, (e.g. for recreation and wildlife), other similar sets of symbols could be added. Another system which might be used is that of the "Limitations" of the Portuguese system (see Table 74, p. 209 and related text). Symbols of the subclasses of the U.S. Bureau of Reclamation (1953) are also applicable.

The "units" indicated as the lowest category in Table 93 (p. 280) are "land suitability units", which are subdivisions of the subclasses; they are similar in most respects, but differ "in their production characteristics or in minor aspects of their management requirements". These may sometimes be definable as differences in detail of their limitations, such as quantities of lime or fertilizers to be applied (see e.g. DE SMET, 1962).

Consideration of Order 2, "Conditionally Suitable Land", has been left until the end of the discussion of this new system of land suitability classification for a definite purpose: this order should only be applied in very special cases. It is defined as "land having characteristics which, in general, render it unsuitable for (sustained) use in the defined manner but which, subject to conditions of management which are not specified in the general definition of the use, could be rendered suitable". The conditions of management might include special systems of tillage and cropping which are not normally applied in a given land utilization type, for example small areas of erodable hills in otherwise flat country. An example given by BRINKMAN and SMYTH (1973) is: "Subclass 2.3 Ht: 'Conditionally marginally suitable', 'Land having limitations of topography which, in general, preclude

Table 96. The land classification system of the U.S.Soil Conservation Service (U.S.Dept. of Agr.), (after STALLINGS, 1957, cited by HUDSON, 1971), copyright: Prentice Hall, Inc.

Class I. Soils in Class I have no, or only slight, permanent limitations or risks of damage. They are very good. They can be cultivated safely with ordinary good farming methods. The soils are deep, productive, easily worked, and nearly level. They are not subject to overflow damage. However, they are subject to fertility and puddle erosion.

Class I soils used for crops need practices to maintain soil fertility and soil structure. These practices involve use of fertilizers and lime, cover and green-manure crops, crop residues, and crop rotations.

Class II. Class II consists of soils subject to moderate limitations in use. They are subject to moderate risk of damage. They are good soils. They can be cultivated with easily applied practices.

Soils in Class II differ from soils in Class I in a number of ways. They differ mainly because they have gentle slopes, are subject to moderate erosion, are of moderate depth, are subject to occasional overflows, and are in need of drainage. Each of these factors requires special attention. These soils may require special practices such as soil-conserving rotations, water-control devices, or special tillage methods. They frequently need a combination of practices.

Class III. Soils in Class III are subject to severe limitations in use for cropland. They are subject to severe risks or damage. They are moderately good soils. They can be used regularly for crops, provided they are planted to good rotations and given the proper treatment. Soils in this class have moderately steep slopes, are subject to more severe erosion, and are inherently low in fertility.

Class III soil is more limited or subject to greater risks than Class II. These limitations often restrict the choice of crops or the timing of planting and tillage operations.

These soils require cropping systems that produce adequate plant cover. The cover is needed to protect the soil from erosion. It also helps preserve soil structure. Hay or other sod crops should be grown instead of cultivated row crops. A combination of practices is needed to farm the land safely.

Class IV. Class IV is composed of soils that have very severe permanent limitations or hazards if used for cropland. The soils are fairly good. They may be cultivated occasionally if handled with great care. For the most part, they should be kept in permanent hay or sod.

Soils in Class IV have unfavorable characteristics. They are frequently on steep slopes and subject to severe erosion. They are restricted in their suitability for crop use. They should usually be kept in hay or pasture, although a grain crop may be grown once in five or six years. In other cases, the soils may be shallow or only moderately deep, low in fertility, and on moderate slopes. These soils should be in hay or sod crops for long periods. Only occasionally should they be planted to row crops.

Class V. Soils in Class V should be kept in permanent vegetation. They should be used for pasture or forestry. They have few or no permanent limitations and not more than slight hazards. Cultivation is not feasible, however, because of wetness, stoniness, or other limitations. The land is nearly level. It is subject to only slight erosion by wind or water if properly managed. Grazing should be regulated to keep from destroying the plant cover.

Class VI. Class VI soils should be used for grazing and forestry, and may have moderate hazards when in this use. They are subject to moderate permanent limitations, and are unsuited for cultivation. They are steep, or shallow. Grazing should not be permitted to destroy the plant cover.

Class VI land is capable of producing forage or woodland products when properly managed. If the plant cover has been destroyed, the soil's use should be restricted until cover is re-established. As a rule Class VI land is either steeper or more subject to wind erosion than Class IV.

Class VII. Soils in Class VII are subject to severe permanent limitations or hazards when used for grazing or forestry. They are steep, eroded, rough, shallow, droughty, or swampy. They are fair to poor for grazing or forestry, and must be handled with care.

Table 96 (continued)

Where rainfall is ample, Class VII land should be used for woodland.
In other areas, it should be used for grazing. In the latter case, strict management should be applied.

Class VIII. Soils in Class VIII are rough even for woodland or grazing. They should be used for wildlife, recreation, or watershed uses.
Within some of the main classes, smaller subclasses are used to specify particular problems. In the American system these are applied only to Classes II, III and IV and shown by the addition of the following letters added after the class.

e = erosion hazard—when vulnerability of the soil is the main problem in its use.
w = wetness—when excess water is the main problem.
c = climate—when climate (eg, temperature or lack of moisture is the main problem).
s = soil—when limitations of the soil (eg, salinity) are the main problem.

Within the subclasses, land capability units may be recognized.

---

economic use in the manner defined but which could be used for this purpose and would be equivalent in suitability to land of Class 1.3, *provided* production was limited to a small range of high value crops requiring intensive methods of production'. The conditions for Order 2 could be 'that only fruit tree crops are grown' (within a land utilization type which also includes arable land and possibly pastures), or 'that farmers with a high level of experience are present', or 'that more irrigation water is available in the dry season than would be normally allowed for'. Most of the conditions applied to the use of Order 2 have therefore to do with the way in which a certain land utilization type has to be applied. If large areas with such conditions are found, they will in general lead to the formulation of a specific new land utilization type, or modification of the land utilization type according to its 'management level'; for this type, the normal use of the Orders 1 and 3 is then foreseen. If, however, in a certain area relatively small surfaces of conditional suitability are found, the use of Order 2 may provide a simpler solution. Because of recent proposals (Rome, 1975), Order 2 will be abolished.

Contributions from Several Countries

The New International Land Suitability Classification is the product of a cooperative effort, the FAO Consultation on Land Evaluation for Rural Purposes (BRINKMAN and SMYTH, 1973), and as such is based on the experience of a number of experts from many different countries, such as the U.S.A., France, Great Britain, Iran, Iraq, Belgium and the Netherlands. In this text, not all these different systems can be described, but the two major systems from the U.S.A. are indicated in Tables 96 and 97. These systems include the 8 classes of the Soil Conservation Service and the system of the Bureau of Reclamation. Both these systems have found applications, often with suitable modifications, in many countries of the world. The new system tries to incorporate their advantages and, by a careful

Table 97. Land classification according to the system of the Bureau of Reclamation (1954)

1. Definitions

Land classification is the systematic appraisal of lands and their designation by categories on the basis of similar characteristics. In the Bureau of Reclamation, land classification is conducted for the specific purpose of establishing the extent and degree of suitability of lands for sustained irrigation. Suitability as herein used connotes a reasonable expectancy of permanent, profitable production under irrigation. It is measured in terms of anticipated relative payment capacity by consideration of potential productive capacity, costs of production and costs of land development. The following terms are defined with specific relation to Bureau of Reclamation usage:

A. *Arable land* is land which, in adequate sized units and if properly provided with the essential improvements of leveling, drainage, irrigation facilities, and the like, would have a productive capacity, under sustained irrigation, sufficient to: meet all production expenses, including irrigation operation and maintenance costs and a reasonable return on the farm investment; to repay a reasonable amount of the cost of project facilities; and to provide a satisfactory level of living for the farm family. The *arable area* comprises all lands delineated in the land classification which have sufficient potential payment capacity to warrant consideration for irrigation development.

B. *Irrigable land* is the arable land under a specific plan for which a water supply is or can be made available and which is provided with or planned to be provided with irrigation, drainage, flood protection, and other facilities as necessary for sustained irrigation. The *irrigable area* comprises that portion of the arable area which is subject to farm use under ultimate development of the project or unit under consideration. It is determined within the arable area by consideration of any limitations imposed by water supply, cost of facilities and service to specific tracts, and of the lands required for additional nonproductive rights-of-way and other purposes. The acreage thus determined will be the irrigable land or area used in Bureau of Reclamation reports and in contracts with the water users' organizations.

C. *Productive land* is the maximum acreage of the irrigable area subject to cropping and provides a basis for determination of water requirements, canal capacities, and payment capacities. The productive area of a project or unit of a project will be less than the irrigable area of the project or unit, the extent of which will depend upon irrigation systems, intensities of farming and other factors. This difference which experience has shown will average 6 percent of the irrigable area is made up of non-productive land uses such as farm roads and feed lots.

D. *Full irrigation service land* is irrigable land now receiving, or to receive, its sole and generally adequate irrigation supply through works or facilities constructed by or to be constructed by the Bureau of Reclamation. This term applies also to previously irrigated land in non-Federal projects where a substantial portion of the facilities has been, or is to be, constructed, rehabilitated, or replaced by the Bureau.

E. *Supplemental irrigation service land* is irrigable land now receiving, or to receive, an additional or re-regulated supply of irrigation water through works or facilities constructed by or to be constructed by the Bureau of Reclamation. Such supply together with the supply from non-project sources will generally constitute an adequate supply.

F. *Gross classification area* includes all the lands mapped and classified in a given survey.

G. *Land class* is a category of lands having similar physical and economic characteristics which affect the suitability of land for irrigation. It is an expression of relative level of payment capacity.

H. *Subclass* is a category within the land class identifying the deficiency or deficiencies.

I. *Informative appraisal* is an evaluation of selected physical factors designed to provide additional information for the planning, development, and operation of irrigation projects.

Table 97 (continued)

---

2. Basic Land Classes

The land classes are based on the economics of production and land development within specific ecological areas. Hence, the production and repayment potentials will differ significantly between such areas. Although all classes will be found in any given ecological area, they will not necessarily be found in a given project area. Four basic classes are used in the Bureau system to identify the arable lands according to their suitability for irrigation agriculture, one provisional class, and one class to identify the non-arable lands. The first three classes represent lands with progressively less ability to repay project construction costs. The excessive deficiency-restricted utility subclasses of Class 4 may have repayment ability ranging from less than that of Class 3 to more than that of Class 1 depending upon the particular utility involved. The number of classes mapped in a particular investigation depends upon the diversity of the land conditions encountered and other requirements as dictated by the objectives of the particular investigation.

Class 1   Arable. Lands that are highly suitable for irrigation farming, being capable of producing sustained and relatively high yields of a wide range of climatically adapted crops at reasonable cost. They are smooth lying with gentle slopes. The soils are deep and of medium to fairly fine texture with mellow, open structure allowing easy penetration of roots, air and water and having free drainage yet good available moisture capacity. These soils are free from harmful accumulations of soluble salts or can be readily reclaimed. Both soil and topographical conditions are such that no specific farm drainage requirements are anticipated, mimimum erosion will result from irrigation and land development can be accomplished at relatively low cost. These lands potentially have a relatively high payment capacity.

Class 2   Arable. This class comprises lands of moderate suitability for irrigation farming, being measurably lower than Class 1 in productive capacity, adapted to somewhat narrower range of crops, more expensive to prepare for irrigation or more costly to farm. They are not so desirable nor of such high value as lands of Class 1 because of certain correctible or non-correctible limitations. They may have a lower available moisture capacity, as indicated by coarse texture or limited soil depth; they may be only slowly permeable to water because of clay layers or compaction in the subsoil; or they also may be moderately saline which may limit productivity or involve moderate costs for leaching. Topographic limitations include uneven surface requiring moderate costs for levelling, short slopes requiring shorter length of runs, or steeper slopes necessitating special care and greater costs to irrigate and prevent erosion. Farm drainage may be required at a moderate cost or loose rock or woody vegetation may have to be removed from the surface. Any one of the limitations may be sufficient to reduce the lands from Class 1 to Class 2 but frequently a combination of two or more of them is operating. The Class 2 lands have intermediate payment capacity.

Class 3   Arable. Lands that are suitable for irrigation development but are approaching marginality for irrigation and are of distinctly restricted suitability because of more extreme deficiencies in the soil, topographic, or drainage characteristics than described for Class 2 lands. They may have good topography, but because of inferior soils have restricted crop adaptability, require larger amounts of irrigation water or special irrigation practices, and demand greater fertilization or more intensive soil improvement practices. They may have uneven topography, moderate to high concentration of salines or restricted drainage, susceptible of correction but only at relatively high costs. Generally, greater risk may be involved in farming Class 3 lands than the better classes of land, but under proper management they are expected to have adequate payment capacity.

Class 4   Limited Arable or Special Use. Lands are included in this class only after special economic and engineering studies have shown them to be arable. They may have an excessive, specific deficiency or deficiencies susceptible of correction at high cost, but are suitable for irrigation because of existing or contemplated intensive cropping such as for truck and fruits; or, they may have one or more excessive, non correctible deficiencies thereby limiting their utility to meadow, pasture, orchard, or other relatively permanent crops, but are capable of supporting a farm family and meeting water charges if operated in units of adequate size or in association with better lands. The deficiency may be inadequate drainage, excessive salt

Table 97 (continued)

content requiring extensive leaching, unfavorable position allowing periodic flooding or making water distribution and removal very difficult, rough topography, excessive quantities of loose rock on the surface or in the plow zone, or cover such as timber. The magnitude of the correctible deficiency is sufficient to require outlays of capital for land development in excess of those permissible for Class 3 but in amounts shown to be feasible because of the specific utility anticipated. Subclasses other than those devoted to special crop use may be included in this class such as those for subirrigation, and sprinkler irrigation which meet general arability requirements. Also recognized in Class 4 are suburban lands which do not meet general arability requirements. Such lands can pay water charges as a result of income derived either from the suburban land and other sources or from other sources alone. The Class 4 lands may have a range in payment capacity greater than that for the associated arable lands.

Class 5   Non-arable. Lands in this class are non-arable under existing conditions, but have potential value sufficient to warrant tentative segregation for special study prior to completion of the classification, or they are lands in existing projects whose arability is dependent upon additional scheduled project construction or land improvements. They may have a specific soil deficiency such as excessive salinity, very uneven topography, inadequate drainage, or excessive rock or tree cover. In the first instance, the deficiency or deficiencies of the land are of such nature and magnitude that special agronomic, economic or engineering studies are required to provide adequate information, such as extent and location of farm and project drains, or probable payment capycity under the anticipated land use, in order to complete the classification of the lands. The designation of Class 5 is tentative and must be changed to the proper arable class or Class 6 prior to completion of the land classification. In the second instance, the effect of the deficiency or the outlay necessary for improvement is known, but the lands are suspended from an arable class until the scheduled date of completion of project facilities and land development such as project and farm drains. In all instances, Class 5 lands are segregated only when the conditions existing in the area require consideration of such lands for competent appraisal of the project possibilities, such as when an abundant supply of water or shortage of better lands exists, or when problems related to land development, rehabilitation and resettlement are involved.

Class 6   Non-arable. Lands in this class include those considered non-arable under the existing project or the project plan because of failure to meet the mimimum requirements for the other classes of land, arable areas definitely not susceptible to delivery of irrigation water or to provision of project drainage, and Classes 4 and 5 land when the extent of such lands or the detail of the particular investigation does not warrant their segregation. Class 6 irrigated land with water rights encountered in the classification will be delineated and designated Class 6W. Such lands will be treated in accordance with special provisions. Generally, Class 6 comprises: steep, rough, broken, or badly eroded lands; lands with soils of very coarse or fine texture, or shallow soils over gravel, shale, sandstone, or hardpan, and lands that have inadequate drainage and high concentrations of soluble salts or sodium. Excluding the position subclasses, the Class 6 lands do not have sufficient payment capacity to warrant consideration for irrigation.

---

definition of land utilization types and land qualities, to avoid some of the pitfalls which the application of a system originating in one country always offers in its application in another country with different land use conditions (see also STEELE, 1967; HUDSON, 1971).

An interesting land use capability classification for grazing lands has recently been produced in Ireland (LEE and DIAMOND, 1972). Some data from this system are given in Table 98.

Table 98. Data from grazing capacity classification of Ireland (LEE and DIAMOND, 1972)

(a) *Classes of grazing capacity with two different fertilizer gifts*

L.U./100 acres[a]		Grazing capacity class	L.U/100 ha	
43 lb. N/acre	206 lb. N/acre		48 kg N/ha	230 kg N/ha
≥ 90	≥ 112	A	≥ 222	≥ 276
85–90	107–112	A_2	210–222	264–276
80–85	102–107	B	197–210	252–264
75–80	92–102	B_2	185–197	227–252
70–75	82–92	C_1	173–185	202–227
65–70	72–82	C_2	160–173	188–202
60–65	—	D_1	148–160	—
55–60	—	D_2	135–148	—
< 55	—	E	< 135	—
—	—	Unclassified	—	—

[a] One Livestock Unit equals one 10.5 cwt cow or equivalent.

(b) *Areas (hectares) of mineral soil associations in Irish Republic and estimates of their grazing capacity*

Soil No.	Area (000 ha)	48 kg N/ha		230 kg N/ha	
		Grazing capacity (L.U./100 ha)	Gross grazing capacity (000 L.U.)	Grazing capacity (L.U./100 ha)	Gross grazing capacity (000 L.U.)
4	187.2	173	324.4	212	389.5
6	64.2	207	133.6	257	165.4
6 (hill)	12.4	185	23.1	232	28.9
6 (Screen)	11.0	190	21.4	237	26.2
7	93.2	227	212.3	284	265.4
8 (South)	249.3	227	567.7	284	709.6
8 (North)	217.9	217	474.6	269	587.8
8 (hill)	108.4	185	201.2	232	252.1
9 (Kerry)	50.9	210	106.8	264	134.8
9	382.4	227	870.8	284	1088.5
10	11.9	210	25.1	264	31.6
11	21.8	136	29.6	—	29.6
12	79.2	148	117.6	—	117.6
13	459.0	156	715.7	—	715.7
15	130.1	178	231.8	207	270.5
17	230.7	136	314.1	—	314.1
18	142.1	195	277.9	247	351.8
19	92.0	195	179.7	247	227.5
20	240.1	202	487.3	252	606.2
21	275.7	215	594.7	269	743.8
22	188.1	203	382.8	252	474.9
23	316.3	212	673.4	267	845.6
24	896.5	212	1908.4	267	2396.6
25 (Meath)	24.2	190	46.2	235	57.0
25	193.0	178	343.9	217	420.2
27	21.0	161	33.9	198	41.7
28 (Wexford)	3.2	183	5.9	227	7.4
28	26.8	173	46.5	212	57.1

Table 98 (continued)

(c) *Grazing capacity of soil series (mineral) in County Wexford*

Soil series	Area (000 ha)	48 kg N/ha		230 kg N/ha	
		Grazing capacity (L.U.100 ha)	Gross grazing capacity (000 L.U.)	Grazing capacity (L.U./100 ha)	Gross grazing capacity (000 L.U.)
Ambrosetown	1 111.0	232	2.58	289	3.21
Baldwinstown	468.6	232	1.16	289	1.36
Bannow	404.0	232	1.00	289	1.17
Broadway	4 120.8	232	9.59	289	11.93
Broomhill	436.3	232	1.01	289	1.26
Carne	387.8	232	0.90	289	1.12
Clonroche (South)	41 805.9	232	97.27	289	121.07
Fethard	1 450.4	232	3.37	289	4.20
Hook Head	484.8	232	1.13	289	1.40
Killinick	3 910.7	232	9.09	289	11.32
Old Ross	2 779.5	232	6.47	289	8.05
Crosstown Complex	3 215.8	220	7.08	274	8.84
Ballindaggan	12 629.0	220	27.82	274	34.70
Clohamon	905.0	220	1.99	274	2.48
Clonroche (North)	55 250.2	220	121.71	274	151.80
Kiltealy	8 387.0	207	17.44	259	21.79
Randallsmill	2 876.5	195	5.62	245	7.04
Slievecoiltia	2 343,2	185	4.35	232	5.45
Screen	11 029.2	190	18.25	237	26.21
Kilmore Slob	1 195.8	183	2.19	227	2.72
Wexford Slob	2 036.2	183	3.72	227	4.63
Rathangan	21 258.5	178	37.88	217	46.30
Ballyknockan	686.8	178	1.22	217	1.49
Kilpierce	18 099.2	161	29.12	198	35.84
Ballinruan	929.2	161	1.49	198	1.84
Macamore	21 028.2	161	33.83	198	41.64
Knockroe	169.7	161	0.27	198	0.34
Templeshanbo	961.5	148	1.43	—	—
Ballywilliam	1 187.8	148	1.80	—	—
Millquarter	517.1	136	0.70	—	—
Coolaknick	1 632.2	136	2.22	—	—
Kilmannock	1 309.0	99	1.30	—	—

Different Kinds of Land Classification

Land suitability classification is one kind of land classification, of which many more kinds exist. Some of these have been mentioned in older publications (VINK, 1963a). The following categories of land classification may be briefly noted (LEWIS, 1952):

(a) Soil Classification,
(b) Land Capability Classification,
(c) Economic Land Use Classification,
(d) Mapping of Major Agricultural Regions.

This list might be extended to include also such systems of land classification as (STEWART et al., 1968):

(e) Land Systems Classification (C.S.I.R.O.),
(f) Terrain Evaluation,
(g) Land evaluation for Engineering,
(h) Land Assessment for Regional Planning,
(j) Land Assessment for Taxation.

Thus, a very unsystematic list develops in which, however, some aspects are still clearly overlooked or understated.

As early as 1941, a systematic approach was started in the U.S.A. (National Resources Planning Board, 1941), which has since been applied and developed (LEWIS, 1952; VINK, 1963a). The original four categories of 1941 have been added to, but the basic principle has been retained: the fact that also land classifications can be characterized according to their inherent characteristics and to the complexity of their approach to the land. The following categories are useful today, starting with the purely "natural science" approach to the land and going through various stages to the final application in land use development:

I. Land classification in terms of inherent characteristics includes all kinds of classifications of the land resources based on their characteristic attributes as described in Chapter 4. Typical examples are: climatic classifications, topographical and geomorphological classifications, geological and soil-taxonomic classifications. Also included are the legends of maps of this kind: climatic, topographical, geomorphological, geological, soil and vegetation maps. Land Systems maps and many terrain evaluation maps also belong to this category.

II. Land classification in terms of inherent qualities, or "*in terms of ecological land conditions*" is the classification of the land conditions as described in Chapter 5. It is a classification which in general is based on the "purely scientific" classifications and maps, and which indicates the direct, technical or biological answers to the requirements of crops and of the different kinds of land use. It is normative in so far as the biological and technological requirements provide normative information. Typical maps include some terrain evaluation maps, drainability maps, salinity maps, engineering classifications.

III. Land classification in terms of present use refers to the classifications used in the "Present Land Use Surveys" described in Chapter 2. This category could, perhaps, have been put in the place of the previous one, as Category 2, but for several reasons its traditional place in the sequence has become third. It is a classification type which stands on its own and which simply notes which kinds of land use and which crops, depending on the scale and the detail of a map, are at present found in a region.

IV. Land classification in terms of responses to management refers to the responses, notably of crops, to different kinds of recurrent management operations as well as to some non-recurrent improvements. The kinds of operations referred to have been described in Para. 5.4.4. Few of these responses have as yet been elaborated into complete classifications. The investigations carried out thus far have in general not been sufficient to classify all land units of an area according to their responses. The results of these investigations are usually incorporated in the suitability classifications of Category V.

V. Land classification in terms of suitabilities, or "*in terms of use capabilities*" is the category to which the New International System of Land Classification and the other systems described in this section, belong. Also "suitability classifications for land improvement", which were discussed in Para. 5.5.3 and 5.5.4, belong to this category, as they are inherent in the potential land suitability classification. The essential feature of the classifications in this category is that they are based on social and economic as well as on ecological and management assumptions. They are concerned with feasibility in so far as the given economic parameters, possibly alternative sets of parameters, make this possible. The classifications in this category are a study of the impact of physical land conditions on land use and land improvement. The economic data are used as parameters and not as variables; the study of the economic and related data as variables belongs to a different category. The classifications of category V lie, however, in the border zone of the physical sciences, where they touch upon the economic and social sciences. A common example is the many "Soil Suitability Classifications" which are an essential part of "Soil Survey Interpretation" (KELLOGG, 1961; VINK, 1960, 1963 a) and which contribute largely to land development in many parts of the world.

VI. Economic Land Use Classification, or "*Land classification in terms of economic and related production variables*" must, at least partially, be based on the data provided by the previously described categories. The fact that this is often not the case derives from a chronic lack of contact and many misunderstandings between economists and those natural scientists concerned with land use and land conditions. The economic variables are in the field of farm economics and of market economics and are mainly concerned with the production systems and with the prices of inputs and outputs (see e.g. FOUND, 1971).

VII. Land classification in terms of recommended use is, in principle, different from the previous six categories. All previous categories are the results of scientific research, based on scientific considerations and on scientifically formulated assumptions. The present category is based on other considerations, essentially those of policy, regardless of the extent to which additional research data, such as on population growth, family composition, industrial development and many others, are utilized. The previous classifications did no more than indicate the possible developments, where necessary with alternative solutions, based on various sets of assumptions. In this classification, also termed "advisory land classification", an advisory body, or a single person, after due consideration of the previously mentioned classifications and of all other available materials, selects the solution which for many reasons is deemed to meet the required purposes in accordance with policy targets. On the relatively simple level of the farm, the advisory classification is made by the agricultural extension officer, on the basis of maps and experimental data and on what he considers the best choice under all given circumstances. On a national level, it is often a National Planning Board or comparable institution which makes the advisory selection. These may be in the form of the selection of one of several alternative maps produced within one of the previously mentioned categories of classification. Often, however, the production of draft plans is the most typical activity within a given project. This might be done in the form of a "minimal project" and an "optimal project", as has been done for the original development of the Lower Medjerda Valley in Tunisia.

VIII. Land classification in terms of program effectuation is where the final decision is made on the kind of land improvement and land development and on the intended future land use which will be effectuated in a given area. It is done by the directly responsible governing bodies. On the farm it is the farmer himself or the director of a state or collective farm, who decides on what is to be done, it is to be hoped after consideration of all previous classifications, or at least of their essential maps and conclusions, with due respect for the recommended use. In a project, the administrative authority of the project decides. If he finds that the alternatives on which to base the decision are still insufficient, he must be free to have other alternatives, at least those from Categories V, VI, and VII, elaborated. If sufficient material of Classifications I through IV is available, there should be relatively few difficulties. It may be that not only an "optimal plan" and a "minimal plan" are needed, but that intermediate steps or phases are necessary because of financial considerations, or that social and political considerations necessitate the formulation of a "maximal plan" (see also FOUND, 1971).

6.5 Land Evaluation Procedures

6.5.1 General

Land Resources Interpretation: "What Can Be Done"

The purpose of land evaluation is prediction: prediction of the land utilization types which can be established on certain lands with and without land improvement. Also included is prediction of the crops which can be grown, the land management which can be, or has to be, practiced and of the land improvements which are technically and economically feasible. These are the general predictions, based on the knowledge of the land resources, of the relevant and foreseeable land utilization types and of the relationships between the requirements of these land utilization types and the land conditions. Such predictions represent the direct application of the knowledge of land resources in the light of possible applications. They provide answers to the question of *what* can be done, but may leave unanswered the question of *how* to arrive at the predicted situations from the point at which a given land use in a given region is carried out under the present circumstances. For the prediction of what can be done, the situation of the present land use is relatively unimportant. Present land use together with its inherent characteristics such as land ownership, field pattern, road conditions, is of no particular interest when answering this question, because it is intended to be changed in the near future. It may be just a source of information about at least some of the crops which will also be grown under future conditions, but only in so far as present conditions, such as on the better tracts of land, with relatively good land-use conditions, give indications for future use (see e.g. VINK, 1963a).

The answer to the question, "What can be done?", with its implications as indicated above, might be indicated as "Land Resources Interpretation", as a parallel to "Soil Survey Interpretation" (see e.g. KELLOGG, 1962). Land resources interpretation may be considered an extension of the domain of the land resources surveyors, for which is required the additional cooperation of agronomists, and for which social and economic parameters have to be provided, but it is a natural extension of their domain, which may even be said to belong to their obligations to human society. It is also a necessary job for the land resources surveyors, since they are the only people who really know the units which they have mapped, with their internal variations and transitions. The job cannot be taken over by others, agronomists or engineers for example, because they have insufficient knowledge of the land. It is also a necessary job for the land resources surveyors in the sense that they have to translate their scientific data and terminology into a language which is readable by non-scientists and to translate their necessarily complicated basic resources maps into maps with fairly simple legends. They must realize that agronomists, engineers and planners as well as administrators have their own jobs to do, and that they cannot be expected to take time off to study the scientific terminology of the many sciences concerned with land resources. Only occasionally, such as when mining engineers use geological maps, do the engineers have the kind of basic knowledge necessary to interpret the basic scientific maps for themselves. Such situations are, however, the exception rather than the rule. In land development the rule is rather that the basic maps are unreadable to outsiders; this is necessary, because land resources are complicated natural phenomena, and it follows that their study and classification are also complicated, but from this the necessity originates, that the land resources surveyors have to do a large part of the job of translating their data and classifications for practical use.

Land Development Classification: "How to Do It"

Answering the question, "What can be done?", however, leaves another important question still unanswered: "How do we proceed from the present conditions toward the predicted possibilities?" This question is the primary concern of land development planners and engineers, and it touches directly upon the problems handled by administrators. These people are therefore directly concerned with the present land use situation (see e.g. BIJKERK et al., 1970). They must determine how the present situation can be transformed into something which approaches the possible land uses, with or without land improvement. Particularly in densely populated areas with already existing intensive land utilization types, the present land use conditions may strongly influence the approach to a land development project. The land use planners often have less of an eye for the general capabilities and constraints of certain kinds of lands, and are more interested in the ways and means of improving and using a particular tract of land. If for instance a certain tract of rather poor land lies very close to a main irrigation canal, it may be more feasible to improve this tract of land than to improve a very good tract of land which lies some kilometers away from the irrigation system.

Some of their attitudes are reflected in an (unpublished) statement given by C. BIJKERK to the FAO Consultation on Land Evaluation (BRINKMAN and SMYTH, 1973). This statement covers the following points:

1. A judgement on the relevance of land uses is a basic issue in each evaluation system. Agricultural land use is first of all an economic process (a process with an economic goal) in which land, labor, capital and non-factor inputs are interacting. So a well-defined economic reconnaissance report (input and output analysis) will have to be the starting point for the physical and technical classification. When such a reconnaissance is not available, at least the economic relevance of technical (physical) subdivisions (of the land) will have to be borne in mind during the procedure.

2. In each land evaluation system a balance between technical (supply of land resources data) and economic (demand for land development planning) factors needs to be taken into consideration. It is no use to develop very detailed physical classifications if there is no or little knowledge on their relationships with the production process.

3. The degree to which factors in land evaluation are investigated and presented in detail will have to be in equilibrium with the relative importance of these factors in the rural production process. In intensive agriculture (or even horticulture) the input of labor and capital in terms of costs is dominant in comparison with land costs. In such situations a classification of, for example, the infrastructure (accessibility, distances from farm to fields, parcellation pattern, size and shape of lots, farm size) will have to be given a heavier weight in an over-all system of land evaluation.

4. A stratigraphy of demand situations may aid in clarifying the structure of land evaluation systems. According to PEARSE (1969), 3 situations can be distinguished: (1) demand is absent (jungles, mountains, eternal snow and ice areas), (2) demand is singular (agriculture, forestry, alpine recreation areas) (3) demand is multiple: (a) not competitive (national parks and large forests), (b) competitive (in densely populated countries). This may be developed for different conditions and land uses.

5. In situations of multiple use, demand curves will have to be deduced for alternative land uses, which give the relationship between price and quantity of these uses. For the optimization of multiple competitive land use, knowledge about the separate uses and their simultaneous application is necessary. Knowledge about the interrelationships among different land uses such as agriculture, forestry, nature preservation, landscaping, outdoor recreation, urbanization and traffic is as yet at a minimum, and such research will have to be promoted in interdisciplinary teams of scientists (see also FOUND, 1971).

6. A systematic approach by linear and non-linear programming techniques of land evaluation systems for alternative land uses in rural areas (in which differences in soil productivity, labor requirements, infrastructure and ecological restrictions can be varied and evaluated) must be one of the main goals of further development in this field. As agricultural production takes place in an integrated process, land evaluation systems will have to be based upon techniques which simulate this process as closely to reality as possible. Linear programming techniques are considered to be the best available ones at the moment.

7. Promoting systematic inventory systems of agrarian infrastructure will enhance the progress in land evaluation systems. The computorized land use inventory system of the Netherlands (BIJKERK et al., 1970) has proved to be of much profit in evaluating land development and rural reconstruction plans.

It is clear that the emphasis and the ambition of this second approach to land evaluation, that of engineers and planners, are different from those of the first approach, which was termed "Land Resources Interpretation". The second approach might be called "Land Development Classification". The integration of the two approaches is necessary for land development in its fullest sense. In any project, only a mimimum of time is available for the evaluation procedures of both and, correctly, the above statement points out that the supply of physical and technical data should be as closely as possible equal to the demand at a given phase of the development process. On the other hand, it is not uncommon that planners and engineers overlook certain aspects of land development. One of these is that land resources may have better possibilities or more serious constraints for the kinds of future land use which are predicted. This may lead to a different appraisal of both the actual and the potential land suitability than can be foreseen if too much emphasis is placed on the existing structural conditions. It should also be foreseen that both with and without the project (actual and potential land suitability), developments take place in agricultural land use, and that the kind and quantity of these developments are considerably influenced by land resources. Finally, land costs as mentioned in the preceding statement do not truly reflect the economic impact of land conditions, because the land prices are the result of a local market, whereas the influence of land conditions works through the differences in productivity of the labor and capital inputs.

Land resources interpretation, however, tends to forget that there is a supply and demand situation for its data and that this situation changes with the different phases of a land development project. Land evaluation procedures have therefore to be attuned to the various phases of a project and have to take into account the usually very limited duration of each of these phases. The two kinds of approaches, "Land Resources Interpretation" and "Land Development Classification", should be integrated in the different stages for optimal efficiency of each procedure. This integration, the "Intersector Approach" to land evaluation (BRINKMAN and SMYTH, 1973) touches upon both the procedures of land evaluation and of land development planning. A "planning of the evaluation" as well as a "planning of the planning" is therefore more necessary than has been understood in the past (DROR, 1971).

6.5.2 Land Resources Interpretation

Physical Classifications and Economic Parameters

Land resources interpretation is based on the many aspects of land use, land attributes and land conditions discussed in the foregoing chapters, notably on: (a) definitions of land utilization types, (b) systematic collections of land resources data, in general in the form of maps and related reports, (c) data and considerations on land use requirements and on land conditions and their possibilities for improvement and hazards of degradation. It is directed towards the production of physical land classifications. These may be based on purely physical and biological data and considerations, in which case several kinds of interpretation maps can be produced:
— Land Quality Maps or Maps of Ecologic Land Conditions,
— Land Limitation Maps,
— Land Degradation Maps, including "soil erosion maps",
— Land Improvement Maps, indicating the purely technical possibilities for improvement,
— Trafficability Maps.

Although these classifications may also be produced in tables, without accompanying maps, it must be understood that the true relations between land conditions and their areal significance can only be indicated on maps.

The use of economic and social considerations, in the form of parameters, for land resources interpretation, leads to the production of land suitability classifications, including classifications of the actual suitability, of the potential suitability and, where applicable, of the suitability for land improvement. The land evaluation procedures described in this paragraph are therefore first and foremost physical evaluation procedures, but they have to be seen in the context of land utilization types, i.e. production units organized as economic entities, the farms. These evaluations are carried out for a definite practical purpose, usually land development of some kind, including land conservation and the conservation of natural habitats. Because land resources interpretation is based on certain sets of assumptions, these assumptions may have to be amended or even completely changed according to findings which lie outside the field of land evaluation. Land resources interpretation as a "self supporting" activity may therefore often only give a first approximation, or a set of alternative approximations, of the true suitabilities to be arrived at. It is therefore often an iterative activity which, through repetitive procedures with feedbacks from planning, arrives at the best possible results for a given moment.

Land Resources Interpretation and Soil Survey Interpretation

Land resources interpretation is more than soil survey interpretation, because in soil survey interpretation the non-soil land resources are often only handled in a very limited sense. Soil survey interpretation is, however, an important part of land resources interpretation, since the soil is one of the central factors, and very often the most important key variable, for land use (KELLOGG, 1961; VINK, 1963a; BARTELLI et al., 1966). The essential difference between land resources interpretation and soil survey interpretation lies in the fact that in the former the complexity of resources data is greater. This is not simply a matter of adding up the results from different surveys; the results, due to the different nature of the resources, are often presented in completely different manners. The latter is partly avoidable by using integrated surveys of the natural environment for the systematic collection of land resources data. The following contains some examples from soil survey interpretation, since sufficient examples from more comprehensive land resources interpretation are not always available. Reference is made to data indicated in Chapter 5 with regard to the more purely physical interpretation of land resources data.

In an ideal case, the results of a land resources interpretation should be fully quantitative, i.e. they should result in a complete mathematical model in which all physical inputs and outputs and all economic and other parameters should be incorporated in a way in which they can be calculated with normal arithmetic methods. In the case of agricultural production, this model must lead to a result presented in "standardized monetary units" (VINK, 1960, 1963a), because: (1) these are the only means of combining the true significance of inputs and outputs in the economic production system of a farm, (2) there is no other reasonable manner for combining such things as labor, fertilizers, machinery operations and farm products. The alternative approach of using non-monetary indicators, such as calories, looks attractive at first view, but it leaves large gaps, e.g. for crops such as flax, fruit, tea, coffee, which cannot be evaluated in terms of calories; it becomes in fact an arbitrary approach which does not fit the actual conditions of agricultural production.

Table 99. Example of a budget of a schematized farm for purposes of quantitative soil suitability classification (VINK, 1960)

Soil type: gray brown podzolic soil, sandy loam
E, T, M: normal, good management/level 1, the Netherlands, A.D. 1960

Rotation		Y	E_1	Gross result	$F. E_2$	$C. E_2$	Net. result
ha	Crop	yield metric tons/ha	monetary units per metric tons	per crop[a] monetary units	fertil. in mon. units per ha	other costs in mon. units per ha	per crop[a] monetary units
1.5	rye[b]	3.4	233				
		4.5	50				
		22.5	5	1695	217	809	+156
2.0	wheat	3.5	263				
		4.0	52	2257	205	793	+261
2.0	oats	3.9	238				
		4.2	42	2210	151	787	+334
1.5	pota-toes	21.4	67				
		5.6	7	2210	350	1603	−720
1.5	sugar-beets	47.0	46				
		36.0	7	3621	461	1663	+435
0.5	maize	4.0	276	552	301	1358	−278
1.0	peas	1.7	536				
		2.8	79	1132	118	834	+180

10.0	Total farm						+368
							Per ha + 37
	general costs of farming						per ha − 120
	S: rate of suitability in monetary units per ha						− 83
	general correction for positive level of all soil types						+470
	S after correction in monetary units per ha						+387

relative suitability if S_{max} is 1200: S rel. $= \dfrac{387}{1200} \times 100 = 32$

[a] per crop = result per ha × planted surface.
[b] from top to bottom the yield data are: grain, straw and second crop (turnips).

General formula for the suitability:

$$S_A = \Sigma\,[(R.Y).E_1 - R(F + C)\,E_2]_{E.T.M.}$$

in which formula S_A means "rate of suitability" of soil type A, R means "rotation" (i.e. acreage of each crop in percentages of the total acreage of the farm), Y means yield of each crop in kg/ha on soil type A, F means fertilizers used for each crop on soil type A, C means all other costs of farming, excepting fertilizers. E_1 and E_2 are economic parameters, valid for a certain technical and economic situation. E, T indicate the economico-technical situation for which the solution is valid. M gives the management level for which the solution was calculated.

Table 100. Some preliminary results of quantitative soil suitability research on various soil types in the Netherlands (VINK, 1960)

Soil type	S_A Soil suitability in monetary units after correction for level $(+470)$
Humus podzol, sand, excessively drained	24
Deeply humose soil, loamy sand, somewhat excessively drained	153
Brown podzolic soil, loamy sand, excessively drained	276
Gray brown podzolic soil, sandy loam, excessively drained	387
Alluvial soil, sandy loam, well drained	1036
Alluvial soil, loam, well drained	1122

Budgetary Models

The quantitative model which forms the basis for standardized calculations in economic units is the farm budget. An example is given in Table 99. The combination of a number of these calculations may produce relative suitability figures of the kind indicated in Table 100.

A full mathematical treatment of these models is possible with the linear programming techniques and with comparable non-linear techniques (FOUND, 1971). An example of the economic interpretation of agronomic data by this technique has been given by SWANSON et al. (1958). It has been indicated previously that this technique is applicable to "land development classification" and to the combination of the latter with "land resources interpretation".

Budgetary models have in fact, although never sufficiently published, been at the base of the German *Bodenschätzung*. The quantitative basis of this was established by investigations of model farms under various representative land conditions of Germany (ROTHKEGEL, 1950; see also WACKER, 1943, 1956).

Calculations on (re)payment capacity in irrigation projects are also based on budgetary calculations. Some results of these were mentioned in Para. 6.3 and in Tables 88 to 92 and in Fig. 6.12 to 6.14.

Budgetary calculations of inputs and outputs are unavoidable for quantitative evaluation procedures in all cases where the differences of inputs have a recognizable influence on the net results. In many extensive systems of land use, i.e. with relatively low inputs per surface area, the growth of the crops as such may be taken as a sufficiently accurate measure of the net production. Typical examples are found particularly in forestry. Some of these are given by VAN ECK and WHITESIDE (1958), DUFFY (1965) and SLAGER and SCHULZ (1969). In Table 101, some data of DUFFY (1965) are shown. It is clear in these cases that land resources interpretation may be independent of the actual exploitation cost of a forest under certain circumstances, but that accessibility and similar factors may still have a great influence on costs. In that case, budgetary calculations may again become unavoidable. They provide the advantage, however, that the inputs are clearly visible as transport costs and related inputs.

Table 101. Summary of forest land productivity levels for the major parent materials in the study area in Alberta, Canada (DUFFY, 1965)

Parent materials	Number of plots	Stand age	Basal area/acre; sq. ft.[a]		Total vol./acre; cu. ft.[a]		Merch. vol./acre; board ft.[a]		Site index at 80 yrs. ft.
			Conifers	All species	Conifers	All species	Conifers	All species	
Productivity Class I									
Lowland alluvial (Alluvium High Prairie)[b]	8	110 ± 20	171 ± 55	197 ± 15	459 ± 1995	7241 ± 444	33913 ± 11072	36223 ± 4214	95
Alluvial-lacustrine (Kathleen) well-drained	10	104 ± 14	151 ± 29	203 ± 12	5081 ± 1292	6833 ± 323	22868 ± 8007	29603 ± 3139	90
Till (Braeburn) well-drained	16	106 ± 25	144 ± 35	179 ± 20	4648 ± 968	5625 ± 786	21433 ± 6922	24950 ± 5957	90
Till with alluvial cap (Braeburn)	11	120 ± 83	158 ± 52	211 ± 31	5308 ± 1690	7029 ± 2244	25646 ± 11198	33069 ± 13751	87
Productivity Class II									
Lacustrine (Donelly) well drained	3	85 ± 16	154 ± 39	190 ± 21	4265 ± 1109	5373 ± 292	15242 ± 7887	17120 ± 5263	84
Alluvial-lacustrine (Kathleen) poorly drained	8	198 ± 28	150 ± 41	177 ± 19	5075 ± 1489	5609 ± 748	22695 ± 9017	24317 ± 6426	84
Till (Braeburn) poorly drained	6	105 ± 19	145 ± 18	176 ± 12	4660 ± 560	5479 ± 365	20661 ± 3642	23877 ± 2443	84
Alluvium (terrace) (Heart)	6	104 ± 3	149 ± 2	103 ± 3	4436 ± 20	4757 ± 6	17380 ± 2165	16322 ± 2513	82

[a] Basis for table: 68 one-fifth acre growth and yield plots.
[b] Range of two standard deviations about the mean excepting the lacustrine condition where total range is given.

Benchmark Soils and Pilot Projects

The collection of fully quantitative data for all land units in a region, in such detail that they can be put into a budget, is not possible; this approach can never be used for more than a relatively small number of units, since the cost of these investigations is very high, and the physical limitations of, and the scarcity of, sufficiently representative farms and experiments on sufficiently representative land units make a large extension impossible. For the determination of future land use, in all cases in which the differences between present and future land uses are great, only the establishment of pilot projects of a particular size provides reliable results. The establishment of these pilot projects is essential, but it has to be limited to lands which, on the basis of more approximative investigations, show sufficient promise for future development. It should be stressed, however, that also here "the proof of the pudding is in the eating" and that only the results of economically run pilot farms, supported by special experiments, can give conclusive evidence on the potential land suitability, as well as for the actual land suitability in all cases where considerable changes in the existing land utilization types are envisaged.

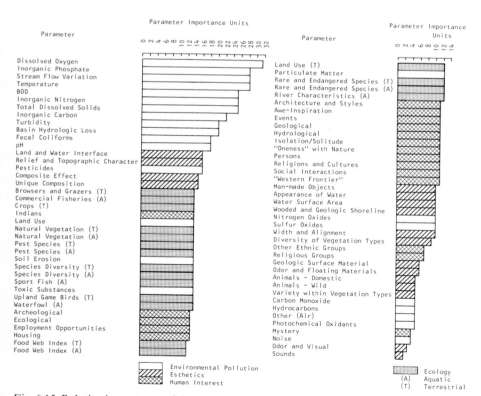

Fig. 6.15. Relative importance of the parameters in an Environmental Evaluation System for Water Resource Planning (Dee et al., 1972)

For a fully quantitative approach to land evaluation, only "bench mark soils" can be selected. In cases where the ecological rather than the economic aspects of land suitability are involved, other models, as nearly quantitative as possible, can be applied; an example is provided by DEE et al. (1972), see Fig. 6.15.

Approximative Methods

In all cases of land evaluation, more approximative methods are necessary. These belong to one of the following kinds:

(a) Schematized model calculations, based on general regularities of growth and production, including the influence of land conditions on outputs and inputs, and, wherever applicable, on environmental conditions; in the FAO Consultation (BRINKMAN and SMYTH, 1973) these have been called: "simulation methods using mathematical growth models based on theoretical growth relationships and relevant land suitability factors at various levels of conceptual detail".

(b) Semi-quantitative methods, in which some data are measured, e.g. yields from some experiments and the related inputs of the experiments and, if possible, some measurements or approximative estimates on the structure of the farm as an economic unity are made. The latter are correlated by empirical methods and by estimates based on general knowledge of relationships between the land conditions on the one hand and growth and production on the other hand; in the previously mentioned document these are called: "empirical assessment based on correlations between measured yields and relevant factors of land suitability at various levels of conceptual detail".

(c) Comparative methods, using both direct observations in the area and in comparable areas in the neighborhood and the systematic transfer of knowledge and experience from other areas with similar land conditions; termed in the FAO Consultation, "Measurement and observation, directly where possible or indirectly in analogous situations".

(d) Analytical methods, which clarify certain growth and production relationships and which, although not directly leading to land evaluation itself, strengthen the understanding of correlations for the preceding methods (RUST and ODELL, 1957; FERRARI, 1950; FERRARI et al., 1957; VAN DER BOON, 1967; VAN NERUM and PALASTHY, 1966).

Schematized Model Calculations

Schematized model calculations, to be sufficiently correct, must be based on analytical investigations on the growth and production relationships of crops under various ecological conditions. Only then can the necessary parameters be developed with sufficient accuracy and the mathematical relationships between variables and parameters ascertained with a sufficiently reliable value for land use predictions. Parametric methods used without the help of sufficient analytical investigations do not produce true models; although they may still be useful under certain conditions (see also NIX. In: STEWART et al., 1968).

There is no doubt, however, that the parametric approach, if developed by good scientists, can lead to forms of schematized model calculations. This is demonstrated by the work of RIQUIER (1972), which is developed on the basis of his original work with parametric methods (see e.g. RIQUIER and BRAMAO, 1964). The general mathematical model is based on the following equation:

$$Y = 100 \times C \times Yp \times Ys \times Yv \times Yo \times Yt \dots,$$

where Y = yield in percent of the maximum genetically possible for the variety specified under optimum conditions,

  C = the growth index of PAPADAKIS, corrected according to climatic, soil and plant requirements (PAPADAKIS, 1952),

  Yp, Ys, Yv, Yo, Yt, etc. = yield in percent as a function of selected diagnostic criteria (e.g. p = effective depth of soil, s = specific surface of soil, v = base saturation of soil, o = percent organic matter content of soil, t = percent salt content of soil, etc. (see also Chapter 5).

Within this model, the following general form has been chosen for each of the yield functions:

$$Q = A\,(1 - e^{-ax}),$$

where Q = predicted yield, A = maximum genetic yield,

  e = Naperian logarithmic base ("natural logarithmic base"),

  a = coefficient differing for each kind of plant.

This is a form of the Mitscherlich growth equation which is easy to calculate and which shows good relations with the majority of experimental results.

In the climatic index of PAPADAKIS (1952), the following climatic factors are taken into account: h = daylength in hours, T_1 = mean temperature in degrees centigrade (corrected for the thermal needs of each plant species), H = an index of humidity related to the water balance of the soil refered to. In some cases, a special factor for radiation intensity is added to the calculation.

The influence of management may be introduced in the equation of RIQUIER through their influence on the yields of the separate crops. The principal aims of RIQUIER's approach are indicated by the author as:

"1. To compare different soils for a specific crop in the same climate,

2. To establish the capacity of a soil for different crops; the crop showing the highest yield is obviously the most desirable if economic factors are also favorable;

3. To study the influence of a single factor; e.g. fertilizer; the action of other factors having been established through calculation, the factor being studied can be better understood;

4. To study the productivity of the same soil in different latitudes and to eliminate the climatic factor;

5. To interpret pedological and climatic observations in terms of the productivity of a crop".

The main goal of RIQUIER's investigations, which led to the development of the present mathematical model (see als RIQUIER et al., 1970), was to reduce the subjective element which is always present in methods of land evaluation. At the present stage of his work, he has arrived at some good possible ways for reducing this subjectivity. His model as it stands today is only concerned with crop yields under specified land conditions and with specific management operations (irrigation, drainage, fertilizers etc.). His formula does not as yet use the economic parameters which are indispensable for arriving at a full mathematical production model. The data derived from RIQUIER's equations are, however, an essential contribution for introduction into a more comprehensive model. Given certain economic and other assumptions, the formula developed by VINK (1960) might well be used for this purpose (see Table 99, p. 300). With some modifications which bring it more in accordance with the general contents of this book as well as with the approach of RIQUIER, the formula can be read:

$$S_{AL} = \Sigma \; [(R.Y) \cdot E_1 - R \cdot (C_i + C_d + C_f + \cdots + C_m) \cdot E_2]_{E.L}.$$

In this formula, the data from RIQUIER's calculations could be incorporated so that the symbols read as follows:

S_{AL} = the suitability of a Land Unit A for a Land Utilization Type L,

R.Y = a vector of the yields according to RIQUIER, in rotation R (percentages of the various crops),

$R \cdot (C_i + C_d + C_f + \cdots + C_m)$ = a vector of the physical cost: management and operation inputs as used in the yield formulas of RIQUIER,

E_1 and E_2 = vectors of the prices of the products and of the inputs, respectively,

E indicates the general economic conditions under which the suitability is determined,

L is the land utilization type for which the suitability is regarded.

The variables C_i, cost of irrigation, C_d, cost of drainage, C_f, cost of fertilizers, and various other costs, according to the inputs used in the yield formulas of RIQUIER may be added. Finally, the general costs of farm management have to be added; these can, at least in their order of magnitude, be estimated for a whole land utilization type under given social and economic conditions.

If a single crop, e.g. a fruit crop (citrus, olives) or a tropical plantation crop (sugar cane, sisal, tea, coffee, tobacco) rather than a crop rotation is planted in a given land utilization type, the formula becomes much simpler, because then no vectors for the rotation have to be used. In that case the formula becomes:

$$S_{AL} = [Y.E_1 - (C_i + C_d + C_f + \cdots + C_m) \cdot E_2]_{,E.L}.$$

In this case R is 100% and can, therefore, in the formula, be taken as R is 1.

In land utilization types in which the mentioned inputs of irrigation, drainage, fertilizers, are not applicable, the relevant C-values become zero.

The formula is suitable for optimization by linear programming techniques and therefore also suits the requirements stated above according to BIJKERK. If necessary, non-linear techniques may also be employed (FOUND, 1971).

Semi-quantitative and Comparative Methods

Semi-quantitative methods are often the best approximation which can be obtained in a given case. The quantitative data are in such cases often derived from existing experimental farms or from experiments carried out under similar land conditions in other regions. The available quantitative data must then be combined with estimates of the order of magnitude of the cost of the various inputs and farm operations, which usually are at least approximatively known to experienced agronomists, farm management experts or farm economists. In principle

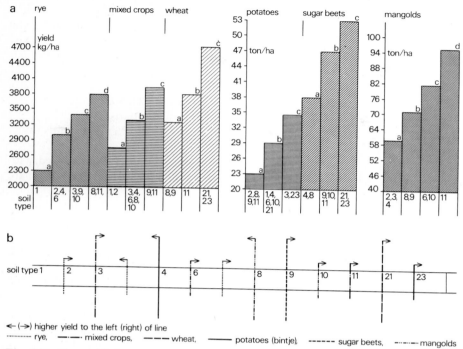

Fig. 6.16. The yield classes and their relationships with some soil mapping units in the Netherlands (VINK et al., 1963)

they have to be known to characterize the land utilization types which exist, or are considered for future establishment, in the region.

For semi-quantitative evaluations, but in fact often also for quantitative evaluations, the variability of the yields measured in practical experiments is often very great. This is due partly to the climatic variations from year to year (see e.g. HAANS and WESTERVELD, 1970) and partly to the natural variability of the land units, but often also to the variations which are an essential aspect of the soils themselves; the latter have been indicated in Para. 5.4.4, Table 52 (p. 163). The result of this variability is that in one region often not more than 3 or 4 yield classes can be ascertained for a single crop with any mathematical reliability. The difference between the different land or soil units is determined in an arable land utilization type, by the different distributions of the classes for the various crops on the various soil units. An example of this is given in Fig. 6.16 (VINK et al., 1963).

The use of semi-quantitative methods is more necessary than is often thought. By comparative methods, without any additional data, the order of magnitude of the net results of production can often be estimated completely incorrectly, particularly if land units from different main land types or physiographical regions have to be compared. The best soil in one region, which as such can be safely determined by comparative methods, may have a much lower quantitative suitability than the poorest soils in another region.

Comparative methods are by far the most commonly used in land evaluation. This is necessary, because they are the only ones which are always available and always applicable. The establishment of differences in land suitability by comparative methods is much less subjective than is often thought. Experience has proved that whole development projects, such as the land classification for the Zuyderzee Polders in the Netherlands, have been based solely on comparisons of the future lands with similar land conditions in other areas (SMITS and WIGGERS, 1959). These methods rest in principle on two kinds of comparisons:

1. direct comparisons of the lands to be evaluated with analogous lands under analogous conditions;

2. comparisons of the various land units in the region to be evaluated with each other and with the requirements of the land utilization types which are considered to be relevant and foreseeable.

The first comparison leads to a scale of evaluation which, although approximative, gives a certain amount of absolute information on the possibilities which exist in an area. The second is necessary for evaluating all the various land conditions in the area concerned, so that proper land evaluation maps, as a basis for future land use and land improvement, can be made. In both cases, comparisons are also made with the general trends of crop requirements and other land use requirements which can be found in the literature or which belong to the experience of the land experts concerned (see Paras. 5.4.2 and 5.4.3).

Parametric Methods

The comparative methods always compare to some extent, the soils of an area with the best soils known in the region or with a hypothetical, "ideal" soil. The comparison is made by judging the limitations of the soils to be evaluated with the real, or hypothetical, standard soil. This approach can be systematized in

Table 102. Actual and potential productivity indexes for irrigated rice in an area of Thailand (FRANKART et al., 1972)

Series	Average rice yield kg/ha	Actual productivity index (C1)	Potential productivity index (C2)	Coefficient of improvement C2/C1
Cm	not used	25	52	2.08
Pm	3 300	90	90	1
St	2 000	60	60	1
Re	1 650	51	60	1.93
Re-l	1 900	63	70	1.11
Re-h	900	40	56	1.4
Nu	450	34	47	1.5
Nu-h	not used	29	52	1.8
Kt	not used	27	45	1.6
Kt-h	not used	12	23	1.9
Rn	—	33	59	1.7
Pp	—	32	68	2.1
V	600	32	45	1.4

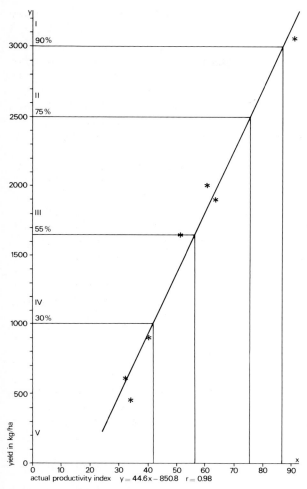

Fig. 6.17. Correlation between the actual productivity index and rice yield in natural conditions
(FRANKART et al., 1972)

different ways, in order to make it less subjective, one of which is the use of
parametric methods. These lead by formulas, not unlike the more theoretically
based model of RIQUIER, to a systematization which, although only approximative, can yield good results if handled by competent experts. The nearer the
parametric methods come to mathematical models, and the more they are based
on quantitative or semi-quantitative data, the more they will approach the true
yields and the true relations of soil productivity. The parametric methods as such
do not usually lead to a complete land evaluation, because they are more concerned with crop growth, a biological process, than with production, an economic
process with biological and other means (see Para. 5.5.1).

Table 103. Grouping of land types in Iran according to their land capabilities (MAHLER et al., 1970). Example: Land zones with arid climates

Land type	Present land capability	Land improvement requirements	Land capability after improvement
Mountains and Hills	Protective grass lands.	Exclosure and soil conservation works	Protective grass lands, occasional grazing at places
Plateaux a) denudated	Protective grasslands	Exclosure	Marginal range
b) with shallow to moderately deep soil mantle	Occasional grazing	Exclosure	Moderately suited for range
Piedmont alluvial plains	Irrigation farming	Flood control	Irrigation farming
River alluvial plains	Irrigation farming	Drainage and salinity control at places	Irrigation farming
Gravelly colluvial fans	Occasional grazing	Exclosure	Marginal to moderately suited for range
		Stone picking at places	Irrigated orchards at places
Gravelly river fans	Occasional grazing	Flood control. Exclosure and range improvement	Moderately suited for range
		Flood control and afforestation	Special trees
Low lands	Occasional grazing	Exclosure and range improvement at places	Marginal to moderately suited for range
		Drainage, salt leaching	Irrigation farming
Flood plains and basins	Occasional grazing	Flood control and range improvement	Moderately for range
		Flood control. Drainage. Salt leaching	Irrigation farming

The main advantage attributed to the parametric methods (BRINKMAN and SMYTH, 1973) is that they provide figures which can be used by economists in their calculations. This fact is very attractive and acceptable as long as sufficiently warranted estimates of the parameters and of their interrelations as well as of their correlations with yields and outputs can be made. An example of this approach is given in Table 102 and in Fig. 6.17. As can be seen from these examples, there is a good correlation between the "actual productivity index" and the yields

Table 104. Assessment of present land capabilities of arid areas in Iran (MAHLER et al., 1970). Tentative guide lines based upon soil depth and slopes

Soil depth class		Slope classes							
		A/a 2%	B/b 5%	C/c 8%	D/d 12%	E/e 25%	F/f 40%	G/g 70%	H/h
120 cm	—	Ir-1	Ir-2t	Ir-3t Ra-2c	Ra-2ct	Ra-3t	Ra-4ct	Ra-4ct	Ra-4ct
80 cm	1	Ir-1	Ir-2t	Ir-3t Ra-2ct	Ra-2ct	Ra-3t	Ra-4ct	Ra-4t	Ra-4ct
50 cm	2	Ir-2s	Ir-3st Ra-2c	Ir-3st Ra-2c	Ra-2ct	Ra-3ct	Ra-4ct	Ra-4t	Ra-4ct
25 cm	3	Ra-2cs	Ra-2cs	Ra-2cs	Ra-2st	Ra-3st	Ra-4st	Ra-4st	Ra-4cst
10 cm	4	Ra-3cs	Ra-2cs	Ra-3cs	Ra-3cst	Ra-4cst	Ra-5cst	Ra-5cst	Ra-5cst

Ir = irrigated agriculture
Df = dry farming
Ra = range
c = climate
t = topography
s = soil

of rice in an area of Thailand (FRANKART et al., 1972). On the basis of this correlation, the estimated "potential productivity index "may be approximatively correct. Whether the "coefficient of improvement", which shows the relation between these two, is of real practical value, will have to be carefully checked by experiments. It should further be realized that the "productivity indexes" are growth indexes and not production indexes and that the improvement coefficient indicates only probable yield relations. Furthermore, the cost of the investments and of the operations and maintenance of the irrigation works and related structures are not included in this system (see also CHAMPROUX, 1967; DESAUNETTES, 1968; MILLETTE et al., 1967).

Other Approaches to Systematization:
The Iran System, Flow Charts

Other approaches to the systematization of comparative land evaluation are possible. Some systems have been elaborated by MAHLER et al. (1970) and by BEEK and BENNEMA (1972). These systems are also related to older systems of land evaluation such as those of the U.S. Soil Conservation Service (see e.g. HUDSON, 1971) and of the Bureau of Reclamation (1953).

The system used in Iran (MAHLER et al., 1970) recognizes three possible approaches to the assessment of land suitability:

1. Comparison of land suitability classifications for different uses,

2. Correlation with similar soils and land units, the capabilities of which have already be ascertained,

Table 105. Assessment of present land capabilities of semi-arid areas in Iran (MAHLER et al., 1970). Tentative guide lines based upon soil depth and slopes

Soil depth class		A/a 2%	B/b 5%	C/c 8%	D/d 12%	E/e 25%	F/f 40%	G/g 70%	H/h
				Slope classes					
120 cm	—	Ir-1 Df-1	Ir-2t Df-2t	Ir-3t Df-3t	Ra-1	Ra-2t	Ra-3t	Ra-4t	Ra-4t
80 cm	1	Ir-1 Df-1	Ir-2t Df-2t	Ir-3t Df-3t	Ra-1	Ra-2t	Ra-3t	Ra-4t	Ra-4t
50 cm	2	Ir-2s Df-2s	Ir-3st Df-3st	Ra-1	Ra-2s	Ra-3t	Ra-3t	Ra-4t	Ra-4t
25 cm	3	Ra-1	Ra-1	Ra-2s	Ra-3s	Ra-3st	Ra-4st	Ra-4st	Ra-4st
10 cm	4	Ra-2s	Ra-2s	Ra-3s	Ra-3s	Ra-3st	Ra-4st	Ra-4st	Ra-4st

Table 106. Characteristics of land suitability classes (BEEK and BENNEMA, 1972)

(A) *Biological characteristics*
   Choice of adapted crops (wide/limited)
   Yield (yield potential)
   Performance reliability (regular/irregular)
   Multiannual yield trend (marginal net return sustained/falling)

(B) *Soil management characteristics*
   Timing of field operations (flexible/fixed)
   Choice of adapted farm equipment (wide/limited)
   Performance of farm equipment (high/low)

(C) *Diversification characteristics*
   Land resource allocation (enterprise proportions free/limited)
   Degree of land use intensity (intensive/extensive)
   Land Resource use alternatives (many/few)
   Elasticity in selection of farm size (free/limited)

(D) *Human aspects*
   Labor productivity (high/low)
   Labor absorbing capacity (high/low employment opportunities)

(E) *Economic aspects*
   Production cost (high/low)
   Benefits (high/low)
   Cost of land improvement/development/conservation (high/low)
   Investment retribution (high/low, short/medium/long term)

3. Judgement of the over-all combination of the land characteristics (climate, soil, topography, drainage limitations, etc.).

The system also places a certain ranking on the various land utilization types which are relevant for Iran:

"When a land is placed in potentiality (suitability) Class 1 or Class 2 for irrigation, its suitability for range should be disregarded and its land capability should

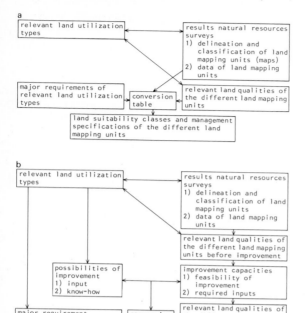

Fig. 6.18. Flow charts for land suitability classification (BEEK and BENNEMA, 1972; BRINKMAN and SMYTH, 1973)

be the one for irrigation. When a land is placed in Class 3 or 4 for irrigation, the land capability class should indicate both its classification for irrigation and its classification for range. When a land is placed in potentiality Class 5 or 6 for irrigation, its land potentiality for range should be given as the land capability". The preceding indications for the arid climates of the country have also been modified for application to the semi-arid and to the subhumid and humid parts of the country.

Correlation tables have been made for comparing similar soils and land units. A draft copy for the arid climates of Iran is shown in Table 103. Other preliminary tables have been drafted in which limitations are used in assessing land suitabilities. In the first instance, only soil depth and slope classes are indicated; these are, however, of great value because they correlate well with other edaphic and production factors under the circumstances prevailing in Iran. Examples are shown in Tables 104 and 105.

BEEK and BENNEMA (1972) developed flow charts for the assessment of land suitability; these are given in Fig. 6.18. The central aspect of their system lies in the use of the major land qualities, either for correlating available experimental data, leading to a semi-quantitative approach, or for developing a systematic approach

Table 107. "Conversion Tables" to estimate land suitabilities (BEEK and BENNEMA, 1972)

a) Without yield potentials

Dry farming

	Suitability classes	Availability nutrients	Availability water	Absence risk salinization	Availability oxygen	Adaptability mechanization	Resistance erosion	Freedom lay-out of the scheme
I	High	1A	3	1	2	1A	1A	1
II	Medium	1A	3	3	3	1A	1A	1
			4	2	2	1A	1A	1
III	Restricted	2A	4	3	3	2A	2A	2
IV	Low	Any grade of the qualities lower than for restricted or any of the improvement inputs higher than for restricted.						

Irrigated agriculture

	Suitability classes	Availability nutrients	Availability water	Absence risk salinization	Availability oxygen	Adaptability mechanization	Resistance erosion	Freedom lay-out of the scheme
I	High	1B	1C	1	1	1	1	1
II	Medium	1B	1D	1	2	1	1	1
			1C	2	2	1	1	2
III	Restricted	1B	2D	2	3	2	1	2
IV	Low	Any grade of the qualities lower than for restricted or any of the improvements inputs higher than for restricted.						

b) With yield potentials

Dry farming

	Suitability classes	Expected yields of wheat	Adaptability mechanization	Resistance erosion	Freedom to select size and shape of fields
I	High	3A	1A	1A	1
II	Medium	4A	1A	1A	1
III	Restricted	4A	2A	2A	2
IV	Low	Any grade of the qualities lower than for restricted.			

Table 107 (continued)

Irrigated agriculture

	Suitability classes	Expected yields of wheat	Adaptability mechanization	Resistance erosion	Freedom to select size and shape of field
I	High	1C	1C	1C	1
II	Medium	1D	1	1	1
		2C	1	1	2
III	Restricted	2D	2	1	2
IV	Low	Any grade of the qualities lower than for restricted.			

c) For non-recurrent input requirements
   (see also Para. 5.4.5)

Grades of relevant land qualities

Levels of input requirements		Availability nutrients	Availability water	Absence risk erosion	Absence risk salinization	Availability oxygen	Availability conditions for mechanization	Freedom lay-out of scheme	Yield potential
(Natural land conditions)	O	3	4	2	2	3	2	1	5
	A	2	4	1	2	2	1	1	4
	B	2	4	1	2	2	1	1	4
	C	1	2	2	3	3	2	1	3
	D	1	1	1	2	2	1	1	2
	E	1	1	1	1	1	1	1	1

n.h. yield potential scale: 1 = very high
                              2 = high
                              3 = medium
                              4 = low
                              5 = very low

to comparative assessments. The main characteristics which are used in this assessment are given in Table 106. Examples of the tables used by these authors to assess the land suitability for a number of land utilization types as well as for some improvements are given in Table 107.

Ways of Obtaining Information

In a previous publication (VINK, 1963a), we mentioned the following ways of obtaining information for land evaluation in those areas where the present land use does not differ too much from the relevant and foreseeable land utilization types:
1. group conferences with good farmers in the region, based on the objective data of the land resources maps, 2. enquiries among individual farmers, 3. judgement of the suitabilities of various individual land units by local experts, e.g. agricultural extension officers, 4. use of available data from all kinds of agricultural experiments and from experimental farms, 5. special investigations of the results of specific crops, 6. special programs for trial harvests and yield assessment on representative land units.

In areas where completely new land utilization types are being considered, even data concerning the crops presently being grown may prove useful, as they can be compared on the basis of crop requirements (see Para. 5.4). Furthermore, the land qualities or ecological land conditions may be compared directly with the crop requirements which are relevant for the land utilization types under consideration, as well as with the other land use requirements of the relevant and foreseeable land utilization types. The land evaluation is also carried out by experts who have themselves a certain "reference level" (cf. VINK in REY et al., 1968), i.e. a certain body of knowledge and experience with regard to lands and their uses. All these together can provide sufficient information, provided that they are systematically carried out, and thus made less subjective, on the basis of good land resources maps of an adequate scale. Finally, the provisional estimates of land evaluation arrived at along the lines indicated above have to be checked and elaborated in pilot projects (see also VINK, 1963a).

Land Evaluation Field Checks

It is often useful to carry out a field check after the provisonal evaluations have been made. The use of this field check, which usually includes the inspection of 10% or less of the area surveyed, is to realize in the field the actual position in the terrain of the units which have been evaluated on the basis of maps or other data. The field check is carried out by the persons who have made the evaluations, if necessary accompanied by some others, either persons who have participated in the original land resources surveys or future users of the evaluations, or both. Land units which have only been seen during the original land resources surveys are once more observed, particularly from the point of view of their variations and similarities, before the next step in evaluation and planning is commenced. In general no special experiments are performed during such a field check and few or no extra measurements are made.

Land Evaluation Experts

To a certain extent, land evaluation has to be carried out as a part-time job by land resources surveyors of various kinds, among whom soil surveyors, and sometimes also vegetation surveyors (range, forests), play a predominant role. These resources surveyors must participate in the land evaluation of each area which they survey, because they are the only persons who truly know all variations and particulars of the different land units. An additional reason is that the need eventually to participate in the evaluation gives them, during the survey stage, an extra inducement to pay enough attention to the ecological consequences of the units distinguished on the basic land resources maps. In other words: they may pay more attention to adapting the legends of their maps for efficient use in land evaluation.

Nevertheless, there exists a growing need for more specialized land evaluation experts, who should, above all, have sufficient knowledge and experience of one or more types of land resources surveys, but they must have enough time to concentrate on the intricacies of land evaluation procedures and on the needs of planners and of other map users. The normal land resources surveyor does not have sufficient time, and often not enough interest, in these aspects. In the same manner in which, in soil surveys, special "soil correlators" take care of special soil taxonomic problems in a survey, "land evaluation correlators" are needed to deal with the various problems in their special areas of expertise. Soil surveyors and other land resources surveyors are primarily students of nature. Land evaluation experts must be aware of land resources as natural phenomena, but their main interest must lie in the ways in which the resources can be used in various land utilization types with various recurrent and non-recurrent inputs. This necessitates a more systematic, theoretical as well as practical, knowledge of these inputs and land utilization types than can be demanded from a normal land resources surveyor. With the development of land use in all parts of the world, the need for land evaluation is growing rapidly. A more systematic education and training of land evaluation experts will therefore become necessary in the near future. They will have to meet the following requirements with regard to their spheres of knowledge and interest: (1) sufficient knowledge and experience in at least one kind of land resources survey at different scales, at a postgraduate level; (2) knowledge of rural, agricultural and non-agricultural land utilization types; (3) knowledge of land evaluation methodology; (4) knowledge of soil and water technology; (5) knowledge of planning methodology and in particular of planning procedures.

Land Evaluation Teams

Occasionally, land evaluation in a particular area for a particular purpose may be performed by one person, who carries out a soil survey or a landscape ecological survey and makes his interpretations for one or more kinds of land use. Usually, however, land evaluation involves teamwork. This teamwork starts with the planning of the survey and continues during its subsequent phases. Investigation of the different kinds of land resources and their relevant diagnostic criteria, and of the ways in which these can be combined in integrated surveys also requires teamwork. Similarly, the land evaluation based on these surveys involves teamwork, even if the original land resources survey was carried out by only one surveyor. The members of the evaluating team must include not only the land resources surveyors, but also experts on land evaluation and on the related branches of the agricultural sciences; in many cases plant production experts, land reclamation engineers and farm economists are needed.

A special function of the members of the evaluating team is the necessity to provide reasonable estimates in all cases in which not enough quantitative data can be provided; these cases are the rule rather than the exception. A team with a sufficiently "all round" composition is needed for this purpose, since they have to combine all land resources and land utilization data from biological, technical and economic points of view. Only such a team can make decisions on: (a) whether the available data are sufficient to make the necessary estimates, calculations and evaluations; (b) whether the gaps in the knowledge can be filled by reasonable estimates and who should assist the team in making these estimates; (c) to what degree certain gaps have to be filled by unavoidable special investigations and how these investigations can be scheduled in the most efficient way, in order to avoid unacceptable delays.

The members of a land evaluation team can also perform valuable work as "liaison officers" with their several branches of rural land use services and institutes. Consequently, too, these institutions can take into account at the earliest possible moment any special wishes with regard to their programs of research which may further the progress of the land evaluation. The team should be formed at the earliest possible moment, i.e. as soon as plans for land evaluation are considered. During the different phases of surveys and evaluation, some changes in its composition may be necessary. It should, however, be clearly stated at the beginning that land evaluation is a multidisciplinary exercise, including biological and technical as well as social and economic aspects, and this diversity should be reflected in the composition of the team.

6.5.3 The Intersector Approach

The Sectors of Land Resources Interpretation and Land Use Planning

The term "intersector approach" originates from Canada. It has been introduced into international discussions on land evaluation at the "FAO Consultation on Land Evaluation for Rural Purposes", Wageningen 1972 (BRINKMAN and SMYTH, 1973). It indicates the fact that, for proper procedures of land evaluation, a combined effort of the "sectors" of land resources interpretation and land use planning is required. The "Land development classification" mentioned in Para. 6.5.1 is also included. The initially prevalent idea that land evaluation is a simple activity which, once it is completed, gives a fixed basis for a planning procedure, again rather simple, has become obsolete through practical experience in both fields. Land evaluation provides many alternatives which cannot all be investigated within a reasonable period of time; therefore the field must be narrowed down to those alternatives which are essential as seen from the viewpoint of planning. Planning includes four aspects (DROR, 1971): A. the general environment of the planning process, B. the subject matter of the planning process, C. the planning unit, D. the form of the plan to be arrived at. It is stressed that "one of

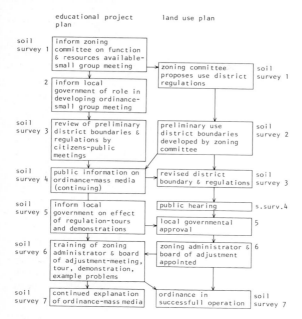

Fig. 6.19. Example of an intersector approach in rural zoning in the U.S.A.: development of a rural zoning ordinance (BEATTY and YANGEN. In: BARTELLI et al., 1966)

the more interesting characteristics of planning is its bidirectional relation with its environment. On the one hand, the planning activity is shaped and conditioned by various environmental factors; on the other hand, planning is in many cases directed at that environment, trying to shape it to a greater or lesser extent" (DROR, 1971).

In rural land use planning, land resources are not only the environment of the planning process, but they are also a part of the second aspect of the planning process, its subject matter. Furthermore, the planning units are to some extent determined by the geographical patterns of the land resources. In rural land use planning also, the form of the plan to be arrived at, although perhaps primarily dependent on the administrative and other executive procedures, cannot be regarded as completely independent of the kind and quantity of the available land resources.

"Planning is the process of preparing a set of decisions for action in the future, directed at achieving goals by preferable means" (DROR, 1971). Land evaluation involves several of these decisions: (1) to what extent and where can action be taken?, (2) for how long a period must the action be taken to be effective (e.g. in desalinization and in maintenance of irrigation systems)?, (3) which goals can be reasonably expected to be attainable?, (4) which means will be preferable because of their effectiveness in the interactions of land utilization type and land resources? An example of the integration which can be achieved by an intersector approach is shown in Fig. 6.19 (after BEATTY and YANGEN in BARTELLI et al., 1966).

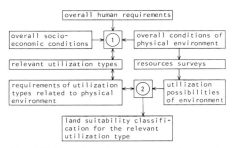

Fig. 6.20. Relations between planning, socioeconomic and land resources knowledge in land evaluation (BEEK and BENNEMA, 1972)

Integration of Procedures

The procedures for land evaluation must, therefore, be integrated with the procedures for planning. This is necessary for the planning itself as well as for the land evaluation as such. It should also be realized that there is nearly always lack of time and of knowledge and that, on the other hand, a certain amount of "tacit knowledge" is available in the minds of both land evaluators and planners (DROR, 1971).

Each group also has its own set of "established (but not always applicable) values" and of assumptions. The exchange of these between the two groups leads to a better and more efficient approach to land evaluation and therefore to land use planning. This is particularly true for those decisions in which the "relevant and foreseeable" land utilization types are selected and for the criteria applied to the feasibility of land improvements. In Fig. 6.20 (after BEEK and BENNEMA, 1972) examples of these relationships are shown. Figure 6.21 (BEEK and BENNEMA, 1972) contains the phases and disciplines for land evaluation. In Fig. 6.22 (BRINKMAN and SMYTH, 1973), a chart of land evaluation activities and their relation to planning and decision-making is shown.

The various steps in the land evaluation procedures are also described in the proposals made by the FAO Consultation on Land Evaluation (BRINKMAN and SMYTH, 1973):

"... the following over all procedure for land evaluation, step by step, may be suggested:

(i) Identification of present land use problems. Formulation of the basic assumptions and of the purpose and scope of the land evaluation.

(ii) Preliminary assessment of relevant land utilization types to establish the major diagnostic criteria (land qualities) which will require to be investigated in land evaluation and thus to determine the required intensity and scope of basic surveys. This assessment is based upon the overall socio-economic and physical conditions of the area which may first require to be broadly investigated.

(iii) Basic inventory of land resources by surveys of landform, geology, soils, present land use and vegetation; by hydrological and climatic studies; and/or by other investigations, where applicable, leading to the identification and delineation of adequately characterized land mapping units.

(iv) Collection of quantitative data relating to each characterized land mapping unit (e.g. production levels, recurrent costs and other socio-economic data). Initiation of experimentation where needed to generate further data and develop improvement specifications.

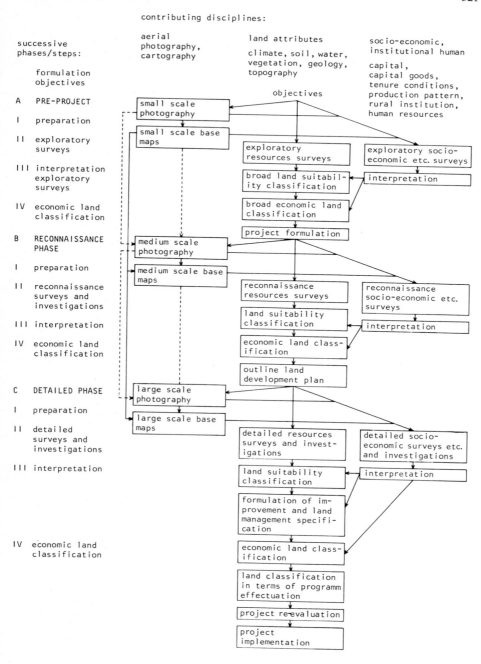

Fig. 6.21. Phases of land evaluation (BEEK and BENNEMA, 1972)

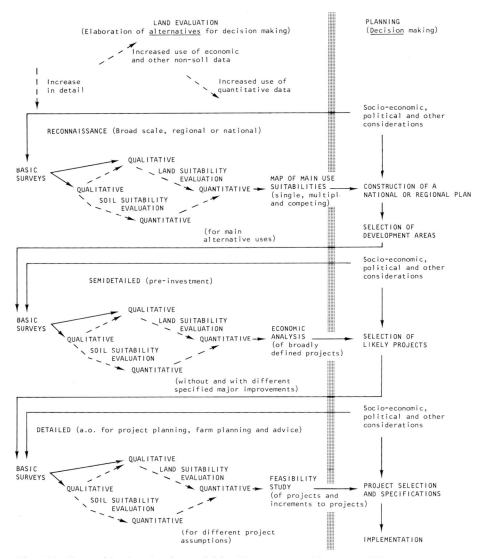

Fig. 6.22. Chart of land evaluation activities (BRINKMAN and SMYTH, 1973)

(v) Decision on the apparently most promising land utilization types for which separate systematic interpretation is required, and precise definition of these land utilization types including the means for their attainment.

(vi) Establishment of specifications for diagnostic criteria (land qualities) that will define interpretative class levels for each land utilization type.

Note: Steps (iv), (v), and (vi) should overlap (iii) to ensure that intensity of survey and data being collected is appropriate.

(vii) Qualitative actual suitability evaluation of each land mapping unit for each land utilization type by a comparison of characteristics (qualities) with the specifications established at step (vi).

(viii) Detailed interpretation of management and minor improvement specifications for each land suitability grouping for each land utilization type.

(ix) Identification, appraisal and classification of desirable major improvements (major non-recurrent inputs), if any, that would create new or improved land use possibilities.

(x) Qualitative evaluation of potential suitability (without and with amortization of major non-recurrent inputs) of each land unit for each utilization type based on estimates of changes, diagnostic characteristics (qualities) due to implementation of major improvements, of recurrent costs for operation and maintenance, and of the level of major non-recurrent inputs.

(xi) Reconsideration, where necessary, of management and minor improvement specifications for each land mapping unit for each relevant land utilization type under conditions following major improvements.

(xii) Field check on accuracy and consistency of suitability and input appraisals also considering the relevance of the land utilization types considered.

(xiii) Conversion of qualitative present and potential suitability evaluations into the corresponding quantitative evaluations when the necessary socio-economic and production data become available or can be reliably estimated.

Note: It is assumed that such socio-economic investigations as fall within the scope of an integrated survey of natural resources, will have proceeded in parallel with the land evaluation activities described".

The relations between planning and land evaluation have thus far not been clearly developed. The understanding that "planning is a process" is still very young and has not yet penetrated everywhere. Also the fact that there is such a thing as "the evaluation of planning", i.e. the evaluation of to what degree the resulting land use and land development have been satisfactory, is still far from common knowledge. As a result, the fact that often a very unsatisfactory use has been made of the possibilities of land evaluation in planning activities has not always penetrated the responsible levels (see e.g. DROR, 1971; HAYES, 1969; VAN DUSSELDORP and LEKANNE DIT DEPREZ, 1970). There is certainly such a thing as "the art of selecting the best project" (GROENVELD, 1960), and this art covers more than is commonly dreamed of in the philosophy of both planners and land evaluators. In particular, the latter often do not see the consequences of the three following levels on which projects may have to be selected (GROENVELD, 1960):

"1. between competing levels in various sectors of the economy;

2. between competing projects of different kinds in the same sector;

3. between competing projects of the same kind."

On the other hand, the planners often do not realize that land evaluation can be done for different kinds of land utilization types and for different levels of recurrent and non-recurrent inputs. Land evaluation is much more flexible than is often realized by either planners or land evaluators; both groups have assumptions and tacit knowledge which can only be made explicit by a regular intersectoral exchange of ideas. Only then can the best solution be found for future land use under the given conditions of human and natural resources and under the prevailing political and socio-economic conditions.

Land Evaluation in Different Dimensions of Planning

VAN DUSSELDORP (1967) distinguishes the following dimensions in multidimensional governmental planning:

1. The levels: national, regional and local which lead respectively to master plans or coordinating plans (national), more detailed general frameworks (regional), and specific clearly delineated objects (local); project planning is a case in itself, as it is usually planned and carried out by special executive organizations.

2. The sectors: related to various activities which take place in society (mining, agriculture, fisheries, industry, commerce, transport etc.): "sector planning may be described as vertical planning in that it is intended to show, in a given sector, the interrelationship at the various levels".

3. The facets: social, economic and physical; these are "so indissolubly linked that it is senseless to speak in terms of separate social, economic or physical planning: in the sense of the facets, all planning is always an integrated, comprehensive type of planning".

4. The phases: (a) formulating the targets, (b) stock-taking and investigation, (c) designing the plan, (d) confirming the plan, (e) implementation, (f) evaluation.

In the third phase, "designing the plan", seven subphases are distinguished: (1) analysis of the present situation and measurement of this against the targets to be reached, (2) determination of, preferably alternative, action programs, (3) determination of the time and of the methods required for the realization of each of the alternative programs, (4) study of the various action programs against the present situation, the available means and the period required for their realization, (5) selection of the optimal and feasible programs, (6) integration of action programs, wherever necessary, (7) delivery of a report on the activities mentioned under 1 to 6 inclusive, the report constituting the actual plan.

Land evaluation is clearly an essential part of different levels, sectors, facets and phases as well as subphases of any plan connected with rural land use. The level of generalization of the land evaluation is directly connected with the levels of planning; this includes the scale of mapping and of other investigations, but it may also include other aspects, e.g. the delineation of areas at the regional level. Delineation of regions for planning may be carried out purely on the basis of administrative divisions, but this may be less than effective if important landscape-ecological relations exist, e.g. with regard to irrigation, drainage and desalinization, land degradation and other land use activities which are directly connected with the nature of the available land resources. Delineation of a project area, if project planning is considered, is still more dependent upon the nature of the land resources. There are cases in which originally intended projects, which were considered insufficiently feasible within the national economy, were easily reduced to a very feasible size by an elementary inventory of the land resources.

Land evaluation for the various "sectors" described by VAN DUSSELDORP is directly related to the various land utilization types. Determination of the relative suitability of certain tracts of land for different, agricultural and other land utilization types, is a typical question which has to be solved by an integrated approach which includes the advice of experts on human and natural resources as well as that of planners. For this purpose, it is particularly necessary to regard the different subphases of the "designing of the plan", in order to obtain adequate results.

The relations between land evaluation and the facets of planning are clear from the fact that in land suitability not only physical data concerning land resources, but also social and economic parameters have to be taken into account. The development of alternative solutions in land evaluation, although theoretically possible on the basis of reasonable socio-economic assumptions, is more effective if the actual assumptions and data available to the planners, as well as their "tacit knowledge", can be used.

With regard to the phases, there occasionally exists the idea that land evaluation provides some of the data for phase b., "stock-taking and investigation", and that from there on the planners take over. If this were done, all land resources data which could possibly be relevant for all further phases of planning would have to be collected in the first instance. This procedure would be very ineffective, as it would lead to excessive detail of the investigations on the land resources with the ensuing cost in time, personnel and money. It is difficult to decide at this step in the procedure, which land utilization types and which non-recurrent inputs may be found feasible in the later phases and subphases. Land resources surveys and the related land evaluation activities have to be carefully timed and coordinated with the various phases and subphases from a to f, inclusive. It is unreasonable to formulate targets without any knowledge of what the land will support; this is often less known in a region than is generally supposed by planners. A rapid reconnaissance by competent land resources experts may shed better light on possible future uses and improvements of the land. In the subsequent phases of the plan, concurrent investigations, each as efficient as possible with respect to the "data-demand" of the planners and of other responsible persons and bodies, have to contribute the necessary information. There is no doubt that, particularly for phase e., "implementation", a large amount of data on land resources, and their evaluation, is required; the detail and the kind of data may vary considerably in various parts of the planning region, according to the selected action programs and targets.

The Ecological Basis of Planning

Planning for agricultural land use always has an ecological basis, but a strong ecological basis also exists in other kinds of regional planning, as GLIKSON (1971) has clearly shown. In this context, the ecological basis refers to the relationships between man and his environment in all its many aspects. In relation to his environment, "man is not a consistent biological unit preserving its identity, but an organism in the process of change", since man can adapt himself to very different ecological conditions. By his adaptation he, or rather his community, modifies nature as a result of the pattern of human rest and movement, of his mobility and of his sedentariness. This new position of sedentariness, which is an acquired biological trait, is used by man to establish a relationship to the land on a new level. This relationship may sometimes be obscured by technological and economic considerations, but it is a very real one, which is essential to planning. Planning has to be done "with the land"; it has to attempt a balance between environmental stability and free human mobility. This goal can only be achieved on the basis of a good system of land evaluation, which has to be interrelated with the various aspects of planning. The increasing degrees of adaptation of the subsequently drained Zuyderzee Polders in the Netherlands provide a good example of increasing "planning with the land"; in the younger polders a much higher "degree of adaptation to the soil map, topography, coast lines and to an overall regional and countrywide plan" is reached than was realized in the older polders of the same scheme (GLIKSON, 1971).

Efficiency of Land Evaluation

Land evaluation and planning have thus far been carried out as very pragmatic activities. This was necessary, because it has only been during the last years that some attempts have been made to view both activities as processes with their own regularities and problems. Both activities must, by definition, be carried out within limited periods of time. Once the political decisions to start planning in a certain region, project or local area have been made, results must be available within a relatively short period, usually within 4 to 10 years. As a result, short cuts are often very inviting and only those methods of land resources inventory and of land evaluation which give adequate results within very reduced periods of time can be used in planning. Thus, land evaluators must realize the need for efficient procedures and for using reasonable estimates, which may be "intelligent guesses", in all cases where the collection of more quantitative data would demand too much time. The continuous collection of more quantitative data, through long-term programs on "bench-mark soils", is a good means for establishing a minimum amount of reliable background information on land productivity and land improvement.

Land evaluation in projects is often carried out together with planning within the apparatus of the project authority. This approach has the advantage that a better intersector approach is likely to develop. The processes as such are often then developed along very pragmatic lines, which may be suitable for the particular conditions of a given project, but may not be so easily applicable in other cases. The processes are also less open to, possibly well-founded, scientific criticism, which might have contributed to obtaining better results. Careful evaluations of the results of such projects is often neglected, and thus they do not contribute to improvement of the general techniques of land evaluation and land-use planning. In other cases, evaluation proceeds along systematic and scientific lines, but it is geared to the particular situation in a given country or region. This is for instance the case with the "Land Development Classification" mentioned in Para. 6.5.1. There is no doubt that this system, developed by BIJKERK and his co-workers (BIJKERK et al., 1970), and which includes a systematic inventory of artifactial land attributes, is well suited to the conditions of the Netherlands. It is, however, of much less importance in many other countries where the artifactial attributes are negligible and where the targets of land-use planning are towards different kinds of land development.

Land evaluation procedures often must be applied in a very pragmatic manner and with a certain degree of subjective influence. Their results may, however, be systematized by careful consideration of the various built-in values and assumptions as well as the levels and categories of evaluation and classification applied. The remaining part of the "tacit knowledge" which cannot be explained should be reduced as much as possible under the prevailing circumstances. It should be realized, however, that some tacit knowledge and some intuition are inherent in all human decisions.

Chapter 7   Development of Land Use
in Advancing Agriculture

7.1 General

A Comprehensive Model

Land use is a way of managing a large part of the human environment in order to obtain benefits for man. Along the lines suggested by WIENER (in Integrated Surveys; 1972; see also Chapter 5, p.176), the complex problems involved in its development may be seen as a comprehensive model. This model encompasses at least three different "geometries", i.e. different subsystems of the total system of the development of land use. These three geometries are:
— the land resources geometry, including all land resources with their interrelationships and their modifications by human activity;
— the human demand geometry, i.e. all demands which men place on the land, for whichever purpose, within the system of rural land use;
— the degradation geometry, which may or may not be avoided, depending on the nature of the land resources and the ways in which they are used.

As indicated by WIENER (in Integrated Surveys, 1972), human demands must be met at different levels according to obvious priorities. These levels are:

"Level One — The metabolism of the body and mind of the individual;
Level Two — The physical habitat of the individual and his close family, his home;
Level Three — The communal habitat—the vital services supplied within the community framework;
Level Four — The wider environment, as we generally consider in the developed world."

These levels were originally devised to systematize some of the problems of water resources and their pollution, but they are, with some modifications, applicable for more general use. Development of land use is essentially a tool for improving the way in which the various priorities indicated in these levels are met, with due regard to both of the other geometries: the land resources geometry and the land degradation geometry. It may then be argued that the levels are too simple to indicate all the true variations of the demand geometry, which is undoubtedly true. It is impossible for an individual to increase his intellectual development above a certain level if his family is starving, and it is impossible for a small family to reach within their home a standard of living which is very much higher than that of the surrounding community. Comparably speaking, the development of luxurious towns in a poor country at least poses serious developmental problems. The ever-increasing number of shanty-towns or "bidonvilles" around nearly all modern towns in many developing countries is proof of these problems.

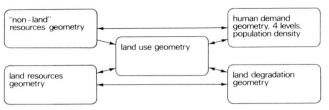

Fig. 7.1. Relations between five geometries in land use

In countries or regions in which the three basic demand levels are reasonably met by the existing system of land use and by all other human activities (commerce, industry, transport), the requirements of the fourth demand level obtain a much higher priority. This is an important change, because then the purpose of land use itself tends to change. When levels one, two or three still have to be satisfied, land use is predominantly an economic activity for society as a whole. The attitude of development planning is directed towards higher production, in the case of dominancy of levels one and two even of higher gross production with the emphasis on food and other primary needs (clothing, fuel, beverages). Attention is drawn towards degradation geometry only to the degree that continuation of the production of the products to satisfy these needs is endangered. The degree to which this is likely to occur depends on other factors. One important factor is population density, as a part of the demand geometry. Another is the resources geometry as such, in relation to the demand geometry and in relation to another subsystem of the model which might be called the "land use geometry".

Land use geometry encompasses all aspects which, in this text, were previously indicated as "land utilization types"; these include, among other things, the level of technical know-how, the available technology and the resulting recurrent inputs. The non-recurrent inputs also find their place in "land use geometry". Finally a fifth geometry, which may be called the "non-land resources geometry", includes the available social, institutional and financial resources which are indispensible for land use and even more for its development. A diagram demonstrating some of the relations among these five geometries is shown in Fig. 7.1.

Land use geometry is situated in the center of the field of tensions caused by the other four geometries. Its present position is also the result of historical growth and therefore reflects previous situations which resulted from older relations among the various geometries. Because land use today in any region of the world is very much the result of past developments, it is never fully adjusted to the present situation and even less to developments which will occur in the future. Tradition plays an important role in all land utilization types, particularly in agriculture. There is nothing wrong with this. Tradition in agricultural land use is largely the result of accumulated and integrated practical experiences of past years and past generations. As has been shown in previous chapters, land resources and land use, as well as land evaluation for land use, are complicated matters which can never be fully calculated from available data. Experience therefore always plays an important role and, seen in this light, traditions in agricultural land use are extremely useful means of transfering knowledge and experience through the successive generations of farmers. To some extent, therefore, tradition is a healthy corrective against unwarranted sudden changes in land use and may therefore act as a buffer among the geometries.

Traditions in Agricultural Land Use

There is, however, one serious danger which results if traditions are overly regarded. Land utilization types are always changing because they have to reflect the relations among the geometries among which they are situated. This has perhaps not always been the case, particularly in typical closed-off types of subsistence farming. It was however true for Mesopotamian arable land farming in the times of the Babylonian empires, some 3000 to 4000 years ago. Today, because agriculture in all parts of the world is advancing and has to advance to meet and solve efficiently the problems posed by the geometries of today, the necessary adaptations of land use types and land use practices have to transgress at several points the limits originally posed by traditions, which may be centuries old.

Tradition, if seen as accumulated and integrated experience, has to be treated the same as all other kinds of experience, i.e. it has to be critically systematized on the basis of the nature and evolution of the land utilization types and on the nature and possible degradations as well as possible improvements of these resources. A careful study of present land use, with its assets and problems, must therefore be carried out to avoid neglecting the good and even today useful experiences transfered by tradition, but it can only be done in a worthwhile manner if it is based on good investigations of the land resources (MAHLER in: Integrated Surveys, 1972).

Traditions are not always old, particularly in those land utilization types which have developed rapidly during the last centuries. Human memory is often not as retentive as is sometimes thought. Many areas in Western Europe which today are considered to be traditionally arable farming regions, in fact supported large herds of cattle before the incidence of the cattle plague in the second half of the eighteenth century. The advent of reliable steam engines for pumping stations in the Netherlands brought about a considerable increase in the drainage of many polders around the beginning of the present century; many polders which today are considered to be typical arable land areas were all in meadows less than a century ago. Changes in land use have always occurred in those areas where land use was practiced within a more or less open market economy, due to changes in the demand geometry and in the "non-land resources geometry" as well as to the technological evolution of land use practices. A typical example of the influence of the "non-land resources geometry" is provided by the large investment of capital, gained through overseas trade, in the reclamation and subsequent land use of the polders around Amsterdam, especially during the seventeenth and eigtheenth centuries.

A much younger tradition is found in the approach to land improvement and land reallotment, which in fact often dates from the years of the "world economic crisis" between 1930 and 1937. In this period, the desire to provide work in land improvement projects for the large numbers of unemployed caused in the Netherlands the first government sponsored projects of any importance; parallels are found in the soil conservation and land reclamation activities started in the U.S.A. under the New Deal. Under the then prevailing circumstances, the economic feasibility of the projects was of minor importance, and the social aspects weighed heavily on two points: (1) providing healthy work for unemployed, and (2) improvement of land resources in socially backward regions. After World War II, the pattern changed in so far as more machinery was introduced, and mechanized land improvement gradually became the only possibility. In addition, changes in the national demand geometries created an emphasis on the feasibility of projects. But at least until some years ago, the original traditions of the earliest period still lived very much in the minds of the staff responsible for their execution. A considerable change in the national demand geometry was provoked during the last years by the increasing integration of urban and rural land uses and by the increased standard of living, accompanied by pollution and other indications of environmental degradation. The demand geometry shifted from social and economic aspects at least partly towards ecological considerations; this shift now causes a complete re-evaluation of the existing traditions and experiences.

Advancing Agriculture: Its Implications

The term "advancing agriculture" itself requires a critical review. Land use is undoubtedly in a period of evolution and development in most parts of the world, and this is meant to lead towards a better adaptation of land use to the various geometries which have been indicated. To what degree can this process be said to lead towards an advancing agriculture and, if so, what kinds of advancements are included? Our generation is less certain of the advantages of progress and development than was that of our grandparents and great-grandparents, who saw the advantages of the Industrial Revolution and the subsequent changes in economic and social conditions of the early twentieth century.

Seen in terms of the geometries, advancing agriculture has to meet as nearly as possible the requirements made upon it by the demand geometry. It must do this, in any given region and period, with the most efficient use of the "non-land resources" and of the "land resources", in a manner which will permit future generations to retain as many "degrees of freedom" for their land use as will be possible. In other words, land use and concurrent land improvement have to leave room for future developments. Finally, land degradation in its widest sense has to be avoided and, in those areas where it exists today, to be remedied if at all possible. Land use in advancing agriculture must therefore develop in such a manner that an optimum use of resources is combined with a minimization of land degradation and a maximization of its attempts to meet human demands.

These requirements lead to different answers in different regions with their considerable differences in all the various aspects of the geometries. The demand geometries of countries broadly classified as "industrialized" and "developing" are quite different, but this very generalized distinction is insufficient to differentiate the many regional problems. There are great differences among the resources as well as among the demand geometries of the different countries, "developing" as well as "industrialized"; and within each country large regional differences occur. Land degradation geometry differs very much among the different regions of the world: arid and semi-arid regions have large natural degradation hazards, and mountainous areas have their own particular hazards in this respect.

Preparation of Decisions

The crucial problem in this situation everywhere is how decisions can be made and by whom. The fact that decisions on policies of land use are necessary is indisputable. But decisions have to be made by farmers, local administrative bodies and by all other bodies at higher levels of organization: project authorities, provincial and state governments, national governments and by some international organizations such as the European Community, often called the "European Common Market" and similar bodies in other parts of the world (see e.g. SSM, 1973). These decisions have to be made with a considerable amount of wisdom, of which it can only be hoped, that our legislators and administrators will receive an abundance. But the decisions must be based upon knowledge which is presented in a form which permits its use for these all-important decisions. Information about the knowledge required has been offered in the previous chapters. In the following paragraphs the spotlight will be turned on those aspects which will weigh heavily in the final decision-making process (see also FOUND, 1971).

Preparation of decisions is today one of the most important activities for all scientists, engineers and others who are concerned with land use and land use planning. Depending upon the scope of a particular decision, these preparations are made with different degrees of generalization and detail. International organizations such as FAO and UNESCO fulfill an important role in the preparation of decisions on an international scale and provide suitable data for decisions on national and large regional scales. Experts of these and of other specialized agencies of the United Nations also help to prepare decisions for projects of regional development within the several countries. Often several institutions help to prepare decisions on land use within each country. In the U.S.A. the Bureau of Reclamation and the Soil Conservation Service are among the important bodies which carry out such work (see e.g. DEE et al., 1972, 1973). A clear preparation, if possible offering several possibilities for decisions and their consequences in terms of the geometries involved, is an essential prerequisite in land use.

Once a decision for land use is made, its consequences are usually felt over a long period and over a surface area which may be much larger than that of the immediately concerned area. The responsibility of experts on land use and on land resources is therefore a great one. Their responsibility includes not only the presentation of the data and of the possible decisions as such, but also the manner in which the data are presented. An easily readable presentation is required, as all decision-makers have an inherent lack of time for each separate project and decision. The presentation should be as objectively presented as possible, but with a clear indication of the positive as well as of the negative aspects of any decision.

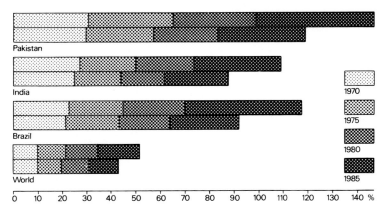

Fig. 7.2. Cumulative increases in annual caloric requirements of Pakistan, India, Brazil and the World, based on high and low population projections for 1970 to 1985. Values are percent increases over 1965 requirements for consumption (not production) and assumed equitable distribution.(President's Science Advisory Committee, 1967)

The use of simple models, to clarify existing relationships, is often helpful (see e.g. Fig. 7.1, p. 328). These models need not necessarily be quantitative to fulfill an important role in the preparation of decisions. To support them with quantitative "bench mark data" may however often be welcome.

7.2 Land Use Improvement and Land Improvement

Stabilization at Attainable Levels

Land resources often allow a much better situation with regard to the geometries indicated above than is found in present land use. This depends on finding the best kinds of land use in relation to the available land resources and "non-land resources" and to the applicable technology for a certain area, at a certain period, with sufficient safeguards against ecological hazards. Land resources surveys, studies of crop and animal requirements and land development planning have to proceed towards a progressive stabilization at a new point, at which an optimum level of production can be combined with an optimum degree of ecological variability and stability. The new stabilization will not be fully permanent, since the geometries will also change in the future, but a certain stabilization over a given period, varying perhaps from 15 years to the duration of one human generation, is in general attainable. The conservation of ecological variability, i.e. of biological conditions within the land use system and within the areas not directly used for agriculture, will to some extent safeguard the possibilities for future development; they will also contribute to a minimum amount of ecological stability. A "cultural steppe" is to some extent unavoidable in arable land farming; it should not,

Table 108. Cultivated land and potentially arable land according to the President's Science Advisory Committee (SIMONSON, 1967)

a) Total land area and arable land by continents

Continents	Total land area[a]	Cultivated land[a]	% of land area cultivated	Potential arable land[a]	Ratio of culti-vated to poten-tial arable land %
Africa	3010	158	5.2	734	22
Asia	2740	519	18.9	627	84
Australia and New Zealand	820	32	3.9	153	21
Europe	480	154	32.1	174	88
North America	2110	239	11.3	465	51
South America	1750	77	4.4	681	11
USSR	2240	227	10.6	356	64
Total	13150	1406	10.6	3190	44

[a] Areas are given in millions of hectares.
Adapted from Table 7-9, p. 434, of The World Food Problem, A Report of the President's Science Advisory Committe, Vol. II, Report of the Panel on the World Food Supply (U.S.A.).

b) Estimated total land area and potential arable land by broad soil groups (± 1965)

Broad Soil Groups	Total area[a]	Potential arable land[a]	Potential arable as % of total area	Potential arable as % of group total	Included orders, 7th Approx.[b]
Tundra soils	517	0	0	0	4, 1
Desert soils	2180	430	3.3	20.7	3
Chernozems and Brunizems	822	450	3.5	54.5	5
Non-calcic Brown soils	291	110	0.8	37.8	7
Podzols	1920	300	2.4	15.6	6, 7
Red-Yellow Podzolic soils	388	130	1.0	34.2	8
Latosolic soils	2500	1050	8.1	42.0	4, 9, 8,
Grumusols and Terra Rossas	325	180	1.3	55.4	2, 7
Brown Forest soils and Rendzinas	101	30	0.2	3.0	4, 5
Ando soils	24	10	0.1	41.7	4
Lithosols	2722	80	0.6	2.9	1, 4, et al.
Regosols	763	70	0.5	9.2	1, 4
Alluvial soils	595	350	2.4	58.8	1, 4
Total	13150	3190	24.2	—	—

[a] Areas are given in millions of hectares.
[b] Orders are indentified by numbers as follows: 1–Entisols; 2–Vertisols; 3–Aridisols; 4–Inceptisols; 5–Mollisols; 6–Alfisols; 8–Ultisols; 9–Oxisols.
Adapted from Table 7-1, p. 423, of The World Food Problem, A Report of the President's Science Advisory Committee, Vol. II, Report of the Panel on the World Food Supply (U.S.A.).

Table 109. Examples of targets of the provisional indicative world plan (FAO, 1969) until 1985

(a) *Selected indicators bearing on agricultural productivity — 1962 and 1985*

	Arable land per caput of total Population		Cropping intensity total arable land		Proportion of Irr. land to total arable land		Consumption of pesticides per ha arable land		Consumption of fertilizer per ha arable land		Tractors per 1000 ha arable land	
	1962	1985	1962	1985	1962	1985	1962[a]	1985	1962	1985	1962	1985
	ha		percent		percent		US$/ha		kg/ha nutrients		numbers	
Africa S. of Sahara	0.90	0.62	42	52	0.7	1.0	0.1	3.0	0.8	6.7	0.3	0.6
Asia	0.31	0.19	100	121	20.9	30.5	0.1	4.5	6.0	79.5	0.4[b]	4.1[b]
Latin America	0.64	0.43	54	60	8.1	10.3	1.2	5.3	11.9	64.2	5.0	8.0
Near East[c]	0.53	0.33	51	59	31.4	31.8	0.7	3.3	11.9	55.4	1.2	3.4
North-West Africa[d]	0.64	0.38	67	81	3.7	6.3	n.a.	2.5	9.2	42.2	2.8	4.2

[a] 1962 estimates taken from FAO on food production resources 1968. 1985 estimate calculated by IWP.
[b] 2-wheeled and 4-wheeled tractors converted into 40 HP units (five 2-wheeled tractors = one 4-wheeled tractor).
[c] 10 countries only, excluding Kuwait and Yemen Arab Republic.
[d] Data refer to 1965 and include area under esparto grass.

Table 109 (continued)

(b) *Estimated area under high-yielding cereal varieties 1967–68: Asia and IWP objectives 1985 (Million ha)*[a]

Country	Rice 1967-8 Total	Rice 1985 Irr.	Rice 1985 N.I.	Rice 1985 Total	Rice Growth %	Wheat 1967-8 Total	Wheat 1985 Irr.	Wheat 1985 N.I.	Wheat 1985 Total	Wheat Growth %	Maize, Millet, Sorghum 1967-8 Total	Maize, Millet, Sorghum 1985 Irr.	Maize, Millet, Sorghum 1985 N.I.	Maize, Millet, Sorghum 1985 Total	Maize, Millet, Sorghum Growth %	Total 1967-8	Total 1985	Total Growth %
Ceylon	0.37	0.90	0.10	1.00	5.6	—	—	—	—	—	—	0.06	—	0.05	+	0.37	1.06	6.1
China (Taiwan)	0.77	0.88	—	0.88	0.8	—	0.02	—	0.02	+	0.02	0.10	—	0.10	9.4	0.79	1.00	1.3
India	1.80	19.00	—	19.00	15.0	2.94	8.60	1.40	10.00	7.1	1.31	4.30	10.00	14.30	14.2	6.05	43.30	11.5
Korea (Rep. of)	0.48	1.18	0.05	1.23	5.4	—	0.40	0.30	0.70[b]	—	0.05	0.02	0.15	0.17	7.0	0.53	2.10	8.0
Malaysia (W)	0.02	0.40	0.03	0.43	18.6	—	—	—	—	—	—	0.04	—	0.04	+	0.02	0.47	+
Pakistan	0.45	7.30	3.60	10.90	19.4	0.91	4.60	0.80	5.40	10.4	0.20	1.80	0.50	2.30	14.5	1.56	18.60	14.7
Philippines	0.40	2.30	0.20	2.50	10.7	—	—	—	—	—	0.01	0.30	0.70	1.00	13.7	0.41	3.50	12.6
Thailand	—	2.50	0.30	2.80	+	—	—	—	—	—	0.04	0.10	0.50	0.60	16.3	0.04	3.40	+
Total	4.29	34.46	4.28	38.74	13.0	3.85	13.62	2.50	16.12	8.6	1.63	6.72	11.85	18.57	14.5	9.77	73.43	11.9

[a] Because of inadequacy of soil, climatic and experimental data for the more remote areas and for rain-fed conditions the maize/sorghum/millet estimates must be regarded as very tentative: similarly in respect of rain-fed wheat/barley in Korea.

[b] Includes barley.

+ = over 20% compound growth rate per annum.

Table 109 (continued)

(c) 1962* Production of other major food crops and IWP objectives 1985

Asia

	Area ('000 ha)		Production ('000 MT)		Growth rate prod. 1962–85	% of prod. from area incr.
	1962	1985	1862	1985		
Starchy roots	1763	3104	15464	37442	3.9	64
Pulses dry	26018	33633	13265	27963	3.3	33
Groundnuts	6962	12753	5125	19611	6.0	45
Other oil crops	8975	12887	2942	7420	4.1	39
Vegetables	6509	9506	33530	82919	4.0	42
Fruits	2937	5274	17093	46676	4.5	58

Latin America

	Area ('000 ha)		Production ('000 MT)		Growth rate prod. 1962–85	% of prod. from area incr.
	1962	1985	1962	1985		
Starchy roots	3215	4304	32626	54400	2.2	59
Pulses dry	5775	8018	3382	6860	3.1	45
Groundnuts	801	1408	1072	1988	2.7	92
Other oil crops	1019	2552	2655	7534	4.6	89
Vegetables	858	1518	7413	16867	3.6	69
Fruits	2616	4669	29172	62645	3.4	76

Africa South of Sahara

	Area ('000 ha)		Production ('000 MT)		Growth rate prod. 1962–85	% of prod. from area incr.
	1962	1985	1962	1985		
Starchy roots	7784	12020	44782	80300	2.6	73
Pulses dry	7339	12372	2701	5749	3.3	70
Groundnuts	4414	6984	3454	7122	3.2	62
Other oil crops	—	—	1806	3242	2.6	n.a.
Vegetables	1228	2679	3152	7040	3.6	94
Fruits	—	—	10455	17314	2.2	n.a.

Near East and North Africa[a]

	Area ('000 ha)		Production ('000 MT)		Growth rate prod. 1962–85	% of prod. from area incr.
	1962	1985	1962	1985		
Starchy roots	152	232	1486	2939	3.0	63
Pulses dry	1472	2422	1234	2908	3.6	61
Groundnuts	1	8	—	12	—	n.a.
Other oil crops	2220	3404	1355	3106	3.7	51
Vegetables	1037	1437	9664	23166	3.9	36
Fruits	1761	2402	7807	17973	3.7	38

Source: IWP Country Study Reports.
Notes: * Average 1961–63.
[a] Data for North Africa are relative to 1965.

Table 109 (continued)

(d) *Value of crop inputs 1962* and proposed 1985 levels (mill. US$ 1962 prices)*

	Fertilizers		Seed		Irrigation		Crop Protection		Mechanization[a]		Total Inputs		Total Input as percent of crop output	
	1962*	1985	1962*	1985	1962*	1985*	1962*	1985	1962*	1985	1962*	1985	1962*	1985
													percent	
Africa South of Sahara	14.2	180.4	295.0	412.1	—	—	13.6	309.0	27.0	101.2	349.8	1002.7	6.4	9.1
Asia	335.0	5180.9	868.6	1258.7	750.7	1186.0	20.4	1215.8	200.9	1153.9	2175.6	9995.3	9.8	18.9
Latin America	218.3	1861.3	276.4	355.7	479.6	896.9	110.0[b]	397.2[b]	438.5	1031.8	1522.8	4542.9	17.1	25.7
Near East[c]	78.7	470.7	108.1	145.7	264.4	350.8	25.0	116.4	36.7	117.3	512.9	1200.9	18.6	19.2
North Africa[d]	18.0	145.0	51.4	72.1	—	—	11.0	38.5	94.0	206.0	174.4	461.6	20.3	25.2
Above regions	664.2	7838.3	1599.5	2244.3	1494.7	2433.7	180.0	2076.9	797.1	2610.2	4735.5	17203.4	11.8	19.2

Growth rates of value. 1962* to 1985 (percent per year)

	Fertilizers	Seed	Irrigation	Crop Protection	Mechanization[a]	Total Inputs
Africa South of Sahara	11.7	1.5	—	14.5	5.9	4.7
Asia	12.6	1.6	2.0	19.4	7.9	6.9
Latin America	9.8	1.1	2.8	5.7[b]	3.8	4.9
Near East[c]	8.1	1.3	1.2	6.9	5.2	3.8
North Africa[d]	11.0	1.7	—	6.5	4.0	5.0
Above regions	11.3	1.5	2.1	11.2	5.3	5.8

[a] Same quantities used also for livestock.
[b] South America only.
[c] 10 countries only excluding Kuwait and Yemen Arab Republic.
[d] 1962* = 1965*.

Table 109 (continued)

(e) *Proposed growth rate in animal production*

Region	No. of countries	Proposed growth rate (% p.a.			Farm gate value of production 1962–85
		Farm gate value of production[b]			
		1962–75	1975–85	1962–85	1962–85
Africa, south of the Sahara	24	3.3	4.3	3.8	3.9
Asia and Far East					
(a)	8	2.7	4.0	3.3	3.3
(b)[a]	(8)	(3.0)	(4.1)	(3.5)	(3.5)
Latin America (excluding Argentina)	17 (16)	3.0 (3.3)	3.7 (4.7)	3.3 (3.9)	3.6 (4.0)
Near East and North West Africa	15	2.6	3.6	3.1	3.1
Total: (a)	64	2.9	3.8	3.3	3.5
(b)	(64)	(3.0)	(3.9)	(3.4)	(3.5)

[a] Asia (b) in this and subsequent tables refers to a variant of the Asian Region which incorporates the figures implied by a higher offtake rate in Indian cattle (see paragraphs 13 and 42).
[b] These columns exclude and the final column includes the increased value of herds due to stock retention.

(f) *Proposed growth rates in output of livestock products*[a] *1962–1985 (% p.a.)*

Region	Ruminant meat	Pork	Poultry meat	Total meat without offals	Milk	Eggs
Africa, south of Sahara	3.1	4.1	6.3	3.4	2.4	4.9
Asia and Far East						
(a)	2.2	4.4	5.6	3.5	2.8	5.9
(b)[b]	(4.9)	—	—	(4.8)	—	—
Latin America	2.9[c]	3.5	4.7	3.1	3.1	4.1
Near East and North West Africa	2.9	−1.8[d]	7.0	3.2	2.6	4.4
Total (a)	2.9	3.9	5.6	3.2	2.8	4.8
(b)[b]	(3.2)			(3.5)		

[a] These growth rates exclude retention of stock to build up inventories (see Table 1).
[b] See footnote 1 to Table 1.
[c] This figure rises to 3.2% if Argentina is excluded from the analysis.
[d] This decline is attributable to the fact that pork is only eaten in non-Moslem communities and in some of these (particularly in North Africa) such communities are expected to decline in numbers during the lifetime of the Plan.

Table 109 (continued)

(g) *Inland[a] fish catch (1965) and technically feasible yields by 1985*

	1965 Production '000 tons	Percent of world fish production	Indicated expansion factor by 1985	Technically Feasible Yields by 1985[b]
Large lakes and reservoirs	1 000	1.9	× 2	2 000
Small lakes, rivers, dams etc.	4 400	8.2	× 3	13 200
Pond culture	1 000	1.9	× 5	5 000
Total	6 400	12.0	× 3.2	20 200

[a] Excludes anadromous species.
[b] Refers only to existing water bodies.

(h) *Total identified annual inputs[a] at 1962 constant prices*

	Africa South of Sahara		Asia and Far East		Latin America		Near East and N-W Africa		Zone C	
	1962	1985	1962	1985	1962	1985	1962	1985	1962	1985
$ million	527	1 408	4 402	15 247	2 514	7 164	946	2 528	8 388	26 347
Index for 1985	100	267	100	346	100	285	100	267	100	314
Increase in percent per annum		4.4		5.6		4.7		4.4		5.1

[a] Comprising those for crops, livestock, fisheries and forestry.

(j) *Identified investments in primary agricultural sector 1963–1985[a]*

	Africa South of Sahara $ million	Asia and Far East $ million	South America $ million	Near East and N-W Africa $ million	Zone C (study countries excl. Central America) $ million	%
Land and water development	2 808	30 272	8 573	5 447	47 100	42
Equipment and machines		22 081	13 737	3 246[b]	39 064[c]	35
Livestock inventory and buildings	1 254	4 578	10 066	2 331	18 229	16
Fisheries: vessels, etc.	265	3 652	359	53	4 329	4
Forestry and logging	391	1 813	825	714	3 743	3
Total	4 718	62 396	33 560	11 791	112 465	100

[a] All figures are gross except those for Africa.
[b] Excl. Morocco.
[c] Excl. Africa South of Sahara.

Table 109 (continued)

(k) *Employment in crop-production — selected Asian countries*

	Total labor days million	Labor days per family	GVP[a] from crops per labor day $	Total labor days million	Labor days per family	GVP from crops per labor day $
	1962*			1985		
Ceylon	301.5	257.7	1.52	548.0	296.9	2.16
India	11429.5	234.4	1.22	19911.6	255.2	1.64
Pakistan	2569.9	195.7	1.35	5021.9	219.6	1.93
Philippines	740.2	244.5	1.07	1433.7	282.1	1.47
Thailand	733.3	183.4	1.19	1189.0	190.5	1.87
W. Malaysia	300.3	436.5	1.72	465.9	388.3	2.80
Total or average	16074.7	227.3	1.25	28570.1	260.7	1.72
Index	100	100	100	178	115	138

[a] GVP = Gross value of production.

(l) *Gross value of agricultural production at constant prices*

	Africa South of Sahara		Asia and Far East		Latin America[b]		Near East and N-W Africa	
	1962	1985	1962	1985	1962	1985	1962	1985
Gross value of agricultural production ($m)[a]	6831	14802	27282	66448	15165	32482	5622	12763
Rate of increase (% per annum)	3.4		3.9		3.4		3.6	

[a] Including higher pig and poultry alternatives.
[b] Continental Latin America.

however, be extended to those parts of an area which may be put to better use in the conservation of natural and semi-natural habitats.

A few years ago, two worldwide attempts were made to estimate some levels which were considered to be attainable. Although the actual data may now have to be changed, some of them are given here as examples of their approach to land use and land resources.

The Indicative World Plan (FAO, 1969) gives some ideas about the levels attainable in the different regions of the world. Some data, as well as some indications developed by an American commission, are shown in Tables 108 and 109 and Fig. 7.2. These two sets of indications do not take into account the specific ecological considerations which have been shown to be of importance during the last few years (see e.g. MEADOWS et al., 1972). These considerations may have a certain impact on a world scale, because the use of mineral fuels in agriculture may become progressively less feasible as their reserves near exhaustion. The same may perhaps be true for some fertilizer materials (phosphates, potassium).

It may also mean that certain kinds of pesticides, such as DDT, may be found to be not completely replaceable and that therefore a less intensive kind of land use has to be accepted on certain lands. These are two different aspects of the "ecological crisis" which may to some extent influence the degree to which the demand geometry of mankind can be met by agricultural land use. Much will depend also on the degree to which population growth, perhaps the most important aspect of the demand geometry, will really proceed according to the predictions of MEADOWS and his co-authors; a continuing exponential growth of the world population may not occur, either because the original extrapolations were based on relatively short-term data, or because mankind adjusts itself to the limits which are certainly imposed on its future growth.

Land Use Improvement

Improvement of land use will, however, have to take into account all relevant data, even if they are based on estimates or extrapolations. Also included are the calculations on the amounts of assimilation products which can be produced in the different latitudes due to differences in insolation (DE WIT, 1966; see Para. 1.3). This provides a goal for land use which will in many conditions not be attainable and which in fact has yet to be attained, but which can be used as a reference for resources studies.

These resources studies must be carried out in much greater detail, because only on the scale of the farm can the resources aspects be compared with the ecological and economic aspects in order to achieve improvements in land use. Improvements in land use will often lead to retrenching of the cultivated area to those lands where the ecological conditions lead to a stable and feasible way of obtaining high production. Advancing agriculture is not always an increasing intensification of agriculture; it is rather an intensification of agriculture, using more inputs to obtain much higher outputs, on suitable lands, accompanied by a decreasing intensity of agriculture, using fewer inputs per surface area to obtain a more feasible production with fewer ecological hazards on all other lands.

This process may lead to an increased overall production of world agriculture, and it is thus not contrary to the demands of the present "demand geometry". New varieties of crops, such as the "Green Revolution" varieties of rice and wheat, will largely contribute to improvements of land use, provided that they are not seen as a panacea for increased production on poor lands, but rather as a means of obtaining increased production on the best lands. Local disappointments and social tensions may result, but world demands as well as economic and ecological considerations point in this direction. These demands are very real, as has been summarized by one of the responsible authors of the Provisional Indicative World Plan (BOERMA, 1969) in approximately the following words:

1. Based on an average annual increase of 6% of the Gross National Product and a population increase of 2.6%, agricultural production in the developing countries has to increase by at least 4% during the period 1965–1985.

2. Approximately half of the agricultural production in the developing countries takes place on subsistence-level farms, whose production may not increase more than is necessary to cope with local growth of the population; the part of agriculture which operates for the more or less open markets will have to increase its production by at least 6% during this period to cope with the other parts of population growth.

3. Agriculture in the developing countries must, first of all, provide for the increased demands for cereal products for human consumption; the increased production of rice and wheat for human consumption will have to be accompanied by an increase in production of cereals as fodder for cattle. A large amount of "non-land resources" will be necessary to effect both aspects of increased cereal production.

4. High priority must be given to the production of high-protein foods, such as milk and meat, but also eggs and fish. Areas such as parts of Latin America and East Africa may be particularly suited for this purpose.

5. Social and economic measures, particularly definite financial measures, will have to be taken to increase applications of both chemical fertilizers and pesticides in the developing countries by approximately 11% per year. Apart from this, large investments will be needed for agricultural mechanization, for cattle breeding, for forestry and for fisheries.

6. Approximately 42% of the total investment will be needed for land reclamation and land improvement.

The first five points involve changes in and extensions of, existing land use. Experience has taught us that large increases in agricultural production as well as in efficiency of farming are possible in this manner. If carried out with careful consideration of the ecology of the lands on which they are practiced, these changes in land use are often much less dangerous than are large projects which, at least during their construction, can cause the occurrence of a very unstable ecological situation and which may lead to the destruction of ecosystems which are ecologically valuable for future land use. The idea, put forward by MEADOWS et al. (1972), that intensification of agricultural land use would always lead to land degradation and hence aggravate the "ecological crisis", is a fallacy. Intensification of land use, if carried out within a land utilization type which is well suited to, and of which the practices are well adapted to, the land conditions of a given area, may even lead to land improvement. The idea of the previously mentioned authors, which has also been put forward by others, e.g. some decades ago by W. VOGT in his book "The Road to Survival", is probably mainly derived from the situation which arose in the U.S.A. during the last decades of the nineteenth and the first decades of the twentieth centuries. The land degradation which followed the opening up of some of the central areas of the U.S.A. was, however, clearly the result of abnormal circumstances: the settling in these areas of farmers whose traditions and experiences derived from the milder climates of the Eastern States and of Western and Central Europe, combined with the invention of large mechanized agricultural techniques, of which no experience at all existed.

The primary objective of land use improvement in the developing areas of the world in the coming decades is to meet the demands for food and for other essentials of human life.

The demand geometry of land use improvement in the more industrialized areas is rather different, although the fundamental objectives remain unchanged. Food and other primary materials for human life remain of great importance in the industrialized areas. Some industrialized areas are characterized by special land and climatic conditions which make them particularly suited for growing particular crops, e.g. vineyards and citrus in various countries of Western Europe and the Mediterranean area. Furthermore, the demand levels of the populations of these areas also have their own requirements, particularly with regard to horticultural products. A legitimate wish of these countries often is to provide at least a minimum quantity of basic food products, to avoid excessive dependency on other countries, which could involve unacceptable political consequences. Finally, some of the high-quality horticultural crops must, for ecological reasons, be grown in rotation with other crops. A typical example is found in the cultivation of flower bulbs in some areas north of Amsterdam, where a rotation with leys and potatoes is the most suitable way of producing good crops of tulips and other flower bulbs under sufficiently stable ecological conditions.

Land use in advancing agriculture will therefore develop in industrialized countries according to a variety of requirements which are related to all of the geometries indicated in Para. 7.1. In some areas, a more extensive land utilization type than has been practiced during the last decades will be required, partly because the existing traditions, and the inherited social conditions, still support the existence of small farms which are really of family size according to the standards of living before World War II. The increased standard of living, due to industrial growth and other economic developments, has created a situation in which these farms must now receive subsidies of various kinds to provide acceptable standards of living for the farmers and their families. Even then, and with a very intensive land utilization type, there is a backlog compared with wages in industry and in the service sectors of the national economies. A natural readjustment of these land utilization types towards more extensive land use on larger holdings is already under way in some areas.

The demand geometry for land use in industrial areas has undergone other changes which increase even more during the coming years. Modern conveniences and improved means of transport have to some extent "urbanized" many rural areas. This process is stimulated by the fact that, in contrast, the industrial population goes to the rural areas for its recreation. The heavy industrialization of the urban areas themselves has also put an increasing ecological pressure on the rural areas. Rural land use is now often seen by the urban populations, which often comprise more than 80% of the total population of industrialized countries, as a "guardian" of the ecological conditions of a country. This "guardianship" includes two demands in particular: (1) that the rural areas maintain or create a landscape which is a pleasant environment for the urban populations when they leave their homes for recreation, and (2) that the rural land use is conducted in such a manner that the ecological variety, which was completely destroyed in the towns, is maintained for the benefit of the whole country.

Both these demands are in themselves realistic and even necessary. They must, however, be met by rural land use which primarily includes agricultural land use, carried out in economic enterprises. New land utilization types, adapted to the new demands as well as to the new socio-economic and ecological conditions, have to be developed to find appropriate solutions. The situation is even more complicated by the fact that industrial and urban land uses sometimes cause serious pollution and damage to crops in the adjoining rural areas. For the latter, financial compensations are sometimes offered to the farmers, which may, in some

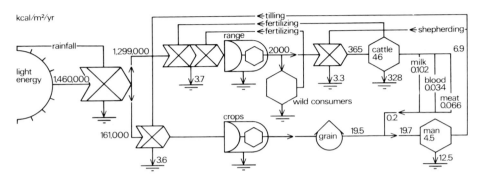

Fig. 7.3. Energy circuit for tribal cattle system in Uganda (ODUM. In: President's Science Advisory Committee, 1967)

Explanation: Example of a simple agricultural system in a pulse climatic, the Dodo tribe in Uganda. Food is derived from grains, meat, blood and milk. Animals serve as storage filter smoothing the pulse and as a nutrition convergence. (Based on an account by DESHLER, 1965). Numbers are kilocalories per square meter per year. There are 70 people per square mile. Dry weights were converted to kilocalories using 4.5 klcal/gm. The basic net production of plant material for dry regions is given by WALTER, 1954, as a function of rainfall. Using 21 inches of rainfall and WALTER's diagram, one is able to determine that 500 g of dry plant material matter are produced per square meter of land each year. As 1 acre is cultivated per person and there are 70 persons per square mile, one finds that 11% of the natural yield area is pre-empted by crops. At 4.5 cattle per person and 560 pounds per cow, 33% of which is dry weight excluding ash and water, one is able to determine that 10.2 g of animal weight is produced per square meter. Seventy people per square mile at 150 pounds per person of which 25% is dry matter is equivalent to 1.0 g per square meter. By integrating the area under curves given for monthly consumption of milk, blood, and meat, one obtains an annual caloric yield per person from the cattle of 3800 cal of milk, 2450 cal of meat, and 1265 cal of blood which provides the per area data in the figure. Calorie requirement per person is given as 2000 cal/person/day or 19.7 cal per square meter per year. The milk, meat, and blood supply only 0.2 of this requirement so crop intake is the remaining 19.5, a net yield much less than the net yield of vegetation of the natural range. Total insolation in this area just above the equator is about 4000-cal/cm²/day based on solar radiation maps for winter and summer for Africa given by DRUMMOND. The work of men in tending the crops and cattle can be taken as a percent of their time involved in this activity (primarily the daylight hours). As the culture is intimately involved with the cattle, one may assume that 1/6 of the daily metabolism of man is devoted to management of the cattle and the same amount is used for production of crops. The rationale for this procedure is that the maintenance requirements of man during his work are necessary to that work. The metabolic activities of 650-pound steers estimated from KLEIBER require 8000 klcal per day or 365 klcal/m²/yr. Some fraction of the cow's time and metabolism goes into refertilizing the range on which it grazes thus reinforcing and maintaining its loop. Part of a cow's day is spent on the move, and parts of its organ systems are involved in the nutrient regeneration system. One-tenth of its metabolism was taken as its work contribution to vegetation stimulation. This system does not involve money, and the economic transactor symbol does not appear

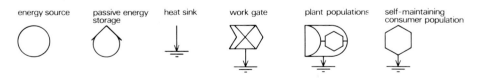

cases, be the only solution, but an over-all national planning of land use may find better answers to these problems.

A special, related demand which is often of considerable importance is the "visual pollution" which is unavoidable in some kinds of horticulture. Fully conditioned hothouses, which cover many hectares, such as between the Hague and Rotterdam, are typical examples of an "industrial" kind of agricultural land use which causes such pollution. They may also cause chemical air pollution through the use of mineral oils in the heating of these complexes. Agricultural land use must meet the demand for the products of these hothouses, but on the other hand, the demand for "clean" landscapes, without visual pollution, is growing more urgent. In contrast, bulb fields provide, at least during one period of the year, a very pleasing impression for the town dweller. Development of agricultural land use must consider all of these aspects.

Land Improvement

Land improvement is mentioned as the sixth point in the series of measures that agriculture must take to meet future demands. It requires, however, as was also indicated, a large share of the investment.

When does land use improvement provide the best solutions for land use in a developing agriculture and when does land improvement, i.e. relatively permanent improvements of the land conditions, provide the best answers? Land use can be improved by applications of recurrent inputs such as: better crop varieties, new crops, better crop maintenance, use of household refuse and other natural manures as well as of chemical fertilizers, better systems of cultivation and of grazing, appropriate use of pesticides. The energy flow diagrams (ODUM in President's Science Advisory Committee, 1967) Figs. 7.3 to 7.5 give information on

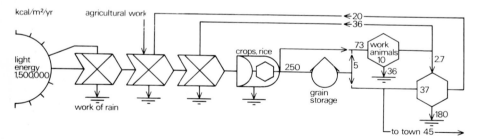

Fig. 7.4. Monsoon agriculture in India. (ODUM. In: President's Science Advisory Committee, 1967)

Explanation: Man in unsubsidized agricultural systems in a climate such as India's which has a sharp seasonal pulse that prevents more diverse systems from excluding the simple one by competitive invasion. Data based on tropical dense populations of 640 persons per square mile. Indian grain yields average 250 kg/acre/yr. One farm animal is shown for each 10 persons. One-half of animal metabolism is considered to be used for work and faecal fertilization. The animal protein intake for India is about six grams/per day. From FAO data, 2 percent of the food crop is fed to animals. Animal metabolism is 8000 kcal/day. Farm work occupies 0.1 of the total man-hours of the population. For explanation of symbols used, see legend to Fig. 7.3

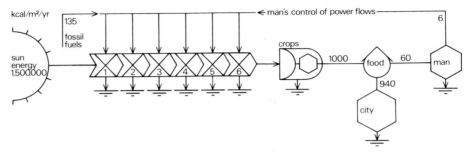

Fig. 7.5. Fuel subsidized industrial agriculture. (ODUM. In: President's Science Advisory Committee, 1967)

Explanation: Man in a United States system of industrialized, high yield agriculture whose energetic inputs include some of the vast flows of fossil fuels which replace the work formerly done by man, his animals, and the network of animals and plants in which he was formerly nursed. Work flows include: (1) Mechanized and commercial preparation of seed and planting replacing natural dispersion systems; (2) fertilizer increments which replace mineral re-cycling system; (3) chemical and power weeding replacing the woody maintenance of a shading system; (4) soil preparation and treatment to replace the forest soil-building process; (5) insecticides and fungicides which replace the system of chemical diversity and carnivores for preventing epidemic grazing or disease; (6) development of varieties which are capable of passing on the savings in work to net food storages; new varieties are developed as disease types appear, thus providing the genetic selection formerly arranged by the forest evolution and choice selection system. One hundred seventy persons per square mile support 32 times this number in cities. The level of United States grain production is about 1000 kcal/m^2/yr. (BROWN). The fuel subsidy is calculated using 10^4 kcal/\$. If production yields \$60 per acre per year in United States production and if the costs were 90% of the gross, then \$54 per acre was the measure of use of materials and services from the industrialized culture. This becomes 54 × 10^4 kcal per acre or 135 kcal/m^2/yr. For explanation of symbols used, see legend to Fig. 7.3

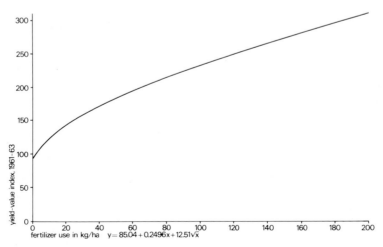

Fig. 7.6. Yield-Value Index *vs.* Fertilizer Use- 1961/63 (President's Science Advisory Committee, 1967)

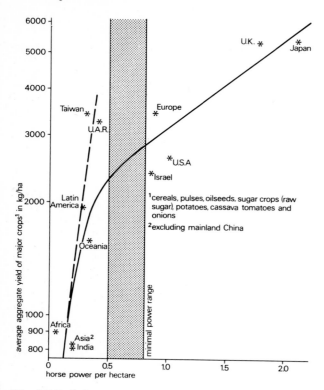

Fig. 7.7. Relationship between yields in kg/hectare and power in horse power per hectare, Major Food Crops (President's Science Advisory Committee, 1967)

how some land use systems work and where the improvements can be directed. General information on the response to some management improvements is given in Figs. 7.6 and 7.7. Many lands of the world are well suited to land use improvements, and the possibly deleterious side-effects of chemical fertilizers for example, may often be overrated. THOMAS (1972), in experiments on red soils from limestone in Kentucky, concluded that there is no discernible influence from nitrate fertilizers on the nitrogen content of the water of rivers in Kentucky streams in agricultural watersheds and that in fact there is no evidence that these streams are higher in nitrate than 50 years ago, when no chemical fertilizers were used in the region. With a view to the rising demand geometry, see e.g. Fig. 7.2, the use of more intensive land utilization types is undoubtedly required on many lands in many parts of the world.

Many lands in the world, however, are not able to carry higher production and may even show decreasing productivity, e.g. due to soil erosion or to increased salinity or waterlogging. Land improvement then, is the only means of arriving at a stable and efficient type of land use improvement; the latter remains the final goal with which agriculture can attempt to meet the requirements of the

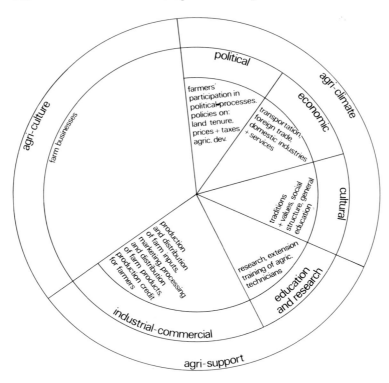

Fig. 7.8. Major factors in agricultural production (President's Science Advisory Committee, 1967)

demand geometry under existing conditions of "non-land" resources (see also Figs. 7.8 and 7.9).

Land improvement in densely populated areas often assumes the shape of land consolidation or land reallotment projects, which involve not only the natural resources aspects of the land but also the artifactial and institutional aspects. This holds true for the Chao Phya Delta of Thailand (SNETHLAGE, 1970; VOLKER and LAMBREGTS, 1963) just as much as for the Mayaga area in Rwanda (VINK, 1968; see Fig. 7.10) and for the rural reallotment projects in Europe (JACOBY, 1961). In all these cases land improvements of various kinds lead to readjusted, or sometimes even completely new cropping patterns and to many improvements in land use. In Fig. 7.11 the diagram for a calculation procedure for rural reconstruction projects is given (LOCHT, 1971); it can be used for a model of regional economic growth.

There is always a tendency in such areas to try to improve all the different kinds of lands in approximately equal measures. The potential suitabilities of the various lands are, however, completely different, and they often differ much more than do the actual suitabilities without land improvement. A careful reconsidera-

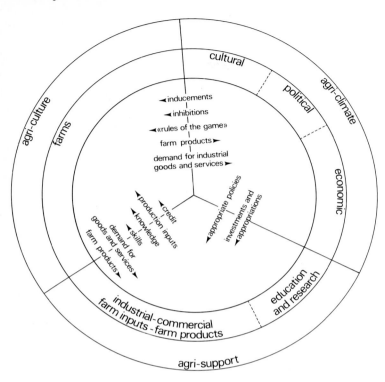

Fig. 7.9. Major interrelationships between agriculture and the total economy (President's Science Advisory Committee, 1967)

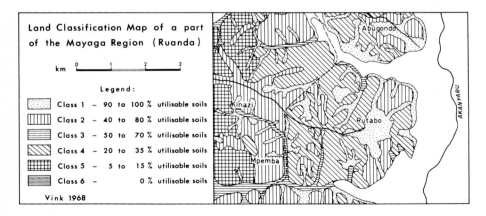

Fig. 7.10. Land classification map of a part of the Mayaga Region (Rwanda) (VINK, 1968)

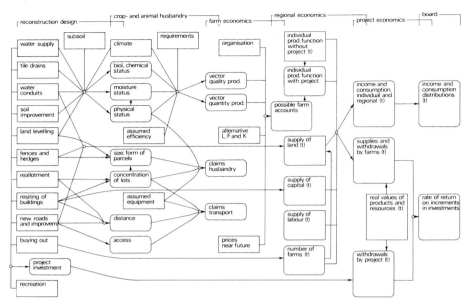

Fig. 7.11. Diagram of the calculation procedure of a rural reconstruction project for regional economic growth (LOCHT, 1969, cited by LOCHT, 1971)

tion of the land suitabilities is therefore necessary; the danger of investing in lands which are not suitable for improvement is twofold: (1) the lands will not be suitable for the new cultural ecosystem and hence land degradation may result, and (2) the effects for the farmers will be deleterious rather than beneficial and will result in grave socio-economic problems. There is always a tendency to provide "equal" improvements on all lands of a region for political and social reasons. In fact, there is often a tendency to invest more in improving the poorest lands than in increasing the productivity of the best lands. In some cases this may be warranted by the results, e.g. if potentially good lands are too dry and can produce large yields if irrigated or if they are waterlogged and can be considerably improved by drainage. In many cases however "improvement of the best soils pays better than improvement of the poorest soils": this maxim should be continuously kept in mind to avoid grave mistakes in land improvement.

Land improvement of empty, or nearly empty, lands may encounter the considerable cultural problems involved in settling a population which has no previous experience with the lands which are opened up or reclaimed. A perhaps even more serious problem occurs when semi-nomadic people must become accustomed to more settled systems of land use. With regard to the technical as well as the economic problems of land use in these cases, the establishment of pilot projects is indispensable. These pilot projects may also be used for gradually schooling the future farmers and their families for their new way of life. The economic aspects of land reclamation within the project itself as well as on a national level have been

Table 110. Itemized list of investments in civil engineering and agricultural works in East Flevoland (50000 hectares, or 125000 acres) (Dutch Agr. Inv. Comm., 1960)

	Millions of guilders (prices first half of 1950)
Civil engineering works:	
Dike (incl. harbours, building excavations)	152.0
Pumping stations (buildings, machinery, pumps)	8.9
Other enclosing work	9.6
Canals, main drainage ditches and ditches dividing plots	34.0
Roads	32.0
Bridges, landing quays and miscellaneous works	9.4
Pumping dry and keeping polder drained	2.1
Maintenance	9.0
Interest during investment period	76.9
General expenses	8.0
Total	341.9
Agricultural works:	
Labor costs	70.6
Costs of plant	21.9
Material for tile drainage	9.6
Material for working land	10.3
Building of farms	73.9
Camp running expenses	3.6
Interest during investment period	20.2
General expenses	12.4
	222.5
less: Proceeds from cultivation during investment period	51.7
Total	170.8

studied for the East Flevoland Polder of the Zuyderzee Works in the Netherlands. Some data are given in Tables 110 to 112.

Land use improvement as well as land improvement may lead to a more intensive use of the best and of the most improved soils, but it may be accompanied by a much less intensive use of the poorer, or more erodible, soils. The original, rather indiscriminate, use of all soils in some parts of the U.S.A. for agriculture changed to a more differentiated use pattern after soil conservation was introduced. This change led to a much better adaptation of land use to the land resources. It must always be kept in mind that an appropriate land use is the best means for conserving the land in a good condition and sometimes even of improving the lands. Appropriate land use on poor soils often means very extensive use, with a very low level of production per acre and with concurrently low recurrent inputs. Improvements of lands and of land uses within a region therefore often mean an increasing differentiation rather than an equal distribution of "benefits" in a project.

This rule is valid in other cases, e.g. in irrigation projects, where the amount of irrigation water is nearly always an important limiting factor. In the best cases, the total amount may be almost sufficient, but its distribution over the seasons

Table 111. Anticipated annual average costs and proceeds of East Flevoland as a private undertaking (Dutch Agr. Inv. Comm., 1960)

	Prices first half 1950	Prices first half 1955
	guilders per hectare	
1. Costs of land and buildings:		
a) Interest on net invested capital	406[a]	451[a]
b) Maintenance and insurance of buildings	20	26
c) Drainage board rates	28	36
d) Depreciation on buildings	18	23
e) Land tax	11	11
	483	547
2. Other costs:		
a) Depreciation	47[b]	58[b]
b) Goods and services	368	501
c) Wages and social charges	334	470
d) Managers salaries	150	200
e) Interest[a]	42[c]	46[c]
f) Indirect taxes	6[d]	7[d]
	947	1282
Total working costs (production phase)	1430	1829
Net profit	− 154	− 285
Total proceeds (production phase)	1276	1544

[a] For 1950 and 1955 on the basis of an interest rate of 4% and $3\frac{1}{2}$% respectively.
[b] Plant.
[c] Plant 22, working Capital 20 and 24 respectively.
[d] Turnover tax.

still shows inadequacies. These inadequacies may be overcome to some extent by the construction of large reservoirs, but the expense is often not warranted for irrigation of the poorest soils. A better procedure is to apply enough irrigation water at appropriate times for adequate intervals to the best soils than to aim at equal distribution. Sometimes, the seasonal distribution of irrigation water favors certain soils and crops in summer and other soils with other crops in winter. This is typically so in Mesopotamia, where in winter the irrigation of wheat, barley and date palms on the loamy river levee soils takes precedence, whereas in summer the irrigation of rice and cotton on the heavy clay soils of the river basin areas is preferable. For the latter, however, only a limited quantity of irrigation water is available due to the low flow of the main rivers during this season.

A more extensive (low-input) land use may on certain lands be preferable because of environmental considerations. The application of chemical fertilizers as well as the harvesting of hay and forage at breeding seasons is often damaging to the vegetation of meadows and to the birds, which may be internationally important migratory species, breeding in the meadows. Other influences of intensive land use may, as indicated in Chapter 5, have deleterious effects through hydrological connections. The aspects of "visual pollution" and the requirements of open-air recreation were mentioned above.

Table 112. National economic yield and employment of East Flevoland (Dutch Agr. Inv. Comm., 1960)

Description	Unit	Eastern Flevoland prices first half of		Supplying and processing industries prices first half of		Total prices first half of	
		1950	1955	1950	1955	1950	1955
1. Average annual net profit	guilders per ha	−18	−268	40	79	22	−189
2. Total annual costs	guilders per ha	1430	1829	1699	2124	1838	2361
3. Ratio of profit to cost (1:2) × 100	%	−1.3	−14.7	2.4	3.7	1.2	−8.0
4. Capital invested	guilders per ha	11300	14400	1200	1600	12500	16000
5. Ratio of profit to capital invested (1:4) × 100	%	−0.2	−1.9	3.3	4.9	0.2	−1.2
6. Ratio of interest plus profit to capital invested × 100	%	3.8	1.6	7.3	8.4	4.2	2.3
7. Employment: a) temporary (in investment period)	1000 man-years	43		—		43	
b) permanent (in working period)	1000 man-years per annum	8		8		16	

7.3 New Land Utilization Types

Evolution of Land Use

Throughout the ages, land use in agriculture has developed and land utilization types have evolved which were better adapted to the resources and demand geometries of a particular region during a particular period (COON, 1962). Occasionally, the new land utilization types resulted from more or less clear decisions of policy. The establishment, during the reign of Charlemagne and his successors, of the three-year crop rotation system: (1) wheat or rye, (2) barley or oats, (3) fallow, may have been the result of such a decision by the Carolingian administration. The Dutch colonial administration in Indonesia, together with private interests, led to some well-defined land utilization types, for example plantations of sugar cane (mostly alternating with irrigated rice of the local population), and of perennial crops such as cinchona, tea, cocoa, coffee and Hevea. Colonial and private interests led also in other colonies, during the second half of the nineteenth century and the first half of the twentieth century, to decisions on the establishment of specific land utilization types. Somewhat similar decisions may perhaps be attributable to the large agricultural schemes of the Cistercian monks and of other religious orders during the Middle Ages in Europe (SLICHER VAN BATH, 1960).

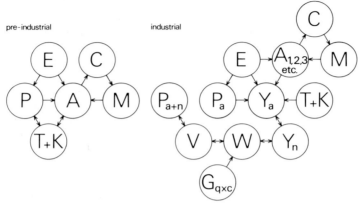

Fig. 7.12. Relation models of evolution in agricultural land use (after SLICHER VAN BATH, 1960)
E = environment, P = population, Pa = agrarian population, Pn = non-agrarian population,
A = agricultural area, A1, A2, A3 = agricultural areas in different parts of a region, C = cattle,
M = manure, T = technique (of agriculture), K = knowledge, Ya = agricultural production,
Yn = non-agricultural production, V = consumption, W = price, Gq = quantity of money,
Gc = rapidity of circulation of money

Very definite decisions on the establishment of new land utilization types
resulted from the Bolshevik Revolution in the Soviet Union, with the development of state farms (Sovchoz) and of collective farms (Kolchoz) in different
regions and with different cropping patterns, often supported by centralized tractor stations with machinery parks.

There exists, however, in agriculture an attitude that new land uses have to
evolve on their own and that a natural development of existing land utilization
types is preferable. The diagrams of this development—the widening relationships
and the concurrently growing possibilities—which occurred in European agriculture between the years 500 and 1850 AD, are shown in Fig. 7.12 (after SLICHER
VAN BATH, 1960). An abrupt change of land utilization types is undoubtedly a
revolutionary act which may carry grave social, economic and ecological consequences. The need for such changes must, however, often be faced today, in
developing regions as well as in highly industrialized areas. The original evaluation of land resources and of land utilization types must be done as objectively as
possible, also taking into consideration the socio-economic as well as the ecological consequences. Whether a particular change will then be acceptable in a particular region during a particular period, is a political decision. The decision should,
however, be made with an eye open to the alternative possibilities.

As was indicated in Chapter 3, land utilization types are characterized by:
(a) social characteristics, (b) infrastructural characteristics, (c) produce ("outputs"), (d) initial inputs (long-term capital), (e) annual production inputs, (f) labor
intensity, (g) source and intensity of farm power. These are used upon land resources which also have their various components and characteristics as shown in
Chapter 4 and 5. Their combination is effected by a systematic procedure of land
evaluation, in which the "relevant" and foreseeable" land utilization types for any
region during any period are used as one of the determinants.

Relevant and Foreseeable Land Utilization Types

The matter now hinges on which land utilization types may be considered relevant and foreseeable for a given area or project. The criteria for this are often influenced by a certain amount of political dogmatism which may lead both to extreme conservatism in the approach to the relevancy of land utilization types and to extreme considerations of changes, whereas an objective approach may lead to better solutions. Only some possibilities will be briefly discussed here, but they are certainly not meant to be comprehensive or exclusive. The "family farm" types are not discussed because they are sufficiently known, in their various forms, in most parts of the world; not because they might not be preferable and relevant in many cases. The family farm has many advantages, but it may not always be the best solution, or it may not be able to stand on its own in certain periods of developing land use. The following broad groups of land use systems are specifically mentioned here:

1. state farms,
2. large private farms,
3. large collective farms,
4. satellite systems of farms,
5. cooperative systems of farms,
6. landscape parks,
7. nature conservancy in agriculture.

Farming Enterprises

State farms are often indicated as a typical form of land use under a socialist system. In our times, the state farms of the Soviet Union are often cited as an example for various purposes. It is known, however, that a type of state farm existed under the Carolingian administration in Western Europe of the ninth century; these farms served as typical bases for the modernization of agriculture in these areas. State plantations for various crops existed under the Dutch colonial administration of Indonesia, and this system has been expanded, for various reasons, under the present regime. Some very extensive and extremely useful state farms have been created in Iraq since the revolution of 1958. Also in the Zuyderzee or "IJsselmeer"-polders of the Netherlands, a certain percentage of the area is, after the initial reclamation, reserved for the establishment of state farms.

The establishment of state farms is not so much a matter of principle as of expediency, as the state is a large investor who can often afford to start enterprises which are run, at least initially, on a low-profit basis, with the intention of developing new land utilization types. It can also afford to pay for high-quality personnel, and it is usually able to provide for this personnel the necessary safeguards with regard to the duration of their employment. Agronomists employed on state farms often also have the possibility of eventually transferring to the Civil Service of the country, e.g. in the Ministry of Agriculture. The state can therefore take risks and at the same time provide the knowledge and the technical methods needed for new approaches to land use. It can do this on farms of various sizes, often very large ones, of the order of 5000 to 10000 hectares of cultivated area per farm. These farms can be developed as independent projects, e.g. with regard to irrigation and drainage. The results provided by these farms may be beneficial for the country as a whole and have at the same time very good effects on the area surrounding a farm; the small farmers of the area may earn money as part-time workers on the state farm and at the same time learn modern methods of crop- and land-management.

The diffusion of practical knowledge by regular contact in actual practice is perhaps the best means of improving agricultural land use in many areas. State farms may be partly used as a basis for special experiments of all kinds, but this is not the essential purpose of such farms: they should as far as possible be run as "business enterprises", and experiments should be delegated to special experimen- tal farms which have a scientific rather than a business purpose and organization. State farms, as well as some of the other kinds of farms mentioned below, have a special advantage in regions where there is a scarcity of personnel who are able to apply the knowledge of modern agronomy on a practical scale; if one good practical agronomist and one or two young assistants with a good schooling in agronomy are put in charge of a state farm, they may produce considerable benefits for the country, and they may gain new experience by their continual applications of modern agronomy under the conditons of the region.

Large private farms are first and foremost business enterprises. They should not be confused with the ownership of large tracts of land, which may be run as one farm or as a whole group of small tenant farms. Large private farms may even be based not on large land ownership at all, but perhaps on special lease con- tracts. This situation existed for the growth of sugar cane in Java under the Dutch colonial administration, where the lands were leased from the population under strict government control, for some decades, with the carefully kept condition that after each sugar cane harvest the population had to have the lands restored to them for harvests of irrigated rice and other crops. The system had some very interesting influences on land use: (1) the sugar cane companies generally im- proved the land, particularly the irrigation and drainage systems, without cost to the population and to their great benefit, (2) sugar cane had to be grown as an "annual" crop with a duration of 18 months, after which the cane had to be completely uprooted to clear the lands for the rice cultivation, (3) the population could work as part-time laborers in the sugar cane fields, which had in general beneficial effects on the economy of the area, although some less beneficial side- effects also occurred. Similar kinds of "land use symbiosis" occasionally existed e.g. between tobacco plantations and farmers in Java (Indonesia), whereby the farmers themselves adopted tobacco as a cash crop, using seeds from, and to- bacco-curing facilities at, the plantations. The influence of a plantation crop in an area has also been experienced in Hevea rubber and in tea cultivation. Hevea rubber, which started in Indonesia as a crop of large plantations, after some decades was grown in small-to medium-sized enterprises on extremely large surface areas by the population of all of the more humid parts of Indonesia.

Large collective farms are, perhaps more than state farms, a feature of the Eastern European and some Asian socialist systems of land use. Like state farms, they have the advantage of the efficient use of scarce, high-quality personnel, but they do not have the other advantages of state farms to the same degree. Depending on socio-economic and political considerations, they may under certain circumstances prove to be efficient in the development of land use in relatively densely populated regions. In those cases where the separate institutionalization of water control in water districts, soil conservation districts, irrigation districts or polders, is not deemed feasible, the organization of land use in collective farms of some kinds may provide an applicable solution to the serious problems of regular and efficient management and maintenance of irrigation and drainage works and of structures for soil conservation. The collective operation of large machinery may also often prove to be an advantage. In some areas, the crop pattern may also be advantageously adapted to land conditions, because in collective farms, the choice of crops may be at least partly independent of the needs of the individual family.

Satellite systems of farms, with a rather large farm, often with processing facilities, as the central part of the system, have been developed from the experience that improvement of land use spreads from the larger, more modern, farms in a region towards the smaller enterprises in the same area. The central farm may be privately run or owned by some public or collective institution. The advantages are the same as those cited for the state farms, but in addition a purposely directed effort is made to bring the surrounding family farms within the orbit of development. In those cases where a central processing plant is indispensable, e.g. in tea growing, the system has had good results.

Cooperative systems of private farms develop in those cases, as in the Netherlands, where technical and economic developments in agriculture make the original family farm less feasible and where private ownership, or long term leases, of farms are firmly established within the social system. This development may, within one generation, lead to the establishment of limited companies for land use as pure business enterprises. In so far as these companies can be maintained in comparison with the feasibility of non-agricultural enterprises, this development may be beneficial for agricultural land use. Similar systems may, under certain conditions, be used in those areas where ecological values are of particular interest, e.g. in landscape parks. The combination of extensive agriculture with suitable maintenance of recreation values may be achieved, if carefully controlled, by profit companies, although in many cases the establishment of non-profit organizations may be preferable.

Landscape Parks and Nature Conservation

Interest in landscape parks is increasing in all industrialized regions of the world, the aim of these parks being to conserve the visual attractions of a combination of "old-fashioned" agriculture with semi-natural vegetation types and with the remnants of old country estates. Often the emphasis is put on the visual aspects, but the true ecological aspects, the conservation of natural variability of the ecosystems, should be seen at least as an equally important purpose. The general intention is to conserve a system of agriculture which as such is becoming less feasible, by providing the farmers with certain subsidies, including a "negative rent" for tenant farmers. A good case may be made for landscape parks in those areas in which otherwise a complete organization for nature conservancy, with all its personnel and other costs would have to be established. Various combinations with cooperative or public non-profit systems appear possible.

Nature conservancy in agriculture is becoming more feasible in all cases where land use shows tendencies towards more extensive systems with lower inputs per surface area. Experience shows that in these cases farmers are often willing, under the guidance of nature conservancy institutions, to sign contracts in which their practices are further regulated for the maintenance of certain kinds of vegetations or of certain species of animals, e.g. migratory birds. A combined land utilization type for agriculture and nature conservation is possible therefore, under certain land conditions and other circumstances.

The systems of land use mentioned above have mainly been related to the institutional aspects of land use. Within this context very different land utilization types are often possible in relation to crop pattern and other aspects. They depend largely on land conditions and market conditions as well as on the availability of "non-land" resources. The demand for higher feasibility of agriculture leading to higher standards of living for the farming populations, combined with the need for careful consideration of ecological conditions and hazards, will lead to a very variegated development of land use in the near future. A careful local study of land utilization types as well as of land resources and land conditions, culminating in a well-balanced land evaluation, will have to guide the steps of all concerned.

7.4 Economic and Ecological Considerations

Social and Economic Aspects

Land use planning, both in developing regions and in industrialized areas, has until recently often been seen primarily as an economic venture with often rather vaguely expressed social considerations. On the other hand, social considerations played a primary role in attempts to uplift backward areas, while economic principles, which in general are firmly based upon the suitability of land conditions for improvement, were neglected. During the last decade, the combination of economic and social aspects of land development and their interrelationships with land resources and land conditions, have become well established. Projects from many different parts of the world, ranging from Ireland to the Far East and to Latin America demonstrate this clearly (RYAN et al., 1969; TOSI in Integrated Surveys, 1966; VAN DUSSELDORP in Integrated Surveys, 1966; VAN DUSSELDORP, 1971).

The Ecological Approach

During the last few years a third aspect, the ecological approach, has gained wide attention. In many past projects of land development also, some ecological considerations were seriously studied and often integrated into land-use planning, i.e. those considerations which clearly involved the maintenance of sustained yields and which were related to soil conservation and to the conservation of suitable vegetation types in forests and in pastoral areas. Today, however, ecology encompasses a much wider scope, which involves may different area of interest. Briefly summarized, these include:

(a) The disturbance of human "ways of life" by different forms of pollution, including the incidence of noise and the disturbance of different ecosystems; this is often indicated as "environmental hygiene".

(b) The decreasing attractiveness of daily life, particularly in urban areas, sometimes indicated as the "spatial environment".

(c) The predictable exhaustion of some natural resources, e.g. fossil fuels and some other resources termed the "limits to growth" or "Club of Rome" approach.

(d) The destruction of natural or semi-natural ecosystems, which may be called the "biological environment".

(e) The existence of unsatisfactory structures in society, leading to "estrangement" between human beings and their societal and other environments, which were noted by Karl Marx during the industrial revolution of the nineteenth century and are perhaps even more valid today, and which may be indicated as the "societal environment".

(f) The tensions between developing human societies and the legislative and administrative structures and institutions which have to cope with the changes in society, to be indicated as the "governmental environment".

These six different kinds of environmental problems are often not clearly distinguishable. They are related, at least to some extent, to different levels of a given society and to different societies with different environmental conditions. It is understandable, and in some cases probably warranted, that in developing countries some increase in pollution and in the destruction of ecosystems will be gladly accepted if it speeds up development. It is also understandable that in an industrialized society with a high standard of living, the requirements of young industrial workers differ considerably from those of young intellectuals and students. There is also a difference between these different ecological approaches in their relations to agricultural and related land uses.

Agricultural land use certainly involves some aspects of pollution (environmental hygiene), and also of the possibility of exhaustion of fossil fuels and of other resources ("Club of Rome") and of the destruction of several kinds of ecosystems. It encompasses, at least in urbanized and industrialized regions, the problems of the "spatial environment", in so far as these enhance the demand for open-air recreation in rural areas. These four approaches to the environment are of importance in all parts of the world, although the decisions taken in a given region at a given time may be quite different.

Decisions in Land Development

Some ways in which these decisions may be made are shown in Fig. 7.13.

In this three-dimensional diagram, the three main contributions to decision making for developments in land use are indicated: economic conditions, social and related (e.g. institutional) conditions and ecological conditions. Each of these lies on one of the three axes of the system. If only one of the three is thought to be of interest, the 100% point for the relevant one is used, and in this point a new plane may be constructed which then is not related to the other conditions but to

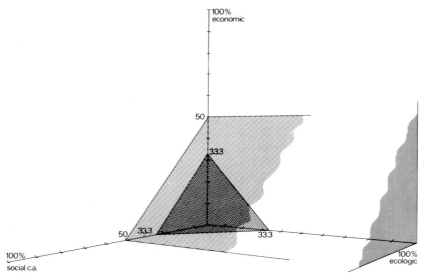

Fig. 7.13. Diagram for considering economic, ecological and social aspects in planning and in related land evaluation

subconditions of the relevant main point; this possibility is indicated at the "100% ecological" point. If all three main conditions are considered to be of equal interest, the plane through the 33.3% points of all three is relevant, and all decisions will have to be made in this plane. Several other principal decisions are possible, e.g. 50% economic and 50% social, as parameters of the ecological conditions; a plane for this example is also indicated. Once the decision in principle has been made as to which basic plane will be used for a given project or area, the relations within the plane can be developed according to the results of the investigations within the area, including the land utilization types which then become relevant.

It is thought that this graph may aid the decision-making process to proceed in a more logical manner than is often used, and it may also be used to clarify the presentation of the available research data and necessary estimates and to prepare materials for alternative solutions.

Problems in land development have grown so much, and their complicated nature is so much better unterstood than some years ago, that the presentation of alternative solutions on the basis of land resources, land conditions and land evaluation in general provides the only practicable approach to decision-making. The presentation of alternative land utilization types and their economic, social and ecological implications is an essential part of this approach. Decisions have to be made by administrators and by legislative bodies, all consisting of persons with only a limited knowledge of the fields of expertise involved. The basic data and the consequences of the decisions should therefore be presented as clear alternatives, and if the decision-making bodies do not find the appropriate answers to their problems, more alternatives should be prepared wherever possible.

Ecology and Development

The relations between land development and ecology have recently been the subject of some general discussions and of several project investigations. The project investigations (BERTHELOT, 1970; WORTHINGTON, 1970) are reports of the situation of a lake in Venezuela and of the general position of ecology and conservation in Jamaica, respectively. It is clear from these reports that also in developing countries, detailed investigations of ecological problems as well as more general inventories of the ecologic and conservation aspects in conjunction with land development are very necessary; they provide useful additions to the more generally accepted investigations of land resources for agricultural land use. The increasing use of water for domestic and industrial uses may cause serious deterioration of lacustrine environments. In addition there is a need in all developing countries for ecological studies to be carried out as an integral part of the assessment of development programs and land-use planning. There is also a need in each country for conservation of appropriate areas as national parks or nature reserves for recreational and scientific purposes. Trained ecologists may therefore play an essential role in development teams of all kinds.

The "Founex Report" (Report, 1971), as it is generally called, is one of the many preparatory documents for the U.N. Conference on the Human Environment, which was held in Stockholm, Sweden in the summer of 1972. Some of the maxims of this report were clearly reflected in the conclusions of this conference. The report itself states that the current concern with environmental issues has emerged from the problems experienced by the industrially advanced countries, but that the developing countries have an obvious and vital stake in these issues to the extent of their impact on the global environment and on the relation between developing countries and industrialized countries. Environmental problems, as is stated in the report, tend, however, to accompany the process of development and are in fact beginning to emerge with increasing severity in the societies of developing countries. The major environmental problems of developing countries are, however, those which reflect urban and rural poverty and the lack of societal development. Not merely "the quality of life", but life itself is endangered by poor water, housing, sanitation and nutrition and by sickness and disease as well as natural disasters. Many of these problems can be overcome by development itself, which remains, therefore, the overriding task in the developing regions of the world.

New dimensions must be added to the development concept itself; social and cultural goals particularly should receive more emphasis, because high rates of economic growth, necessary and essential as they are, do not themselves guarantee the easing of urgent social and human problems. "To the extent that these objectives support or reinforce economic growth—and it can be shown that some of them do—their place in the pattern of priorities would be more easily established. But where conflicts are involved, particularly of a short or medium term, more difficult choices would have to be made regarding the "trade-off" between these and the narrower growth objectives. These choices can only be made by the countries themselves in the light of their situations and development strategies and cannot be determined by any established rules a priori".

Several ecological problems are likely to emerge along with the process of development. The processes of agricultural growth and transformation, for example, involve the construction of reservoirs and irrigation systems, the clearing of forests, the use of fertilizers and pesticides and the establishment of new communities. Industrialization results in the release of pollutants and acts on the environment in a number of ways. The entire economic infrastructure of transport and communications has consequences for the ecological system. Urbanization, already an urgent problem in many developing countries, will lead to some of their cities experiencing problems common to those of the industrialized countries. Unless resolute action is taken, these problems will assume formidable dimensions in the decades ahead; corrective action is therefore urgently needed. The formulation of mimimum environmental standards may be one of a series of useful procedures in this process. International economic relations may also have to be readjusted for this purpose. Various ecological considerations should be included in the guidelines for project appraisal. Different kinds of institutional arrangements will be required for effecting these various objectives.

Some of these objectives have been further elaborated in a recent symposium under the aegis of UNESCO (Integrated Surveys, 1972). The matters mentioned therein were discussed in Chapters 5 and 6. The importance of systematic approaches to environmental planning, decision-making and implementation will be stressed here. Particular attention is also paid to the impact of urbanization in the developing countries, taking into account that the developing countries "are now largely responsible for the rapid urbanization of the world as a whole" (McLOUGHLIN in Integrated Surveys, 1972). Education and training for urban and environmental management will have to have a primacy in providing the solutions in all countries.

The "impact of urbanization on man's environment" was the special subject of an earlier symposium sponsored by the United Nations (Symposium Environment, 1970). How can the structures of government and society in the poorer nations survive and withstand the shock of human tide that, according to the report of this symposium, will continue to mount throughout the next three decades? It is estimated that the urban population will increase fivefold over the next generation. Taking into account that the urban facilities are already overloaded and that the environment is being dangerously polluted, each increment of urban growth will lead to a further deterioration of the environment. Apart from the urgent need for better planning and implementation of urban development programs, the solution lies largely in a sound approach to the problems of the rural areas. Increased agricultural production is necessary in all developing countries; at the same time, the prevention of health risks may be one of the important aspects for development. Therefore, development of land use is a necessity in the advancement, not only of agriculture, but of human society as a whole. Urban and rural land uses are interrelated, and their combined study in the decades ahead may be the only means of arriving at suitable solutions for development and economic growth as well as for the social and environmental problems which are facing the whole world of today.

Integrated Rural Development

Industrialized countries are, to a much greater extent than developing countries, being faced with "the limits to growth" which undoubtedly exist, perhaps on a world scale, but certainly in many regions. As was indicated previously (Chapter 5), the interrelationships between urban and rural land uses are becoming more and more important every year. In the Upper Silezian Industrial District, according to PASZINSKY (1958), industrial air pollution has caused a weakening of the solar radiation by 36% of the solar constant. The deposited pollution materials, especially sulphur and zinc, may at some times reach an order of magnitude of 100 grams per square meter per day. Fruit trees and other crops, as well as the soil itself, are seriously affected by this. Although this case is clearly an extreme one, the tendency reflected by these figures is well recognized today in most industrialized countries. As a result, the urban populations are increasingly aware of, as well as in need of, open-air recreation in unpolluted rural areas. But agricultural land use must develop into feasible systems. Integrated rural development is therefore definitely necessary (MOSHER, 1972).

Depending on the objectives desired, there exist various types of integrated rural development programs, such as those geared to an increase in agricultural production or in agricultural efficiency, or wholly or partly, to an increase in various satisfactions in rural living and urban recreation. The latter may be either economic or strictly non-economic in their approach. Integrated rural development in developing regions does not basically differ from that in industrial areas. It is the quantitative aspects which differ widely, and not only if very underdeveloped areas and highly industrialized areas are compared. Each case has to be judged with respect to its own basic geometries and to the main social and political aims put forward by the responsible institutions. The particular land resources and the special demand geometry of an area have to be very carefully considered. For each tract of land, decisions have to be made as to its future use or non-use in agricultural and other land utilization types.

Non-Use of Land

A decision "not to use a certain tract of land" is often more difficult to make than any other decision with respect to land use. Farmers and agronomists as well as land reclamation engineers, do not like to have certain tracts of land "lie waste". Throughout the ages, land has been "lying waste" in all parts of the world. This situation was, however, often not due to any special decision, but to the fact that the available technology was not sufficiently applicable to a particular kind of land resource. At the present stage of technological development, nearly all lands can be used if sufficient inputs are invested in their improvement and use. In some cases, the establishment of a development project or program, although technically possible, is clearly not economically feasible. In a still rarer number of cases, the execution of a project cannot be carried out because of too great technical obstacles.

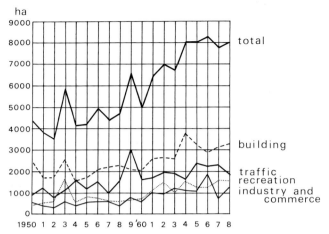

Fig. 7.14. Increase of non-agricultural land use in the Netherlands 1950–1968 (PRILLEVITZ, 1969)

In most cases, however, we are dealing with land resources of moderate suitabilities and with projects or programs which have advantages as well as disadvantages. To decide under such conditions how to use the land is always a problem, as has been discussed previously. To decide that a certain tract of land should *not* be used is then often a much more difficult decision. In order to make this decision, the whole range of economic, social and ecological criteria should be considered. The first priority goes to those criteria which relate to the economic feasibility and social acceptability of the way of life for the farmers which will result from the program. It is a simple matter of social ethics that the people whose entire life is tied to the land and who are completely dependent upon its production, should be considered with the highest priority. It will, however, often be seen that it is also to the advantage of the farmers to leave certain lands unused, since agricultural land use on lands which are poorly suited for ecological reasons is usually not very rewarding to the farmer.

It is even more difficult to take lands out of use which have already been used for some generations, than to leave lands out of use which have not been previously used or which were only very occasionally used. The decision by the late HUGH H. BENNETT and his co-workers in the early 1930's to establish a Class-VIII of lands which should not be used at all but be left to wildlife, was a very courageous one, but this decision has today to be faced by many people and in many countries, also for reasons which have little to do with soil conservation. On a national scale, it is more urgent in industrialized countries than in developing regions. In the latter, agricultural land use as a whole still has to expand, whereas in the former, agricultural land use has to contract, to meet both the economic conditions and the ecological circumstances.

The establishment of "land balance-sheets" in land use for national and regional purposes may be one of the best means for clarifying the situation at a given moment and for guiding the future developments of land use. PRILLEVITZ

Table 113. Soil balance sheet in hectares of the changes in agricultural land use in the Netherlands, 1963–1968 (PRILLEVITZ, 1969)

	1963	1964	1965	1966	1967	1968
Increase:						
Polders	569	6 583	2 716	4 917	2 007	2 285
Reclamation of waste land	135	259	374	264	246	216
Other causes	56	304	111	67	6 056	202
Total	761	7 146	3 201	5 249	8 309	2 703
Decrease:						
Non-agric. l. u.	3 505	4 040	4 375	3 701	3 530	3 408
Building	4 878	3 981	5 810	4 479	3 573	4 302
Other causes	177	238	714	626	4 474	227
Total	8 561	8 259	10 898	8 806	11 577	7 937
Saldo	− 7 800	− 1 113	− 7 697	− 3 557	− 3 268	− 5 234

(1969) did this for the Netherlands in order to obtain a better knowledge of all kinds of land use for the application of decisions within the framework of the European Community and for the planning of land use in the newly reclaimed polders. In Tables 113–115 the land balance sheet for agricultural land use and the increase for the various kinds of non-agricultural land uses during a number of years are given. The latter is also indicated in Fig. 7.14.

In relation to the general land balance sheets, specific balance sheets reflecting land conditions may be given; these are of particular use for making decisions on the future "non-use" of lands in agriculture. An example of this, reflecting the areas with specific limitations for "rational dairy farming", one of the predominant land utilization types in the Netherlands, is given (Table 115); in this table the lands are specified per province, the main administrative units of the country. Data have been provided from the Soil Map of the Netherlands, scale 1:200000. Finally, a decision is suggested that between 1970 and 1980 a total surface area of 160000 hectares should be taken out of agricultural land use in the Netherlands. This surface area could be divided among different non-agricultural uses as follows (PRILLEVITZ, 1969):

1. Nature conservation, for increase of nature reserves — 60000 hectares

2. Landscape reserves or landscape monuments — 10000 hectares

3. Increase of water surface for recreation, by "de-poldering" — 5000 hectares

4. Holiday-bungalow complexes — 30000 hectares

5. Afforestation for landscaping, recreation and wood production — 55000 hectares

This is only a prognosis, but some elements of this are being realized during this period.

Table 114. Increases of non-agricultural land uses in the Netherlands, 1963–1967, in hectares (PRILLEVITZ, 1969)

	1963	1964	1965	1966	1967
Taken in use for					
Building	2639	3738	3256	2912	3159
Industry and commerce	1201	1119	1081	1864	765
Recreation	1007	1533	1294	1275	1568
Traffic	1914	1669	2410	2253	2307
Total	6761	8059	8041	8304	7799
Of which taken from:					
Agric. lands	3505	4040	4375	3701	3530
Forests	203	254	259	162	271
Waste lands	77	245	156	492	316
Reserve of building lands	2825	3405	2959	3775	3567
Other lands	151	115	292	174	115
Total	6761	8059	8041	8304	7799

Table 115. Surface areas (hectares) in the Netherlands of lands with limitations for "rational dairy farming", per province and kind of lands (PRILLEVITZ, 1969)

Provinces	Gro-ningen	Fries-land	Drente	Over-ijssel	Gelder-land	Utrecht	N-Hol-land	Z-Hol-land	Zeeland	N-Brabant	Lim-burg	Total
Categories of lands:												
a) Dry and sandy	—	16100	6100	32100	121500	20600	23900	7800	5100	38000	30400	301600
b) Weak and peaty	21050	34260	23480	26450	4850	21100	48330	59300	100	7460	1550	247930
c) Very poorly drained	6900	7600	37000	33300	24150	2320	2140	4920	2000	17700	13750	151780
Total	27950	57960	66580	91850	150500	44020	74370	72020	7200	63160	45700	701310

Note: 1% of surface area of the Netherlands is approx 30000 hectares.

Nature Conservation

The reservation of lands for nature conservation merits a brief discussion. One approach to this is to let those lands which "belong to Class VIII" of the U.S. Soil Conservation Service simply revert to wild lands because of their low productivity and often generally low suitability for agricultural land use. There is, however, a more positive approach possible. Especially in industrialized areas, at least some room should be reserved for the maintenance and conservation of the remnants of natural and semi-natural ecosystems. These need not be large areas, at least if their conservation can be assured on small surface areas without undue interference from other land uses in their proximity (pollution of air and water, pesticides). The importance of this type of conservation lies in its scientific importance as well as in the wish to conserve at least some of the potential natural variability; the latter is done in order to prevent destruction of values which may prove to be of great importance to future generations. The reserving of rest and feed areas for migratory birds in industrialized areas is often of the greatest importance for the conservation of ecological conditions in far-away regions: it is known that some of the migratory birds passing annually through the Netherlands form the total bird population of certain parts of Northern Siberia. Sometimes, these birds start to use the newly constructed dikes and polders in preference to some of their old resting and feeding grounds. As a rule, however, it is very easy to destroy a natural or semi-natural ecosystem but it is nearly impossible to establish a similar one in a period of duration shorter than some centuries.

The choice of areas for nature conservation should also involve the consideration of the existence of natural variability of the existing plant and animal communities as well as of their habitats. These are generally found in "gradient situations" i.e. in those zones where ecological conditions of soil, water and relief, change within short distances. Gradient situations may also arise from variations caused by human land use. They are characterized by a very complicated ecological pattern and by a great stability of the internal ecological processes (VAN LEEUWEN, 1966). These situations occur mainly in border areas of the more homogeneous surfaces in which agricultural land use is situated. There need not, therefore, be competition between agricultural land use and nature conservation. Agricultural land use is best carried out on rather large homogeneous surfaces. These surfaces usually alternate with border zones which are appropriate for nature conservation because of their existing or potential natural variability. Some impression of this situation, for the Netherlands, can be obtained from Fig.7.15 (after "Tweede Nota", 1966). The diversity of biological communities can, therefore, be conserved in conjunction with, rather than in competition with, agricultural land use. One aspect is of great importance: that technology be used with discretion and that wherever necessary or warranted it be used to improve those areas which have a natural suitability for agricultural land use, rather than to create homogeneous lands in those zones where a biological diversity is required and indicated by the natural land conditions. As was indicated previously, this is not only the best choice for ecology, but it is the most feasible choice from the standpoint of economy (see e.g. WESTHOFF, 1970).

Fig. 7.15. Sketch map of the Netherlands showing the main border-zones with gradient situations of national importance: black lines and coastal dune areas (TWEEDE NOTA, 1966)
1 = Dune areas with many variable border zones
2 = Narrow border zones with ecological gradients
3 = Lower courses of the main rivers with transitions between fresh and salt waters and with increasing tidal influences
4 = Areas with relatively many transitions between fresh water and salt or brackish water influences
5 = Parts of the country with many plant species

In many cases, the design of new plans for rural and urban landscapes can be guided by similar considerations. Gradient situations in land areas may be detected by land resources surveys, even in those situations where the biological diversity has been destroyed by previous land use. By using these, in so far as warranted by the basic geometries described above, of which the human demand geometry is a crucial one, it may be possible to "design with nature" (McHARG, 1969) and to create in this manner new land uses which are economically feasible, ecologically warrantable and socially acceptable, as well as pleasing to the eye. In industrialized areas and their adjoining rural districts, the latter is of increasing importance. The new discipline of "landscape building" is a natural counterpart to nature conservation as well as to modern agricultural land use.

Nature conservation as well as landscape building has its own particular kinds of land utilization types. In a nature reserve surrounded by other land uses, where the natural succession of plant and animal communities has to be conserved, some measures must be taken to prevent undue outside influences. In many cases, however, the object is to conserve a particular step in a succession, e.g. heath areas on the sandy soils of northwestern Europe. These heath areas are the result of the old agricultural land utilization types which included the grazing of sheep on the moors. Now that the sheep have gone, the natural succession means an invasion by pine trees and other plants on these moors. Their conservation means an entire complex of management measures, including the cutting or otherwise removing of the young trees. The conservation of bird reserves in meadows usually can only be carried out by some kind of agricultural land use. Nature conservation which is accompanied by recreation, often possible and even useful, also necessitates definite combinations of inputs and management practices and therefore is also recognizable as a whole series of non-agricultural land utilization types. Various "management models" have been constructed for the various kinds of reserves, depending on their origin, their outside influences and inside requirements and on the rapidity with which the natural biological succession tends to develop (WESTHOFF, 1973).

Land Use in Developing Agriculture

Where does land use lead in developing agriculture? Certainly to a better solution of the world food problem and to a better satisfaction of the other legitimate demands of human beings in all parts of the world. These demands, as well as the land conditions and the land utilization types, show great variations. Development of land use therefore must itself be varied to meet the demands under the varying natural and social conditions. Even modern mechanized systems of agriculture, if transferred to other parts of the world, will have to be modified and adapted. With this, a natural variability also has to develop, or be conserved in agriculture itself. In addition, the preservation of mankind requires that a great biological variation be conserved and even, in many lands, developed. The thought that we shall strive, not for a homogenized technological world, but for a very variegated agricultural, social and biological world, in which economy and technology have their important place as essential tools, is indeed very fascinating and warrants the application of our knowledge and science.

References

AANDAHL, A. R.: Soil survey interpretation—theory and purpose. Soil Sci. Soc. Am. Proc. **21**, 152–154 (1957).

AANDAHL, A. R. et al.: Productivity of soils in the North central region of the United States. Agr. Exp. Stal. Bull. 710, University of Illinois, Urbana, IL. (1965).

ABMEIJER, W., CAMPBELL, H. V.: Soil survey of Shawnee county. Kansas. Soil Conserv. Service, U.S. Dept. Agric., Washington (D.C.) (1970).

ADDISON, H.: Land, water, and food. London: Chapman & Hall 1961.

ALBERTZ, J.: Sehen und Wahrnehmen bei der Luftbildinterpretation. Bildmessung und Luftbildwesen **38**, 25–34 (1970).

AL-JAWAD, S. B. et al.: Possible communication between ground water in the Dibdibba Sandstone aquifer of the Zubair area and adjoining aquifers. Techn. Rep. No. **9**, UNSF/UNESCO, Inst. Appl. Res. Nat. Resources, Baghdad (1970).

AL-JAWAD, S. B. et al.: On the delimitation of ground water recharge areas around Berjesiyah. Techn. Rep. No. **12** UNSF/UNESCO, Inst. Appl. Res. Nat. Resources, Baghdad, Iraq (1970).

An Forais Taluntais: West Donegal survey. Dublin: An Forais Taluntais 1969.

A Priority Scheme for Dutch land consolidation projects. Publ. **6**, Intern. Inst. Land-reclamation and Improvement Wageningen: ILRI 1960.

ARENS, R., KRÄMER, F., LANGNER, CH.: Über die Bodenstruktur, den Wasserhaushalt und die Ertragsfähigkeit von Pseudogleyen und gleyartigen Braunerden. Z. Acker-Pflanzenbau **107**, 67–98 (1958).

ASHRAF ALI, M., BRINKMAN, R., RAFIQ, CH. M.: Economics of water use in the irrigated plains of West Pakistan. Eng. News Quant. W. Patr. Eng. Congr. **17**, 7–23 (1972).

ATUJAH, E.: The Arabs. Beirut: Lebanon Bookshop 1968.

BAEYENS, L. et al.: Orienterend onderzoek over de produktiviteit van Cox's Orange Pippin op E. M. Type IX op verschillende bodems. Agricultura **12**, 263–340 (1964).

BALL, A. G., HEADY, E. O., BAUMANN, R. V.: Economic evaluation of the use of soil conservation and improvement practices. U.S. Dept. Agr. Techn. Bull. 1162, Washington (1957).

BARR, D. J., MILES, R. D.: SLAR imagery and site selection. Photogramm. Eng. **36**, 1155–1170 (1970).

BARTELLI, L. J. et al.: Soil surveys and land use planning. Soil Sci. Soc. Am. (1966).

BASTUSCHEK, C. P.: Ground temperature and thermal infrared. Photogramm. Eng. **36**, 1064–1072 (1970).

BAZILEVICH, N, I., PANKOVA, YE. I.: Tentative classification of soils by salinity. Soviet. Soil Sci. 1477–1487 (1969).

BEEK, K. J., BENNEMA, J.: Land evaluation for agricultural land use planning, an ecological methodology. Mimeograph, Afd. Bodemkunde and Geologie. Wageningen: Landbouwhogeschool 1972.

BEEK, K. J., BENNEMA, J.: Evaluacion de tierras para la planificacion del uso rural — un metodo ecologico. Boletin Latinamericano sobre fomento de tierras y aquas, 3, Oficina Regional FAO, Santiago de Chile (1973).

BEEK, M. A.: Atlas of Mesopotamia. London/Edinburgh: Nelson 1962.

BENNETT, H. H.: Soil conservation. New York: McGraw Hill 1939.

BERTHELOT, R.: Venezuela, examen des perturbations écologiques et hydrologiques du Bassin du Lac Valencia. Paris: UNESCO 1970.

BIJKERK, C., LINDHORST, TH. J., VAN WIJK, C.: Cultuurtechnische inventarisatie van Nederland. I.C.W. Wageningen, Mixed reprints 102. Tijdschr. Kon. Ned. Heidemij **81**, 255–292.

Summ.: A method of machine processed survey of the division of rural areas, as practiced in the Netherlands (1970).

BIRSE, E. L., DRY, F. T.: Assessment of climatic conditions in Scotland. 1. Based on accumulated temperature and potential water deficit. Aberdeen: Soil Survey of Scotland 1970.

BIRSE, E. L., ROBERTSON, L.: Assessment of climatic conditions in Scotland. 2. Based on exposure and accumulated frost. Aberdeen: Soil Survey of Scotland 1970.

BISWAS, A. K., SANYAL, D. K.: Rainfall and irrigation. Part I: In: Two and a bud, Vol. 2, Tocklai Exp. Sta., Tea Research Assoc., Jorhat (India), 12–19 (1971).

BLEVINS, R. L.: No-tillage-suitability of Kentucky soils. In: Agronomy notes, Vol. 3, No. 2. Dept. of Agronomy. Lexington: Univ. of Kentucky 1970.

BLEVINS, R. L. et al.: Influence of no-tillage on soil moisture. Agronom. J. **63**, 593–596 (1971).

BOERMA, A. H.: De plaats van de landbouw in het Tweede Ontwikkelingsdecennium. Landbouwk. Tijdschr. **81**, 304–310 (1969).

BOUMA, J.: Evaluation of the field percolation test and an alternative procedure to test soil potential for disposal of septic tank effluent. Soil Sci. Soc. Am. Proc. **35**, 871–875 (1971).

BOUMA, J. et al.: Soil absorption of septic tank effluent, a field study of some major soils in Wisconsin. Inform. Circ. **20**. Madison (Wisc.): Univ. of Wisconsin-Extension 1972.

BRADFORD, J.: Ancient landscapes, studies in field archeology. London: Bell Sons 1957.

BRADY, N. C.: The nature and properties of soils, 8th Ed. New York: MacMillan, 1974.

BRINKMAN, R., SMYTH, A. J. (Ed.): Land evaluation for rural purposes. Publ. **17**, Wageningen: Intern. Inst. Land Reclam. and Improvement (ILRI) 1973.

BROEKHUIZEN, S. et al.: Agroecological atlas of cereal growing in Europe. Amsterdam/PUDOC, Wageningen: Elsevier 1969.

BROWN, L. H.: Problems of wildlife in the grazing areas of Africa. In: Seminar, 1967. Integrated Surveys, Publ. S. **21**, Delft. [In: Proceedings 2nd Intern. Seminar Integr. Surveys. Integr. Surveys of Natural Grazing Areas (1967)].

BUCKMAN, H. O., BRADY, N. C.: The nature and properties of soils, 7th ed. London: Macmillan, 1969.

Bureau of Reclamation: Manual, Vol. V. Irrigated land use: Part 2: Land classification. Denver, Colorado: U.S. Dept. Interior 1953.

Bureau of Reclamation: Instructions for the conduct of feasibility grade land classification surveys of the Lam Nam Oon project, Thailand. U.S.B.R. Engin. and Res. Cent. Denver, Colorado: U.S. Dept. Interior 1967.

BURINGH, P.: Soils and soil condition in Iraq. Baghdad: Min. of Agriculture 1960.

BUIJCKX, E. J. E., FRANKART, R., LIBEN, L.: Interprétation de photos aériennes pour la délimitation des biotopes de Glossina Morsitans Westw. au Bugesera (Rwanda). ITC Publications B **40**, Delft (1966).

CALHOUN, J. W., WOOD, G. J.: Soil survey of Ben hill and Irwin counties, Georgia. Soil Conserv. Service. Washington (D.C.): U.S. Dept. Agric. 1969.

CAPPER, P. L., CASSIE, W. F., GEDDES, J. D.: Problems in engineering soils. London: Spon Ltd. 1971.

CARDOSO, J. V. DE CARVALHO: The soil survey of Portugal and its main applications. Geneva: U.N. Nat. Res. Conf. 1963.

CARSON, M. A., KIRKBY, M. J.: Hillslope form and process. Cambridge: University Press 1972.

CASTRI, F. DI, MOONEY, H. A. et al.: Mediterranean type ecosystems. Ecological Studies **7**. Berlin-Heidelberg-New York: Springer 1973.

CHAMPROUX, J. P.: Productivité et potentialité des sols-préliminaires à l'aménagement, application aux régions naturelles du Mayaga Bugesera, République du Rwanda. Louvain: Thesis Univ. Cathol. 1967.

CHEVALLIER, R.: Panorama des applications de la photographie aérienne. Annales: economies, sociétés, civilisations, No. 4, pp. 677–698. Paris: Colin 1963.

CHEVALLIER, R.: Les applications de la photographie aérienne aux problèmes agraires. Etudes rurales 13-4, pp. 120–124. Paris: Ecole Pratique des Hautes Etudes 1964.

CHEVALLIER, R., BURGER, A.: Les multiples applications de la photo-interprétation à l'urbanisme. Bull. Soc. Franc. Photogramm. **23**, 33–55 (1966).

CHORLEY, R. J., KENNEDY, B. A.: Physical geography, a systems approach. London: Prentice Hall 1971.

COLWELL,R.N.: Potential uses of satellite photography for natural resources surveys, pp. 34–38. In: Peaceful uses of photo-reconnaissance satellites. Washington (D.C.): Hoover Inst. War, Revel. Peace 1965.

COLWELL,R.N. et al.: Manual of photographic interpretation. Washington (D.C.): American Soc. of Photogrammetry 1960.

CONKLIN,H.E.: The cornell system of economic land classification. Author's reprint (1957).

COON,C.S.: The history of man. London: Penguin Books 1962.

DAN,J., YAALON,D.H., KOYUMDJISKY,H.: Catenary relationships in Israel. 1. The Netanya catena on coastal dunes of the Sharon. Geoderma **2**, 95–120 (1968).

DAN,J. et al.: The soil association map of Israel. Israel J. Earth Sci. **21**, 29–49 (1972).

DE BOER,TH,A.: Der Zusammenhang zwischen Grünlandvegetation und Bodeneinheiten. Bericht Int. Symp. Pflanzensoc.-Bodenk., Stolzenau/Weser, pp. 74–82. Angewandte Pflanzensoziologie, Heft **15**, Stolzenau/Weser (1958).

DEE,N. et al.: Final report on environmental evaluation systems for water resource planning. Columbus, Ohio: Bureau of Reclamation, U.S. Dept. Interior 1972.

DEE,N. et al.: An environmental evaluation for water resource planning. Water resources research **9**, 523–535 (1973).

DE FORGES,J.M.: Research on the utilization of saline water for irrigation in Tunisia. In: Natural resources. Paris: UNESCO 1970.

DE LANGE,L., SMIT,A.: Report of a vegetational survey of the island of Elba, Italy. Geoforum **8**, 55–58 (1971).

DELVER,P.: Properties of saline soils in Iraq. Neth. J. Agr. Sci. **10**, 194–210 (1962).

Department of Regional Economic Expansion: Land capability for outdoor recreation. The Canada Land Inventory, Report No. **6**, Ottawa (1969).

DESAUNETTES,J.R.: Etude pédologique du casier pilote de Ornolde, Sénégal, mimeogr. rep. Rome: FAO 1968.

DE SCHLIPPE,P.: Shifting cultivation in Africa, the Zande system of agriculture. London: Routledge and Kegan Paul 1956.

DE SMET,L.A.H.: Het Dollardgebied. Wageningen: PUDOC 1962.

DE SMET,L.A.H.: Grondverbeteringsmogelijkheden en hun betekenis in de Groninger veen-kolonien. Cultuurt. Tijdschr. **7**, 252–267 (1968).

DE SMET,L.A.H.: De Groninger veenkolonien (westelijk deel), bodemkundige en landbouw-kundige onderzoekingen in het kader van de bodemkartering. Versl. Landbouwk. Ond. **722**, Wageningen: PUDOC 1969.

DE VISSER,C.: Een gewasopname in de omgeving van Wageningen. Boor en Spade **VIII**, pp. 84–99. Wageningen: Stichting voor Bodemkartering 1956.

DE WIT,C.T.: Overbevolking zonder Ondervoeding. In: Alberda,Th. (Ed.): De Groene Aarde, pp. 425–436. Utrecht/Antwerpen: Aula pocket 250. (1966).

DIELEMAN,P.J. et al.: Reclamation of salt affected soils in Iraq. Publ. 11. Wageningen: ILRI 1963.

DIELEMAN,P.J., DE RIDDER,N.A.: Studies of salt and water movement in the Bol Guini Polder, Chad Republic. Journ. Hydrol. 1, pp. 311–343, Bull. 5. Wageningen: ILRI 1964.

Dokuchaev Soil Institute: Soil-geographical zoning of the USSR. Jerusalem: Israel Prog. Sci. Transl. 1963.

DÖRR,R.: Das Verhalten von sechs Bodenarten unter gleichem Klima als Ackerboden während 20 Jahre. Trans. Commissions II and IV, Intern. Soc. Soil. Sci., Hamburg, pp. 119–124 (1958).

DOUGRAMEJI,J.S.: Water requirements of some crops in the Baghdad region. Techn. Report No. **11**. Inst. for Applied Research on National Resources (UNSF-UNESCO-Ins. Iraq). Iraq: Abu Ghraib 1970.

DRAEGER,W.C., PETTINGER,L.R.: A regional agricultural survey using small-scale aerial photography. Photogrammetria **28**, 1–15 (1972).

DROR,Y.: Ventures in policy sciences. New York: American Elsevier 1971.

DUCHAUFOUR,P.: Précis de Pédologie. Paris: Masson 3ème éd. 1970.

DUDAL,R.: Arable land, 13–29. In: Ann. Rept. Int. Inst. Landreclam. Improvement. Wageningen: ILRI 1969.

DUDAL,R.: Key to the units of the soil map of the world. Rome: FAO 1970.

DUDAL,R. et al.: Legend of the World Soil Map. Paris: UNESCO 1974.

DUFFY,P.J.B.: A forest land classification for the mixedwood section of Alberta. Publ. 1128. Ottawa: Dept. Forestry 1965.

DUFFY,P.J.B., SHEPHERD,R.F.: Australian forestry highlights. In: The Forestry Chronicle (Canada), Vol. **45, 14**, pp. 1–6 (1969).

DURAND,J.H.: Le choix des sols irrigables en Algérie. In: Trans. 6th Intern. Congr. Soil. Sci., Paris, VI-10, pp. 537–542 (1956).

DURY,G.H. et al.: Essays in geomorphology. New York: American Elsevier 1966.

Dutch AGR(Icultural) INV(Estment) COMM(Ission): An assessment of investments in land reclamation. Publ. 7. Wageningen: Intern. Inst. Land Reclam. and Improvement 1960.

EDELMAN,C.H.: Studien over de bodemkunde van Nederlands Indie. Reprinted 1947. Wageningen: Veenman 1941.

EDELMAN,C.H.: Soils of the Netherlands. Amsterdam: Noordholl. Uitg. Mij. 1950.

EDELMAN,C.H. et al.: Een Veluws dorp. Bennekom (Neth.): Stichting "Oud-Bennekom" 1958.

EDELMAN,C.H., EEUWENS,B.E.P.: Sporen van de Romeinse landindeling in Zuid-Limburg. Ber. Rijksd. Oudheidk. Bodemond **9**, 40–56 (1959).

EDMINSTER,F.C.: Finding the potentials for rural recreation. J. Soil Conservation 32 (cited by Van Lier, 1972) (1966).

EMBERGER,L.: Une classification biogéographique des climats. In: Rec. Trav. Lab. Botan., Fac. Sci. Montpellier, Fasc. **7**, 3–43 (1955).

EYRE,S.R.: Vegetation and soils, a world picture, 2nd ed. London: Edw. Arnold 1970.

FAO: Provisional indicative world plan for agricultural development. Rome: Food and Agricultural Organization of the United Nations Conference, C 69/4, Vol. 2 (1969).

FAO-UNESCO: Soil map of the world, 1:5000000, Vol. I. Legend Vol. IV. South America. Paris: UNESCO 1971, 1974.

FERRARI,TH.J.: Growth factors and soil productivity. Amsterdam: Trans. 4th Int. Congr. Soil Sci. Vol. **1**, 348–352 (1950).

FERRARI,TH.J. et al.: Factor analysis in agricultural research. Neth. J. Agr. Sci. **5**, 211–221 (1957).

Field Book: Veldbook voor land- en waterdeskundigen (fieldbook for land and water experts). Int. Inst. Landreclam. Impr. Wageningen: ILRI (1972).

FINK,J.: Veränderungen der Böden in der Kulturlandschaft. Mitt. Österr. Geogr. Ges. **105**, 453–460 (1963).

FLAWN,P.T.: Environmental geology. New York: Harper and Row 1970.

FOUND,W.C.: A theoretical approach to land use patterns. London: E. Arnold 1971.

FRANKART,R., SIJS,C., VERHEYE,W.: Contributions to the use of the parameter method for the evaluation of the classes in the different categories of the land evaluation proposed by the working group. Wageningen: Mimeogr. rept., FAO Consultation on Land Evaluation 1972.

FRINKING,H.D.: Crop identification in the Netherlands by means of aerial false-color film. Neth. J. Agr. Sci. **20**, 261–271 (1972).

GAESE,D., MUSHTAG,M.A., SCHLICHTING,E.: Wirkung einer Meliorationskalkung in leh-migen Böden der Braunerde-Gruppe. Landwirtschaftliche Forschung **24**, 316–327 (1971).

GALJART,B.F.: Itaguai; old habits and new practices in a Brazilian land settlement. Wageningen: Thesis 1968.

GAUSMANN,H.W., ALLEN,W.A., CARDENAS,R., BOWEN,R.L.: Color photos, cotton leaves, and soil salinity. Photogram. Eng. **36**, 454–459 (1970).

GEERTZ,C.: Agricultural involution, the process of ecological change in Indonesia. Ass. As. Stud. Mon. XI. Berkeley-Los Angeles-London: Univ. Cal. Press 1971.

GLIKSON,A.: Edited by: Mumford,L.: The ecological basis of planning. The Hague: Nijhoff 1971.

GOOSEN,D.: Aerial photointerpretation in soil survey. Soil Bulletin 6. Rome: FAO 1967.

GOOSEN,D.: Physiography and soils of the Llanos orientales, Colombia. Publ. Fys. Geogr. Bodemk. Lab. Amsterdam: Univ. of Amsterdam No. 20 (1971).

GRICE,D.G. et al.: Soil survey of Mercer county, Pennsylvania. Soil Conserv. Service, Washington (D.C.): U.S. Dept. Agric. 1971.

GRICE, W.J.: Catchment planning and contour planting for safe water disposal, water and soil conservation in the plains areas of North-East India. Memor. No. 28. Jorhat (Assam): Tocklai Exp. Sta. Tea Research Assoc. 1971.

GROENVELD, D.: The "art" of selecting the best project. Ann. Rept. Int. Inst. Land Reclam. Improvement (ILRI) 7–13. 1960.

HAANS, J.C.F.M., WESTERVELD, G.J.W.: The application of soil survey in the Netherlands. Geoderma **4**, 279–309 (1970).

HAANTJENS, H.A.: Agricultural land classification for New Guinea land resources surveys. Techn. Memor. 65/8. Canberra: CSIRO 1965.

HAANTJENS, H.A.: The relevance for engineering or principles, limitations and developments in land systems surveys in New Guinea, pp. 1–22. Canberra: Sympos. terrain eval. engineering 1968.

HADDAD, R.H. et al.: Preliminary studies on groundwater in Samarra-Tikrit area. Techn. Rep. No. 13. Baghdad: UNSF/UNESCO Inst. Appl. Res. Nat. Resources 1970.

HAEBERLI, R.: Levé cartographique agricole des stations végétales de la Côte (Canton de Vaud, Suisse). Thèse 4196. Zürich: ETH 1968.

HAEBERLI, R.: Carte des dangers de gel tardif printanier dans le Canton de Vaud. Cahiers de l'aménagement régional. Off. Vaud. Lausanne: Urban 1971a.

HAEBERLI, R.: Carte écologique-physiographique des sols du Canton de Vaud. Cah. amén. rég. 12, Off. Vaud. Lausanne: Urban 1971b.

HAEBERLI, R.: Carte du potentiel naturel des surfaces agricoles du Canton de Vaud. Cah. amén. rég. 13, Off. Vaud. Lausanne: Urban 1971.

HAEFNER, H.: Der Strukturwandel der Alpwirtschaft im Luftbild (am Beispiel des Dischmatales). Geographica Helvetia **4**, 218–228 (1964).

HAEFNER, H.: Airphoto interpretation of rural land use in Western Europe. Photogrammetria **22**, 143–152 (1967).

HAGAN, R.M. et al.: Irrigation of agricultural lands. Agronomy Series 11. Madison (Wisc.): Amer. Soc. Agron. 1967.

HARROLD, L.L.: Studies in hydrology of agricultural watersheds. Agric. Res. Service. Coshoction (Ohio): U.S. Dept. of Agric. 1962.

HAURWITZ, B., AUSTIN, J.M.: Climatology. New York-Lausanne: McGraw Hill 1944.

HAYES JR., S.P.: Evaluating development projects. Paris: UNESCO 1969.

HELLINGA, F.: Local administration of water control in a number of European countries. Publ. 8. Wageningen: ILRI 1960.

HESLOP, R.E.F., BOWN, C.J.: The soils of Candacraig and Glenbuchat. Bulletin No. 1. Soil survey of Scotland. Aberdeen: The Macaulay Inst. for Soil Res. 1969.

HIDDING, A.P.: Aanpassing van de bodemgesteldheid aan het agrarisch gebruik in het bijzonder in de tuinbouw. Landbouwk. Tijdschr. **79**, 378–381 (1967).

HOFSTEE, E.W., VLAM, A.W.: Opmerkingen over de ontwikkeling van perceelsvormen in Nederland. Boor en Spade **5**, pp. 194–235. Wageningen: Stichting voor Bodemkartering 1952.

HUDSON, N.: Soil conservation. Ithaca (N. Y.): Cornell University Press 1971.

HULSBOS, W.C., BOUMANS, J.H.: Leaching of saline soils in Iraq. Neth. Agr. Sci. **8**, 1–10, (1960).

Integrated Surveys: Proceedings of the first international seminar on integrated surveys and land development. Delft: ITC-UNESCO Centre for Integr. Surv., Publ. S 1/14, 1966.

Integrated Surveys: Proceedings of the second international seminar on integrated surveys of natural grazing areas. Delft: ITC-UNESCO Centre f. Integr. Surv., Publ. S 15/28, 1967.

Integrated Surveys: Proceedings of the third international seminar on transportation problems and integrated surveys. Delft: ITC-UNESCO Centre for Integr. Surv. 1968.

Integrated Surveys: Proceedings of the fourth international seminar on integrated surveys for river basin development. Delft: ITC-UNESCO Centre for Integr. Surv. 1969.

Integrated Surveys: Proceedings of the international symposium on integrated surveys and environmental management. ITC-UNESCO Centre for Integr. Surv. Enschede. Enschede: ITC-Journal, Special Issue, 1973-2 (1972).

ISRAELSEN, O. W., HANSEN, V. E.: Irrigation principles and practices, 3rd ed. New York: Wiley 1962.

JACKS, G. V. et al.: Soil chemistry and fertility: Transactions Comm. II and IV. Aberdeen: Intern. Soc. Soil Sci. (1967).

JACOBY, E.: Flurbereinigung in Europa (Land reallotment in Europe), Publ. 3, Intern. Inst. Land Reclam. Impr. Wageningen: ILRI 1961.

JANITZKY, P.: Salz und Alkaliböden und Wege zu ihrer Verbesserung. Gießener Abhandl. Agr. und Wirtsch. Forsch. Europ. Ost, Band 2. Gießen: Schmitz 1957.

JONGERIUS, A. et al.: Micromorphology of soils. Special (Kubiena) Issue. Geoderma 1, 3/4 (1967).

KELLER, R.: Gewässer und Wasserhaushalt des Festlandes. Leipzig: Teubner 1962.

KELLOGG, CH. E.: Soil interpretation in the soil survey. Soil Conservation Services. Washington (D. C.): U.S. Dept. Agric. 1961.

KELLOGG, CH, E.: Soil surveys for use. In: Trans. Intern. Soils Conf., Wellington, New Zealand, pp. 529–535 (1962).

KIEMSTEDT, H.: Zur Bewertung der Landschaft für die Erholung. Beiträge zur Landespflege, Sonderheft 1. Stuttgart: Eugen Ulmer 1967.

KING, H. H.: Farmers of fourty centuries. New York: Harcourt, Brace, and Co. 1910.

KINORI, B. Z.: Manual of surface drainage engineering. Amsterdam: Elsevier 1970.

KLINGEBIEL, A. A.: Soil survey interpretation-capability groupings. Soil Sci. Soc. Am. Proc. 22, 160–163 (1958).

KOCH, L.: The East Greenland Ice. Kopenhagen: Meddelser on Grönland 1947.

KÖPPEN, W., GEIGER: Handbuch der Klimakunde. Berlin (1928).

KOSTROWICKY, J.: The typology of world agriculture, a preliminary scheme. Mimeograph., Internat. Geographical Union 1972.

KOUWENHOVEN, J. K., TERPSTRA, R.: Characterisation of soil handling with mould-board ploughs. Neth. J. Agric. Sci. 20, 180–192 (1972).

KOVDA, V. A.: Laws of migration and distribution of salts on continents. In: Problems of soil science and reclamation. Paris: UNESCO (mimeograph) 1964.

KOVDA, V. A., EGOROV, V. V.: Landscapes in relation to irrigation, danger of salinity, and need for drainage. In: Problems of soil science and reclamation. Paris: UNESCO (mimeograph) 1964.

KOVDA, V. A. et al.: Irrigation drainage, salinity. Hutchinson/FAO/UNESCO (1973).

KRANTZ, B. A.: Soil survey interpretation—interpretation of soil characteristics important in soil management. Soil Sci. Soc. Am. Proc. 21, 155–156 (1957).

KREIG, R. A.: Aerial photographic interpretation for land use classification in the New York State land use and natural resources inventory. Photogrammetria 26, 101–111 (1970).

KUIPERS, H. et al.: Papers on zero-tillage. Neth. J. Agric. Sci. 18, 219–320 (1970).

LEAMY, M. L.: The soils of central Otago. Proceed. 28th Conf., New Zealand, Grassland Association, pp. 7–18 (1966).

LEE, J., DIAMOND, S.: The potential of Irish land for livestock production. Dublin: An Foras Taluntais 1972.

LEWIS, A. B.: Landclassification for agricultural development. Dev. Paper 18. Rome: FAO 1952.

LEWIS, A. J., MAC DONALD, H. C.: Mapping of mangrove and perpendicular-oriented shell reefs in Southeastern Panama with sidelooking radar. Photogrammetria 28, 187–199 (1972).

LOCHT, L. J.: Evaluation of rural reconstruction projects with the aid of a model of regional economic growth. In: Kendall, M. G. (Ed.): Cost-benefit analysis. London: Engl. University Press 1969.

LOCHT, L. J.: Evaluation of rural reconstruction projects with the aid of a model of regional economic growth. Techn. Bulletin 74. Wageningen: Inst. Land and Water manag., Res. 1971.

LUTHIN, J. N. et al.: Drainage of agricultural lands. Madison (Wisc.): Am. Soc. Agron. 1957.

MAAS, F. M.: Toekomstmodel voor natuur en landschap. Baarn: Wereldvenster 1971.

MABBUTT, J. A., STEWART, G. A.: The application of geomorphology in resource surveys in Australia and New Guinea. Rev. de Géomorphologie dynamique 14, 97–109 (1963).

MACAN, T. T., WORTHINGTON, E. B.: Life in lakes and rivers. London: Collins 1968.

McCormack, R. J.: The Canada land use inventory: a basis for land use planning. Soil Water Cons. **1971**, 141–146.

McHarg, I. L.: Design with nature. New York: Natural History Press 1969.

Mahler, P. J. et al.: Manual of multipurpose land classification. Teheran: Soil Institute of Iran, Ministry of Agriculture 1970.

Mahler, P. J.: Integrated surveys and environmental problems associated with land development in developing countries. Integrated Surveys 1972.

Maletic, J. T.: Land classification survey as related to the selection of irrigable lands. Sao Paulo (Brazil): Pan Am. Soil Cons. Congr. 1966.

Maletic, J. T.: Land classification principles. Soil Scient. Train. Inst. (mimeograph). Denver (Colorado): U.S. Bur. Reclamation 1970.

Maletic, J. T., Bartholomew, O. F.: The relationship between selected climatic parameters to crop production on Western irrigated land. Denver (Colorado): West. Reg. Techn. Work-Plann. Conf. for Soil Survey 1966.

Maletic, J. T., Hutchings, T. B.: Selection and classification of irrigable land. In: R. M. Hagan (Ed.): Irrigation of agricultural lands. Agronomy 11. Madison (Wisc.): Am. Soc. Agron. 1967.

Marcaccini, P.: Il limite dell'olivo nella Romagna e in genere nell'Italia continentale. Rivista Geogr. Ital. **80**, 28–49 (1973).

Marinet, J.: Coordination et planification des ressources naturelles. Photogrammetria **19**, 72–83 (1964).

Martin, H. B.: Louisiana range handbook. Soil Conserv. Service. Alexandria (Louisiana): U.S. Dept. Agric. 1956.

Marr, R. L.: Geländeklimatische Untersuchung im Raum südlich von Basel. Basler Beiträge zu Geographie, Heft 12. Basel: Geogr. Ethnol. Ges. 1970.

Meadows, D. H. et al.: The limits to growth. London: Earth Island 1972.

Meienberg, P.: Die Landnützungskartierung nach Pan-, Infrarot- und Farbluftbildern. Münchener Studien Sozial u. Wirtsch. Geogr., Bd. 1. Regensburg: Verl. Larsleben Kallmeier 1966.

Meier, H. K.: Color-correct aerial photography? Bildmessung und Luftbildwesen **5**, 206–214 (1967).

Meyer de Stadelhofen, M. C.: Exemples de contribution de la géophysique aux travaux de l'ingénieur. Bull. Techn. Suisse Romande **10**, 1–5 (1947).

Millette, G. et al.: Etudes pédohydrologiques, Togo; rapport final, rept. Rome: FAO/SF, 13/TOG, FOA 1967.

Mohr, E. C. J., van Baren, F. A., van Schuylenborgh, J.: Tropical soils, third revised, and enlarged edition. The Hague-Paris-Djarkarta: Mouton-Ichtiar Baru-Van Hoeve 1972.

Mohrmann, J. C. J.: Some aspects of sprinkler irrigation in tropical regions. Neth. J. Agric. Sci. **7**, 118–133 (1959).

Mohrmann, J. C. J., Kessler, J.: Water deficiencies in European agriculture. Wageningen: Intern. Inst. Land Reclam. and Improvement 1959.

Mosher, A. T.: Custom-made systems. In: Ceres, pp. 33–37. Rome: FAO-Journal 1972.

National Resources Planning Board: Land classification in the United States. Washington (D. C.): Govt. Printing Off. 1941.

Nelson, J. G., Chambers, M. J. (Ed.): Vegetation, soils, and wildlife. Toronto: Methuen 1969.

Neubert, R. W.: Sick trees. Photogramm. Eng. **35**, 472–475 (1969).

Newcomb, R. L.: Celtic fields in Himmerland, Denmark, as revealed by vertical photography, at a scale of 1:25000. Photogrammetria **27**, 101–113 (1971).

Newcomb, R. M.: Two keys for the historical interpretation of aerial-photographs. In: The California Geographer, pp. 37–46 (1966).

Nielsen, A. D.: Economics and soil science—copartners in land classification, paper presented at Region 7 land classification meeting (mimeograph). Denver (Colorado): U.S. Bur. Reclam 1963.

Northey, R. D.: Correlation of engineering and pedological soil classification in New Zealand. New Zealand Journ. Sci. **9**, 809–883, Soil Bur. Publ. 390 (1966).

Nunnally, N. R., Witmer, R. E.: Remote sensing for land use studies. Photogramm. Eng. **36**, 449–453 (1970).

OLBERTZ, M., SCHWARZ, K.: Die Meliorationswissenschaftliche Forschung in der Deutschen Demokratischen Republik. In: Sitzungsberichte 15, pp. 5–58. Berlin: Akad. Landeswirtschaft DDR 1966.

OLIVER, R., Fage, J. D.: A short history of Africa. London: Penguin African Libr. 1962.

OLSON, R. E.: A geography of water. Dubuque (Iowa): Wm. Brown 1970.

PAPADAKIS, J.: In: Papadakis (Ed.): Agricultural geography of the world. Buenos Aires 1952.

PAPADAKIS, J.: Crop ecology and agricultural development. Field Crop Abstracts **17**, 85–88 (1964).

PAPADAKIS, J.: Climates of the world and their agricultural potentialities. Buenos Aires 1966.

PAPADAKIS, J. S.: Ecologic agricole. Gembloux: Ducilot 1938.

PAPE, J. C.: Plaggen soils in the Netherlands. Geoderma **4**, 257–278 (1970).

PASZYNSKI, J.: Investigation of local climate in the upper silesian industrial district. In: Problems of Applied Geography, pp. 83–95 (1958).

PEARSE, P. H.: Principles for allocating wildlife among alternative uses. Can. J. Agric. Econ. **17**, 1 (1969).

PERRET, N. G.: Land capability classification for wildlife. The Canadian Land Inventory, Rep. No. **7**. Ottawa: Dep. Reg. Econ. Exp. 1969.

PESSL, F., LANGEN, W. H., RYDER, R. B.: Geologic and hydrologic maps for land-use planning in the Connecticut Valley, with examples from the folio of the Hartford North Quadrangle, Connecticut, Circular 674. Washington (D. C.): Geological Survey 1972.

PESTRONG, R.: Multiband photos for a tidal marsh. Photogramm. Eng. **35**, 453–470 (1969).

PHILPOTTS, L. E., WALLEN, V. R.: IR for Crops disease identification. Photogramm. Eng. **35**, 1116–1125 (1969).

PONS, L. J.: Soil requirements for mechanized rice cultivations in tropical alluvial plains, with special emphasis on Surinam (South America). Djarkarta: Second Asian Soil Conference 1972.

President's Science Advisory Committee: The world food problem. Washington (D. C.): The White House 1967.

PRILLEVITZ, P. C.: Gronden uit de cultuur. Landbouwk. Tijdschr. **81**, 311–319 (1969).

RASMUSSEN, J. J.: Soil survey of Benton county area (Washington). Washington (D. C.): Soil Conserv. Service, U.S. Dept. Agric. 1971.

RAUSCHKOLB, R. S.: Land degradation. Soil Bulletin 13. Rome: FAO 1971.

REIJMERINK, A.: Microstructure, soil strength, and root development of asparagus on loamy sands in the Netherlands. Neth. J. Agric. Sci. **21**, 24–43 (1973).

Report: Development and environment, submitted by a panel of experts convened by the secretary general of the UN conference on the human environment. Founex (Switzerland), 4–12 June 1971. Geneve (Switzerland): United Nations GE 71-13738 (1971).

REY, P. et al.: Aerial surveys and integrated studies. Natural Resources Research VI. Paris: UNESCO 1968.

REYNDERS, J. J.: The analysis of shifting cultivation areas. In: Symposium Photointerpretation. Delft: Arch. Int. Photogramm. **14**, 171–176 (1962).

RID, H.: Die Stellung der pseudogleyten Böden im Acker- und Pflanzenbau. Trans. Commissions II and IV, Intern. Soc. Soil Sci. (Hamburg), pp. 99–104 (1958).

RIQUIER, J., BRAMAO, D. L.: Soil resources of Nigeria. In: Agricultural Development in Nigeria 1965-1980, pp. 386–391. Rome: FAO 1964.

RIQUIER, J., BRAMAO, D. L., CORNET, J. P.: A new system of soil appraisal in terms of actual and potential productivity (first approximation) (mimeograph), AGL:TESR/70/6. Rome: FAO 1970.

RIQUIER, J.: The parametric method of land evaluation, (mimeograph), ACL:Misc/71/12. Rome: FAO 1971.

RIQUIER, J.: A mathematical model for calculation of agricultural productivity in terms of parameters of soil and climate (advance Summary of a paper to be published by Orstom, Paris). Rome: FAO 1972.

RODE, A. A.: Soil science. Israel Progr. Sci. Transl., Jerusalem (1962).

ROTHKEGEL, W.: Geschichtliche Entwicklung der Bodenbonitierungen und Wesen und Bedeutung der deutschen Bodenschätzung. Stuttgart-Ludwigsburg: Ulmer 1950.

RUBINSTEIN, E. S., ALISSON, B. P., DROSDOW, O. A., RUBINSTEIN, E. S.: Lehrbuch der Klimatologie. Berlin: VEB Deutscher Verlag der Wissenschaften 1956.

RUMNEY, G. R.: Climatology and the world's climate. New York: MacMillan 1968.

RUSSELL, E. W. et al.: Effects of intensive fertilizer use on the human environment. Soils Bull. No. 16. Rome: SIDA/FAO 1972.

RUST, R. H., ODELL, R. T.: Methods used in evaluating the productivity of some Illinois soils. Soil Sci. Soc. Am. Proc. **21**, 171–175 (1957).

RUXTON, B. P. et al.: Lands of the Safia-Pongani area. Melbourne: CSIRO 1967.

RYAN, P. et al.: Trace element problems in relation to soil units in Europe. World Soil Resources Report 31. Rome: FAO 1967.

RYAN, P. et al.: West Donegal resource survey. Dublin: An Forais Taluntais 1969.

SALGUEIRO, T. A. et al.: The land capability map of Portugal. In: Trans. 8th Intern. Congr. Soil Sci (Bucharest), V, pp. 837–845 (1964).

Salinity Laboratory Staff: Diagnosis and improvement of saline and alkali soils. Agriculture Handbook No. **60**. Washington (D. C.): U.S. Dept. of Agric. 1954.

Salinity Seminar, Baghdad: Irrigation and drainage paper. Rome: FAO of the UN 1971.

SARFALVY, B. et al.: Land utilisation in Eastern Europe. Budapest: Akademia Kiadó 1967.

SCHEFFER, F., LIEBEROTH, I.: Was versteht man unter Bodenfruchtbarkeit-Ertragsfähigkeit und -Ertragsleistung? In: Deutsche Landwirtschaft **8**, 272–275 (1957).

SCHEFFER, F., SCHACHTSCHABEL, P.: Lehrbuch der Bodenkunde. Stuttgart: Enke Verlag 1970.

SCHELLING, J. et al.: Soil survey research in the Netherlands. Special Issue. Geoderma **4**, **3** (1970).

SCHILSTRA, J.: Irrigation as a soil and relief forming factor in the lower Mesopotamian plain. Neth. J. Agr. Sci. **10**, 179–193 (1962).

SCHREIBER, K. F. et al.: Natur-, betriebs- und marktgerechter Obstanbau. Obstbau **78**, 1–16 (1959).

SCHREIBER, K. F. et al.: Naturbedingte Entwicklungsmöglichkeiten für den Erwerbsobstbau im Rahmen einer landwirtschaftlichen Gesamtplanung in Baden-Württemberg. Stuttgart: Min. Ernähr., Landw. Baden-Württemberg 1967.

SCHREIBER, K. F.: Les conditions thermiques du Canton de Vaud. Lausanne: Off. Cant. de l'Urbanisme (1968).

SCHREIBER, K. F.: Ökologische Probleme der Landschaftsnützung und deren Konsequenzen für die Landschaftsplanung. In: 8, Landwirtschaftlicher Hochschultag. Mainz: Min. Landwirtschaft, pp. 12–33 (1972).

SCHWAAR, D. C.: Method and procedure by photointerpretation for survey of rubber plantations in Thailand. Kingdom of Thailand. Bangkok: Report SSR-85 (1971).

SELDON, T. H., WALKER, L. D.: Economic evaluation and selection of lands for irrigation. Soil Survey Seminar. Dept. Land Dev., Bangkok, Thailand: Min. Nat. Devel. 1968.

Serviço de Reconhecemento e de Ordenamento Agrario: Carta de capacidade de uso do solo de Portugal, bases e normas adoptadas na sua elaboraçao. Regiao à Sul do Rio Tejo. Madrid: Ministeria de Economia 1963.

SHAY, J. R. et al.: Remote sensing, with special reference to agriculture and forestry. Washington, D. C.: National Academy of Sciences 1970.

SHRADER, W. D. et al.: Estimated crop yields on Iowa soils. Special Rept. 25. Ames (Iowa): Agric. Exp. Sta. 1960.

SIMONSON, R. W.: Present and potential usefulness of soil resources. In: Annual Report Int. Inst. Land Recl. Improvement, pp. 7–25. Wageningen: (ILRI) 1967.

SLAGER, S., SCHULZ, J. P.: A study on the suitability of some soils in the Northern Surinam for *Pinus caribaea*, var. Hondurensis. Neth. J. Agr. Sci. **17**, 92–98 (1969).

SLICHER VAN BATH, B. H.: De agrarische geschiedenis van West-Europa (500–1850). Utrecht–Antwerp: Aula 1960.

SMALL, R. J.: The study of landforms, a textbook of geomorphology. London: Cambridge Univ. Press 1972.

SMITS, H., WIGGERS, A. J.: Soil survey and land classification as applied to reclamation of tea bottom land in the Netherlands. Publ. 4. Intern. Inst. Landrecl. Improvement. Wageningen (ILRI) 1959.

SMYTH, A. J.: Selection of soils for cocoa. Soils Bull. 5, Rome: FAO 1966.

SNETHLAGE, P.: The role of land consolidation in the Northern Chao Phya area of Thailand. In: Ann. Rept. Intern. Inst. Land Reclam. and Impr., pp. 13–27. Wageningen: (ILRI) 1970.

Soil Survey Staff: Soil survey manual. Washington D.C.: U.S. Depth Agric. Handbook 18 (1951).

Soil Survey: Selected chapters from the unedited text of the soil taxonomy of the national cooperative soil survey. Washington (D.C.): U.S. Dept. Agric. 1970.

SONNEVELD, S.: Precipitation deficits in the Netherlands. Neth. J. Agric. Sci. 5, 61–70 (1957).

SOUSA, A.: Irrigation and civilisation in the land of the twin rivers. Baghdad: Publ. by the author 1969.

SSM: Congress: much adò about land-use. Environmental Sci. Technol. 7, 4 (1973).

STAMP, L. D.: The Land of Britain, its use and misuse. 2nd ed. London: Longmans Green 1950.

STAMP, L. D.: Land for tomorrow, the underdeveloped world. Bloomington: Indiana Univ. Press 2nd pr. 1953.

STAMP, L. D.: The underdeveloped lands of Britain. London: A Howard Memorial Lecture, the Soil Association 1954.

STAMP, L. D.: The measurement of land resources. The Geological Review, Vol. 48, pp. 1–15. New York: American Geographical Society 1958.

STAMP, L. D.: Applied geography. London: Pelican A 449, 2nd ed. 1961.

STAMP, L. D. et al.: A history of land use in arid regions. Paris: UNESCO, Arid Zone Research XVII 1961.

STARR, C. et al.: Energy and power. Sci. Am. 225, 3, 37–224 (1971).

STEELE, J. G.: Soil interpretation and its use. Soils Bulletin 8. Rome: FAO 1967.

STEINER, D.: Zur Technik und Methodik der Landnützungsinterpretation von Luftbildern. Berichte 2. Deutsche Landeskunde 29, 99–130 (1962).

STEINER, D.: Aerial photography for land use mapping, cattle inventories, yield forecasting and crop diseases determination. Third. Intern. Aviation Congress, The Hague, pp. 334–361 (1966).

STEINER, D.: Time dimension for crop surveys from space. Photogramm. Eng. 36, 187–194 (1970a).

STEINER, D.: Annotated bibliography of bibliographies on photointerpretation and remote sensing. Phorogrammetria 26, 143–161 (1970b).

STEINER, D.: Towards earth resources satellites: the American ERTS and SKYLAB programs. Photogrammetria 27, 211–251 (1971).

STEINER, D., MAURER, H.: The use of stereo-height as a discriminating variable for crop classification on aerial Photographs. Photogrammetria 24, 223–241 (1969).

STELLINGWERF, D. A.: Volume assessment through aerial photographs in a forest area in Belgium. Photogrammetria 22, 161–169 (1967).

STEWART, G. A. et al.: Land evaluation. Canberra 1968.

STORIE, R. E.: Rating soils for agricultural forest and grazing use. Trans. IV. Amsterdam: Int. Congr. Soil Sci. 1, pp. 336–339 (1950).

STORIE, R. E.: Land classification as used in California for the appraisal of land for taxation purposes. Leopoldsville (Congo): Trans. V Int. Congr. Soil Sci. VI-10 (1954).

SWANSON, E. R., TYNER, E. H., PETERSON, G. A.: Economic interpretation of agronomic data by the linear programming-technique. Soil Sci. Ann. Proc. 22, 132–136 (1958).

Symposium, Photointerpretation (1st). Archives Internationales de Photogrammétrie, Vol. 14, Delft (1962).

Symposium, Photointerpretation (2nd). Archives Internationales de Photogrammétrie, Vol. 16, Paris (1966).

Symposium, für Photointerpretation. Dresden (DDR): Berichte des — (1970).

Symposium, Environment. On the impact of urbanisation on man's environment. Rept. 70-44816. New York: United Nations 1970.

TADMOR, N. H., ORSHAN, G., RAVITZ, E.: Habitat analysis in the Negev desert of Israel. Bull. Res. Comm. Israel, D. Botany, 11 D 3, 148–173 (1962).

TASCHENMACHER, W.: Bodenschätzungskarten 1:5000 aus den Ergebnissen der Boden-schätzung. Z. Pflanzenernähr. Düng. Bodenk. 65, 215–228 (1954).

TAVERNIER, R. et al.: Soil map of Europe on scale 1:2 500 000. Rome: FAO 1966.

THAER, A.: Über die Wertschätzung des Ackerlandes. Berlin 1811.

THOMAS, G. W.: The relation between soil water characteristics, water movement and nitrate contaminations of ground water. Research Rept. **52**, Univ. of Kentucky, U.S. Dept. Interior (1972).

TRICART, J.: Principes et méthodes de la géomorphologie. Paris: Masson 1965.

TROLL, C.: Landscape ecology. Publ. S 4, ITC-UNESCO. Delft: Centre for Integrated Surveys 1966.

TSCHEBOTARIOFF, G. P.: Soil mechanics, foundation and earth structures. New York–London: McGraw Hill 1953.

Tweede Nota: Over de ruimtelijke ordening in Nederland. The Hague: Staatsuitgeverij 1966.

TYURIN, I. V., SOKOLOV, A. V.: Soil types and efficiency of fertilizers. Trans. Comm. II and IV, Intern. Soc. Soil Sci. (Hamburg), pp. 60–72 (1958).

TYURIN, I. V. et al.: Soil Survey, a guide to field investigations and mapping of soils. Jerusalem: Isr. Progr. Sci. Transl. 1965.

ULRICH, H. P. et al.: Soil survey of La Porte county (Indiana). Bur. of Plant Industry, Soils and Agric. Eng. Washington, D.C.: U.S. Dept. Agric. 1944.

UNESCO: International co-ordinating council of the Program on man and the biosphere (MAB) — First Session — Final Report. Paris: UNESCO 1971.

UNESCO: Curricula and syllabi in hydrology. Technical Paper in hydrology 10. Paris: UNESCO 1972a.

UNESCO: Teaching aids in hydrology. Technical Paper in hydrology 11. Paris: UNESCO 1972b.

UNESCO-FAO: Bioclimatic map of the Mediterranean zone, explanatory notes, arid zone research XXI. Paris: UNESCO 1963.

UNESCO/UNDP: Tunisia, research, and training on irrigation with saline water. Techn. Rept. TUN 5. Paris: UNESCO 1970.

VAN DAM, J. G. C.: Geschiktheid van de grond voor tuinbouw. Landbouwk. Tijdschr. **79**, 299–305 (1967).

VAN DAM, J. G. C.: Bodemgeschiktheidsonderzoek, in het bijzonder bij asperges, appels en stooktomaten. PUDOC, Wageningen: Ph. D. Thesis 1973.

VAN DE GOOR, G. A. W., ZIJLSTRA, G.: Irrigation requirement for double cropping of lowland rice. Publ. 14, Int. Inst. Land Reclam. and Improvement. Wageningen: (ILRI) 1968.

VAN DER BOON, J.: Analyse van de bodemvruchtbaarheid volgens de proefplekkenmethode bij een meerjarig tuinbouwgewas, de aardbei op zandgrond. Thesis, Wageningen: The Hague: Verslagen Landbouwk. Onderzoekingen 1967.

VAN DER MAAREL, E., LEERTOUWER, J.: Variation in vegetation and species diversity along a local environmental gradient. Acta Botan. Neerl. **16**, 211–221 (1967).

VAN DUSSELDORP, D. B. W. M.: Meerdimensionale overheidsplanning. Wageningen: Veenman 1967.

VAN DUSSELDORP, D. B. W. M., LEKANNE DIT DEPREZ, B. E. J. C.: Problems connected with evaluation of the process of planned regional development. Neth. J. Agric. Sci. **18**, 3–11 (1970).

VAN DUSSELDORP, D. B. W. M.: Planning of service centres in rural areas of developing countries. Publ. 15. Wageningen: ILRI 1971.

VAN DYNE, G. M. et al.: The ecosystem concept in natural resource management. New York/London: Academic Press 1969.

VAN ECK, W. A., WHITESIDE, E. P.: Soil classification as a tool in predicting forest growth. Forest Soils Conf. (USA), 218–226 (1958).

VAN HEESEN, H. C.: Presentation of the seasonal fluctuation of the water table on soil maps. Geoderma **4**, 257–278 (1970).

VAN ITTERSUM, A.: A calculation of potential riceyields. Neth. J. Agric. Sci. **19**, 10–21 (1971).

VAN LEEUWEN, C. G.: A relation theoretical approach to pattern and process in vegetation. Wentia **15**, 25–46 (1966).

VAN LIER, H. N.: Zwemwater in strandbaden. Journal H_2O **3**, 10 (1970).

VAN LIER, H. N.: Research on some technical aspects of outdoor recreation, as part of multipurpose rural reconstructions in the Netherlands. Neth. J. Agric. Sci. **20**, 154–179 (1972).

VAN LIERE, W. J.: Survey of soil, present land use and land capabilities of the Jezireh (Syria). Rome: FAO-ETAP Rept. No. 2075 (1965).

VAN LYNDEN, K. H.: De houtsoorten in verband met de bodem. Bosbouw **39**, 3–22 (1967).

VAN NERUM, K., PALASTHY, A.: Studie van de bodemgeschiktheid voor de aspergeteelt. Agricultura **14**, 251–288 (1966).

VAN 'T LEVEN, J. A., HADDAD, M. A.: Surface irrigation with saline water on a heavy clay soil in the Medjerda Valley (Tunisia). Neth. J. Agric. Sci. **15**, 281–303 (1967).

VAN WIJK, A. L. M., VAN DEN HURK, J. A.: Geschiktheid voor speel-en ligweiden en bos, Rept. 1. Werkgroep Bodem en Water Twiskepolder. Wageningen: Inst. Land Water Manag. Res. 1971.

VAN WIJK, W. R. et al.: Physics of plant environment. Amsterdam: North Holland Publ. Cy., 2nd ed. 1966.

VEENENBOS, J. S.: De bodemgesteldheid van het gebied tussen Lemmer en Blokzijl in het randgebied van de Noordoostpolder. Thesis, Wageningen. Versl. Landbouwk. Ond. 55, 12. The Hague 1950.

VERBOOM, W. C.: Planned rural development in the Northern province of Northern Rhodesia. Delft: ITC Publications, B 12/13 (1961).

VERBOOM, W. C.: The use of aerial photographs for vegetation survey in relation with tsetse control and grassland surveys in Zambia. Delft: ITC Publication, B 28 (1965).

VERSTAPPEN, H. TH. et al.: Aerospace observation techniques, Geoform 2. Oxford-New York-Braunschweig: Pergamon/Vieweg 1970.

VERSTEEGH, P. J. D.: Notes on tropical forestry development and aerial photo-interpretation. Delft: ITC Publication, B 34, (1966).

VIKTOROV, S. V., VOSTOKOVA, YE. A., VYSHIVKIN, D. D.: Short guide to geobotanical surveying. Oxford: Pergamon 1964.

VINK, A. P. A.: Proeven en problemen met betrekking tot bemesting en schaduw in een theecultuur. Archief voor de Theecultuur, Bogor, pp. 33–91 (1953).

VINK, A. P. A.: Quantitative aspects of land classification. In: Trans. 7th Int. Congr. Soil Sci. V, 52, Vol. 4, pp. 371–378 (1960).

VINK, A. P. A.: Observations and experiences with some soils in Indonesia. In: Boor en Spade XII, pp. 33–48. Wageningen: Stichting voor Bodemkartering 1962a.

VINK, A. P. A.: Soil survey as related to agricultural productivity. J. Soil Sci. **14**, 88–101 (1962b).

VINK, A. P. A.: Aspects de pédologie appliquée. Neuchâtel (Switzerland): La Baconnière 1963a.

VINK, A. P. A.: Planning of soil surveys in land development. Publ. 10. Wageningen: ILRI 1963b.

VINK, A. P. A.: Die Interpretation von Bodenkarten für landwirtschaftliche Zwecke. Albrecht-Thaer Archiv **11**, 1021–1029 (1967).

VINK, A. P. A.: The rôle of physical geography in integrated surveys of developing countries. Tijdschr. Econ. Geogr. **59**, 294–312 (1968).

VINK, A. P. A.: Methology of air-photo-interpretation as illustrated from the soil sciences. Bildmessung und Luftbildwesen **1**, 35–44 (1970a).

VINK, A. P. A.: Soils, land reclamation, and pilot projects. Report to the Government of Iraq. Rome: FAO, rept. TA 2760 (1970b).

VINK, A. P. A.: Ricerche sui suoli e i paesaggi nel Lazio e in Toscana. Rivista Geografica Italiana **80**, 261–277 (1973).

VINK, A. P. A. et al.: Enkele onderzoekingen over de bodemgeschiktheidsclassificatie voor akker- en weidebouw. Bodemkundige studie 6. Wageningen: Stichting voor Bodemkartering 1963.

VINK, A. P. A., VAN ZUILEN, E. J. (Ed.): De geschiktheid van de bodem van Nederland voor akker- en weidebouw. Wageningen: Stichting voor Bodemkartering 1967.

VINK, A. P. A., VAN ZUILEN, E. J.: A soil suitability map of the Netherlands for arable land and grassland. Wageningen: Stichting voor Bodemkartering 1974.

VINK, G. J.: De grondslagen van het Indonesische Landbouwbedrijf. Wageningen: Thesis 1941.

VOLKER, A., LAMBREGTS, C. P.: Flood control, land reclamation, and agricultural utilisation of the deltaic areas in the Far East. In: Ann. Rept. Int. Inst. Land Reclamation and Improv., pp. 5–29 (1963).

VOLKER, A. et al.: Het Veluwemeer, schakel tussen oud en nieuw land. Dienst der Zuiderzeewerken. 's-Gravenhage: Staatsdrukkerij 1969.

WACKER, F.: Die Reichsbodenschätzung, Erläuterung des Verfahrens, der Klassenzeichen und der Wertzahlen. Peterm. Geogr. Mitt., Heft 11/12, pp. 332–335 (1943).

WACKER, F.: Zur Auswertung der Bodenschätzung. Zeitschr. Pflanzenernähr. Düng. Bodenk. 72, (117), 224–231 (1956).

WARRINER, D.: Land reform and development in the middle East. 2nd ed. London: Oxford Univ. Press 1962.

Water Resources Council: Principles for planning water and land resources, report to the water resources council by the special task force. Washington, D. C.: U.S. Water Res. Counc. 1970.

WEAVER, J. C.: Crop combination regions in the middle west. Geographical Rev. 44, 175–200 (1954 a).

WEAVER, J. C.: Crop combination regions for 1919 and 1929 in the middle West. Geographical Rev. 44, 560–572 (1954 b).

WEISCHET, W.: Die Geländeklimate der Niederrheinischen Bucht und ihre Rahmenlandschaften. Münchener Geografische Hefte 8. Kalmünz/Regensburg: Lassleben 1955.

WEISCHET, W., BARSCH, D.: Studien zum Problem der Deformation von Baumkronen durch Wind. Freiburger Geografische Hefte 1. Geogr. Inst. Albert. Freiburg i. Br.: Ludwigs-Universität 1963.

WERKGROEP: De gemengd agrarisch-recreatieve gebieden. Capita Selecta. Wageningen: Landbouwhogeschool 1970–1971.

WESTHOFF, V.: New criteria for nature reserves. New Sci. 1970, 111–113.

WESTHOFF, V.: Quelques aspects de la conservation de la nature aux Pays Bas. Natura Mosana (Liège) 24, 33–35 (1971).

WESTHOFF, V.: 1. Vegetatie-ontwikkeling, 4. Reservaten. In: Natuurbeheer in Nederland, Samson, Alphen a/d Rijn (Netherlands), pp. 46–54 and 180–189 (1973).

WIELING, H.: Yield pattern of grassland in terms of farm management. Neth. J. Agric. Sci. 19, 57–66 (1971).

WIENER, A.: Water resources development and environmental management in developing countries. Transactions ITC-UNESCO Symposium on Environmental Management and Integrated Surveys. Enschede: ITC 1972.

WIESLANDER, A. E., STORIE, R. E.: Vegetational approach to soil surveys in Wild-land areas. Soil Sci. Soc. Am. Proc. 17, 143–147 (1953).

WOBBER, F. J.: Orbital photos applied to the environment. Photogramm. Eng. 36, 852–864 (1970).

World Atlas of Agriculture. Novara: Istituto Geografico de Agostini. 1973.

WORTHINGTON, E. B.: Jamaica, ecology, and conservation. Rept. Paris: UNESCO 1970.

YAHIA, H. M.: Soils and soil conditions in sediments of the Ramadi Province (Iraq). Amsterdam: Thesis 1971.

YARON, D., DANFORS, E., VAADIA, Y. (Ed.): Arid zone irrigation. Berlin-Heidelberg-New York: Springer 1973.

Yearbook of Agriculture: Climate and man. Yearbook of agriculture. Washington (D.C.): U.S. Dept. Agric. 1941.

Yearbook of Agriculture: Soil. Washington (D.C.): U.S. Depth. Agric. 1957.

Yearbook of Agriculture: Land. Washington (D.C.): U.S. Depth. Agric. 1958.

Yearbook of Agriculture: A place to live. Washington (D.C.): U.S. Depth. Agric. 1963.

ZONNEVELD, I. S.: Zusammenhänge Forstgesellschaft-Boden-Hydrologie und Baumwuchs in einigen Niederländischen Pinus-Forsten auf Flugsand und auf Podzolen. In: Anthropogene Vegetation, Symp. Stolzenau/Weser. The Hague: Verlag Junk 1966.

ZONNEVELD, I. S.: Land evaluation and land(scape) science. ITC Textbook of Photo-Interpretation, Vol. VII, 4. Enschede: ITC 1972.

ZSILINSKY, V. G.: The practice of photointerpretation for a forest inventory. Photogrammetria 19, 42–58 (1964).

Subject Index

* The word is continuously used in the book from hereon.